FOUR CORNERS

KATHLEEN BRYANT

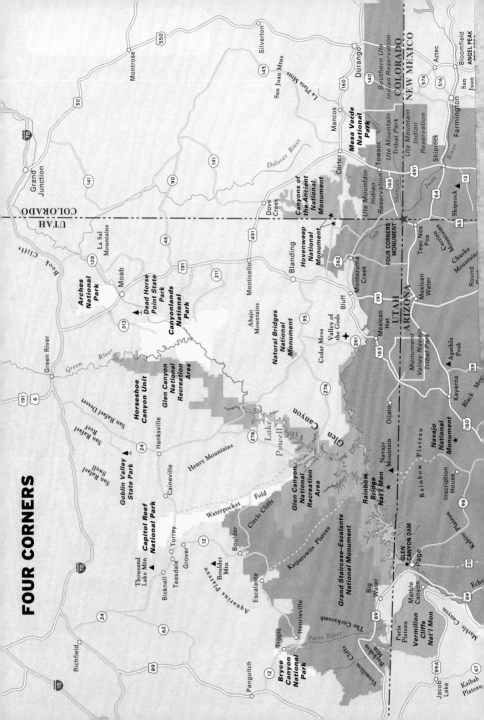

Contents

Discover
the Four Corners

At Four Corners Monument on the Navajo reservation, imaginary lines cross a high sagebrush plain. This X marks the heart of the Southwestern United States, where mountains meet desert and the past is close enough to touch. But no surveyor's mark can convey the vastness that is the soul of the Four Corners.

Here, powerful rivers have cut through millions of years of stone layers, peeling open the earth's secrets. Wind and rain have sculpted hoodoos and arches, and volcanoes have left domes, columns, and pinnacles scattered like old bones across the uplifted Colorado Plateau.

Here, too, Navajo, Hopi, Zuni, and Ute people continue traditions hundreds, even thousands, of years old, stretching from the palatial ruins of Mesa Verde to the humble farmsteads of Canyon de Chelly. When Spaniards, Mexicans, and Americans arrived, native cultures accommodated new traditions without losing their own, creating an intriguing blend of crafts, cuisines, and customs.

Nor can a surveyor's mark represent the Four Corners' convergence of extremes: After spring melt or summer showers, wildflowers burst from seemingly bare rock. Lazy brown rivers change to white-water rapids. Forested mesas and snow-topped mountains surround sparse deserts and sagebrush flats. Sun-drenched expanses transform at night to velvety black skies studded with countless stars.

Little wonder that this curious and remote region has drawn humans for centuries. From hidden Escalante canyons to the windswept ruins at Homolovi, the Old Ones left spiraling petroglyphs or pictographs to symbolize their journeys across the landscape. Their ancient footpaths and trade routes became surveyors' routes and wagon trails. In turn, these became paved highways, where oases of blinking neon welcomed travelers and promised a taste of the Old West: trading posts piled with native crafts or curiosities like petrified wood, a ride on a Victorian train, or a tour of an ancient city.

More than a dozen parks and monuments preserve stunning scenery and historical treasures. Charming small towns like Bluff, Utah, and Aztec, New Mexico, offer comfortable lodgings and home-style cooking, while livelier cities like Flagstaff, Arizona, and Durango, Colorado, host a dazzling array of adventure sports and cultural events. For those who prefer solitude, millions of acres of roadless backcountry hold slot canyons, rock towers, forest trails, trout streams, and the stone dwellings of the Old Ones. One of the last areas in the United States to be mapped, the Four Corners still imparts a sense of discovery to those who visit its expanses.

Planning Your Trip

▶ WHERE TO GO

Navajo and Hopi Country

Arizona's northeast corner contrasts the geologic wedding cake of the **Grand Canyon** with the snowy crests of the **San Francisco Peaks. Flagstaff,** the region's tourist hub, is an active city with enviable outdoor offerings, an outstanding cultural museum, and a lively college scene. The metaphysical mecca of Sedona is only a short hop away, as are the evocative expanses of the **Navajo and Hopi Reservations,** ranging from the lush river bottom of **Canyon de Chelly** to the airy reaches of the **Hopi Mesas.** Where else can you hike into one of the Natural Wonders of the World one day, explore 1,000-year-old ruins the next, and bargain with native artisans over handwoven rugs or finely wrought jewelry the day after that?

New Mexico and Colorado

The United States' archaeological heartland covers the northwest corner of New Mexico and the southwest corner of Colorado. It's anchored by two world-class historic sites: **Mesa Verde National Park,** with its famed Cliff Palace, and **Chaco Culture National Historical Park,** whose monumental ruins stand open beneath the desert sky. Other outstanding sites in the area include **Hovenweep** and **Aztec Ruins,** both national monuments, and **Salmon Ruins** in Bloomfield. You can learn all about the Old Ones at the Anasazi Heritage Center or the Crow Canyon Archaeological Center near Cortez, or see centuries-old traditions come alive in contemporary pottery, weavings, stone carvings, and dance performances at Zuni Pueblo and Gallup. **Durango** is the most entertaining city in southern Colorado, with hiking, skiing, mountain biking, and camping, and the historic narrow-gauge railroad to the former mining camp of Silverton.

IF YOU HAVE...

Delicate Arch is Utah's most iconic landform.

- **ONE WEEK:** Starting from **Arizona,** visit Flagstaff, Grand Canyon National Park, the Hopi Mesas, and Monument Valley.

- **TWO WEEKS:** Add Canyon de Chelly National Monument, Page, and Glen Canyon National Recreation Area.

- **THREE WEEKS:** Add Canyonlands National Park, Arches National Park, and Moab.

- **FOUR WEEKS:** Add SR 12 (Escalante, Boulder, Capitol Reef National Park), Mesa Verde National Park, and Durango.

If you are starting from **Utah,** begin in Moab and follow the route from the opposite direction.

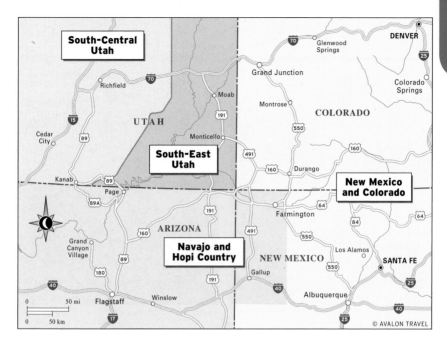

Southeast Utah

It's easy to feel small in Southeast Utah, whether you're standing on the edge of a 1,000-foot precipice or gazing up at a red stone arch that could hold an office building. **Canyonlands and Arches National Parks** are both wonderlands of geology and less than an hour from the adventure-sports hotbed of **Moab.** Take a mountain bike ride on the famous **Slickrock Trail,** climb a desert tower, raft the **Colorado River,** or watch the sun set from Grandview Point on the **Island in the Sky.**

South-Central Utah

It takes a little more tire tread and boot leather to explore this vast corner of America's Outback, but the rewards are incredible scenery, from the monumental geology of Capitol Reef to the hidden slot canyons of the Escalante canyons, and memorable experiences, from picking apples or cherries in Fruita's desert orchards to floating lazily across Lake Powell's hallucinatory blue expanse. The small towns of **Escalante** and **Boulder** offer access to the canyons of the gigantic **Grand Staircase-Escalante National Monument,** and **Page** is tucked neatly between the Navajo Reservation and **Glen Canyon Dam.** Beyond that, you're more or less on your own. If it's solitude you seek, you'll find it in abundance here.

Hovenweep's enigmatic towers were built on canyon edges.

Wild sunflowers grow along the Colorado River near Moab.

▶ WHEN TO GO

In terms of weather, the best times to visit the Four Corners are in **spring** and **fall.** Warm days give way to cool nights, and the skies are mostly crystal-clear. **Summer** is hotter, making a venture into the backcountry (especially the Grand Canyon, the Escalante canyons, and Utah's canyonlands) an exercise in getting from one water source to the next as much as anything else.

Summer also brings the monsoon season, with sweltering mornings frequently relieved by afternoon downpours. Increased rainfall can turn dirt roads into mud bogs and slot canyons into raging sluices. It's still possible to have a great time here in summer by timing outdoor activities for mornings and evenings, when it's cooler. Or follow the lead of many locals and head into the hills, where temperatures are cooler and running water more abundant.

In the **winter,** when the lower angle of the sun bathes canyon walls in golden light, you'll have many of the region's sites to yourself. However, many local businesses and even some visitors centers limit their hours or close for the season.

► BEFORE YOU GO

What to Take

Water, water, water. When traveling in the Southwest, you should always keep a water bottle close at hand and a couple of extra gallons in the car. Many hikers and bikers swear by backpack hydration systems. Sun protection is just as important: light-colored, long-sleeved shirts, pants, sunglasses, and a hat with a wide brim are ideal. Otherwise, slather on the sunscreen. (A bandanna or scarf is handy to protect your neck from the sun.)

A warm layer such as a light fleece jacket or sweater comes in handy for cool evenings. Synthetic fabrics are light, breathe well, and dry almost instantly. Cotton clothing is cool but the fabric can chafe when it gets damp and chill you quickly when it gets wet. Bring a swimsuit if you want to take a dip in a river or your hotel pool.

If you plan on doing any hiking, pack a light pair of boots (already broken in) or hiking shoes. Consider a walking stick or a pair of trekking poles for backpacking. Waterproof sport sandals are comfortable for everything but hard-core hiking. They're particularly good in situations where your feet are constantly getting wet, such as rafting.

Camping brings its own gear list. For a night under the desert stars, you can get by with a tarp (or nothing at all) instead of a tent. Remember that you'll have to carry more water than you're probably used to for extended hikes and backpacking trips, so bring bottles or bladders enough to carry at least a gallon, and perhaps more. The rest is standard gear: compass, sleeping bag and pad, cook set and stove, water filtration, and the like.

Outfit your car with a good map, binoculars, and a sunshade or towel to keep dark upholstery from turning into a frying pan. High elevations and dry air mean the sun there is intense. And, unless the moon is full or close to it, the nights are inky black. Be sure you have a flashlight for after-dark rambles.

Square Tower House is Mesa Verde's tallest cliff dwelling—rising to four stories.

Explore the Four Corners

▶ THE BEST OF THE FOUR CORNERS

Even if you only have two weeks to explore this huge expanse, and no particular interest to sculpt your itinerary, it's still possible to see most of the highlights before you have to head home. Like the rest of these itineraries, this one starts and finishes in Flagstaff, the closest city to a major airport (Phoenix) in the region.

Day 1

Visit the **Museum of Northern Arizona** for an overview of the Four Corners' art, history, and native cultures, and spend the afternoon hiking or riding the chairlift to the top of Humphrey's Peak. If possible, attend an evening viewing program at **Lowell Observatory.** Sleep in Flagstaff.

Day 2

Head north on U.S. 89, stopping at **Wupatki** and **Sunset Crater National Monuments** en route. Have lunch at **Cameron Trading Post,** and tour Glen Canyon Dam or stroll or bike a section of the Rim Trail before spending the night in **Page.**

Day 3

Spend the day hiking and photographing **Antelope Canyon,** tour **Lake Powell** and **Rainbow Bridge,** or float the Colorado River through **Glen Canyon** to **Lees Ferry.** Sleep in Page again.

Day 4

Continue east from Page on SR 98, a good introduction to the backcountry of the **Navajo Reservation.** Continue on U.S. 160 to Kayenta, with an optional stop at **Navajo National Monument** to hike the short trail for an overlook of the Betatakin cliff dwelling. North of Kayenta is **Monument Valley,** which

The Betatakin cliff dwelling is tucked into an alcove at Navajo National Monument.

The Around the Peaks Loop north of Flagstaff is a colorful autumn drive.

you should aim to reach for sunset. (Don't miss sunrise either, if you can help it.) Sleep here or in Mexican Hat, Utah.

Day 5

Head north into Utah on U.S. 163, where you'll pick up SR 261 and climb onto Cedar Mesa. When the road ends at SR 95, turn west and spend a few hours hiking and driving **Natural Bridges National Monument.** Keep going west across the upper reaches of Lake Powell and the Burr Desert. If you're camping, sleep among the weird formations at **Goblin Valley** or near the trailhead into **Horseshoe Canyon,** a detached portion of Canyonlands's Maze District. If not, continue on to I-70 and **Green River,** stopping if time permits.

Day 6

In Green River, visit the **John Wesley Powell River History Museum** before turning back south toward **Moab** on U.S. 191. Catch the sunset from **Grandview Point** in the Island in the Sky District of **Canyonlands National**

Park if you have time. If not, drive a few miles along Potash or River Roads and watch sunset cliffs reflecting in the Colorado River. Spend the night in Moab.

Day 7

Explore **Arches National Park,** which can easily take a full day if you do some of the hiking trails. Sleep in Moab.

Days 8-9

Moab and its environs are well worth a few days' exploring. Take your pick from a short raft trip on the **Colorado River,** a ride on one of the many **mountain bike trails** nearby, or a hike in the **Needles District** of Canyonlands, an hour south. Sleep in Moab.

Day 10

Head south on U.S. 191 to Monticello, where you can turn east onto U.S. 491 toward Colorado. If you have time, stop at **Lowry Pueblo** or continue through Monticello and turn west at SR 262 to spend a couple of hours

Gallup's historic El Morro Theater was built in 1928.

at **Hovenweep National Monument.** Get a hotel room or campsite in **Cortez.**

Day 11

Spend the day touring **Mesa Verde National Park.** Enjoy a stroll through historic downtown **Durango** or along the Animas River before spending the night in Durango.

Day 12

Head south from Durango on U.S. 550 to **Aztec,** a tidy little town near two Chaco outliers: **Aztec Ruins National Monument** and **Salmon Ruins** in Bloomfield. Sleep in Aztec or **Farmington.**

Day 13

Continue west to **Shiprock,** near the pinnacle of the same name, and south on U.S. 491 across the eastern edge of the Navajo Reservation to **Gallup,** where you should do some trading-post browsing.

Day 14

For your last day you have two route choices: One is to stick to I-40, stopping off at the many interesting sights as you edge the Painted Desert: **Petrified Forest National Park, La Posada** and "**Standin' on the Corner Park**" in **Winslow,** and **Meteor Crater** or **Walnut Canyon National Monument** to the west. Otherwise, for a final dose of native culture, head north from Gallup to SR 264 through Window Rock to **Ganado,** where you can visit the **Hubbell Trading Post National Historic Site.** Continue on SR 264 across the mesa-top villages of the **Hopi Reservation,** eventually reaching U.S. 160 at **Tuba City,** where more trading posts await. Turn south on U.S. 89 soon after. Either way, you'll be back in Flagstaff before you know it.

▶ SOAK UP THE SCENERY

This route is for those who don't plan on venturing far from the pavement but still want to maximize their oohing and aahing opportunities.

Day 1

From **Flagstaff**, head east on I-40, stopping off at **Meteor Crater**. Take the scenic drive through **Petrified Forest National Park**. Have lunch or dinner at **La Posada's Turquoise Room** in Winslow, and spend the night in **Holbrook**.

Day 2

Head up U.S. 191 though Ganado to **Canyon de Chelly National Monument**. You can tour this one your own or descend into the canyon itself on a guided tour. Spend the night here camping or at the **Thunderbird Lodge**.

Day 3

Take U.S. 191 to U.S. 160 and then U.S. 163 to get to **Monument Valley** on the Arizona-Utah border. To make sure you catch the stupendous colors of sunset and sunrise, spend the night here.

Day 4

Head north into Southeast Utah, stopping for a peek at the **Goosenecks of the San Juan** near Mexican Hat. Climb the precipitous Moki Dugway (SR 261) up onto **Cedar Mesa,** and don't miss the views from Muley Point Overlook at the top. Stop at **Natural Bridges National Monument** before returning to U.S. 191 via SR 95, the Trail of the Ancients. Spend the night in **Bluff, Blanding,** or **Monticello.**

Days 5-7

Colorado is a short distance east on U.S. 491 and offers the Cliff Palace of **Mesa Verde National Park**, near Cortez. This is worth at least a full day or more, as is the **San Juan Skyway** that loops in the mountains north of **Durango**. Spend a few nights in the area, and then head back west toward Moab.

At Canyonlands National Park views extend from Island in the Sky to the La Sal Mountains.

Golden columbine grows in shady forests and along waterways.

Days 8-9

Use **Moab** as a home base to visit **Arches National Park** and the Island in the Sky District of **Canyonlands National Park,** where stunning panoramas are easily accessed along paved roads. Sleep in Moab.

Day 10

Continue north on U.S. 191 to I-70 and head west through Green River to reach the turn-off for SR 24 south to **Hanksville.** Here the surroundings get downright weird, from the sawtooth bulwarks of the **San Rafael Swell** to the melting mudstone of **Goblin Valley State Park.** Make it to **Torrey** by nightfall.

Day 11

In nearby **Capitol Reef National Park,** a short scenic drive gives access to a surprising chunk of the park's stupendous sights. Spend a day touring it and spend another night in Torrey.

Day 12

Turn south onto **scenic SR 12,** one of the most spectacular drives in the country. SR 12 winds up onto Boulder Mountain for amazing views before descending into the slickrock wildness of the northern **Grand Staircase-Escalante National Monument.**

Days 13-14

Keep going on SR 12 to **Bryce Canyon National Park,** whose wonders can be absorbed in a day from the rim. Take U.S. 89 south to Kanab, where you should hop south across the state line and drive U.S. 89A up onto the Kaibab Plateau, with the option of a detour to the **North Rim of Grand Canyon.** U.S. 89A continues east along the base of the Vermilion Cliffs to **Marble Canyon** and the impressive twin spans of **Navajo Bridge.** Allow some time to drive down to **Lees Ferry** and linger along the Colorado River.

Eventually you'll find yourself back on U.S. 89 heading south toward Flagstaff. You can take SR 64 west from Cameron to visit the **South Rim of Grand Canyon,** or else continue south to Flagstaff to finish the loop.

BACKCOUNTRY BEAUTY

The Bisti/De-Na-Zin Wilderness Areas encompass eroded badlands and hoodoos.

If a beautiful view makes you want nothing more than to run out and disappear into it for as long as possible, then here are the places to head for. Check routes carefully to see if a four-wheel-drive vehicle is a necessity, take plenty of water, and keep the gas tank half full.

- **Petrified Forest National Park:** Grab a free permit to backpack amid the colorful palette of the Painted Desert north of I-40.

- **Canyon de Chelly National Monument:** Sign up for a guided hike among the Navajo farms and orchards at the bottom of this gorgeous canyon system, or hike on your own down to White House Ruin.

- **Bisti/De-Na-Zin Wilderness Areas:** Wander among otherworldly rock formations south of Farmington, and stick around for a sunrise or sunset here or in the badlands surrounding Angel Peak.

- **Durango:** Mountain bike or hike the foothills of the trail-packed San Juan National Forest, or try rafting or kayaking the wild upper Animas River.

- **San Juan River:** Make a one- to three-day raft trip from Bluff to Mexican Hat, bouncing through sand waves and stopping to view rock art.

- **Grand Gulch:** Hike this canyon loop below Cedar Mesa, rich with ruins and rock art, or take the less-trafficked Owl and Fish Creek Canyons loop.

- **Moab:** Visit the undisputed adventure epicenter of Southeast Utah's outdoor playground for hiking, rock climbing, river rafting and, of course, mountain biking.

- **San Rafael Swell:** Explore twisting slot canyons near the odd landscape of Goblin Valley National Park.

- **Grand Staircase-Escalante National Monument:** Enjoy a backcountry smorgasbord in this gigantic expanse of high desert, highlighted by the sinuous canyons along the Hole-in-the-Rock Road, south of Escalante.

- **Paria Canyon:** Embark on one of the region's most amazing multiday hikes, starting with the peerless slot canyon of Buckskin Gulch.

- **North Rim of the Grand Canyon:** Less crowded than the South Rim, and cooler, too, this part of the park has plenty of shady rim-side trails and the North Kaibab Trail, which leads into the gorge to end all gorges.

- **Needles District of Canyonlands National Park:** Some of the best day hikes in the Southwest are here, with many loop options through the distinctive stone formations.

▶ HISTORIC TREASURES

The past is everywhere you turn in the Four Corners, from ancient ruins and trading posts, museums, and movie locations to Old Route 66. If history is your forte, this is your itinerary.

Day 1

Start your journey in Flagstaff, spending some time at the excellent **Museum of Northern Arizona,** followed by the ruins at **Wupatki.** Spend a night in town.

Day 2

Heading east on I-40, stop to walk along the cliff dwellings of **Walnut Canyon National Monument.** Choose among two **classic hotels** of very different character: La Posada in Winslow and the Wigwam Motel in Holbrook. Continue up U.S. 191 onto the Navajo Reservation to the **Hubbell Trading Post National Historic Site** in Ganado. Take SR 264 east to Gallup and spend the night at vintage El Rancho Hotel.

Day 3

Your next destination is just a stone's throw away, but without four-wheel drive, you'll have to go all the way up to Farmington, over to Bloomfield on U.S. 64, and down U.S. 550 to reach the turnoff to **Chaco Culture National Historical Park,** the center of one of the Southwest's greatest prehistoric cultures. Camping at the park will give you the most time for touring the ruins and rock art here.

Day 4

Visit a pair of Chaco outliers at **Aztec Ruins National Monument** and **Salmon Ruins,** near the cities of Aztec and Bloomfield, respectively. Sleep in Aztec or Farmington.

Day 5

Take U.S. 550 north from Aztec to **Durango,** where you'll leave the ancient past for the Victorian era. Spend a day and night here, grabbing a cocktail at the Strater Hotel's Diamond Belle Saloon before settling in for

Durango Mountain Resort (also known as Purgatory) has 88 ski trails.

Vintage cars sit outside Bluff's Cow Canyon Trading Post.

NATIVE INFLUENCES

Navajo dancers perform at the Gallup Inter-Tribal Indian Ceremonial.

Experience the ways the original Americans live on a visit to one of the Four Corners' largest Native American tribes: Navajo, Hopi, Zuni, and Ute. You can visit each without going far out of Arizona.

- **Cameron, AZ:** Savor a Navajo taco at the Cameron Trading Post and peruse the wares, from the rug room in back to the gallery of Indian arts and antiques out front.

- **Hopi Reservation, AZ:** Tour a timeless stone village perched on one of three long mesas, visit an artist's studio, or learn about different kachina carvings at one of the local galleries.

- **Canyon de Chelly National Monument, AZ:** Hike to the bottom of this stunning canyon to view White House, an Ancestral Puebloan cliff dwelling, while experiencing the agrarian setting, little changed after centuries of Navajo occupation.

- **Crownpoint, NM:** Join local residents and visitors from around the world for an authentic handmade rug auction, held the second Friday of every month.

- **Gallup, NM:** The "Gateway to Indian Country" teems with trading posts and galleries full of crafts made by tribes from across the Southwest, and hosts traditional dance performances on the plaza on summer evenings.

- **Zuni, NM:** Make the scenic drive from Gallup to Zuni Pueblo for an arts-and-crafts festival or a tour of the Spanish Colonial mission.

- **Ute Mountain Tribal Park, CO:** Ancient ruins here rival those at Mesa Verde, but with far fewer visitors.

- **Monument Valley, AZ:** This Navajo tribal park protects red sandstone towers and mesas sacred to the Navajo and famous worldwide thanks to Western movies.

Ismay trading post sits at the edge of the Ute Mountain Ute Reservation.

the night in a grand 1880s hotel or a Queen Anne–style B&B.

Days 6-7

West of Durango on U.S. 160 is a place that will have you awestruck all over again: **Mesa Verde National Park,** whose cliff dwellings have to be seen to be believed. The area around Cortez and the Four Corners itself is rich in archaeology, including the boulder-perched towers of **Hovenweep National Monument,** the sprawling **Canyons of the Ancients National Monument,** and the **Anasazi Heritage Center** near Dolores. Spend two nights in Mesa Verde or Cortez.

Days 8-9

Continue west on U.S. 491 into Southeast Utah at Monticello. On your way toward **Moab** to the north, you'll pass the turnoff for the Needles District of **Canyonlands National Park,** a treasure trove of rock art and ruins. The huge petroglyph panel of **Newspaper Rock** is a mere 10 miles down pretty SR 211. More petroglyphs line roads near Moab, a good home base for a couple of nights.

Day 10

The full-day trip via Green River to the **Horseshoe Canyon** portion of Canyonlands's Maze District (and back) rewards you with one of the most impressive walls of pictographs you'll ever see, the **Great Gallery.** You may see riders heading into the Maze, a network of canyons that served as a hideout for Butch Cassidy and other outlaws.

Day 11

Drive south on U.S. 191 to a pair of museums in Blanding, the **Edge of the Cedars State Park Museum,** full to the rafters with pottery and other artifacts, and the **Dinosaur Museum,** with fossils and realistic models. Take an afternoon detour west onto Cedar Mesa to visit some ruins along SR 95. Spend the night in Blanding or Bluff.

Day 12

Keep going south along U.S. 191, which becomes U.S. 163 as it enters Arizona at **Monument Valley,** the backdrop for dozens of Westerns. Nearby are two **trading posts** not

Petroglyphs cover Newspaper Rock.

to be missed—Goulding's and Oljato. The first is now a museum; the second is closed but affords a picturesque drive that lets you travel back 100 years to the reservation's trading days. Spend the night in Monument Valley and enjoy sunset and sunrise.

Days 13-14

South of Kayenta on U.S. 163 is **Navajo** **National Monument,** where you can see two large cliff dwellings. View Betatakin from a short rim-side trail or get closer on a ranger-guided day hike. For most, visiting Keet Seel is an overnight hike. More trading posts await as you return on U.S. 160 and U.S. 89 to Flagstaff, including the **Tuba City Trading Post** and the **Cameron Trading Post** (which serves up some tasty fry bread). Finish in Flagstaff.

▶ CIRCLING THE CORNERS

In the 1920s the Union Pacific Railroad promoted its Grand Circle Tour through a tight concentration of national parks. Even if your vacation is limited to a week, you can explore the region on a park-bagging auto tour that takes in some of the Four Corners' finest views. To make the most of every minute, try to time your park visits to early morning or late afternoon, when crowds are thinnest and rock formations are bathed in golden light. Enjoy scenic routes by taking well-timed breaks to stretch or eat lunch. Make reservations in advance so you don't lose time searching for a motel room or campsite.

Day 1

Beginning in Flagstaff, drive to the **North Rim** of the Grand Canyon and spend the night at historic Grand Canyon Lodge.

Day 2

Head north to **Bryce Canyon National Park** and stay overnight to enjoy sunset and sunrise.

THE FOUR CORNERS' TOP TEN

In Canyonlands National Park, Mesa Arch frames a stunning view.

Fascinating and fun, dazzling and delicious, here are a dozen of the Four Corner's finest events and attractions:

- **Balloon Festival** (Gallup, NM):Colorful balloons float among towering sandstone cliffs during December's **Red Rock Balloon Rally.**

- **Beer** (Durango, CO): The "City of Brewerly Love," **Durango** has four major brewers crafting beers from pale ale to porter.

- **Scenic Drive** (Escalante, UT): Utah's **Highway 12,** which edges the Grand Staircase–Escalante National Monument, boasts jaw-dropping views with plenty of opportunities for side explorations.

- **Ruins** (Mesa Verde National Park, CO): The cliff dwellings of **Mesa Verde** offer a fascinating glimpse into the Colorado Plateau's urban scene of 800–1,500 years ago.

- **Art Festival** (Sedona, AZ): Over an October weekend more than a hundred artists display their work at the **Sedona Arts Festival** in inspiring red rock surroundings.

- **Trading Post** (Gallup, NM): The Four Corners area is rich with historic and modern trading posts, but if you have time to browse only one, make it **Richardson's Trading Company.**

- **Scenic Overlook** (Canyonlands National Park, UT): The park's Island in the Sky district boasts some of the most breathtaking panoramas in the West, including the view framed by **Mesa Arch.**

- **Fry Bread** (Hopi Reservation, AZ): When tribes were forced onto reservations and given rations of flour and lard, they invented fry bread, now a standby at powwows, fairs, and regional restaurants. Health food it's not, but the blue corn version at the Cultural Center restaurant on **Second Mesa** is delectable, especially with honey.

- **Visitors Center** (Natural Bridges National Monument, UT): Small but mighty, the visitors center at **Natural Bridges National Monument** has excellent displays, an intriguing gift shop selection, and a welcoming staff.

- **Museum** (Flagstaff, AZ): Flag is a science-focused town, and its **Museum of Northern Arizona** offers an impeccable overview of the entire Four Corners region, from paleontology to contemporary art.

The Colorado River runs through Canyonlands National Park.

Day 3

Drive scenic Highway 12 to Torrey, Utah. Stop en route to see **Kodachrome Basin State Park** or hike along the Escalante River. Make Torrey your base for visiting nearby **Capitol Reef National Park.**

Days 4-5

Drive to Moab, taking time to stop at **Goblin Valley State Park.** Spend a couple days exploring **Arches National Park** and the **Island in the Sky** district of Canyonlands.

Days 6-7

Choose between traveling east to **Mesa Verde National Park** or heading south for **Monument Valley.** Side trip possibilities include **Hovenweep** or **Navajo National Monument.** End your trip in Durango or return to Flagstaff.

NAVAJO AND HOPI COUNTRY

Northeastern Arizona contains some of the loneliest yet most extraordinary acres of the Colorado Plateau, averaging between 5,000 and 7,000 feet in elevation, where sagebrush, yucca, and desert grasses march to the rims of deep canyons and mountains are dusted with snow in winter. The wide-open country is a textbook of geology. Mesas, buttes, and volcanic features from cinder cones to lava dikes thrust above the otherwise flat expanse. Badlands, scarps, and canyons reveal colorful layers of sandstone, limestone, and shale. Ninety minutes northwest of Flagstaff, the largest ponderosa pine forest in the world spreads to both rims of the Grand Canyon, the biggest gorge of them all.

Flagstaff alone could keep a curious traveler occupied for weeks, with three national monuments, some of the Southwest's best museums, a ski resort, and miles of trails leading around the 600-plus volcanic peaks that dot the skyline. But it is the indigenous cultures that truly define this part of the Four Corners. Despite almost overwhelming odds, the Navajo and Hopi tribes have maintained their traditions into the 21st century. Farming, ranching, herding, and tourism provide an income for many, and tribal artisans continue to weave rugs, carve katsina figurines, or make silver jewelry.

With the exception of Flagstaff, the larger cities on or near the reservations, including Kayenta, Window Rock, and Winslow, are not very big, and the surrounding poverty can make them as sobering as they are inviting. Yet they offer riches of experiences: shopping

© KATHLEEN BRYANT

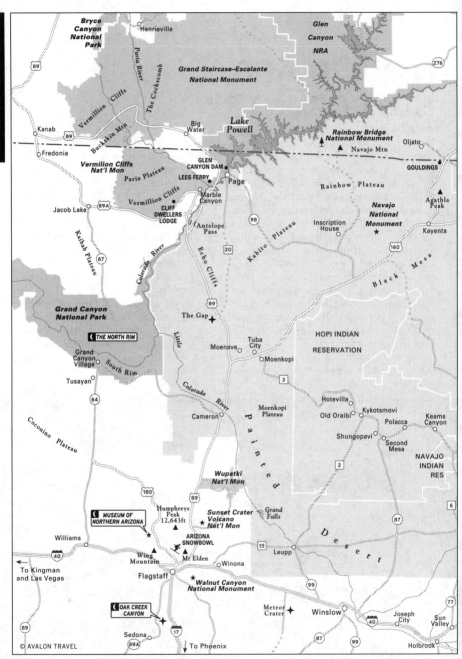

© AVALON TRAVEL

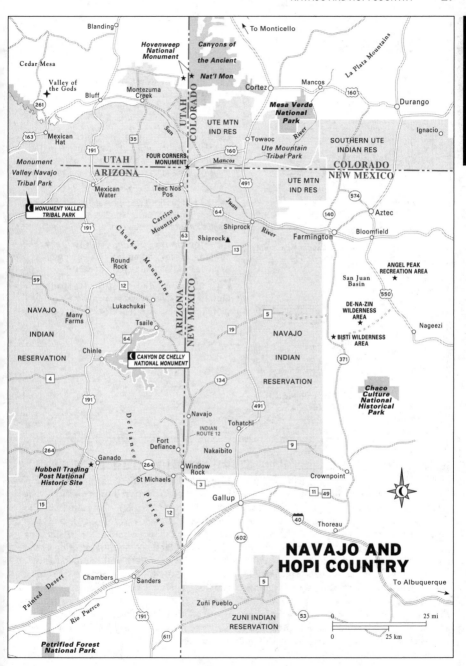

Blanding

To Monticello

Cedar Mesa

Hovenweep
National
Monument

Canyons of
the Ancient
Nat'l Mon

Valley of
the Gods

261

Bluff

Montezuma
Creek

UTAH
COLORADO

Cortez

Mancos

La Plata Mountains

160

Durango

163

Mexican
Hat

191

35

San

UTAH
ARIZONA

UTE MTN
IND RES

Mesa Verde
National
Park

Ignacio

Monument
Valley Navajo
Tribal Park

FOUR CORNERS
MONUMENT

160

Towaoc

Ute Mountain
Tribal Park

SOUTHERN UTE
INDIAN RES

Mancos

COLORADO
NEW MEXICO

MONUMENT VALLEY
TRIBAL PARK

Mexican
Water

Teec Nos
Pos

491

UTE MTN
IND RES

574

Aztec

191

Carrizo
Mountains

64

Juan

140

550

Bloomfield

59

Chuska

63

Shiprock

Shiprock▲

River

Farmington

ANGEL PEAK
RECREATION AREA

Round
Rock

13

San Juan
Basin

NAVAJO

12

Mountains

Many
Farms

Lukachukai

DE-NA-ZIN
WILDERNESS
AREA

Nageezi

INDIAN

Tsaile

5

19

NAVAJO

★ *BISTI WILDERNESS*
AREA

RESERVATION

64

CANYON DE CHELLY
NATIONAL MONUMENT

INDIAN

371

4

Chinle

191

134

RESERVATION

Chaco
Culture
National
Historical
Park

Defiance

491

Navajo

INDIAN
ROUTE 12

Tohatchi

264

Fort
Defiance

Nakaibito

9

Hubbell Trading
Post National
Historic Site

Ganado

264

Window
Rock

Crownpoint

St Michaels

3

11 49

15

Plateau

12

Gallup

40

Thoreau

602

NAVAJO AND
HOPI COUNTRY

Chambers

Sanders

Painted Desert

191

5

To Albuquerque

Zuñi Pueblo

611

ZUNI INDIAN
RESERVATION

53

Rio Puerco

0   25 mi

0   25 km

Petrified Forest
National Park

HIGHLIGHTS

◖ **Museum of Northern Arizona:** An extensive collection, clearly presented, focuses on the cultural and natural history of the Colorado Plateau region (page 31).

◖ **Oak Creek Canyon:** Rugged cliffs shelter this recreation area between Flagstaff and Sedona, a riparian oasis of sycamores and pines, swimming holes, hiking trails, and sparkling spring-fed waters (page 46).

◖ **The North Rim:** Less visited and cooler in the summer, the Grand Canyon's northern rim seems a world apart from its southern one (page 54).

◖ **Monument Valley Tribal Park:** Towering mesas and buttes make up one of America's best-known vistas (page 65).

◖ **Canyon de Chelly National Monument:** A gorgeous canyon system preserves a timeless slice of Navajo life (page 68).

LOOK FOR ◖ TO FIND RECOMMENDED SIGHTS, ACTIVITIES, DINING, AND LODGING.

at trading posts and galleries; taking in breathstopping views of Canyon de Chelly National Park, Monument Valley, or the Grand Canyon; walking the timeless villages of the Hopi Reservation. Ancestral Puebloan cliff dwellings are scattered throughout the region, with those at Navajo National Monument rivaling anything in Colorado or Utah.

Though the largest towns on the reservations have hotels, food choices and tourist services are limited, and it may be an hour or more to the next gas station. But for those who bring a sense of adventure and an open mind along with their sunscreen and hiking boots, this is a region where legend and landscape meet.

PLANNING YOUR TIME

Flagstaff makes a convenient hub for exploring northern Arizona's Indian country. The forested college town is an appealing place to spend several days, including at least a half day to peruse the collection of the outstanding **Museum of Northern Arizona.** Visiting **Grand Canyon National Park** will require at least a day, and for anything longer than a short hike, you'll need gear, permits, and some strong legs. **Sedona,** down lovely Oak Creek Canyon, is worth another day or two if you plan on soaking up some of the groovy local energy or redrock scenery.

The Big Rez (as residents refer to the vast

Navajo Nation) has impressive attractions of its own, and each could take a day to explore. The sandy bottoms and sheer cliffs of **Canyon de Chelly** have sheltered humans for centuries. **Monument Valley** is a visual icon for good reason: The stone monoliths rising from the stark red-dirt plateau make up one of the most awesome sights in the American West. In the center of the larger Navajo Nation, the traditional Hopi villages can be explored in a day, though the motel on Second Mesa makes a pleasant overnight.

The Route 66 towns of Flagstaff, Winslow, and Holbrook lie along I-40, which parallels the southern border of the Navajo Reservation. The interstate passes the gaudy palettes of the Painted Desert and cuts through Petrified Forest National Park as it continues east to New Mexico. South of Flagstaff, I-17 leads to Phoenix. U.S. 89 runs north from Flagstaff, splitting off into U.S. 89A before reaching Page and the Utah border.

U.S. 160 leads northeast across the Navajo Reservation from Tuba City to Shiprock via Kayenta, where U.S. 163 heads north to Monument Valley and the Utah border. From Tuba City, you can also take SR 264 through the Hopi Mesas to Ganado, Window Rock, and Gallup, New Mexico. U.S. 191 travels north-south, through Ganado and Chinle to Mexican Water, Utah. Countless paved and dirt roads reach much of the rest of Indian land. Some of these tracks can be very rough, particularly in bad weather, and some are unmarked; the AAA *Guide to Indian Country* (familiar to Tony Hillerman fans as Jim Chee's map of choice) is your best weapon against getting lost.

Flagstaff and Vicinity

"Flag" (pop. 65,000) is a mountain town, and outdoor recreation centers around the ponderosa-and-aspen-covered San Francisco Peaks, which tower above the city's northern edge. It may be hard to believe as the heat waves shimmer up off the Sonoran and Mohave Deserts to the south and west, but at 7,000 feet, Flagstaff is actually the second-snowiest metropolitan area in the country after Syracuse, New York, with an average of 108 inches of snow yearly.

Flag is also a city aware of its heritage, from landmarked historical buildings to the blinking neon motel signs along Route 66. This has always been a railroad town—an average of 60 trains still roar through daily, though the city recently spent close to a million dollars to quiet the whistles downtown. Founded in 1899, Northern Arizona University (NAU) has a student population of 20,000 that helps keep the local music and art scenes lively.

Three national monuments are within a half hour of the city, which is surrounded by the Coconino National Forest. City and county parks host dozens of summertime festivals, and Lowell Observatory keeps an eye on the starry night skies year round. Skiing the Arizona Snowbowl, hiking the Grand Canyon, visiting the outstanding Museum of Northern Arizona, taking a day trip to Sedona or a nearby Indian reservation—whatever your interests, Flagstaff has plenty to offer.

History

People were living in scattered pit houses and canyon-edge dwellings in the foothills of the San Francisco Peaks when a series of eruptions from 1040 to 1100 covered 800 square miles of the surrounding countryside with lava and ash. The cinders acted as a moisture-preserving mulch, and the region's population shifted to larger pueblo-style villages that became centers of agriculture and trade. By 1250 many villagers had moved on.

After the 1848 treaty ceding Mexican lands to the United States, U.S. military engineers and surveyors explored the area, following prehistoric routes that later became wagon trails, railroads, and highways. An 1857 survey expedition was led by Lt. Edward F. Beale, whose camel corps established the Beale Road used by gold-seekers and immigrants. In 1876 a group of settlers arrived from Boston, and on July 4 they raised an American flag on a peeled pine at Antelope Springs, not far from present-day Thorpe Park. The early settlement didn't last, but the flagpole did, and travelers heading west were told to keep an eye out for the good campsite it marked.

Eventually, some settlers stayed, and so did the name Flagstaff. The post office and railroad both arrived in 1881, and by 1886 this was the biggest city on the tracks between Albuquerque and the Pacific Ocean. The Arizona Lumber and Timber Company made a fortune from the abundant forests, shipping logs out cheaply by rail. Sheep and cattle ranches provided additional jobs. Coconino County, established in 1891, was named for the Cohonina Indians, ancestors of today's Havasupai tribe.

Three years later, Percival Lowell established an observatory on a hill overlooking Flagstaff, and in 1930 Lowell Observatory astronomer Clyde Tombaugh discovered Pluto (now considered by many scientists to be a dwarf planet). In 1926 Route 66 replaced the old Beale Wagon Road and decades later was in turn replaced by I-40. The route has become a gateway for visitors discovering the wonders of the Petrified Forest, Painted Desert, the Grand Canyon, and Indian Country.

SIGHTS
San Francisco Peaks

The peaks forming Flagstaff's distinctive northern skyline were named by Spanish explorer-priests after St. Francis of Assisi, the founder of their order. The Navajos refer to the peaks as Dook'o'oosliíd ("abalone shell mountain"), the Sacred Mountain of the West. The Hopis call them Nubat-i-kyan-bi ("place of the snow peaks") and believe that their kachina spirits live among the summits for part of every year before returning to the Hopi mesas in the form of nourishing rain clouds. The ever-shifting play of light over the peaks makes it easy to see why all the region's native tribes revere them. The 1930s Works Progress Administration (WPA) guide to Arizona notes, "At sunrise they appeal gold; at noon they are Carrara marble against a turquoise sky; at sunset they are polished copper, ruby, coral, and finally amethyst."

The tallest is **Humphreys Peak,** Arizona's highest point at 12,633 feet, home to a ski resort and miles of hiking trails. The views there are fabulous, from flower-splashed meadows all the way down to the Painted Desert and— if it's a clear day—the Grand Canyon. The 18,960-acre **Kachina Peaks Wilderness** encloses the highest slopes of the San Francisco Peaks, which were formed during the mountain's most recent eruption, about two million years ago. At their center is a huge caldera, the Inner Basin, filled with aspens, pines, and firs.

The easiest way to explore the peaks is via the paved road to the **Arizona Snowbowl,** which leaves Highway 180 seven miles north of downtown and climbs another seven to the ski resort. In the winter, 32 runs are served by four lifts. During summer months, the **Arizona Snowbowl Skyride** (928/779-1951, www.arizonasnowbowl.com, 10 A.M.–4 P.M. Fri.–Sun. and holiday Mon., Memorial Day–mid-Oct., $12 adults, $8 seniors and youth, under seven free) carries visitors to 11,500 feet for panoramic views. At the base of the lift, the Peak Side Café serves snacks and sandwiches for lunch ($10 and under).

Schultz Pass Road (FR 420), a dirt road suitable for passenger cars or bikes, loops 26 miles, passing trailheads and shady meadows where it's easy to while away a couple hours picnicking or watching for elk, wild turkey, and other forest creatures. To get there, drive two miles north of Flagstaff, turning right (east) just after passing the Museum of Northern Arizona. The road ends east of the peaks on U.S. 89, where you can turn right (south) and continue back to Flag. The 2010 Schultz Fire damaged some sections; check with the Flagstaff Ranger District (928/526-0866, www.fs.usda.gov/coconino) for current road conditions.

The **Around the Peaks Loop** is a scenic 44-mile dirt and gravel route that's open April–November, weather permitting. This drive is especially pretty in autumn, when the aspens are turning gold. To do the loop counterclockwise, drive 14 miles north of Flagstaff on U.S. 89 to FR 418, west 12 miles to FR 151 (also known as the Hart Prairie Road), and then south 8 miles to rejoin U.S. 180 about 10 miles north of Flagstaff. The **Nature Conservancy** (928/774-8892, ext. 5, www. nature.org) administers a 245-acre preserve at Hart Prairie, with guided nature walks on Sundays, mid-June–mid-October.

◖ Museum of Northern Arizona

Founded in 1928, this outstanding museum located three miles northwest of downtown Flagstaff (3101 N. Fort Valley Rd., 928/774-5213, www.musnaz.org, 9 A.M.–5 P.M. daily, $7 adults, $4 children) makes an ideal introduction to the human and natural history of the Colorado Plateau. Displays on anthropology, biology, geology, paleontology, and fine art are comprehensive without being exhausting, even though the museum curates more than 600,000 artifacts. The histories of the Colorado Plateau's tribes are a main focus, and exquisite weavings, katsina carvings, baskets, pottery, jewelry, and other crafts are displayed. The museum's Kiva Gallery recreates a kiva with a modern mural by the late Michael Kabotie and Delbridge Honanie, founders of Group Hopid, artists who took tribal traditions in new directions. Changing exhibits examine such topics as the role of Native Americans in Westerns. Programs include monthly behind-the-scenes tours of museum archives, hands-on activities for kids and adults, and guided excursions to locations around the Colorado Plateau. MNA's celebrated summer heritage programs spotlight Zuni, Hopi, Navajo, and Latino traditions, with arts and crafts, dances, storytelling, food, and other activities filling the museum's courtyard and grounds one weekend a month.

Pioneer Museum

The 1908 Coconino County Hospital for the Indigent was converted to a boardinghouse and then a museum in 1963. Today the northern division of the Arizona Historical Society administers the museum (2340 N. Fort Valley Rd., 928/774-6272, http://arizonahistoricalsociety.org, 9 A.M.–5 P.M. Mon.–Sat., $5 pp

adults, children free). The collection includes more than 10,000 bits of Flagstaff's past, from an old iron lung to farm gear and clothing. Nearby are a 1910 barn, a 1912 steam locomotive, and a historic cabin that was moved there from the east side of the San Francisco Peaks. In summer and fall, the museum hosts walking tours of historic downtown, the annual Wool Festival, and other events featuring reenactors, craft demonstrations, music, and cookouts.

Lowell Observatory

Boston aristocrat-turned-astronomer Percival Lowell founded this observatory (1400 W. Mars Hill Rd., 928/774-3358, www.lowell. edu, 9 A.M.–5 P.M. daily, from noon Nov.–Feb., $10 adults, $4 children) in 1894. He spent 15 years gazing at Mars through the 24-inch refractor telescope, convinced that he was looking at the remains of canals built by an intelligent race. On that matter he was way off, but his hunch about "Planet X" orbiting beyond Uranus proved correct: 14 years after Lowell's death in 1916, Pluto was discovered by Clyde Tombaugh, and Lowell is given most of the credit. Today the privately owned observatory sits at 7,260 feet in the clear mountain air above Flagstaff, and it is still used for serious research. The observatory offers daily tours and evening programs throughout the year. Highlights include the original telescope inside historic Clark Dome (built of native ponderosa pine in the days before power tools), the spectrograph used to prove that the universe is expanding, and photographic plates with the first images of Pluto. During summer months (June 1–Aug. 31), music and food are available on the patio 6 P.M.–8 P.M. Tuesday–Thursday, and telescope viewing programs begin every evening at 8:30 P.M., weather permitting. Held rain or shine, interactive planetarium presentations begin at 7 P.M.

Riordan Mansion State Historic Park

Brothers Timothy and Michael Riordan successfully operated the Arizona Lumber and Timber Company near the turn of the 20th

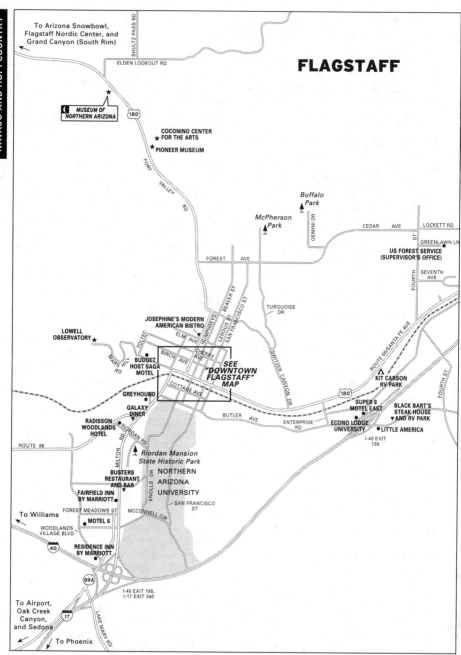

FLAGSTAFF

To Arizona Snowbowl, Flagstaff Nordic Center, and Grand Canyon (South Rim)

SHULTZ PASS RD

ELDEN LOOKOUT RD

MUSEUM OF NORTHERN ARIZONA

180

COCONINO CENTER FOR THE ARTS

PIONEER MUSEUM

FORT VALLEY RD

Buffalo Park

McPherson Park

GEMINI DR

CEDAR AVE

LOCKETT RD

GREENLAWN LN

US FOREST SERVICE (SUPERVISOR'S OFFICE)

FOREST AVE

SEVENTH AVE

FOURTH ST

TURQUOISE DR

JOSEPHINE'S MODERN AMERICAN BISTRO

HUMPHREYS
LEROUX ST
BEAVER ST
SAN FRANCISCO ST
ELM AVE

LOWELL OBSERVATORY

MARS HILL RD
TOLTEC

BIRCH AVE
CHERRY AVE
COTTAGE AVE

SEE "DOWNTOWN FLAGSTAFF" MAP

SWITZER CANYON DR

ROUTE 66/SANTA FE AVE

KIT CARSON RV PARK

180

FOURTH ST

BUDGET HOST SAGA MOTEL

GREYHOUND

GALAXY DINER

RADISSON WOODLANDS HOTEL

BUTLER AVE

ENTERPRISE RD

SUPER 8 MOTEL EAST

BLACK BART'S STEAK HOUSE AND RV PARK

ECONO LODGE UNIVERSITY

LITTLE AMERICA

ROUTE 66

MILTON RD
RIORDAN RD

I-40 EXIT 198

Riordan Mansion State Historic Park

KNOLLS DR

NORTHERN ARIZONA UNIVERSITY

BUSTERS RESTAURANT AND BAR

FAIRFIELD INN BY MARRIOTT

SAN FRANCISCO ST

To Williams

FOREST MEADOWS ST

MCCONNELL CIR

MOTEL 6

WOODLANDS VILLAGE BLVD

40

RESIDENCE INN BY MARRIOTT

89A

I-40 EXIT 195, I-17 EXIT 340

To Airport, Oak Creek Canyon, and Sedona

17

LAKE MARY RD

To Phoenix

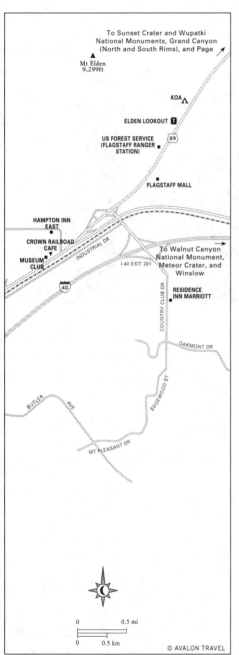

To Sunset Crater and Wupatki
National Monuments, Grand Canyon
(North and South Rims), and Page

Mt Elden
9,299ft

KOA

ELDEN LOOKOUT

US FOREST SERVICE
(FLAGSTAFF RANGER
STATION)

89

FLAGSTAFF MALL

HAMPTON INN
EAST

CROWN RAILROAD
CAFE

MUSEUM
CLUB

INDUSTRIAL DR

I-40 EXIT 201

To Walnut Canyon
National Monument,
Meteor Crater, and
Winslow

40

RESIDENCE
INN MARRIOTT

COUNTRY CLUB DR

OAKMONT DR

EDGEWOOD ST

BUTLER

AVE

MT PLEASANT DR

0   0.5 mi

0   0.5 km

© AVALON TRAVEL

century. Each of the two brothers married one of the Metz sisters, cousins of the famous Babbitt Brothers traders. In 1904 they commissioned the architect of the Grand Canyon's El Tovar Hotel to build them a monumental home of logs and volcanic stone, which they called *Kinlichi* (Navajo for "red house"). The Riordan Mansion (409 W. Riordan Rd., 928/779-4395, www.pr.state.az.us, 8:30 A.M.–5 P.M. daily, from 10:30 A.M. Nov.–Apr., $7 adults, $3 children) is actually two separate homes joined by a large rec room—13,000 square feet in all. Michael's side of the 40-room duplex has displays on Flagstaff's lumber industry, and Timothy's side is open for tours. Original fixtures and hand-carved American Craftsman–style furniture give a taste of life at the high end in early Flagstaff. Reservations are a good idea for the guided tours, held hourly, beginning at 9 A.M. in the summer and 11 A.M. in winter. Brown bag lunches and evening slide presentations, offered on a monthly basis, explore such topics as stagecoach lines or Flagstaff's volcanic past.

The Arboretum at Flagstaff

More than 2,500 species of plants from across the Colorado Plateau thrive at the country's highest research botanical garden (4001 S. Woody Mountain Rd., 928/774-1442, www.thearb.org, 9 A.M.–5 P.M. daily Apr.–Oct., $7 adults, $3 children). The arboretum's 7,150-foot elevation gives it a brief 75-day growing season, yet some 2,500 species are successfully cultivated there, half of which are native to the Four Corners. The collection includes the largest herb garden in the Southwest. Wildflowers are particularly impressive during the summer monsoon season—the best time to visit. Several miles of trails wind through the garden's 200 acres, and guided tours are given daily at 11 A.M., 1 P.M., and 3 P.M. Other activities include weekly bird walks, occasional summer wildflower walks, concerts, classes and workshops, and educational programs for kids.

Elden Pueblo

About 900 years ago, a group of Ancestral Puebloans referred to by archaeologists as the

The Museum of Northern Arizona is a good introduction to the land and cultures of the Colorado Plateau.

Sinagua (see-NAH-wa) Indians constructed this village situated below Mt. Elden, a lava dome. Their descendants, the Hopis, call the 60- to 70-room pueblo Pasiovi. Since 1978 the Forest Service has administered Elden Pueblo as a public archaeology project to educate visitors. You can tour the ruins (one mile north of the Flagstaff Mall along U.S. 89) year-round, weather permitting. In summer and fall, the Elden Pueblo Project hosts an archaeological field school there. Occasional public dig days are offered. For more information about classes and special events, contact the Elden Pueblo Program Manager at the Coconino National Forest Supervisor's office (928/527-3452).

Sunset Crater Volcano National Monument

The youngest of more than 600 extinct volcanoes in the San Francisco Volcanic Field, Sunset Crater is a cinder cone, 1,000 feet high and nearly a mile wide at its base. Its name comes from the multicolored mineral deposits on the crater rim, which appear to glow with inner fire at sunset. Between A.D. 1040 and 1100, Sunset Crater began to erupt. Flowing lava and forest fires lighted the night sky, and spewing ash traveled 800 square miles. Cinders piled up around the vent, and molten rock oozed through cracks in the earth, transforming the landscape into a stark expanse of cinder drifts and lava hardened into chunks and rough swirls.

A 36-mile **loop road** off U.S. 89 north of Flagstaff connects Sunset Crater (8,029 feet), the Strawberry Crater Wilderness (in the Coconino National Forest), and Wupatki National Monument. It's a fascinating drive through an altered landscape that is slowly transforming once more. Pines, sagebrush, and wildflowers—bursts of bright pink and yellow among the black- and rust-colored cinders—have re-colonized the scorched habitat.

Sunset Crater is on the southern end of the loop. To begin there, turn right 12 miles north of Flagstaff and go two more miles to the newly

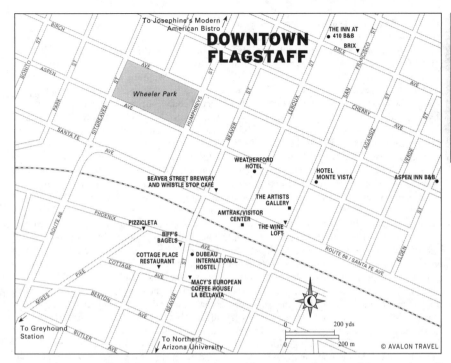

To Josephine's Modern
American Bistro

DOWNTOWN FLAGSTAFF

THE INN AT
410 B&B

BRIX

Wheeler Park

WEATHERFORD
HOTEL

BEAVER STREET BREWERY
AND WHISTLE STOP CAFÉ

HOTEL
MONTE VISTA

ASPEN INN B&B

THE ARTISTS
GALLERY

AMTRAK/VISITOR
CENTER

PIZZICLETA

THE WINE
LOFT

BIFF'S
BAGELS

COTTAGE PLACE
RESTAURANT

DUBEAU
INTERNATIONAL
HOSTEL

MACY'S EUROPEAN
COFFEE HOUSE/
LA BELLAVIA

To Greyhound
Station

To Northern
Arizona University

200 yds

200 m

© AVALON TRAVEL

renovated **visitor center** (928/526-0502, www.
nps.gov/sucr, 8 A.M.–5 P.M. daily May–Oct.,
9 A.M.–5 P.M. Nov.–Apr., $5), where you'll find
displays on volcanism, including a seismograph,
as well as a bookstore, picnic tables, and information on daily guided walks and evening
programs. Across the road is the U.S. Forest
Service's **Bonito Campground** (928/526-0866,
mid-May–mid-Oct., $18 per vehicle).

The steep **Lenox Crater Trail** begins a mile
east of the visitor center, climbing 0.5 mile to
the top of a cinder cone. The elevation and deep
cinders will have all but the fittest gasping for
breath by the time they reach the top, which
offers views of the San Francisco Peaks and
surrounding volcanic features. Another half a
mile down the park road is the beginning of the
Lava Flow Trail, a mile-long loop past jagged
lava flows, spatter cones, lava tubes, and cinder
drifts that look like black snow. A quarter-mile
portion of the trail is paved and accessible to
wheelchairs.

The entrance fee is good for a week at all
three Flagstaff area monuments—Sunset
Crater, Wupatki, and Walnut Canyon. A **local
passport** ($25) is good for one vehicle for a year.

Wupatki National Monument

Human presence in the Wupatki Basin
stretches back 10,000 years. During the 12th
century A.D., Ancestral Puebloan clans built
several multistory pueblos there after the eruption of nearby Sunset Crater. Prehistoric farmers found growing conditions improved by the
water-retaining layer of ash and cinders, using
it as a mulch to make up for the area's dry location in the rain shadow of the San Francisco
Peaks. (About seven inches of precipitation fall
there every year.) Wupatki Pueblo became the
largest in the area, home to perhaps 100 people,
with several thousand more living nearby in
smaller villages. It was a hub of different cultures and influences, evidenced by the adjacent
Mesoamerican-style ball court and artifacts

that included parrot feathers, copper bells, and shell jewelry. By the mid-13th century, however, most clans moved on to the north, east, and south, where they were assimilated into other villages and cultures.

The **visitor center** (928/679-2365, www.nps.gov/wupa, 9 A.M.–5 P.M. daily, $5 adults) has a picnic area, vending machines, and a bookstore. Interpretive exhibits explain how people subsisted in the Wupatki Basin and surrounding areas and provide an excellent overview of cultural relationships in the Southwest. Ask about orientation programs and guided hikes, held occasionally in summer and more often in spring and fall.

A short self-guided trail leads to the multistory **Wupatki Pueblo,** constructed from reddish Moenkopi sandstone and chunks of volcanic basalt. The trail circles the 100-room pueblo, passing rooms once used to house rangers. The nearby ball court is the northernmost one yet found. The trail to the ball court passes a blowhole, a small opening that expels or draws in air depending on barometric pressure, one of many fascinating geological features found inside the monument.

A side branch from the loop road leads 2.5 miles to **Wukoki,** which may have housed two or three families and is arguably the monument's most striking pueblo, rising high atop a stone outcropping. The loop road leads northwest to several other pueblos. The 30-room **Citadel** stands like a castle on a small butte above **Nalakihu,** which is about half as big. **Box Canyon Pueblo** is perched on either rim of a small canyon en route to pretty **Lomaki.** All these ancient villages share views of the San Francisco Peaks, which continue to be revered by contemporary Indian cultures.

Walnut Canyon National Monument

This deep, lush canyon eight miles east of Flagstaff was home to at least 100 members of the Sinagua culture in the 12th and 13th centuries. Villagers built masonry dwellings in shallow alcoves on the canyon's steep walls and raised corn, beans, and squash in fields among the pine forests at its rim. Limestone ledges are

embedded with marine fossils, and the sandstone gorge continues to shelter abundant vegetation and wildlife. Eventually the Sinaguas moved on; today some Hopi clans trace their ancestry to Walnut Canyon.

Six miles of the 20-mile canyon are protected today, including more than 300 masonry ruins. The **visitor center** (928/526-3367, www.nps.gov/waca, 8 A.M.–5 P.M. May–Oct., 9 A.M.–5 P.M. Nov.–Apr., $5 adults) sits on the edge of the 400-foot-deep canyon, with exhibits on the Sinagua culture and a bookstore. Ranger-guided hikes are held in summer. Allow an hour for the self-guided, paved **Island Trail** (one mile round-trip), which climbs down into the canyon past the ruins of 25 cliff dwellings. The trail's steepness and the altitude (6,700 feet) make it harder than you'd think. The shorter, easier Rim Trail leads past canyon overlooks, a pit house, and a small pueblo.

Watch for the canyon's varied wildlife, which inhabits several overlapping ecological communities. About 70 species of mammals in the area include coyotes, mule deer, elk, mountain lions, black bears, pronghorn antelopes, and a host of smaller critters. Most species are crepuscular (active at dawn and dusk), but you'll see and hear some of the 121 resident bird species, such as canyon wrens, Cooper's hawks, turkey vultures, and white-throated swifts.

To get there, take I-40 east to exit 204 and drive south three miles to the visitors center.

ENTERTAINMENT AND EVENTS

Thanks to its large student population and its role as Northern Arizona's major city, Flagstaff is a shopping hub and entertainment center, with dozens of venues, from concert halls to pool halls. For the latest word on events, as well as restaurant reviews, movie schedules, and current entertainment listings, pick up a copy of *Flagstaff Live!,* the free local weekly that hits the streets Thursday mornings.

Nightlife

Built in 1931, **The Museum Club** (3404 E. Rte. 66, 928/526-9434) has evolved into one of the best country-music roadhouses in the United

VISITING ANCIENT SITES

The Four Corners region is in many ways an outdoor museum, and the dry, rocky environment has preserved a vast collection of artifacts and dwellings over hundreds, even thousands, of years. With increased visitation, these fragile resources are showing wear, and land managers are often faced with the dilemma of limiting access to preserve scientific and historic values versus encouraging public appreciation and enjoyment. There's something magical about looking up from a hike to spot a Sinaguan granary tucked into a shadowy alcove, or coming across a finely crafted obsidian point and imagine its maker. To help preserve that sense of discovery for those who travel after you, practice the following ethics:

- Don't stand, sit, or climb on walls. Supervise your children. It only takes a moment to destroy something that has stood for centuries (and you wouldn't want to become part of a site for future archaeologists to uncover).

- Don't remove artifacts or pile them up like booty. Context is part of the archaeological record, and once a potsherd or stone flake is moved, that clue to the past is missing.

- Don't camp or burn anything in sites, including cigarettes, incense, or candles.

- Don't eat your lunch in a ruin. Crumbs attract rodents, and rodent activity can undermine walls or damage artifacts.

- Don't allow pets to dig, urinate, or defecate in sites.

- Don't deface rock art. This includes touching. You may think your hands are squeaky-clean, but your skin has oils that can damage the patina and impact future scientific study.

Archaeology is an evolving science, and new research methods are being developed all the time. Activities we don't think twice about today may impact future research. An oft-repeated tale focuses on a pioneer archaeologist who burned roof beams in his campfires, blithely unaware that a nifty new technique for dating ruins would develop from dendrochronology (tree-ring dating).

All archaeological sites on public land and Indian lands are protected by the Archaeological Resources Protection Act (1979) and other laws. Violation can result in felony prosecution, with imprisonment, impoundment, and very stiff fines. If you see someone vandalizing a site, contact the land manager (park service, national forest, or BLM) as soon as possible.

States. Enter through the split-pine archway onto the state's largest wooden dance floor. Five more ponderosas support the A-frame roof, and the mahogany bar in the back dates to the 1880s. For more live music, you can head downtown to **Mia's Lounge** (26 S. San Francisco, 928/774-3315), **Altitudes** (2 S. Beaver, 928/214-8218), or the **Green Room** (15 N. Agassiz, 928/226-8669), a few of the establishments popular with the college crowd. There you'll also find several brewpubs within walking distance, including **Flagstaff Brewing** (16 E. Rte. 66, 928/773-1442).

The Arts

NAU's College of Arts and Letters (928/523-8632, www.nau.edu/cal) holds a variety of exhibits, performances, and events at various venues around campus. The **Richard E. Beasley Gallery** (928/523-4612, 10 A.M.–5 P.M. Tues., Thurs., Fri.) displays rotating exhibits of contemporary art by students and faculty on the second floor of the School of Art. Eighteenth-century furniture, glassware, silver, and art fill the **Marguerite Hettel Weiss Collection** on the third floor of the Old Main building. These galleries are both under the auspices of the **Old Main Art Gallery and Museum** (928/523-3471, www.nau.edu/artgallery, noon–5 P.M. Tues.–Sat) on the northern end of campus. Old Main's varied collection is open to the public.

The **Flagstaff Symphony Orchestra** (928/774-5107, www.flagstaffsymphony.org)

has been entertaining northern Arizona audiences since 1949. Performances are held in NAU's Ardrey Auditorium September–April, and tickets are available online.

The stately redbrick **Orpheum Theater** (15 W. Aspen St., 928/556-1580, http://orpheumpresents.com) drew movie audiences for decades. Renovated and reenvisioned, the Orpheum now hosts film, concerts, and special events. **Theatrikos** (11 W. Cherry Ave., 928/774-1662, www.theatrikos.com), a community theater company, stages five productions yearly at its historic downtown theater (once home of the Flagstaff Library) and offers outreach programs for kids and adults interested in the dramatic arts. **Coconino Center for the Arts** (2300 N. Fort Valley Rd., 928/779-2300, www.culturalpartners.com, 11 A.M.–5 P.M. Tues.–Sat.), managed by Flagstaff Cultural Partners, hosts a diverse mix of exhibits, film, concerts, art markets, fundraisers, and other events sponsored by local arts organizations.

Events

Every month, dozens of downtown businesses and galleries serve up art, entertainment, and refreshments during Flagstaff's hugely popular **First Friday ArtWalk.** Officially, this street party lasts 6–9 P.M., though many venues continue the celebration into the wee hours.

Annual events begin on New Year's Eve with Flagstaff's very own Pinecone Drop, when crowds huddle in the crisp mountain air to watch as a giant lighted pinecone is lowered from the third-story veranda of the historic Weatherford Hotel. You could say it's both the first and last event of the year because the pinecone drops twice, at 10 P.M. (midnight New York time) to accommodate families and again at midnight Arizona time. In February, Flagstaff's **Winterfest** rolls together more than 100 events, including skiing and sled-dog competitions, sleigh rides, and themed dinners.

Flagstaff may be a winter wonderland, but spring brings a slew of outdoor events. May marks the beginning of the Museum of Northern Arizona's **Heritage Program,** highlighting the food, music, dance, arts, and traditions of the Colorado Plateau's diverse cultures. The **Hopi Festival** is scheduled around the Fourth of July weekend, with Navajo, Zuni, and Latino festivals held in the months preceding and following.

June weekends are chock-full of activities, from the **Pine Country Pro Rodeo** to the **Flagstaff Folk Festival,** many taking place under shady pines or glittering stars. Fourth of July festivities include a summer pops concert, art fair, and a parade (but not fireworks, when the surrounding forests are tinder-dry). On Labor Day weekend the **Coconino County Fair** takes over 413-acre Fort Tuthill County Park with livestock competitions, exhibits, rides, food, and music. The **Route 66 Festival** rumbles into town mid-September, and the **Flagstaff Festival of Science** (www.scifest.org) stretches into October, when the peaks' aspen groves turn gold.

SHOPPING

It makes sense that Flagstaff—surrounded by mountains, deserts, canyons, and forests—has plenty of good sporting-goods stores. Within a few short blocks downtown, you'll find **Aspen Sports** (15 N. San Francisco St., 928/779-1935), **Babbitt's Backcountry Outfitters** (12 E. Aspen Ave., 928/774-4775), **Mountain Sports** (24 N. San Francisco St., 928/226-2885), and **Peace Surplus** (14 W. Rte. 66, 928/779-4521).

You'll also find stunning landscape photography and Native American arts and crafts. **The Artists Gallery** (17 N. San Francisco St., 928/773-0958) is a cooperative of more than 30 local contemporary artists whose works range from blown glass and paintings to sculpture and furniture. Just down the street, the **Artists Coalition of Flagstaff** (13 N. San Francisco St., 928/522-6969) displays members' works. **Winter Sun Trading Company** (107 N. San Francisco St., 928/774-2884) sells jewelry, old-style kachina dolls, and baskets in the front of the shop. If you'd like to learn more about ethnobotany, head to the back room, where you can buy traditional Hopi herbs or sample one

© KATHLEEN BRYANT

Flagstaff's historic downtown has numerous shopping and dining options.

of the sumptuous skincare products formulated by the owner's daughters. For more Native American crafts, try **Puchteca Indian Crafts** (20 N. San Francisco St., 928/774-2414).

RECREATION
Hiking

From mild strolls to strenuous hikes, Flagstaff boasts some of the best trails in Arizona this close to a city. The 50-mile **Flagstaff Urban Trails System** (FUTS) connects open space to neighborhoods and businesses, and is used by bicyclists, hikers, and runners.

Several trails within the **Mount Elden/Dry Lake Hills Trail System** start from the **Mount Elden trailhead,** near the National Forest Service's **Flagstaff Ranger Station** (5075 N. Hwy. 89, 928/526-0866, 8 A.M.–4:30 P.M. Mon.–Fri.). To get there, take Route 66 east until it becomes U.S. 89, and look across from the Flagstaff Mall. The trails climb up through boulders and huge junipers and piñon pines. **Fatman's Loop** (two miles round-trip, easy) overlooks the city and is named as a warning: A

narrow gap between rock formations filters out those who aren't fit. A connecting steep, three-mile trail (one-way) climbs 2,400 feet and leads to the **Elden Lookout Tower** at 9,300 feet, with views as good as you'd expect.

The city's **Buffalo Park** has miles of biking and hiking trails, and serves as a trailhead for the **Oldham Trail** (11 miles round-trip, moderate), climbing through aspen, spruce, pines, and firs to views stretching as far as Oak Creek Canyon, Sunset Crater, and the Painted Desert. To get to Buffalo Park, take San Francisco Street north, turn right on Forest Avenue, which becomes Cedar, and then left on Gemini.

North of town off U.S. 180, the road to **Arizona Snowbowl** offers access to a number of trails, including the popular **Kachina Trail** (10 miles round-trip, moderate) which skirts the San Francisco Peaks, and the challenging **Humphreys Peak Trail** (nine miles round-trip) leading to the highest point in Arizona. (Note that hiking is not allowed off trails above 11,400 feet to protect the fragile tundra vegetation.)

© KATHLEEN BRYANT

The Kachina Trail leads through mountainside forest and meadows.

The **Weatherford Trail** (8.7 miles one-way) follows a historic roadbed and is popular with families for its moderate climb and good views. This trail, accessible from Schultz Pass Road (FR 420), crosses the Fremont Saddle (11,354 feet) before connecting with the Humphreys Peak Trail from the Arizona Snowbowl. Schultz Pass Road (Apr.–Nov., weather permitting) leaves U.S. 180 just north of the Museum of Northern Arizona. The trailhead is at Schultz Tank, about six miles up the dirt road, which is accessible for most passenger cars.

Northeast of Flagstaff, the trail to the fire tower on top of 8,965-foot **O'Leary Peak** (10 miles round-trip, strenuous) offers excellent views of the Painted Desert, the Inner Basin of the San Francisco Peaks, and nearby Sunset Crater. Like Mount Elden, O'Leary Peak is a lava dome, formed when thick magma oozed up through the earth's crust. To get there, take U.S. 89 north 12 miles, turning right (east) at the road to Sunset Crater Volcano National Monument. Turn left on paved FR 545A just before the campground and visitors center. The

trail begins at the parking area, about a quarter mile down the road.

An easier climb with good views is to the top of 5,589-foot **Doney Mountain,** a cinder cone located on forest land at the edge of Wupatki National Monument. To get to the trail (1 mile round-trip, easy), drive 22 miles north of Flagstaff and turn right (east) at the road to Wupatki. Drive another 9.5 miles to the Doney picnic area and trailhead. Interpretive signs tell about prospector Ben Doney and the two prehistoric ruins that lie along the trail. At the top, you can see the Hopi Buttes—dark volcanic cores that rise above the desert 40 miles away. (The buttes serve as horizon markers for the Hopis' ceremonial calendar.)

For detailed information on these and many other trails, pick up a local hiking guide at one of Flagstaff's numerous outfitter stores.

Biking

Road bikes can get you around town on the **Flagstaff Urban Trails System** (FUTS), which has 50-plus miles of trails and another

80 miles in the works. About half of the existing trail miles are paved, and the rest are hard-packed aggregate. Trail maps are available at city offices and in shops around town.

Mountain bikers can tackle the 19.6-mile **Mount Elden Loop,** which circles the San Francisco Peaks clockwise by connecting the Schultz Creek, Little Elden, Pipeline, Oldham, and Rocky Ridge Trails. This is a popular all-day ride, and most of it is moderately difficult single-track. The trailhead is 3.2 miles north of town on U.S. 180; at milepost 218, turn right and proceed to the intersection of Schultz Pass Road (FR 420) and the Mount Elden Lookout Road (FR 557), where you can park. Head north on the Schultz Creek Trail to begin the loop. **Mount Elden Lookout Road** (FR 557) makes another good ride, one of many in the national forests near town—just be sure to stay out of the wilderness area, where bikes aren't permitted.

Absolute Bikes (202 E. Rte. 66, 928/779-5969, www.absolutebikes.net) sells and rents full-suspension mountain bikes and in-town cruisers; they host group rides several times a week. **Single Track Bikes** (575 W. Riordan Rd., 928/773-1862) is another good source of local riding info, gear, and service.

Winter Activities

The **Arizona Snowbowl** (928/779-1951, 9 A.M.–4 P.M. daily Dec.–mid-Apr., depending on snow conditions) hosts a ski school and has 32 runs for downhill skiers and snowboarders. Lift tickets ($25–50 for adults) provide full- or half-day access to the slopes. Two lift-side lodges have snack bars and rental shops, with overnight lodges and cabins at the base of the mountain.

For cross-country skiing and snowshoeing, head for the **Flagstaff Nordic Center** (928/220-0550, www.flagstaffnordiccenter. com, 9 A.M.–4:30 P.M. daily mid-Dec.–Mar., depending on snow conditions, $8–18 pp) for miles of groomed trails, plus full moon tours, skiing clinics, and equipment rentals. The Nordic Center is 16 miles north of Flagstaff off U.S. 180 at mile marker 232. Other cross-country skiing trails and a snow-play area can be found on Wing Mountain (602/923-3555,

9 A.M.–4 P.M. daily, depending on snow conditions, $12 per vehicle), eight miles northwest of Flagstaff via U.S. 180 and FR 222B.

Guided Tours

In addition to being a popular home base for Grand Canyon river trips, Flagstaff is the starting point for a variety of adventures near and far. **Four Season Outfitters & Guides** (1051 S. Milton Rd., 928/525-1552 or 877/272-5032, www.fsguides.com) organizes hiking, backpacking, climbing, and kayaking tours throughout the Four Corners. Day hikes into the Grand Canyon are $179, including transport, food, and park admission, and can be lengthened up to a week and more. Four days in the Escalante canyons are $985 per person. They have a retail shop on the premises where you can buy or rent gear.

The Museum of Northern Arizona's **Ventures** programs (928/774-5211, ext. 230, www.mnaventures.org, ventures@musnaz. org) explore the Colorado Plateau's canyons and Indian reservations. Offerings range from day trips around Flagstaff's volcano country to wilderness trips in the Grand Canyon or the Escalante. MNA will also put together custom trips for groups. Trip leaders include professional geologists and archaeologists, and prices range $350–1,600, with hotel-based trips on the higher end.

Hitchin' Post Stables (928/774-1719) leads trail rides ($85–150) into Walnut Canyon, southeast of Flagstaff. Riders might spot wildlife like elk or porcupines, or view prehistoric Indian ruins tucked into cliff alcoves.

The **Nature Conservancy** (928/774-8892, ext. 5, www.nature.org) leads 90-minute nature walks focusing on the flora and fauna of Hart Prairie. The free tours depart from the Fort Valley Shopping Center at 10 A.M. each Sunday morning, mid-June–mid-October.

ACCOMMODATIONS

As northern Arizona's main tourist center, Flagstaff has an abundance of lodging options, from primitive camping to resorts. Rates fall by as much as half in the off-season.

Under $50

Between downtown and NAU, two highly regarded hostels operate under single management, **Grand Canyon International Hostel** (19½ S. San Francisco, 928/779-9421 or 888/442-2696, www.grandcanyonhostel.com), open year-round, and **Dubeau International Hostel** (19 W. Phoenix, 928/774-6731 or 800/398-7112), closed in winter. Both offer dorm-style rooms ($18–20) or private doubles ($44–48). Breakfast is included, and it's a good idea to book private rooms a few weeks or even a month in advance, especially in the summer. They organize trips to Sedona ($60 pp) and the Grand Canyon ($85 pp) several days a week, and offer Internet access, a cable TV/VCR room, and laundry services.

Many inexpensive motels (some with great old neon signs) line Route 66 on its way out of town. The **Budget Host Saga Motel** (820 W. Rte. 66, 928/779-3631, www.budgethost.com) has rooms for under $50.

$50-100

On January 1, 1900, John W. Weatherford opened a hotel in the dusty frontier town of Flagstaff, and it still bears his name. The ◖ **Weatherford Hotel** (23 N. Leroux St., 928/779-1919, www.weatherfordhotel.com, $90–140) has gone through various incarnations since then—billiard hall, theater, and radio station to name a few—but after two decades of work it has been restored to its glory days. Zane Grey penned *The Call of the Canyon* while staying there. Period touches include a 19-foot lobby ceiling, the wraparound third-floor balcony, and a huge wooden bar in the ballroom, built for a Tombstone saloon over a century ago. (They have rooms with shared bath for $50–80.) Downstairs, **Charly's** serves breakfast, lunch, and dinner ($5–25) and hosts live music several evenings each week.

The ◖ **Hotel Monte Vista** (100 N. San Francisco St., 928/779-6971 or 800/545-3068, www.hotelmontevista.com, $65–125) is Flagstaff's other historical (and, purportedly, haunted) lodge downtown. Since it was built in 1927, it has hosted presidents and Hollywood

stars, including John Wayne, who reported a friendly ghost in his room. Most of the 50 rooms on its four floors have good views, and all are named after famous guests. Downstairs, the **Rendezvous** is a coffeehouse by day and martini bar by night, and the cool **Monte Vista Lounge** has billiard tables and live bands on weekends.

A number of chain hotels also fall into this price category, including the **Motel 6** (2475 S. Woodlands Village Blvd., 928/779-3757) and the **Super 8 Motel East** (3725 Kasper Ave., 928/526-0818).

$100-150

You'll also find a number of chain hotels in this range. Try the **EconoLodge University** (914 S. Milton Rd., 928/774-7326) or the **Fairfield Inn by Marriott** (2005 S. Milton Rd., 928/773-1300 or 800/574-6395). Other choices include Best Western, Hampton Inn, Hilton, Holiday Inn, Howard Johnson, La Quinta, and Quality Inn. Several are located near the south end of Milton Rd., with quick access to I-17 and I-40 and numerous nearby stores and restaurants.

Over $150

C. B. Wilson, cousin to Wyatt Earp, built the graceful 1912 home three blocks from downtown that has been turned into the **Aspen Inn Bed & Breakfast** (218 N. Elden St., 928/773-0295 or 888/999-4110, www.flagstaffbedbreakfast.com, $130–170). The owners speak German, Spanish, Italian . . . and English.

Some of the nine rooms at ◖ **The Inn at 410 Bed & Breakfast** (410 N. Leroux St., 928/774-0088 or 800/774-2008, www.inn410.com, $150–200) have fireplaces and/or whirlpool tubs. The owners of the 1894 Craftsman home, which was at one time the home of NAU's Sigma Nu fraternity, offer gourmet breakfasts and can arrange packages that include a tour of the Grand Canyon. They've repeatedly won awards as one of the best bed-and-breakfasts in the state.

Situated on 500 acres of ponderosa pines, **Little America** (2515 E. Butler Ave., 928/779-7900 or 800/865-1401, www.littleamerica.com/flagstaff, $140–200) has 247 units decorated with imported marble, a heated outdoor pool, and a restaurant. For suites with kitchens, head to the north edge of town and the **Residence Inn by Marriott** (3440 N. Country Club Dr., 928/526-5555 or 888/236-2427, $140–220). The **Radisson Woodlands Hotel** (1175 W. Rte. 66, 928/773-8888, $160–200) offers a heated outdoor pool, the Sakura Japanese restaurant, and a café.

Campgrounds

Year-round choices include **Black Bart's RV Park** (2760 E. Butler Ave., 928/774-1912), which has 174 wooded tent and RV sites for $26–30 near I-40 exit 198. They also have a saloon and an antiques store, and host a musical revue in the steakhouse. The **Flagstaff KOA** (5803 N. Hwy. 89, 928/526-9926 or 800/562-3524) offers both campsites ($30–50) and cabins ($55), five miles northeast of town near I-40, exit 201.

You can camp just about anywhere in the national forest that surrounds Flagstaff; just make sure you're not on private land (signs, fences, and houses are good clues), and be very careful with fires in this tinderbox woodland. Some forest roads close due to winter conditions; contact the Flagstaff Ranger District (5075 N. Hwy. 89, 928/526-0866, www.fs.usda.gov/coconino, 8 A.M.–4:30 P.M. Mon.–Fri.) for more information. Coconino National Forest manages **Bonito Campground** on the loop road near Sunset Crater Volcano National Monument, with 43 sites open April–October for $18.

FOOD

Flagstaff has an impressive variety of places to eat, with plenty of options—including pizza joints, sandwich shops, and ethnic restaurants—priced for student budgets.

Downtown

Many restaurants are located in the rapidly gentrifying area south of the train tracks on Beaver Street, close to NAU. **La Bellavia** (18 S. Beaver St., 928/774-8301, breakfast and lunch daily, $5–10) is a comfy spot that has earned Flagstaff's "best breakfast" title many times

since they opened in 1976. Try their signature Swedish oat pancakes. The smell of fresh-roasted coffee permeates **Macy's European Coffee House, Bakery and Vegetarian Restaurant** (14 S. Beaver St., 928/774-2243, all meals daily) thanks to the big red roaster by the tables. The creative menu includes soups, salads, and sandwiches for $5–10. A few blocks away **Biff's Bagels** (1 S. Beaver St., 928/226-0424, 7 A.M.–3 P.M. Mon.–Sat., 8 A.M.–2 P.M. Sun.) serves breakfast, coffees, and bagels, with sandwiches in the $5 range. They also have Internet access.

Pizza lovers will have a hard time choosing among the options, but if Neapolitan-style pie is your fave, check out **Pizzicletta** (203 W. Phoenix Ave., 928/774-3242, 5 P.M.–9 P.M. Tues.–Wed., 5 P.M.–10 P.M. Thurs.–Sun., $9–13) and its 900-degree wood-burning oven that turns out crispy, chewy circles of joy. Pizza is also on the menu at the **Beaver Street Brewery and Whistle Stop Café** (11 S. Beaver St., 928/779-0079, lunch and dinner daily, $8 and up), along with bratwurst platters and other casual meals meant to go with their home-brewed ales.

Occupying a restored 1909 bungalow, the ◖ **Cottage Place Restaurant** (126 W. Cottage Ave., 928/774-8431, dinner Wed.–Sun.) may just be Flagstaff's finest. This intimate spot serves appetizers such as escargots for $7–15 and a wonderful two-person chateaubriand for $75 (à la carte entrées are $20 and up). Their wine list has earned *Wine Spectator* magazine's Award of Excellence six times. Reservations are recommended.

Brix (413 N. San Francisco St., 928/213-1021, dinner daily) is a "farm-focused" restaurant and wine bar in a turn-of-the-century brick carriage house downtown. The menu changes seasonally, with entrées like lamb ragout or pan-roasted scallops ($23–35). There's a well-chosen wine list and wide variety of cheeses to enjoy at the long candlelit bar.

Also downtown is **The Wine Loft** (17 N. San Francisco St., 928/773-9463), serving a light menu daily starting at 3 P.M. (2 P.M. Fri. and Sat.). They offer wines by the glass and Belgian beers, with occasional live music and wine tastings on the first Saturday of each month. **Josephine's Modern American Bistro** (503 N. Humphreys St., 928/779-3400, lunch Mon.–Fri., dinner daily, brunch Sat. and Sun.), housed in a historic *malpais* (volcanic rock) bungalow, serves gourmet lunch sandwiches around $10 and dinner entrées running $20–30. The menu's culinary influences range from Southwestern to Mediterranean and Asian, with such imaginative concoctions as short-rib "pie" topped with sweet potato gnocchi.

Route 66

There's no shortage of restaurants and diners along Route 66, which makes a swing through town from the northeast, but only a handful will give you a sense of traveling back in time to the days of the Mother Road. **Miz Zip's** (2924 E. Rte. 66, 928/526-0104, all meals daily) dishes up down-home meals for less than $10, but be sure to bring cash—credit cards aren't accepted. Meat loaf sandwiches, malts, movie posters, and waitresses in Hawaiian shirts sum up the **Galaxy Diner** (931 W. Rte. 66, 928/774-2466, all meals daily), a neon-and-silver faux Route 66 café that does American road staples for $5 and up. You may feel a bit silly driving through (literally) the **Dog Haus** (1302 E. Rte. 66, 928/774-3211, 6:30 A.M.–10 P.M. Mon.–Sat.), but this popular spot lures 'em in with breakfast burritos, burgers, Polish sausages, and chili dogs for less than $5.

Elsewhere in Town

Busters Restaurant and Bar (1800 S. Milton Rd., 928/774-5155, lunch and dinner daily, $10–25) is an animated place with all-American steaks, seafood, and chicken dishes. Northern Arizona's finest sushi bar is probably **Sakura,** in the Radisson Woodlands Hotel (928/773-9118, lunch Mon.–Sat., dinner daily). They also serve teppanyaki, with entrées starting at $15 for dinner.

If you like music with your prime rib, head to **Black Bart's Steak House and Musical Revue** (2760 E. Butler Ave., 928/779-3142, dinner daily), a Western-themed place where

students in NAU's voice program serenade diners over oak-broiled steaks and chicken.

INFORMATION AND SERVICES

The **Flagstaff Convention and Visitors Bureau** (928/774-9541 or 800/842-7293, www.flagstaffarizona.org) runs a **visitors center** in the old train station at 1 East Rte. 66 (8 A.M.–5 P.M. Mon.–Sat., 9 A.M.–4 P.M. Sun.). Stop by the **Flagstaff Ranger District** offices (5075 N. Hwy. 89, 928/526-0866, www.fs.usda.gov/coconino, 8 A.M.–4:30 P.M. Mon.–Fri.) for information about recreation on the Coconino National Forest or to buy maps, passes, or permits. You can pick up an America the Beautiful interagency pass there. You'll find similar information at the Forest Supervisor's office (1824 S. Thompson St., 928/527-3600, www.fs.usda.gov/coconino, 7:30 A.M.–4:30 P.M. Mon.–Fri).

Flagstaff Medical Center (928/779-3366) is the region's largest hospital, with 24-hour emergency services. **Concentra Clinic** (1100 E. Rte. 66, Ste. 100, 928/773-9695) provides walk-in urgent care.

At the main branch of **Flagstaff Public Library** (300 W. Aspen Ave., 928/779-7670, 10 A.M.–9 P.M. Mon.–Thurs., 10 A.M.–7 P.M. Fri., 10 A.M.–6 P.M. Sat.) visitors can use the Internet up to 30 minutes daily at no charge and purchase additional time.

The main post office (2400 Postal Blvd., 928/527-2440) is on Flagstaff's northeast side. There's also a downtown branch (104 N. Agassiz, 928/779-2371).

GETTING THERE AND AROUND

Flagstaff is located at the intersection of I-40, which travels from Albuquerque to Kingman, and I-17, which leads north from Phoenix and Tucson. From Phoenix, Flagstaff is a two-hour drive up I-17.

The **Mountain Line** bus service (928/779-6624, www.naipta.az.gov) operates five different routes daily every 30–60 minutes. **A Friendly Cab** (928/774-4444, www.afriendlycab.com) and **Sun Taxi & Tours** (928/779-1111) offer in-town taxi services as well as service to Phoenix and the Grand Canyon's South Rim.

Open Road Tours (602/997-6474 or 855/563-8830, www.openroadtours.com) offers sightseeing tours from Flagstaff, Phoenix Sky Harbor International Airport, and other locations to Grand Canyon, Sedona, and Indian Country. **Arizona Shuttle** (928/226-8060, ext. 1303, or 800/888-2749, www.arizonashuttle. com) has daily shuttle service from Flagstaff to Sedona, Williams, and the Grand Canyon, with runs several times daily to Phoenix Sky Harbor International Airport.

Greyhound (399 S. Malpais Ln., 928/774-4573) takes advantage of the city's location on I-40 with service to major cities to the east and west. **Amtrak**'s (928/774-8679 or 800/872-7245) Southwest Chief stops at the Flagstaff depot (1 E. Rte. 66, 4:15 A.M.– 11:45 P.M. daily), arriving from Los Angeles or Albuquerque. **US Airways** (800/235-9292, www.usairways.com) flies daily between Phoenix and Pulliam Airport, three miles south of town along I-17. (However, it's usually cheaper to fly to Phoenix and take a bus or shuttle from there.)

Sedona

South of Flagstaff on SR 89A is one of Arizona's most beloved destinations. Equal parts art town, resort retreat, and New Age nexus, Sedona (pop. 10,000) is blessed with unearthly red-rock scenery, a moderate climate at 4,500 feet, and (according to many) a number of "energy vortexes" scattered among the stones. With more massage therapists, yoga teachers, spirit guides, and artists per capita than any other place in the West—not to mention spas and luxury accommodations galore—Sedona makes for a fascinating and wonderfully scenic short trip from Flagstaff.

Getting there is half the fun. SR 89A descends through Oak Creek Canyon for almost half of the 30 miles from Flagstaff to Sedona, a gorgeous drive past rocky cliffs, swimming holes, trailheads, and rustic lodges. The canyon can be very crowded on summer weekends, so consider arriving midweek or during the off-season. The same applies to Sedona itself; it's definitely not off the beaten track, with some four million people making the pilgrimage every year.

History

Some 10,000 years ago, hunter-gatherers wandered red-rock canyons in search of plants and game. After the beginning of the last millennium, people began relying increasingly on agriculture, digging irrigation canals and tanks, outlining garden plots with stone, and employing other strategies for conserving water. The Southern Sinaguas moved from scattered pit houses around A.D. 1100, building stone pueblos inside alcoves, where they lived until congregating in larger hilltop villages during the latter half of the thirteenth century. For a time, these Ancestral Puebloans coexisted with seminomadic bands who arrived from the south around A.D. 1300. But by A.D. 1450, Sinaguan clans had moved on, though many individuals likely stayed behind, intermarrying with the Yavapais, who were visited in turn by Spanish explorers, Mexican and American trappers, prospectors, and eventually settlers and soldiers. The army forcibly removed the Yavapais and Apaches to a reservation in 1875.

Oak Creek Canyon's first Anglo resident was J. J. Thompson, who arrived in 1876 and built a cabin on a site where Indian crops were still growing. He named it Indian Gardens. More families arrived and settled farther down the creek, digging irrigation ditches to water crops and raise orchards. The remote farming community was named in 1902 after the wife of settler T. C. Schnebly, who established the town's first post office. He chose the name Sedona partly because it was short enough to fit on a cancellation stamp.

Author Zane Grey helped popularize the landscape with his novel *The Call of the Canyon,* and Hollywood arrived in the 1940s and 1950s, filming dozens of Westerns, including *Angel*

© KATHLEEN BRYANT

Sedona's red rocks bear names like Coffee Pot, Ship Rock, and Steamboat.

and the Badman (1949) and *Broken Arrow* (1950). In the ensuing decades a new cadre of visitors was drawn by the town's stunning location. Artists, tourists, and retirees came for the scenery and stayed for a variety of reasons, and Sedona gradually became one of the top destinations in the Southwest. The New Age movement of the 1980s brought an influx of seekers. The city was incorporated in 1988, but half of its 19 square miles belongs to the federal government as Coconino National Forest. High-end tourism has begun to replace the desert-love-in vibe of Sedona's early years, but metaphysical inquiry and alternative therapies continue to prevail, along with outdoor recreation and art.

SIGHTS
◀ Oak Creek Canyon

Colorful stone cliffs and pine forests above lush riparian habitat make Oak Creek Canyon one of the most inviting spots in this dry state, drawing hikers, anglers, and swimmers, especially on summer weekends. The canyon mixes public and private land, and SR 89A travels its length from Uptown Sedona to the rim at the top of a series of switchbacks. Three Forest Service campgrounds, numerous picnic areas, and several trailheads are located along the canyon's 14-mile length, along with rustic lodges, residences, and a few shops and restaurants. You can take a dip in Oak Creek at **Grasshopper Point** or at **Slide Rock State Park** (928/282-3034, 8 A.M.–7 P.M. daily in summer, $20 per vehicle), where you can slide down smooth rocks and hike three short trails (all less than a half mile). The park is 6 miles north of Sedona.

At the top of the canyon, **Oak Creek Vista** (9 A.M.–4:30 P.M. daily, weather permitting) offers a splendid overlook. The Forest Service visitor center located there is open March–October. During summer months, Navajo artisans sell jewelry and other crafts under the shade of the vista's ponderosa pines.

Jordan Historical Park

The Sedona Historical Society operates a

© KATHLEEN BRYANT

Oak Creek Canyon is an oasis of shade and cascading waters.

museum (735 Jordan Rd., 928/282-7038, www.sedonamuseum.org, 11 A.M.–3 P.M. daily, $5) on the site of the home and orchards of Walter and Ruth Jordan. During the 1930s, the Jordans built an irrigation system that developed into Sedona's first commercial water supply. Their apple-packing barn has displays on the town's farming history, and the Jordans' red-rock cabin has exhibits on movie-making, ranching, and forestry.

Chapel of the Holy Cross

Sedona's celebrated Chapel of the Holy Cross (780 Chapel Rd., 928/282-4069, www. chapeloftheholycross.com, 9 A.M.–5 P.M. daily, from 10 A.M. Sun.) soars up from a red sandstone outcropping, supported by the large cross that also serves as its central design feature. This Catholic chapel is open to people of all faiths, who come for the panoramic views as well as for the spiritual energy that seems to emanate from the chapel and its surroundings. To get there, take SR 179 south toward the Village of Oak Creek for three miles; then turn left on Chapel Road.

Prehistoric Ruins and Rock Art

Sedona's red-rock canyons and cliffs provided shelter and food to the prehistoric Sinagua Indians. The finest red-rock cliff dwelling in the area is **Palatki** (928/282-3854, 9 A.M.–3 P.M. daily), occupied 800 years ago. A short trail leads to a series of alcoves holding more than 5,000 pictographs and petroglyphs, with docents and rangers on hand to answer questions. Reservations are strongly recommended. To get there, take SR 89A eight miles west of the Y intersection. Just past mile marker 365, turn right on FR 525, a good dirt road suitable for most passenger cars unless it's been raining or snowing. Continue for five miles to a fork; stay right, continuing on FR 795 to the parking lot. After your tour, you can make a scenic loop back to Sedona by turning left (east) on the Boynton Pass Road (FR 152C), which changes from a rough dirt road to pavement after a couple miles. Continue to a T, where you'll turn right, and then right again at the next T onto Dry Creek Road, which will return you to modern civilization.

If you have a sturdy vehicle, you can venture even farther into the cliffs and canyons to visit **Honanki** (10 A.M.–6 P.M. daily, weather permitting). This village and rock art site tucked below Loy Butte is four miles away from Palatki via FR 525. It's a good idea to check in first with the Forest Service (928/282-4119) or the rangers at Palatki (928/282-3854) for directions and current road conditions, or arrive via a Pink Jeep tour.

The **V-V Heritage Site** (9:30 A.M.–3 P.M. Fri.–Mon.) preserves the densest concentration of petroglyphs (rock art pecked into stone) in the area, including a possible solar calendar. It's a short (0.3 mile) stroll to the site, where docents can tell you more about the Sinagua culture. To get there, take SR 179 south of Sedona toward I-17. Continue under the freeway, where the road becomes FR 618. It's three paved miles to the parking lot.

EVENTS

For several years running, Sedona has been named one of the nation's top small art towns, and many annual events revolve around music and the visual arts. The fabulous **Sedona International Film Festival** (www.sedonafilmfestival.com) arrives the last week of February with parties, workshops, and more than 100 independent movies.

The event calendar peaks in autumn, when the weather is at its best. One of the first fall festivals is **Jazz on the Rocks** (http://sedonajazz.com) with concerts and master classes. Early in October, the weekend-long **Sedona Arts Festival** hosts more than 150 artists, followed by a couple of weeks later by the **Plein Air Festival** (www.sedonapleinairfestival.com), when painters work out-of-doors on sidewalks and trails and by creeks. The latter event is sponsored by **Sedona Art Center** (15 Art Barn Rd., 928/282-3809), a beloved community institution with a gallery and classrooms in Uptown.

Mild winters—think red rocks dusted with snow—are the backdrop for outdoor holiday celebrations like Tlaquepaque's candlelit **Festival of Lights,** held on a single evening in early December, and **Red Rock Fantasy,** which sparkles from late November to New Year's Day.

A handful of restaurants host live music on weekend evenings, and there's often something happening at **Oak Creek Brewing Company** (2050 Yavapai Dr., 928/204-1300). You'll find entertainment listings in *Kudos* (www.kudos-az.com), a free newsweekly published on Wednesdays.

SHOPPING

More than 80 galleries and shops sell everything from red-dirt T-shirts to fine art. A good place to start is **Tlaquepaque** (336 Hwy. 179, 928/282-4838, www.tlaq.com), constructed in the 1970s along Oak Creek to resemble the colonial town outside Guadalajara, Mexico, bearing the same name. Tlaquepaque's sycamore-shaded courtyards and arched walkways are home to more than 30 galleries and shops, as well as four restaurants with outdoor dining.

Many other galleries are concentrated along this pleasant, walkable section of SR 179, such as **Sedona Pottery, Garland Rugs** (specializing

in Navajo weavings), **Hozho,** and the **Hillside Sedona** shops and restaurants. On the first Friday evening of each month, a trolley (free) provides transportation between "gallery row" and Uptown, when participating venues host receptions and offer light refreshments.

If you're interested in learning more about Sedona's spiritual side, the **Center for the New Age** (928/282-2085, www.sedonanewagecenter.com), across SR 179 from Tlaquepaque, operates a bit like a clearing house for various practitioners and services. There you can sign up for a guided vortex tour, get a horoscope chart, find a massage therapist, or have your aura cleansed, and then stop next door at **Crystal Castle** (313 SR 179, 928/282-5910), for a psychic reading on the shady porch. In West Sedona, **Crystal Magic** (2978 W. Hwy. 89A, 928/282-1622) and its sister store **Clothing Magic** (2970 W. Hwy. 89A, 928/203-0053) sell New Age music, metaphysical books, Birkenstocks, and, of course, crystals.

RECREATION

There are a gazillion red rocks and almost as many ways to explore them, from bouncing down a dirt road on a jeep to floating overhead in a hot air balloon. Tour options abound, and scenic views are as easy as stepping out the door. A Red Rock Pass ($5 daily, $15 weekly) is required to park at many national forest trails and viewpoints in the Sedona area. Additional fees are charged for popular recreation areas like Call of the Canyon, Grasshopper Point, and Crescent Moon Ranch. Stop in at a visitors center or contact the **Red Rock Ranger District** (928/282-4119 or 928/203-7500, www.redrockcountry.org) for more information.

Hiking

More than 300 miles of hiking trails wind through the forest or traverse reddish sandstone buttes and mesas with names like Coffee Pot Rock, Snoopy, and the Cockscomb. If you're curious about Sedona's energy vortexes, the most easily accessed is at the saddle of **Airport Mesa.** To get there, turn left on Airport Road as you enter West Sedona. Look for a parking area on the left about halfway up the mesa. It's a short scramble to the saddle, which offers excellent views of Munds and Lee Mountains to the east.

At **Cathedral Rock,** said to be another vortex, you'll find an invigorating slickrock climb to the spires at the heart of this dramatic formation. Acrophobes should think twice about this moderately difficult hike: Though it's a mere 1.5 miles round-trip, it's steep, with ledges and toeholds in some places. For the trailhead, drive 3.5 miles south on SR 179 from the Y intersection. Turn right at Back O' Beyond Road and continue a half mile to the parking area on the left.

Every bit as inspiring is **Boynton Canyon** northwest of Sedona. To get there, take U.S. 89A through West Sedona, turning right (north) on Dry Creek Road and traveling about three miles to the T intersection. Turn left, taking Boynton Pass Road 1.6 miles to another T. Turn right toward Enchantment Resort. The large trailhead parking area outside the resort entrance, often full on weekends, offers access to three trails, including Boynton Canyon Trail (moderate, five miles round-trip). The entire canyon is said to be diffused with energy, though some people say the vortex is centered on Boynton Spires, reached by the short (less than one mile) Vista Trail. In any case, it's all scenic, and by now you may be thinking it's hard to distinguish between vortex energy and the thrill of being outdoors in such a beautiful place.

To continue your experiment, you could hike a "non-vortex" trail to see if you detect a difference. For **Doe Mountain,** a moderate 3.6-mile round-trip climb up a mesa with 360-degree views, take Boynton Pass Road another 1.2 miles to the trailhead. If you'd like a more challenging hike, head across the road from Doe Mountain to the **Bear Mountain Trail** (five miles round-trip, strenuous). This trail alternates between steep climbs and plateaus, and the scenery changes with each section, making it feel like three or four hikes in one. The summit of 6,506-foot Bear Mountain has views all the way north to Flagstaff's San Francisco Peaks.

For more information on Sedona's superb hiking, pick up a copy of a local trail guide or stop in at a visitors center for maps. Another option is to hire **Sedona Private Guides** (928/204-2201, www.sedonaprivateguides. com), who mix good humor and hospitality on a range of outings, from metaphysical-themed walks to challenging hikes.

Biking

Though bikes are not allowed inside Sedona's three wilderness areas, forest roads and trails offer miles of rides. Friendly local bike shops provide trail information and lead tours. Among them are **Absolute Bikes** (6101 SR 179, Ste. C, 928/284-1242, www.absolute-bikes.net/sedona) and **Bike & Bean** (6020 SR 179, 928/284-0210, www.bike-bean.com), both in the Village of Oak Creek, and **Over the Edge** (1695 W. SR 89A, 928/282-1106, www. otesports.com) in West Sedona. Bikes rent for $40–70 per day.

Single-track enthusiasts like **Cathedral Loop** (11.4 miles round-trip, mixing road and trail) and **Little Horse Trail** (3.2 miles round-trip, technical). Paved **Bell Rock Pathway** (seven miles round-trip) is a better choice for road bikes and families with small children. It travels between the Little Horse parking area (south of the Chapel of the Holy Cross) and Courthouse Butte in the Village of Oak Creek.

Scenic Drives and Tours

A half-dozen jeep tour companies call Sedona home, each with its own flavor and at least one exclusive route. Tours start around $50 at **Red Rock Jeep** (270 N. Hwy. 89A, 928/282-6826 or 800/848-7728, www.redrockjeep.com), whose guides dress in Old West garb. **Pink Jeep** offers several options, including a jeep tour ($72) to **Honanki Pueblo,** a 700-year-old cliff dwelling, or a comfy van excursion ($125) to the Grand Canyon.

All tour companies travel **Schnebly Hill Road,** a scenic but rocky route you can explore on your own if you don't mind wear and tear on your vehicle (and your nerves). A high-clearance 4WD is strongly recommended for this adventure. The road begins at the roundabout at the Oak Creek bridge, about a half mile south of the U.S. 89A/179 intersection. At one mile, the pavement ends at a large parking area with picnic tables and trailheads. From there, Schnebly Hill Road changes to a rock-studded route as it winds its way up to the Mogollon Rim, passing the softly rounded red sandstone buttes known as the Cowpies at about three miles. In winter, the road is often closed just past the Merry-Go-Round, a red sandstone formation circled by blocks of gray limestone that make up the carousel "horses." Beyond the Schnebly Hill Vista, a dirt parking area with great views at about six miles, the road levels out and continues another seven miles toward I-17 through a juniper woodland. Instead of continuing to the freeway, most drivers will want to flex their knuckles (now white from gripping the steering wheel), turn around, and head back to Sedona, taking in the views from the other direction.

For a milder scenic drive with a side trip to **Red Rock Crossing,** head a couple miles west of town on SR 89A and turn left (south) on Upper Red Rock Loop Road. The paved road travels past the high school before winding down toward Oak Creek. En route, several pull-outs provide photo opportunities of **Cathedral Rock.** For a closer look or a splash in the creek, turn left on Chavez Road, cross the bridge, and turn right, following the signs for Red Rock Crossing and Crescent Moon Ranch. The **picnic area** (8 P.M.–8 P.M. daily, Memorial day–Labor day, closing at dusk during the off-season, $9/vehicle) is often crowded, and at sunset, photographers flock there for the money shot, when Cathedral Rock's sandstone cliffs turn bright orange and reflect in the waters of Oak Creek.

For less-crowded creek views (but no swimming), continue on the loop road (which changes to a good dirt road for about two miles) to **Red Rock State Park** (928/282-6907, 8 A.M.–5 P.M. daily, $10/vehicle). There you can hike, picnic, and linger along the creek to watch for blackhawks and other wildlife. Nature hikes and programs are offered daily. Twice a month from April–October, park naturalists lead moonlight walks (reservations

required). The loop road rejoins SR 89A in another three miles.

Fishing

Anglers can try their luck in Oak Creek Canyon, where cold springs nurture trout introduced at the fish hatchery upstream. The section from Call of the Canyon picnic area south to Junipine is catch-and-release. At Rainbow Trout Farm (3500 N. Hwy. 89A, 928/282-5799, daily), you keep what you catch, and you can use the grills provided for a creekside picnic. Jim McInnis of **Gon' Fishin'** (928/282-0788), a fount of local wisdom, guides trips to favorite canyon fishing holes. Fishing licenses are available at Bashas' grocery store in West Sedona or on the Arizona Game and Fish Department's website (www.azgfd.gov).

ACCOMMODATIONS

Sedona Schnebly was the first to lodge guests in the town named for her, and her legacy of hospitality extends today from rustic canyon lodges to sprawling resorts. Most offer off-season specials, and if you're willing to submit to a timeshare sales pitch, you can shop around for a bargain package that might include a tour and spa services.

Sedona boasts a number of award-winning B&Bs and small inns. In the Village of Oak Creek, the **Canyon Villa Inn of Sedona** (40 Canyon Circle Dr., 800/453-1166, www.canyonvilla.com, $210–320) offers rooms designed around monumental views of Bell Rock and Courthouse Butte, an outdoor heated pool, and gourmet breakfasts. Another AAA four-diamond option, **Casa Sedona B&B Inn** (55 Hozoni Dr., 800/525-3756, www.casasedona.com, $140–280) is located in West Sedona. **El Portal** (95 Portal Ln., 928/203-9405 or 800/313-0017, www.elportalsedona.com, $260–450) re-creates early 1900s Arts-and-Crafts style a few steps away from sycamore-shaded Oak Creek and Sedona's gallery district.

If your budget permits, you can spring for a casita at **Enchantment Resort** (800/826-4180, www.enchantmentresort.com, $400 and up) nestled between the gorgeous red-and-buff sandstone walls of Boynton Canyon. One of the resort's three dining rooms has a telescope focused on a centuries-old cliff dwelling. Amenities include a kids' camp, tennis courts, and the fabulous Mii amo spa.

Even on a modest budget, you can have stunning views, a pool, and a pretty garden for strolling at **Sky Ranch Lodge** (1105 Airport Rd., 928/282-6400 or 800/708-6400, www.skyranchlodge.com, $90–150), perched atop Airport Mesa. (If you're concerned about noise, don't be: Sedona's airstrip is rarely used after dark, and the hotel sits 500 feet above city traffic.) Guests at **Lo Lo Mai Lodge** (50 Willow Way, 928/282-2835, $55–95) in West Sedona are granted access to its sister property in nearby Page Springs, where you can enjoy a cool dip in Oak Creek or a spring-fed pond. In the Village of Oak Creek, the **Sedona Village Lodge** (105 Bell Rock Plaza, 928/284-3626 or 800/890-0521, $50–90) has both standard rooms and suites with kitchenettes.

At-large camping is restricted to certain areas in the forest's Red Rock Ranger District. Contact Coconino National Forest (928/282-4119, www.fs.usda.gov/coconino or www.redrockcountry.org) for details. The Forest Service operates three seasonal campgrounds in Oak Creek Canyon ($16–18, mid-Mar.–mid-Oct.) Some sites can be reserved (877/444-6777, www.recreation.gov), but most are on a first-come, first-served basis and fill quickly on summer weekends. None have utility hookups, and only Pine Flat and Cave Springs can accommodate small RVs. A better choice for RV travelers is **Rancho Sedona** (135 Bear Wallow Ln., 928/282-7255 or 888/641-4261, http://ranchosedona.com, $40–60), a shady creekside oasis just off Schnebly Hill Road.

FOOD

Sedona's food choices range from simple fare to fine dining, including a handful of ethnic choices, a natural-foods deli, and Uptown's tempting sweet shops. What you won't find there are a slew of ubiquitous chains: Even McDonald's forgoes the usual golden arches in favor of a verdigris M.

The **Mesa Grill at the Sedona Airport** (928/282-2400, all meals daily, $8–27) has good food, but the main draw is the awe-inspiring panorama from atop Airport Mesa. Plane buffs can pick a window seat overlooking the mesa's notoriously tricky runway; the rest can feast on red-rock views from the dining room or patio.

Also in West Sedona, the **Heartline Café** (1610 W. SR 89A, 928/282-0785, dinner daily, $15–30) has earned repeat best-restaurant honors. Breakfast and lunch ($6–12) are served next door at Heartline's **Gourmet Express** (928/282-3365). Both locations have pleasant patios for meals al fresco. A bit farther west is **Cuisine of India** (1910 W. SR 89A, 928/204-2300, lunch and dinner daily), serving a mildly spicy lunch buffet for $8.

The elegant **Rene at Tlaquepaque** (336 Hwy. 179, Ste. 118, 928/282-9225, lunch and dinner daily) has an extensive wine list and continental cuisine. Entrées are $8–13 for lunch, $18–28 for dinner. The Southwestern-themed **Cowboy Club** (241 N. SR 89A, 928/282-4200, lunch and dinner daily, $10–35) is a lively venue that occupies one of Sedona's historic Uptown buildings.

◀ Elote (771 SR 179, 928/203-0105, dinner Tues.–Sat., $17–22) is popular with locals and visitors alike. Those who manage to get a table (reservations are taken only for parties of five or more) will be wowed by Chef Smedstad's reinterpretation of Mexican cuisine, such as the chiles rellenos stuffed with vegetable-nut *picadillo* and goat cheese.

If you're feeling weak after navigating Uptown's long gauntlet of shops, a stop at **Sedona Memories Bakery & Café** (321 Jordan Rd., 928/282-0032, $5–10) will fortify you with giant sandwiches and cookies. In the Village of Oak Creek, the **Blue Moon Café** (6101 SR 179, Ste. B, 928/284-1831, all meals daily, $7 and up) is a breakfast-all-day kind of place, with hand-tossed pizzas and Philly cheesesteaks.

INFORMATION AND SERVICES

For more information on Sedona and the surrounding area, contact the **Sedona-Oak Creek Chamber of Commerce** (1 Forest Rd.,

928/282-7722 or 800/288-7336, www.visitsedona.com, 8:30 A.M.–5 P.M. Mon.–Sat., 9 A.M.–3 P.M. Sun.).

The **Red Rock District visitors center** (8375 SR 179, 928/282-4119 or 928/203-7500, www.redrockcountry.org, 8 A.M.–5 P.M. daily) lies south of the Village of Oak Creek along SR 179. Along with informative displays and a retail area with books and maps, it offers a wide veranda with awesome views of Bell Rock, Courthouse Butte, and other formations. The ranger district's northern gateway is at the vista overlook at the top of Oak Creek Canyon, open 9 A.M.–4 P.M. daily, March–October, weather permitting.

The **Sedona Library** (3250 White Bear Rd., 928/282-7714, Mon.–Sat.) has computers for visitors who want to check their email. (Be sure to pause at the library's entrance and admire the statue of Sedona Schnebly made by sculptor Susan Kliewer.)

The main **post office** (928/282-3511) is located at the intersection of SR 89A and SR 179. Sedona Medical Center (3700 W. SR 89A, 928/204-3000 or 928/204-4100) has 24-hour emergency services. Nonemergencies can be handled at Sedona Urgent Care (2530 W. SR 89A, 928/203-4813).

GETTING THERE AND AROUND

Sedona is roughly divided into three areas along SR 89A and SR 179: Uptown, the bustling strip of shops along SR 89A north of its intersection with SR 179; West Sedona, a quieter, mostly residential section west of the intersection; and the Village of Oak Creek, an unincorporated area of residences, resorts, and shops approximately seven miles south of the intersection en route to I-17. If you stop to ask for directions, keep in mind that locals still refer to the 89A/179 intersection as "the Y," even though it has been reconfigured into a double roundabout.

Though less than 30 miles south of Flagstaff,

allow an hour for the winding drive through Oak Creek Canyon on SR 89A to Sedona. Sedona is about two hours north of Phoenix via I-17. You can exit the freeway at SR 260 (exit 289) or SR 179 (exit 311). The former route passes through Cottonwood and joins SR 89A for the Dry Creek Scenic Road. The latter follows the Scenic Red Rock Byway between the Village of Oak Creek and Sedona. Whichever route you choose to get there, the views are great.

Though it's easy to get around in your own vehicle, if you prefer to have someone else introduce you to the sights, the **Sedona Trolley** (276 Hwy. 89A, 928/282-4211, $12) has two routes that give riders a narrated overview of the town's layout and vistas. The **Verde Lynx** (928/282-0938, $2) connects Sedona to the Verde Valley community of Cottonwood, making several in-town stops and running until early evening. Sedona is known to roll up the sidewalks early, but if you're out late, you can call **Bob's Taxi** (928/282-1234) or hire **White Tie Transportation** (928/203-4500) to usher you around in a limo or luxury SUV. (A lot of folks tie the knot in Sedona, so livery options are plentiful for a small town.)

Jeep rental companies like Barlow's (928/282-4344 or 888/928-5337) will provide maps and information about 4WD trails. Barlow's is located next to Hertz (3009 W. SR 89A, 928/282-0878 or 800/654-3131). At the airport terminal, Discount Rent-a-Car (877/467-8578) offers hourly rentals in addition to standard rates.

The **Sedona Airport** (235 Terminal Dr., 928/282-1046, www.sedonaairport.org) hosts five fixed-wing and helicopter tour companies, charter air services, and a restaurant.

The **Sedona-Phoenix Shuttle** (928/282-2066, $50 one-way, $90 round-trip) travels from Sky Harbor Airport in Phoenix to the Village and West Sedona.

Grand Canyon National Park

One of the world's greatest natural wonders awaits a mere 90 minutes northwest of Flagstaff. The Grand Canyon's mile-deep chasm reveals layers of rock laid down over two billion years and then carved out by the relentless force of flowing water. This colorful gash through the high Colorado Plateau is the canyon to end all canyons: 277 miles long and up to 18 miles wide, with countless side gorges, each of which could be a national park in itself.

The Colorado River flows through the canyon's heart, tumbling over 160 rapids and dropping more than 2,000 feet by the time it reaches the Grand Wash Cliffs marking its western edge. The canyon's diverse environments, from riparian to desert to boreal forest, are home to more than 2,000 species. Regional tribes have revered the Grand Canyon for centuries, and yet it was one of the last places in the United States to be mapped. Established in 1919, Grand Canyon National Park (928/638-7888, www.nps.gov/grca, $25 per vehicle for one week) has become one of the country's greatest tourist draws, and justifiably so. The view from the edge is something you'll never forget, and a trip to the bottom—particularly a raft voyage through the famous Colorado River rapids—is almost beyond words.

THE SOUTH RIM

Most visitors approach Grand Canyon National Park from its south side, which offers the quickest access from Flagstaff and Phoenix. As a result, the South Rim has more tourist amenities than the canyon's remote North Rim. From Flagstaff, three routes lead to the South Rim's main tourism center, Grand Canyon Village. The shortest is from downtown Flagstaff via U.S. 180 (78 miles). You can also take I-40 to Williams and then SR 64 to the canyon (80 miles). To enter the park at its less-used East Entrance Station, take U.S. 89A to SR 64. Though this route is twenty miles longer, you'll travel through the Navajo Reservation and along Desert View Drive en route to Grand Canyon Village.

Grand Canyon Village

The heart of the park's largest developed area is historic Grand Canyon Village, where you'll find lodges and buildings dating to the early 1900s, including the train depot, El Tovar Hotel, and several of architect Mary Colter's fabulous creations: Lookout Studio, Hopi House, Hermits Rest, and Bright Angel Lodge. Between the South Rim Entrance Station and the village are a post office, a bank, medical services, and the main visitors center (8 A.M.–5 P.M. daily) at **Canyon View Information Plaza.** The plaza, where you'll also find parking, shops, restrooms, a theater, and informative kiosks, is located across from **Mather Point.**

The **Rim Trail,** accessible from Mather Point and several locations within Grand Canyon Village, offers a pleasant walk to scenic overlooks, where you can get a sense of the vastness of the canyon and its tributaries. The mostly paved trail is 12 miles long, but it can easily be hiked in sections.

Hermits Rest Road

West of Grand Canyon Village, an eight-mile paved road leads to Hermits Rest, a historic building designed by architect Mary Elizabeth Jane Colter, now a visitors center and gift shop. The **Hermit Trail** begins there, the start of a multiday backpacking trip for those with permits, or an invigorating day hike to Santa Maria Spring or Dripping Springs. En route to Hermits Rest are some of the South Rim's most panoramic overlooks, including **Hopi Point, Pima Point,** and the **Abyss,** where the canyon's cliffs plummet a mile deep. The park's free shuttles travel the road March–November. During winter months, the road (also known as West Rim Drive) is open to passenger cars, weather permitting.

© KATHLEEN BRYANT

Mather Point is a popular overlook on Grand Canyon's South Rim.

Desert View Drive

State Route 64 runs east from Grand Canyon Village for 25 miles along the edge of the canyon, where it's called Desert View Drive or East Rim Drive. Along the way are ruins, scenic overlooks, and the **Desert View Watchtower,** a stone structure designed by Mary Colter for the Fred Harvey Company in 1932 and lined with murals that represent different cultural periods. SR 64 continues east to Cameron.

Accommodations and Food

Six national park lodges offer accommodations on the South Rim, including the grand old **◖ El Tovar,** built in 1905. Rooms range $166–300, depending on the season. For reservations, contact Xanterra Parks & Resorts (303/297-2757 or 888/297-2757, www. grandcanyonlodges.com). Most of the lodges have restaurants. You can camp at **Mather Campground** (877/444-6777, www.recreation. gov, $18 per vehicle, open year-round) and its attached **Trailer Village** ($25 per vehicle) in Grand Canyon Village, or at **Desert View Campground** (May–Oct., $12 per vehicle, no reservations or hookups), 26 miles east.

More tourist services are available a couple miles south of park boundaries in the town of **Tusayan,** on SR 64.

Getting There and Around

Shuttle companies in Flagstaff make daily runs to Grand Canyon Village and Tusayan. From Williams, you can take the charming **Grand Canyon Railway** (800/843-8724, www.thetrain.com). The 2.5-hour ride is $65–170 per person ($35–100 children), but various packages including tours and lodging are available.

The park's free shuttle-bus system runs between Grand Canyon Village, Mather Point, and the South Kaibab trailhead, extending spring through fall to cover Hermit Road. For those staying in Tusayan, just south of the park's entrance, a commuter shuttle operates during summer months.

◖ THE NORTH RIM

Though only about 10 miles from the South Rim as the raven flies, the less-developed North

© KATHLEEN BRYANT

Grand Canyon's cooler and quieter North Rim is open from mid-March to mid-October.

Rim is more than 200 miles away by road, so it sees far fewer visitors. You can still depend on stupendous views and precipitous trails—but you'll have several thousand fewer people to share them with. Plus, since it's over 1,000 feet higher, the North Rim is significantly cooler in summer . . . and closes due to heavy snows in the winter.

Bright Angel Point

The North Rim's main developed area is at Bright Angel Point, where you'll find the **North Rim Visitors Center** (8 A.M.–6 P.M. daily May–Oct.), as well as lodging, camping, dining, and shopping options.

Day hikes near the lodge include the paved **Bright Angel Point Trail** (0.5-mile one-way, easy) and the **Transept Trail** (3 miles one-way, easy) from the lodge to the campground. Three longer trails start a couple of miles north of the lodge, including the popular **North Kaibab Trail,** which leads backpackers 14 miles into the canyon, where it connects to trails originating on the South Rim. Day hikers can take the

North Kaibab Trail to the Coconino Overlook (1.5 miles round-trip, moderate) or Roaring Springs (10 miles round-trip, strenuous).

Cape Royal Drive

A paved 23-mile scenic drive leads to **Cape Royal,** passing a half-dozen overlooks along the way, many with picnic areas and short trails. From Cape Royal, you can see all the way across to the South Rim's Grand Canyon Village and Desert View Watchtower. A short side route leads to **Point Imperial,** the highest overlook on the North Rim, with views of Mount Hayden and the Marble Platform.

Accommodations and Food

Built in 1928, the log-beam **❨ Grand Canyon Lodge** boasts two porches and an octagonal sunroom with huge windows to take advantage of the panorama. Cabins start at $120 per night, and it's a good idea to make reservations as far ahead of time as possible through Forever Resorts (888/386-4383, www.foreverlodging.com). The same goes for the **North**

The North Kaibab Trail leads into the depths of Grand Canyon.

Rim Campground (877/444-6777, www.recreation.gov) with sites for $18–25, showers, laundry facilities, a grocery, and a general store. The lodge restaurant (928/638-2611, ext. 760, $5–35) serves all meals, but reserve a table well in advance if you want to eat dinner while watching the sunset through the dining room's tall windows. Other options are the deli next to the lodge (all meals daily, $5–10) or the daily chuck-wagon cookout ($35 adults, $22 children).

Getting There
State Route 67, which originates at Jacob Lake, is the only paved route to the North Rim. U.S. 89A intersects SR 67 from the east (Marble Canyon area) and northwest (Fredonia/Kanab). Many North Rim visitors begin their trip to the North Rim from Las Vegas (275 miles), where it's easy to sign up for a tour or rent a car. You can also get there via the Trans Canyon Shuttle (928/638-2820, www.transcanyonshuttle.com, $150), which travels the

212 miles from the South Rim daily during summer months.

The nearest sizable city is St. George, Utah (156 miles). United and Delta fly into the St. George airport from Los Angeles and Salt Lake City. Flagstaff is 207 miles away, or about five hours.

The Kaibab Plateau
En route to the North Rim Entrance Station, U.S. 89A climbs into the cool evergreen forests of the Kaibab Plateau, and at almost 8,000 feet hits Jacob Lake, where it joins with SR 67. At the intersection, the **Jacob Lake Inn** (928/643-7232, www.jacoblake.com) has a year-round restaurant, rooms ($120–140), and cabins ($90–140). It's also where you'll find the **Kaibab Plateau Visitor Center** (928/643-7298, 8 A.M.–5 P.M. daily mid-May–mid-Oct.), with shorter hours later in the season) run by the Forest Service.

Across the road, **Allen's Guided Tours** (Jacob Lake, 435/644-8150 or 435/689-1370, $15–75) organizes horseback trips into the Kaibab National Forest, and the Forest Service **Jacob Lake Campground** (928/643-7395, May 15–Nov. 1, depending on snowfall) has primitive sites for $17. A quarter mile south is the **Kaibab Camper Village** (928/643-7804 or 800/525-0924, May 15–Oct. 15, http://kaibabcampervillage.com) with full hookup sites ($35), tent sites ($17), and a cabin ($85). From there, SR 67 reaches almost 9,000 feet as it winds through the parklike meadows and pine-clad hills of the Kaibab National Forest, one of the prettiest in the lower 48. Buried by snow in winter, the road is open mid-May–mid-October, weather permitting.

Tuweep
For the adventurous, this "back door" to the North Rim of the Grand Canyon offers something that may seem unbelievable if you've ever been to the South Rim in tour-bus season: solitude. To get there you'll have to negotiate about 60 miles of dirt roads; don't try it with a low-slung car or when it's wet, and keep in mind that the Park Service recommends carrying not just one but two spare tires. From

Fredonia, drive seven miles west and turn off onto BLM Road 109 (the "Sunshine Route"), following the signs through BLM, wilderness, and ranch land to the Tuweep Ranger Station. It's another rough six miles to the campground. There aren't any tourist facilities (or water), but you can drive to the edge of the canyon and camp for free, often with only a handful of other people around. It's a whole other facet of the Grand Canyon, which looks more like a steep-walled gorge there, rather than a mountain range seen from above.

There are no barriers at this overlook and nothing between you and the 3,000-foot drop to the Colorado River. Far below is Lava Falls, the meanest rapid in the park: Sometimes you can hear it roar or see tiny rafts negotiating their way through the rocks. Eleven primitive campsites (first-come, first-served) are available near the rim, with picnic tables, fire grates, and composting toilets. Contact the park (928/638-7888, www.nps.gov/grca) for more information.

© KATHLEEN BRYANT

Tuweep is a remote area along Grand Canyon's northwest rim.

THE INNER CANYON

First, the warnings: Since it gets hotter as you descend into the gorge, and it typically takes twice as much time, energy, and water to climb back out, *and* it can hit over 100°F down there in summer, the inner canyon is as dangerous as it is beautiful. Don't go unprepared, gear- and fitness-wise. It's frighteningly easy to underestimate how challenging hiking in the Grand Canyon is. The combination of altitude, steep terrain, and lack of water claims victims every year.

The best times to venture into the canyon are in spring and fall; March, April, October, and November are ideal. From May to September, temperatures at the rim can be in the 90s and can climb to over 100°F in the canyon.

Permits are necessary for overnight camping in the backcountry ($10 plus $5 pp per night). These can be requested in person, by fax, or by mail, but be warned that the park receives about 20,000 requests every year and only grants 13,000. So apply early—up to four months ahead, on the first of the month. See the backcountry hiking portion of the park's website (www.nps.gov) for details and permit applications.

Hiking

From the South Rim, the **Bright Angel Trail** heads 9.3 miles downhill to **Phantom Ranch** at the river. A bunk in the men's or women's dorms is $42/night, and meals are also available. Reserve rooms through Xanterra Resorts (303/297-2757 or 888/297-2757, www.grand-canyonlodges.com). A wealth of other trails lead down into the gorge. One popular hike is the **Grandview Trail** from Grandview Point to Horseshoe Mesa, an old Indian route improved by miners more than a century ago (6 miles round-trip, strenuous).

From the North Rim, you can take the **North Kaibab Trail** (28 miles round-trip, strenuous) to Phantom Ranch. The steeper and more remote **Bill Hall Trail** also leads to the river (10 miles and 5,200 feet down). Near the bottom it passes **Thunder River,** which gushes out of a sheer limestone cliff before flowing right into the Colorado, making it by some estimates the shortest river in the world.

Rafting the Canyon

Riding the rapids of the Colorado River ranks high up on the list of Things You Should Do Before You Die. Follow in the footsteps of daring explorers as you hike up side canyons, float the placid stretches, and shrink in significance next to billions of years of geology. Unlike John Wesley Powell and other pioneer canyon adventurers, you'll enjoy gourmet meals and the (relative) luxury of sleeping bags on a sandy beach beneath the stars.

Commercial outfitters in Flagstaff and other regional cities offer many different options for guided river trips, and reservations are often available within months or even weeks. (In contrast, it can take years to win the lottery for a private trip permit.) Choose from motorized rafts, oar or paddle rafts, or classic hard-shell dories. The full 226 miles from Lees Ferry to Diamond Creek takes 11–19 days by oar or 6–8 days with a motor. Alternatively, you can join or leave a trip at Phantom Ranch, cutting your travel time considerably. The park's website (www.nps.gov/grca) includes a page on river trips, with links to outfitter/guides. Also helpful is the website of the **Grand Canyon River Outfitters Association** (www.gcroa.org).

Commercial outfitters include **Canyoneers** (928/526-0924 or 800/525-0924, www.canyoneers.com), which traces its origins to 1936, when Norman Nevills first guided a trip down the San Juan River. Their Grand Canyon offerings range from weeklong trips on motorized rafts ($1,959 pp) to 14-day excursions on oar boats ($3,250 pp). **Arizona Raft Adventures** (800/786-7238, www.azraft.com) offers motorized, paddle, oar, and hybrid Grand Canyon

raft trips. If you need help sorting through the options, Tim and Pam Whitney have been running the Grand Canyon since 1973, and in 1986 they founded **Rivers and Oceans** (928/526-4575 or 800/473-4576, www.riversoceans.com). They provide a central reservation service for outfitted trips through the Grand Canyon, as well as trips on rivers in southern Utah and Idaho.

For those lucky souls who've landed a permit for a private river trip, planning and outfitting is easier with the services of a trip support company. **Canyon REO** (800/637-4604, www.canyonreo.com) has gear rentals, kayak instruction, meal planning, and shuttles.

Tours and Activities

Besides boot leather, another classic way to enter the canyon is on a **mule tour.** These sturdy animals have carried visitors up and down the canyon's trails for over a century. The Phantom Ranch mule tour (303/297-2757 or 888/297-2757, www.grandcanyonlodges.com, $482 one night, $674 two nights) departing from the South Rim is the only mule trip with an overnight in the canyon.

The **Grand Canyon Field Institute** (928/638-2485 or 866/471-4435, www.grandcanyon.org/fieldinstitute) organizes a wealth of guided educational overnight trips into the canyon March–November.

Helicopter tours over the canyon have been a contentious subject, with the machines' noise and intrusiveness jarring visitors who came to get away from it all. If you can't resist, **Maverick Helicopters** (928/638-2622 or 888/261-4414, www.maverickhelicopter.com) offers flights departing from the South Rim ($210–250 pp for 25–50 minutes).

Navajo Nation

At 27,000 square miles, the Big Rez (pop. 250,000) is larger than several U.S. states. Even so, the present-day reservation is smaller than Diné Bikeyah, the traditional Navajo homeland that stretched between the four sacred peaks: Sis Naajiní (Mount Blanco) in the east, Tsoodzil (Mount Taylor) to the south, Dook'o'ooslíid (the San Francisco Peaks) to the west, and Dibé Nitsaa (Mount Hesperus) in the north.

Four is an important number in Navajo cosmology. The Diné emerged from three previous worlds before entering this, the Fourth or Glittering World. The holy people—Spider Woman, Talking God, and others—arranged four sacred stones (black jet, white shell, turquoise, and abalone or coral) to mark tribal boundaries, and then placed the sun, moon, and stars and made clouds, trees, rain, and other necessities. The Navajo Nation flag and seal depict the four sacred mountains and their associated colors.

Though many Navajos work wage jobs today, tradition is strong in this land where landscape and culture are woven together as tightly as a Two Grey Hills rug. Ranching, herding, and farming are still central to the reservation economy. Artisans continue to produce silver and turquoise jewelry, though it's common now to see traditional craftsmanship applied to gold, sugalite, and other minerals. (By some estimates, 70 percent of the reservation's workers are associated with arts and crafts.) Hogans, traditional octagonal-shaped homes, still dot the landscape. Medicine men continue to conduct healing ceremonies, employing chant, sandpainting, and other techniques to restore *hozho,* or harmony.

A journey into Navajoland can encompass incredible scenery and fascinating history, from towering sandstone monuments and sculpted canyons to storied trading posts, where you can watch a rug weaver or listen to the Navajo language, famously used as a code by the U.S. military during World War II. A few of the reservation's scenic highlights—such as Monument Valley—are immediately recognizable across the world. Many other wonders are seldom seen by non-Navajos. Most are rich with cultural meaning or legend. Although Navajos graciously welcome visitors to the reservation, the tribe requires that non-Navajos obtain a pass ($5 pp per day) for camping, hiking, or backcountry explorations.

CAMERON AND VICINITY

The Navajo government is organized around 110 chapters, similar to counties or townships. The name for the Cameron chapter is Na ni' ah' hasani, which translates as "old structure across," in reference to the suspension bridge that crosses the Little Colorado River near the trading post. Cameron (pop. 1,200) is located on the reservation's western edge. There, the Painted Desert is a pastel landscape of rounded hills banded in lavender, rose, green, and gray. SR 64 meets U.S. 89 in Cameron, making this small community the gateway to the section of Grand Canyon's South Rim known as Desert View or the East Rim. The sprawling trading post complex north of the intersection is an interesting place to linger on the way to the Grand Canyon, Page, or Tuba City and the Hopi Mesas.

Sights

In 1911 a suspension bridge (named for Arizona Senator Ralph Cameron) was built over the Little Colorado River about 50 miles north of Flagstaff. Now closed, the **historic Cameron Suspension Bridge** is listed on the National Register. Five years later, Hubert and C. D. Richardson established a trading post where the Navajo and Hopi exchanged wool, blankets, and livestock for dry goods. Today the **Cameron Trading Post** (978/679-2231 or 800/338-7385, www.camerontradingpost. com) is employee-owned. The complex of stone buildings there—post, gallery, hotel, RV park—is a lovely enclave and a perfect home

THE LAUGHING PARTY

Part of Navajo tradition is the Chi Dlo Dil, or Laughing Party, held for newborns. At first, babies are considered to be of two worlds—the human world and the world of the holy people. The baby's laughter (at about six weeks) is a sign that the child is ready to be fully human and participate in the community. The first person to make the baby laugh, it is thought, will play an important role in the child's life. That person also is expected to host a feast, where friends and relatives gather to eat and play with the baby.

base for exploring the western reservation and the Grand Canyon.

Steep walls of Kaibab limestone and Coconino sandstone confine the Little Colorado River, dubbed the LCR or "Little C," to a narrow gorge on its final run to the Grand Canyon, where it joins the Colorado River. About 10 miles west of the Cameron junction, SR 64 edges the **Little Colorado River Gorge,** a Navajo Nation Tribal Park. The tribe charges a small entry fee to stop at the main overlook.

Shopping

The **Navajo Arts and Crafts Enterprise** (www.gonavajo.com) has represented regional artists since 1941, with five locations around the reservation. At the U.S. 89/SR 64 junction, NACE operates a store (928/679-2244) with jewelry, rugs, and other crafts.

The **Cameron Trading Post,** approximately a mile north of the U.S. 89/SR 64 junction, has a vast inventory of Native American art, from jewelry to rugs, but it also remains an active post where locals buy craft supplies and sundries and sell wool and piñon nuts. Make sure you don't miss the adjacent **gallery,** which has a museum-quality collection of antique and contemporary native art. Rugs, concho belts, pottery, kachina carvings, baskets, and Old West memorabilia fill the place from wooden floor

to wide-beamed ceiling. More pieces are on display upstairs, in a series of rooms restored to look like living quarters.

Roadside stands, like the ones at the Little Colorado River Gorge along SR 64, are places where you can purchase jewelry and other items directly from artists or their families.

Accommodations and Food

About a mile north of the intersection of U.S. 89 and SR 64, the **Cameron Trading Post** (reservations 800/338-7385) has an RV park ($25) and lodge with 66 rooms ($60–180) that feature hand-carved furniture and balcony views of the Little Colorado River. Many rooms are arranged around the hotel's lovely gardens, where Chinese elms, fruit trees, and rosebushes mingle with native plants. A large stone fireplace, pressed-tin ceiling, and gorgeously woven Navajo tapestries decorate the dining room, which serves all meals daily ($5–25).

Simpson's Market (928/679-2340), located at the junction of U.S. 89/SR 64, is a grocery with a deli serving sandwiches and other inexpensive bites.

Information and Services

Near the U.S. 89/SR 64 intersection, you'll find the **Cameron Visitor Center** (928/679-2303, www.navajonationparks.org), which provides information and issues permits for sites on the western Navajo Nation. Across the intersection is Simpson's convenience store and gas station. About a mile north at the Cameron Trading Post complex, you'll find gas pumps and a **post office.**

Grand Falls of the Little Colorado

In the spring (or after summer thunderstorms), chocolate-colored meltwater roars over the edge of this 185-foot cascade. The falls, which are higher than Niagara Falls, are about 50 miles northeast of Flagstaff at the edge of the San Francisco Volcanic Field. A tongue of lava from Merriam Crater created this pourover about 100,000 years ago. To get there, take exit 211 off I-40 east of Flagstaff and drive 2.3 miles north to Indian Route 15 (Leupp Road). Take IR 15 east 20 miles to the Grand Falls Bible

© KATHLEEN BRYANT

Cameron Trading Post combines shopping, dining, and lodging along the Little Colorado River.

Church sign, between mileposts 5 and 6. Turn left onto a dirt road that ends at the falls overlook, about 9.5 miles. A high-clearance vehicle is recommended. In the spring or after a storm, when the falls are running, the dirt road can be muddy and impassable. For those planning to do any hiking in the area, the Cameron Visitor Center (928/679-2303, 8 A.M.–5 P.M. Mon.–Fri., hours vary seasonally), at the junction of U.S. 89/SR 64, is the nearest parks office issuing permits.

TUBA CITY AND VICINITY

One of the Navajo Reservation's most diverse communities, Tuba City (pop. 8,500) sits off U.S. 89 between Flagstaff and Page, about 45 miles northwest of the Hopi Mesas. The Navajo name for Tuba City is To'Nanees'Dizi (Water Scattered). Mormon settlers called it Tuba City after a Hopi chief called Tuuvi, who established the nearby village of Moenkopi as a summer farming community in the 1870s.

Tuuvi was the first Hopi to meet Brigham Young, and after converting to the Mormon faith, Tuuvi donated a plot of land to the church on the condition that Mormon settlers would protect the Hopi from Navajo and Paiute raiders. Moenave was a small spring-fed oasis west of Tuba City along the Honeymoon Trail. Trailblazer Jacob Hamblin established a settlement there, and it became a popular stop for Mormon couples traveling between their Little Colorado River farms and St. George, Utah, the nearest temple where wedding vows could be solemnized. The last Latter-Day Saint left Moenave near the turn of the 20th century, when the area was added to the Navajo Reservation.

The Hopi village of Moenkopi, "the place of running water," sits across SR 264 from Tuba City. From there, Moenkopi Wash cuts across the desert to the Hopi Mesas. Hopis who farmed at Moenkopi would run between their fields and their home village of Oraibi—a distance of over 30 miles—several times a week.

The Navajo Reservation, like much of the United States, observes daylight saving time. The Hopi Reservation, like the rest of Arizona,

NAVAJO CRAFTS

The Diné tell how Spider Woman taught their ancestors to weave on looms built by her husband. The introduction of curly-horned Churro sheep by the Spanish in the 17th century, along with the adoption of pueblo-style looms as well as a more sedentary lifestyle, allowed the tribe to become expert weavers. Today their **rugs** can hold their own among the world's finest handmade textiles. Women traditionally own the sheep and weave the rugs, which can take months to make. (The Churro sheep had almost become extinct by the 1970s but is being pulled back from the brink through a process of careful breeding.)

Navajo rugs combine Mexican and Spanish stylistic influences with geometric designs and representations of natural phenomena. At the advice of early Anglo traders, the weavers expanded their repertoire to include more intricate patterns. True Navajo rugs are woven from sheep wool, and a quick sniff will reveal an earthy aroma. Other things to look for in a quality rug include symmetry, straight edges, coloration, and a tight, flat weave. You'll often find a "spirit line" running to the border, included to keep the weaver's spirit from being trapped inside the pattern.

Styles include the geometric Two Grey Hills, made of natural white, gray, and brown wool; the pastel vegetals (plant-based dyes) of the Burnt Water style; the elaborately banded Wide Ruins; and the self-explanatory Eye Dazzlers and Pictorials. Some rug patterns are identified by their colors, such as Ganado (deep red) and Klagetoh (gray). Yei rugs depict the Holy People, and Yeibichai illustrate ceremonies in which the Holy People are impersonated by human dancers. Prices range anywhere from the low hundreds to well into the thousands, with a quality 3-by-5-foot rug generally going for about $500-750. This is an exacting art and, sadly, a dying one, since fewer young weavers are learning the old techniques. For this reason, a quality rug will hold its price well and probably even climb in value. Good rugs will also last for years—some old ones have endured over a century of boot traffic.

The Navajos originally learned the technique of **silversmithing** from Mexican smiths, and by the 1860s the craft was spreading throughout the region. Early Navajo silver was made from silver coins, but traders began stocking materials and tools, and smiths expanded their repertoire. By the early 1900s Navajo silver encompassed chunky bracelets, elaborately detailed concha belts, rings inlaid with turquoise and coral, and gorgeous "squash blossom" necklaces. Traditional Navajo silver jewelry is often sand- or tufa-cast, polished to a bright luster, and die-stamped with decorative details. Navajo matriarchs still go out in their best necklaces and bracelets, with enough turquoise to ransom a princess. Men wear the *ketoh* (bow guard), a wide forearm band that is now purely decorative. Turquoise remains the most common stone, but new techniques have seen the addition of gold and a veritable rainbow of precious and semiprecious stones.

Navajo **sandpaintings** re-create the ceremonial designs drawn on hogan floors by medicine men, which are gathered and scattered to the winds when the ritual is finished. Sandpaintings are drawn with glue on plywood or particleboard and then sprinkled with minerals collected on the reservation. Look for precise workmanship, and know that you're not getting a true religious artifact—small details are changed in the paintings to avoid offending the Holy People.

One of the most widely recognized types of baskets made in the Southwest is the Navajo **ceremonial basket,** a wide, shallow dish woven of sumac and mahogany fibers. These baskets are made using a concentric coil technique and have geometric designs in muted colors. They are most commonly used in traditional weddings.

Tribe members produce many other types of crafts and fine arts. These include pottery, leatherwork, wood carvings, ceramic and alabaster sculpture, **"folk art"** (figurines carved from wood or fashioned from clay), oil or acrylic paintings, drums, cedar flutes, stained glass, and furniture.

does not. Thus, when you cross the highway between Tuba City and Moenkopi during summer months, you change time zones. Keep this in mind when you are traveling from one area to the next.

Although predominantly Navajo, Tuba City has many residents who belong to the Hopi and other tribes, as well as Anglos. The Bashas' grocery store (928/283-5250), at the junction of SR 160/SR 264, serves as the unofficial community gathering place. Though many travelers zip past without a second glance on their way to Page or the North Rim, the oasis of Tuba City makes an interesting and pleasant stop en route to the Hopi Mesas.

Sights

Next to the Tuba City Trading Post, the **Explore Navajo Interactive Museum** (Main St. and Moenave Rd., 928/283-5441, 8 A.M.–6 P.M. Mon.–Sat., noon–6 P.M. Sun., $9 adults, $6 children) holds exhibits on the tribe's history and culture, including crafts and the Navajo Code Talkers of WWII.

Tuba City sits on a mesa north of U.S. 160 in one of the most striking expanses of the **Painted Desert.** About two miles east on U.S. 160 from U.S. 89, a dirt turnoff leads to the top of a small hill, a great place to take photos and enjoy the view.

Three more miles brings you to another turnoff marked by a hand-lettered sign for **Moenave,** the site of the original Mormon settlement. Near the turnoff are a set of **dinosaur tracks** laid down by the nine-foot Dilophosaurus in the late Triassic mud. Navajo children are usually on hand to give you a short tour (a small tip is expected) and will point out the three-toed footprints, petrified eggs, and even an embedded claw. The settlement of Moenave itself, at the base of Hamblin Ridge, is a green oasis fed by springs. John D. Lee, of Lees Ferry, hid out there for a while before being tracked down and executed for his role in the Mountain Meadows Massacre.

Fifteen miles southeast of Tuba City along SR 264, beautiful **Coal Mine Canyon** secrets a collection of colorful hoodoos and cliffs.

This treasure is easy to miss: The canyon is less than a mile long, and there are no signs to indicate its presence on the barren landscape. Look for a dirt road leading to a windmill between mile markers 336 and 337. The Navajo call this serrated landscape *hááhonooji* (jagged), and the Hopi tell of Quayowuuti, the Eagle Woman from Old Oraibi who stepped from the edge of the canyon to her death. Her ghost is said to appear under the full moon. Permits for visiting and hiking the canyon are available at the Cameron Visitor Center (928/679-2303, 8 A.M.–5 P.M. Mon.–Fri., hours vary seasonally), at the junction of U.S. 89/SR 64 in Cameron.

Red Lake Trading Post (928/283-5194) also known as Tonalea Trading Post, is 20 miles northwest of Tuba City along U.S. 160. The building dates to 1891, when the Babbitt Brothers Trading Company built it using Arbuckle coffee boxes for some of the walls. The post has a rich and storied history, including being the scene of a tragic love triangle and appearing in Zane Grey's novel *Rainbow Trail.* It was used as a location for *The Dark Wind* (1991), based on the Tony Hillerman novel and produced by Robert Redford. Today it's a convenience market where you can stop and get a cool drink before continuing your drive. A mile north, you'll see the **Elephant Feet,** a pair of stocky sandstone pillars on the west side of the highway.

Shopping and Events

The **Tuba City Trading Post** (10 N. Main, 928/283-5441), established in 1870, was operated for a time by the Babbitt family. Teddy Roosevelt stayed there in 1913 on his way back from hunting mountain lions on the North Rim of the Grand Canyon, and Zane Grey also visited. The present octagonal-shaped building was constructed in the 1930s out of local blue limestone with logs from the San Francisco Peaks. Today the trading post displays a wealth of quality crafts, including Navajo rugs woven in the bold geometric storm pattern developed in the Tuba City area.

Every Friday the **Tuba City Flea Market**

coalesces behind the chapter house. A little bit of everything is for sale—car parts, used clothing, medicinal herbs, turquoise jewelry—and when you need a break from browsing, you can listen to the lilting sounds of the Navajo language over a bowl of mutton stew and fry bread.

The **Western Navajo Fair** is held every October on the first weekend after Columbus Day. Make hotel reservations early if you plan to attend this popular event, which includes a rodeo, beauty pageant, dances, and a Yeibichei ceremony.

Accommodations and Food

At the intersection of U.S. 160 and SR 264, the recently completed **Moenkopi Legacy Inn & Suites** (928/283-4500, http://experiencehopi. com, $100–220) has 100 rooms and suites with amenities that include a pool and fitness center. It's one of only two hotels on Hopi tribal land, and the lobby, anchored by a three-story fireplace designed by Eddie Calnimptewa, showcases their art and culture. Next to the Tuba City Trading Post, the **Quality Inn** (928/283-4545, 10 N. Main, $120–165) has a restaurant and an RV park with six tent sites. Students at the Greyhills Academy High School run the 32-room **Greyhills Inn** (U.S. 160 and Warrior Dr., 928/283-6271, ext. 142, $62) as part of a training program in hotel management.

Dining options are limited in Tuba City. At the U.S. 160/SR 264 intersection, the **Tuuvi Café** (928/283-4374, all meals daily, $5–10) serves American food and a few Hopi dishes like hominy stew. Drive north along SR 264 and you'll spot a handful of chains, as well as the **Hogan Restaurant** (928/283-5260, all meals daily, $5–15) at the Quality Inn, serving American and Mexican dishes with a few local specialties and a salad bar.

KAYENTA AND VICINITY

The largest city (pop. 5,000) in the northern part of the Navajo Reservation takes its name, loosely, from the Navajo *teehindeeh,* meaning "bog hole" or "natural game pit," after the gluelike soil around a nearby spring that mired livestock. The Navajo also call it Tódínéeshzheé, meaning "water spreading out like fingers."

Once the center of the Ancestral Puebloan world, Kayenta is now a dusty town of pickup trucks and cowboy hats, home to miners and farmers. Kayenta's chief attraction is its access to nearby Navajo National Monument and Monument Valley Tribal Park, and it makes a convenient stop en route to Four Corners National Monument. You'll find a few motels, inexpensive restaurants, and a shopping center at the intersection of U.S. 160 and 163.

There, as elsewhere in Navajo country, landscape and story are inseparable. As you drive U.S. 160 northeast, you'll parallel **Comb Ridge,** a 100-mile-long sandstone monocline that Navajos say represents the earth's backbone. Across the highway north of town is a cluster of hoodoos known as **Baby Rocks Mesa.** One of the reddish spires is said to be a girl who refused to share bread with a baby sister. The Holy People turned her into stone, and she stands today as a warning against selfishness.

Views encompass diatremes, or volcanic necks, thrusting up from the high desert floor. One of these, **Aglatha Peak,** is located along U.S. 163, marking the gateway to Monument Valley. Among the many stories associated with this peak is one identifying it as the center of the world, where the Holy People propped up the sky. Kit Carson renamed it El Capitan when he rode through there in his 1863–64 campaign against the Navajos.

Sights

The Navajos have a long, proud warrior tradition, and many young men volunteered for military service during World War II. Some 400 were trained as Code Talkers and sworn to secrecy about their roles in order to preserve the code. It wasn't until 1968, when the U.S. government declassified their story, that their unique contributions to the war were acknowledged. Another 30-odd years passed before the Code Talkers were officially honored with Congressional Medals of Honor, awarded at a ceremony in 2001. Inside the Burger King restaurant, located just west of the U.S. 160/U.S. 163 intersection, one wall is dedicated to an exhibit of letters, uniform parts, and other artifacts relating to the **Navajo Code Talkers.**

Next door to the restaurant, the **Navajo Cultural Center** (928/697-3170) has examples of male and female hogans and the Shadehouse Museum, which displays additional Code Talker memorabilia. The shadehouse was built by Richard Mike, whose father was a Code Talker.

Shopping and Events

Crafts, Western wear, and craft supplies are sold at the **Navajo Arts and Crafts Enterprises** (928/697-8611, 9 A.M.–6 P.M. Mon.–Fri. spring-fall, with limited weekend hours in winter) near the U.S. 160/U.S. 163 intersection. The **Kayenta Fourth of July Rodeo** is a hugely popular multi-day event with live Western music and fireworks.

Accommodations and Food

Kayenta has only a few chain hotels, all near the intersection of U.S. 160 and 163, including the **Best Western Wetherill Inn** (928/697-3231, $80–140) and the **Holiday Inn** (928/697-3221, $90–170).

At the main intersection, the **Blue Coffee Pot** (928/697-3396, 6 A.M.–9 P.M. Mon.–Fri.) is a local favorite, serving good steaks, Mexican, and Navajo dishes for $5–9. About 10 miles west on U.S. 160, the Hampton Inn's **Reuben Heflin Restaurant** (928/697-3170, dinner daily) serves seafood, steak, and Southwestern cuisine.

NAVAJO NATIONAL MONUMENT

Twenty miles southwest of Kayenta, this small national monument protects two of the most impressive and intact prehistoric pueblos in the Four Corners. The monument lies within the Navajo Reservation on the Shonto Plateau, nine miles off U.S. 160 at the end of SR 564. The ruins, both cliff dwellings, are open for visitation. Start at the **visitors center** (928/672-2700, www.nps.gov/nava, 8 A.M.–6 P.M. Memorial Day–Labor Day, otherwise 9 A.M.–5 P.M., free), which has a museum and bookstore. Local Navajo artists demonstrate their crafts there on occasion. The monument observes daylight saving time.

Sights and Hikes

Two short, easy trails lead along the canyon rim

to overlooks of **Betatakin** (Navajo for "ledge house"), a 125-room pueblo tucked into a dramatically arched stone alcove. The only way to experience this cliff dwelling up close is to take a ranger-led tour, offered from spring through fall. The five-mile round-trip tour requires some effort—the trail is sandy and steep, like walking up the stairs of a 70-story building at 7,300-foot elevation—but it's worth every sweaty step.

The Betatakin tour departs twice daily on summer mornings. Allow three–five hours for the strenuous hike, which can be particularly trying in summer heat. (Tours are available on some winter weekends, depending on staffing.)

Keet Seel (Navajo for "broken pottery") is more than eight miles from the visitors center, meaning you can spend a night at the small, primitive campground near the ruin or do the whole 17-mile round trip in an epic one-day push. Either way, you'll be able to follow a ranger through this 100-room settlement tucked under a cliff overhang. Only a handful of visitors are allowed on each tour, and the experience is haunting: Decorated potsherds and corncobs lie scattered around the silent village, and wood ladders and beams poke out of masonry rooms, as though the inhabitants simply walked away and never returned. Many archaeologists consider it among the best-preserved Southwestern ruins.

Accommodations and Food

The monument has two free **campgrounds,** one with 31 sites and another with 11 sites. The closest lodgings are in Tsegi Canyon, about 14 miles southeast on U.S. 160. The **Anasazi Inn** (928/697-3793) has 57 rooms ($95–120) and a small café serving all meals daily. The rooms and menu are simple, but you can't beat the setting in the pink sandstone gorge.

◖ MONUMENT VALLEY TRIBAL PARK

Drive north of Kayenta on U.S. 163 toward the Utah border, and you may feel like you've entered a Western movie sunset just as the credits started to roll. Rising from the flat plain like

Betatakin is one of the cliff dwellings preserved at Navajo National Monument.

© KATHLEEN BRYANT

the gods' own rock garden, the stone monoliths of Monument Valley are the unmistakable icon of the American West, recognizable worldwide, thanks to countless movies, television commercials, and photographs. Director John Ford, the first to put Monument Valley on the big screen, called it the "most complete, beautiful, and peaceful place on earth."

The Navajo consider all of Tsébii'nidzisgai (the "valley within the rocks") to be one huge hogan, with the traditional east-facing door situated near the visitors center. Chief Hoskininni led many Navajos to the valley for refuge there during Kit Carson's scorched earth campaign of 1863–64, and about 100 people still live and farm there. The valley became the Navajos' first tribal park in 1958. Visitation is limited to a single loop road and permitted tours. (Rock climbing there—or elsewhere on the reservation—is forbidden, regardless of what you saw in *The Eiger Sanction* or *Vertical Limit*.)

The floor of Monument Valley is a weathered, river-deposited siltstone laid down more than 200 million years ago. Iron oxide within the siltstone gives it a reddish color. Over the millennia, the softer siltstone has eroded, revealing vertically jointed slabs of sandstone in the form of massive buttes and spires with names like Totem Pole, the Yei Bi Chei, the Three Sisters, and the Mittens. Many Monument Valley formations are capped by harder Moenkopi shale and Shinarump. Dark, jagged peaks on the valley's southern edge are volcanic remnants.

Visiting Monument Valley

At an intersection on the state line, a short road leads east to the **Monument Valley Navajo Tribal Park** (435/727-5870, www.navajonationparks.org, 6 A.M.–8 P.M. daily, 8 A.M.–5 P.M. Oct.–Apr., $5 pp). The recently constructed hotel and visitors center complex is at the edge of the valley, situated to take in the glorious view from large windows and a multilevel terrace. The visitors center has exhibits on Navajo culture and a gift shop with native crafts, books, and souvenirs.

From there, the 17-mile, self-guided **loop**

road descends into the valley, past many Navajo homes and a viewing point named for director John Ford. Allow at least two hours for the dirt road, which is suitable for most two-wheel-drive vehicles and closes shortly before sundown. It's also a great mountain bike ride.

If you'd prefer to sit back and enjoy while someone else does the driving, or if you'd like to get off the main road, dozens of local operators offer guided trail rides, hikes, and vehicle tours. One of them, **Sacred Monument Tours** (435/727-3218, www.monumentvalley.net), has hiking, jeep, and horseback riding tours starting at $70, with an all-day horseback-riding tour for $300 per person. Longer tours leave the loop road for backcountry petroglyphs and ruins. **Roland's Navajoland Tours** (928/697-3524) leads Monument Valley tours out of Kayenta.

For the classic road-trip shot of Monument Valley—the place where Forrest Gump finally stopped running—approach from the north on U.S. 163, the **Monument Valley-Bluff Scenic Byway.** A little more than 13 miles north of the Utah-Arizona border there's a small hill, with the highway heading straight as an arrow toward the valley below: You'll recognize the view.

Adjacent to the visitors center, the recently opened **View Hotel** (435/727-5555, www.monumentvalleyview.com, $150–300) has rooms with balconies overlooking the valley's formations, a deli counter, and a restaurant serving all meals daily. The aptly named hotel is often fully booked months in advance by tour companies during peak season, but cancellations are possible. Nearby is access to the **Wildcat Trail** (four miles round-trip), which circumnavigates one of the Mittens and is the only park trail where non-Navajos can hike without an authorized guide.

Mitten View Campground sits at the edge of the valley near the visitors center. Of its 100 campsites, sites 24 and 25 have the best views, making it well worth getting up for sunrise. Group, tent, and RV sites are available ($10, no hookups) year-round, with restrooms and coin-operated showers open in high season.

The View Hotel sits on the edge of Monument Valley.

Goulding's Lodge and Trading Post

At the north end of the valley at the Arizona-Utah state line is a trading post established in a 10-person tent by Harry Goulding and his wife, Mike, in the 1920s. Harry, called **Dibé Nééz** ("Tall Sheep") by the Navajo, purchased 640 acres at the base of Black Door Mesa in 1937 for $320. Goulding bought local crafts, settled disputes, and acted as a liaison between the Navajo and the government. Hoping to bring jobs to the area during the Great Depression, he traveled to Hollywood to persuade director John Ford that the local scenery would make an ideal movie location. The rest is celluloid history. Monument Valley has been the backdrop for countless movies, including the classic Westerns *Stagecoach* (1939), *My Darling Clementine* (1946), and *Fort Apache* (1948). As Hollywood started to arrive, the Gouldings opened a lodge that became a second home to stars like John Wayne. Movie memorabilia and trading-post artifacts fill the original trading post, which has been turned into a museum (open daily year-round). A suggested donation of $2 is put toward scholarships for local children.

The modern **lodge** (435/727-3231, www.gouldings.com) has 62 rooms ($80–200) and the Stagecoach Dining Room, built for the filming of *She Wore a Yellow Ribbon* (1949). You can rent a Western movie to watch in your room . . . or just gaze from your balcony at the real thing. A year-round **campground** has views of the valley as well, with cabins ($80–100) or sites for tents ($25) and RVs ($44). Amenities include a coin laundry, hot showers, and shuttles to the lodge's heated indoor pool, grocery store, and dining room. Sign up at the lodge for Navajo-guided **tours** to nearby ruins, petroglyphs, crafts demonstrations, and movie locations.

Oljato

Eight miles past Goulding's, the **Oljato Trading Post** was opened in 1905 by cowboy archaeologist John Wetherill. The present building was constructed in 1921 and served the local population for decades before closing its doors. Once, more than 150 posts dotted the Navajo reservation. Locals depended on trading posts until highways improved, automobiles replaced horse travel, and distant regional shopping centers offered a greater variety of goods at lower prices. Of the handful of posts remaining in business today, most have modernized by adding gas pumps and tourist conveniences. Oljato is a fine example of a traditional post—simply built and remotely located. Though you can no longer see the interior of the low-roofed stone building, the drive there is well worth it for the scenery and ambiance.

◖ CANYON DE CHELLY NATIONAL MONUMENT

Joseph Campbell, international guru of mythology, once called this canyon system in northeast Arizona "the most sacred place on earth." The four canyons there—del Muerto, Black Rock, de Chelly, and Monument canyons—sheltered Ancestral Puebloan farmers, and later, acted as a Navajo stronghold. Navajos consider this to be the spiritual heart of Diné Bikeyah, the traditional homeland bounded by the four sacred mountains.

Covering 130 square miles of precipitous gorges and fertile canyon bottoms, Canyon de Chelly (de-SHAY) has the ageless quality of a place inhabited for thousands of years, and Navajo families continue to farm and tend orchards and herds of animals beneath its soaring sandstone cliffs. Navajo families still own the land that comprises the monument, which is administered by the National Park Service. Roads run along the north and south rims, with sweeping overlooks that take in rock spires, ancient ruins, and farmland. Aside from a single trail to the bottom, the only way to visit the canyon depths is to join a Navajo-led tour.

The canyon rims range 5,000–7,000 feet in elevation. Down the center runs the Rio de Chelly, from its beginnings in the Chuska Mountains in the east to the mouth of Canyon de Chelly near the town of Chinle, meaning "the place where the water flows out." The glowing red sandstone walls are over 1,000 feet high in places and as sheer as the side of a skyscraper. Temperatures range from well below 0°F in winter to over 100°F in summer, but the river-deposited sediments and reliable water supply make the canyon bottom excellent for farming. Side streams dry up in summer and rage with flash floods during the summer rainy seasons and spring snowmelt. Quicksand is often a concern in wet, sandy spots.

History

The earliest people to shelter in this canyon system were nomadic bands, who camped seasonally in alcoves while hunting game and foraging plants. Beginning about 2,500 years ago, during what is known as the Basketmaker Phase, people began experimenting with agriculture. They pecked hand-and-foot trails in cliff faces and progressed from dispersed jacal shelters and pit houses to impressive multiroom cliff dwellings cultivating canyon bottoms. Around A.D. 1300, Ancestral Puebloan villagers migrated from the canyon, joining other clans to establish pueblos near the Little Colorado River.

Their descendants, the Hopis, farmed Canyon de Chelly sporadically thereafter, and members of other tribes fled there after the Pueblo Revolt of 1680, but by 1700 Navajos were using the canyons and upland plateaus. The Navajo families who settled there brought livestock and peach trees introduced by the Spanish, having learned farming techniques and weaving from the pueblo tribes. They called the canyons Tséyi', meaning "within the rocks," but it is the Spanish mispronunciation of the word that has stuck.

For more than a century, the canyons' cornfields and peach orchards were a refuge from repeated raiding between various tribes and Spanish colonists. The Navajos fortified the canyons with stone walls, hidden trails, and food caches. Even so, Spanish, Ute, and later U.S. military parties occasionally managed to get past the defenses. Some of these attacks are memorialized by pictographs painted or drawn on the canyon walls.

Beginning in 1863 Kit Carson's merciless campaign drove hundreds of Navajos from their homes. Soldiers entered this canyon stronghold in the winter of 1864, killing or capturing those sheltered there, later destroying orchards and hogans and slaughtering livestock so that any survivors could not return. Those who survived the assault were forced on the Long Walk to eastern New Mexico, where they were incarcerated for four years before being allowed to return to a reservation established by treaty in 1868.

The canyons were declared a national monument in 1931, under a rare arrangement in which management is shared by the tribe and the National Park Service. The Navajo still grow melons, corn, beans, and squash on the fertile canyon bottom, where sheep and goats wander among cottonwoods and peach orchards.

Visiting Canyon de Chelly

Just east of the town of Chinle, the sandstone cliffs lower to about 30 feet, forming a natural gateway to the canyon system. You can take the rough road leading into the canyons only if you're on a guided tour or if you're a resident. Three miles east of Chinle, the **visitors center** (928/674-5500, www.nps.gov/cach, 8 A.M.–5 P.M. daily) has exhibits on the area's history and geology, as well as restrooms and drinking water. Entrance to the monument is free. Navajo Parks and Recreation charges a small fee for **Cottonwood Campground** (928/674-2106), open year-round. (The campground doesn't have hookups and can't accommodate RVs longer than 40 feet.) Nearby is the beautiful **Thunderbird Lodge** (just inside the park entrance on South Rim Drive, 928/674-5841 or 800/679-2473, www.tbirdlodge.com), which began as a trading post built by Sam Day in 1902. The original post building is now the cafeteria, decorated with Navajo rugs and open for all meals daily, featuring fry bread, chili, and other inexpensive Navajo and American dishes. The lodge is open year-round, with 73 rooms ($115–171). Rates drop by almost half in winter months. The lodge has a fine gift shop and offers half- and full-day canyon excursions ($52–83) in Unimogs, dubbed "shake-and-bake" tours by locals.

Canyon de Chelly's four main gorges and numerous side canyons slice generally eastward into the Defiance Plateau. Narrow paved roads parallel the northern and southern edges of the canyon system, where overlooks offer fantastic views of rock formations and ruins tucked into shadowy alcoves. Short trails lead to the cliff edges. Be careful at the overlooks: There are sharp drop-offs and the occasional car theft; don't leave anything of value in plain view.

North Rim Drive

This 17-mile section of Indian Route (IR) 64, which connects Chinle to Diné College and Tsaile, runs along Canyon del Muerto, Spanish for "Canyon of the Dead" (also referred to as North Canyon by locals). Archaeology buffs will find this drive especially interesting for its combination of tribal history, rock art, and well-preserved ruins. At the first of four overlooks, you can see 900-year-old Ledge Ruin and—if your eyes are sharp—a line of toeholds leading to a separate room.

At seven miles is **Antelope House Overlook,** above a ruin named for pictographs of running antelopes painted by a Navajo artist around 1830. The ruins and pictographs left by Ancestral Puebloans are at least 1,000 years older. Directly across the canyon, above the junction of Canyon del Muerto and Black Rock Canyon to the south, is the **Navajo Fortress,** an aerie where Navajo warriors hid from attackers, sneaking down at night for water and food.

Drive another nine miles, turn right, and take the right-hand fork for **Mummy Cave Overlook,** named by archaeologist Earl Morris for two mummified corpses found below. The ruins, thought to have been occupied between A.D. 300 and 1300, are situated in two cliff alcoves with a three-story Mesa Verde–style tower in between. The left-hand fork leads to **Massacre Cave Overlook.** When Lieutenant Antonio de Narbona led a punitive expedition into the canyon in 1805 to quell Navajo raids, the Spaniards found a group hiding in this cave. Over the course of two days, Spanish riflemen killed 115 people in the cave by bouncing bullets off its ceiling from the rim above. The bones of the victims remain in the cave untouched, per Navajo custom. It's a short walk to **Yucca Cave Overlook,** where you can see a small cliff dwelling and granary, connected by a series of toeholds.

South Rim Drive

This road parallels Canyon de Chelly (also called South Canyon), with views of the Chuska Mountains as well as the canyon system. You can stop at the **Tunnel Overlook** and **Tsegi Overlook** for views of the lower canyon and farms en route to **Junction Overlook,** about four miles from the visitors center. There, Canyon del Muerto joins Canyon de Chelly, and the rim is less than 500 feet above the creek. **First Ruin** and **Junction Ruin** are both visible.

It's another two miles to **White House Overlook,** which offers not only a great view but also the only way to reach the canyon bottom without a guide. The steep, rocky trail down to **White House Ruin** (2.5 miles round-trip, easy) descends 600 feet, passing through short tunnels and near a farm and orchard before crossing the wash on a footbridge. The trail ends in front of the well-preserved upper and lower ruins, named for the white-painted plaster finish on one of the rooms. Long streaks of desert varnish (manganese oxide) extend from the rim to the alcove, making this site a favorite of photographers. Nearby, you'll find restrooms and Navajo vendors selling jewelry and other items. Bring plenty of water, as the trail is sun-exposed. Respect the privacy of the families living in the canyon; don't wander off the trail without a guide.

Drive six more miles for the turnoff to **Sliding House Overlook.** The ruins there are named for the sloping alcove floor. A couple of miles farther along South Rim Drive is the **Spider Rock Campground** (928/674-8261, www.spiderrockcampground.com). Owned by local resident Howard Smith, this year-round campground has tent sites for $10 and RV sites for $15, as well as solar-heated showers and two hogans starting at $30. At **Face Rock Overlook,** twenty miles east of the visitors center, the canyon rims are now 1,000 feet above the wash. The ruins there are named for the stone spire nearby.

Follow the paved road northeast another mile, where it ends at **Spider Rock Overlook,** the park's most outstanding viewing point. An 800-foot rock tower thrusts from the canyon bottom where three canyons come together, one of the most breathtaking sights in the Southwest. Navajos call this monolith Tse' Na' ashjé'ii and tell of the supernatural being who lives on top. Spider Woman teaches weaving on a loom whose warp is the rays of the sun. Navajo mothers once warned their children to behave or else Spider Woman would carry them to her perch, said to be white with bones.

Tours

Canyon de Chelly Unimog Tours (928/674-5433, www.canyondechellytours.com) offers tours of the canyon bottom in jeeps, the military-looking, natural-gas powered Unimog, or your own vehicle. Tours start at $66 adults ($44 children) for a half day. They can also organize an overnight campout in the canyon.

Authorized Navajo guides offer driving tours (your vehicle—high-clearance, 4WD recommended) for $15 per hour. They lead hiking tours (15 people maximum) for the same price—an absolute bargain granting access to some of the canyon's most amazing historical and scenic treasures. Ask at the visitors center for details and trail suggestions. Some local residents, including James Yazzie, Jr. (928/674-5647), can arrange for overnight treks or horseback tours.

Chinle

The town of Chinle (pop. 5,300), situated at the mouth of Canyon de Chelly, is surrounded by farms and ranches, making it a busy shopping hub for rural residents. At Bashas' grocery store, look for labels in Navajo. For jewelry and other crafts, try the **Navajo Arts & Crafts Enterprises** at the main intersection. The Chinle area is known for crossbanded rugs woven with wool in vegetal dyes, though other styles are also woven there. The Chinle Comprehensive Health Care Facility (928/674-7001) combines traditional Navajo healing practices with modern medicine; it

even includes a hogan for ceremonies. Food and accommodation can be found at **Best Western** (100 Main St., 928/674-5874), with 100 rooms for $110, and a **Holiday Inn** (928/674-5000, from $115), close to the canyon on IR 7 at the site of the Garcia trading post. Both have heated pools and restaurants open daily for all meals, and both offer bargain winter rates.

HUBBELL TRADING POST NATIONAL HISTORIC SITE

The oldest continuously operating trading post on the Navajo Reservation was built on the banks of Pueblo Colorado Wash in 1871. Clerk and interpreter John Lorenzo Hubbell bought the post seven years later, and it stayed in his family until the National Park Service purchased it in 1965. Over the decades, Hubbell built one of the most successful trading empires in the Southwest, buying out and opening other posts throughout the Four Corners and earning the nickname Don Lorenzo, a Spanish term of respect, for his fair dealing and hospitality.

Hubbell learned the Navajos' culture and language, counseling them and treating their sick during an 1886 smallpox epidemic. He advised weavers on which designs would fetch the best prices. (The handsome Ganado pattern, with its deep red wool and cross motif, is still woven.) He brought a silversmith from Mexico to teach the art to locals. The Hubbells—Lorenzo, his wife, Lina, Rubi, and their four children—amassed one of the largest art collections in the Southwest in their home next to the post.

Today the original 160-acre homestead, one mile west of Ganado on SR 264, is administered by the National Park Service (928/755-3475, www.nps.gov/hutr, 8 A.M.–6 P.M. May–early Sept., until 5 P.M. in winter, free). The old trading post is operated by the Western National Parks Association (928/755-3254, www.wnpa.org). The post still buys and sells crafts, food, and supplies, though most sales now are to tourists. The rug room in back boasts a king's ransom in Navajo textiles.

Hubbell Trading Post is the oldest continuously operated post on the Navajo Reservation.

Demonstrations and auctions of Native American crafts are held throughout the year, and daily tours take visitors into the Hubbell home ($2 pp), which has retained all its original furnishings, excluding rugs. The ceiling in the main hallway is covered with dozens of woven baskets, and works by artists who visited the family adorn the walls, including portraits by Maynard Dixon and E. A. Burbank done with red Conté crayon.

WINDOW ROCK

The administrative center of the Navajo Nation straddles the New Mexico–Arizona border 24 miles northwest of Gallup on Highway 264/3. Window Rock (pop. 3,000) owes its importance to John Collier, commissioner of Indian Affairs in the 1930s, who brought the reservation's various offices together there as the Navajo Central Agency. He is remembered for his sympathetic ear in matters such as the tribe's education and health care, including the replacing of boarding schools with day schools for children.

Sights

The **Navajo Nation Museum** (928/871-7941, 8 A.M.–5 P.M. Mon.–Fri., until 8 P.M. Wed., 9 A.M.–5 P.M. Sat., free) is near the intersection of SR 264 and IR 12. The museum has well-done displays on tribal history, geology, and archaeology. Sharing the same parking lot are the **Navajo Parks & Recreation Department** (928/871-6647, www.navajonationparks.org, 8 A.M.–5 P.M.), where you can pick up permits for camping on the reservation, and the small **Navajo Nation Zoo and Botanical Park** (928/871-6574, www.navajozoo.org, 10 A.M.– 4:30 P.M. Mon.–Sat., free), which houses animals injured or otherwise unfit for the wild. The collection includes a cougar, black bears, bobcats, and a pair of Mexican Gray Wolves. (Pets are not allowed.)

The headquarters of the Navajo tribal government encompass the tribe's executive offices and—attention, readers of Tony Hillerman's novels—police headquarters. The **Navajo Tribal Council Chambers** is an octagonal structure built of rock, representing a hogan. Depending on the council's schedule, you may be able to join a tour for a look inside at the log ceiling and colorful murals depicting Navajo history and daily life. Most council business is conducted in the Navajo language. To get there, take a right a half mile north of the intersection of SR 264 and IR 12.

Window Rock Tribal Park (8 A.M.–5 P.M. daily, free) centers around Tségháhoodzání (the "perforated rock"). This natural window is important as one of four sites where Navajo medicine men collect water for the Water Way ceremony, held to ensure abundant rainfall. The park is laid out in a quartered circle, the form of a medicine wheel, and features a veterans memorial honoring the many Navajos who served in the military. The graceful structure was designed with input from veterans and medicine men, and symbolism includes 16 steel pillars representing bayonets. The memorial includes a sanctuary for healing and reflection with a sandstone fountain and a statue that depicts a World War II Navajo Code Talker.

St. Michael's Mission, established in 1898, is now a museum (928/871-4171, 9 a.m.–5 p.m. Mon.–Fri., Memorial Day–Labor Day) documenting the work of Franciscan friars who taught school and catechism there.

Scenic Indian Route 12, also known as Diné Biítah ("Among the People"), passes through Window Rock on its way north from I-40 to Tsaile. Tune the radio to KNNN 660 AM, sit back, and enjoy the views from the paved highway, which parallels gorgeous sandstone cliffs and softly rounded buttes edging small farms and ranches. Four miles north of Window Rock, **Fort Defiance** was where the Navajos' Long Walk began in 1864. The Episcopal Church built a hospital mission there in 1897, and the building was later used as an orphanage and boarding school. **Wheatfields Lake,** 40 miles north of Window Rock at the base of the Chuska Mountains, has areas for picnicking and camping. You can continue north, turning west at Tsaile for Canyon de Chelly, or take IR 134 through the forested **Chuska Mountains** to join U.S. 491, another scenic road that travels south to Gallup or north to Shiprock. (When traveling the reservation, stay on main roads and do not approach private property unless invited. Keep a watchful eye out for livestock.)

Shopping and Events

A large selection of traditional and contemporary jewelry, rugs, Western clothing, Pendleton blankets, and more awaits at the **Navajo Arts & Crafts Enterprises** store (928/871-4090 or 866/871-4095, www.gonavajo.com, 9 a.m.–5 p.m. Mon.–Fri) near the Navajo Nation Inn. NACE began as a craft guild in 1941, and artisans still buy supplies there. NACE also repairs and restores jewelry.

Thousands of people flock to **Navajo Nation Fair** (928/871-6478, www.navajonationfair.com), held early in September, for its rodeo, parade, music, exhibits, and pageantry. Held since 1938 to showcase Navajo agriculture and artistry, it's the largest Indian fair in North America.

Accommodations and Food

Most tourist activity in Window Rock centers around the **Quality Inn** (48 W. Hwy. 264, 928/871-4108 or 800/662-6189, www.explorenavajo.com, $90–100), a comfortable place with 56 rooms near the main intersection. The hotel's **Diné Restaurant** (all meals daily) is a local favorite, serving good food (plates $6 and up), including a breakfast buffet, burgers, Navajo tacos (of course), and mutton stew. Three miles west on SR 264 in St. Michaels, the Navajoland Inn (392 W. Hwy. 64, 928/871-5690, $70–90) has an indoor pool and spa. A handful of fast-food outlets are scattered along SR 264, from St. Michaels east across the border.

Hopi Reservation

The 1.5-million-acre Hopi reservation (pop. 7,000) is a cultural island surrounded by the larger Navajo reservation. Once, Hopi lands encompassed over 18 million acres, from the Grand Canyon east to the Lukachukai Mountains, and from Navajo Mountain to the southern edge of the Colorado Plateau. According to the Hopis' long oral history, when their ancestors emerged into this world, they were greeted by the earth god Maasau, who told them they would leave their footprints in many places before reuniting at the center of the universe.

A millennium ago, having left footprints in the form of ruined villages, rock art, and potsherds, the clans gathered at what are known today as the Hopi Mesas, three high, finger-like projections extending from Black Mesa. Surviving there—with less than 10 inches of annual rainfall and a 7,000-foot elevation—required cooperating with each other and with nature. Each arriving clan contributed

WHERE TO SHOP

There are two main options when it comes to purchasing native crafts (well, three, if you count paying five times as much at a boutique back home): buy directly from the artists themselves or buy from a trading post or gallery. Buying from the creator, either in his or her home or at a roadside or flea market stand, adds not only the personal touch but also the opportunity to get the best price. It helps to know what you're looking for in this situation and to have an idea of how to judge quality and a fair price. To be honest, a good number of items for sale at tourist spots like Monument Valley are mere trinkets. (But if something pleases you, why not buy it and enjoy it?)

Trading posts and galleries charge higher prices, and at an established post, you can be assured that you're getting a quality product, with the reputation of the store behind it. Employees are happy to let you browse and to lend their expert advice if necessary, and they can pack up and ship your purchases back home. Some off-reservation posts have pawn departments, and unredeemed goods (known as dead pawn) may be offered for sale or auction.

Wherever you buy an item, try to find out where and when it was made and ask for a **certificate of authenticity,** or else a receipt with the name and contact information of the artist or gallery, the artist's name and tribal affiliation, and the price, including the original price if you received a discount.

The **Indian Arts and Crafts Act of 1990** prohibits the misrepresentation of Native American arts and crafts (defined as a tribe member or artisan certified by a tribe) produced after 1935. For more information, contact the Indian Arts & Crafts Board of the U.S. Department of the Interior (202/208-3773 or 888/278-3253, www.doi.gov/iacb).

The nonprofit **Indian Arts and Crafts Association** (505/265-9149, www.iaca.com) offers consumer tips and other information on their website.

© RICHARD MAYER

Richardson's, on Gallup's historic Route 66, is a prime example of a traditional post that has endured into the present.

ceremonies and married into other clans, creating community ties. Together, they became Hopituh Shinumo, the peaceful or well-mannered people.

Today Hopi life continues to center around a dozen villages scattered on or below the mesas. A few of the Hopi villages have been inhabited for over eight centuries. The mesas are quiet and isolated, and an almost tangible sense of tradition hangs in the clear air. Many Hopis are farmers or artisans, and those with off-reservation wage jobs are likely to return there for weekends or ceremonies or to tend family fields below the mesas.

The Hopis welcome visitors, and they expect you to behave yourself. Unless you are in the company of a guide or local resident, stick to paved roads and village plazas. Don't wander down back alleys, particularly during ceremonies, and get permission from a village

TRADITIONAL HOPI ARTS AND CRAFTS

Ancestral Puebloans began making pottery when they settled in villages and raised crops that required long simmering, such as beans. The first pots were utilitarian, but as villages grew and skills became more specialized, pottery designs evolved and flourished. Today's Hopi **pottery,** still made by coiling and scraping and firing over an open flame, is exceptionally fine-walled, with intricate designs and a satin finish.

Hopi artisans also make woven, coiled, and plaited **baskets** from local materials such as sumac, rabbitbrush, yucca, or galleta grass. Coiled and wicker plaques are especially colorful, with kachina designs or geometrics. Basketry is made on all three mesas, and many baskets are used in ceremonies, such as traditional weddings or the basket dances marking the fall harvest.

Sikyatala, the first Hopi silversmith, learned his craft from artisans at the Zuni pueblo in the 1890s. Veterans returning from World War II developed the striking Hopi **overlay style,** in which a design is cut from a flat sheet of silver and set in front of another sheet that has been textured and oxidized until black. Hopi jewelry is marked with the artist's name, clan, or village, and the design may be pictorial or abstract. Gold and gemstones are sometimes used.

Kachina (katsina) dolls are some of the most distinctive souvenirs of the Southwest. Carved from cottonwood roots, kachina dolls were originally used to teach children about the spirit beings who live in the San Francisco Peaks and bring rain. When collectors began purchasing the dolls, carvers began making them with stands, sometimes depicting them in action. After the 1970s, when the use of migratory bird feathers was restricted, some carvers began to fashion feathers from wood, leading to astounding detail and craftsmanship. Sculpture-style dolls, often created from a single piece of wood, took artistry even further, with flowing forms and complex symbolism. Proving that everything old is new once again, a popular carving style today is based on the oldest of designs—the flat dolls first used in Hopi homes. Referred to as old-style or traditional, these kachina dolls are often embellished with feathers and natural mineral pigments.

Kachina dolls come in all sizes, and the quality of the carving and painting varies as widely as the price. Prime examples are true works of art and justifiably fetch thousands of dollars. Among the kachinas depicted as dolls are Mongwa, the Great Horned Owl; Angak'china, whose long, flowing hair represents rain; and the whimsical Koyemsi and Koshare clowns.

leader, or *kikmongwi,* if you plan on spending more than a few hours in any village. The tribe guards its privacy and traditions, so photography, videotaping, sketching, and any other methods of recording are *strictly* prohibited—no exceptions. Accept the fact that this is one part of your journey you'll have to recall from memory, because if you're caught breaking this rule, you will be asked to leave.

Early explorers arrived from the east; thus First, Second, and Third Mesa were named from east to west. The mesas are strung together by SR 264, and SR 87 travels north to Second Mesa from the town of Winslow and I-40. But no matter which route you take to get there, if you want to make the most of your visit, it's a good idea to begin in the middle, at the Cultural Center on top of Second Mesa, where you can arrange for a guided tour or find out about local events.

SECOND MESA

Of the three mesas, Second Mesa (pop. 800) extends the farthest south, offering commanding views. This mesa is home to the tribe's cultural center, as well as a number of galleries carrying coiled basketry (a Second Mesa specialty) and other types of Hopi arts and crafts. Three villages are located atop Second Mesa. To the northeast are Sipaulovi (shi-PALL-o-vee) and Mishongnovi (mi-SHONG-no-vee), located at the very top of the mesa beneath the twin stone pillars known as **Corn Rock.** Nearest the cultural center is **Shungopavi** (shon-GO-pah-vee) ("water place where reeds grow"). The largest of the Hopis' traditional villages, Shungopavi was relocated to the top of the mesa after the Pueblo Revolt of 1680, but its roots reach back to the mesas' very first settlement, established by the Bear Clan before the 1100s.

Sights and Tours

Along SR 264, west of its intersection with SR 87, the **Hopi Cultural Center** (928/734-2401, www.hopiculturalcenter.com) encompasses a motel and restaurant adjacent to a museum of Hopi crafts and interpretive displays (928/734-6650, 8 A.M.–5 P.M. Mon.–Fri., 9 A.M.–3 P.M. Sat. and Sun., $3 pp). While you're at the museum, be sure to try some traditional paper-thin *piki* bread, made with blue-corn flour and baked on top of a heated stone.

If you haven't made tour reservations prior to your arrival, you can find out about guided tours there. Traveling with a guide is the best—and in many cases the only—way to experience Hopi culture. No hiking is allowed without a guide, and visitors are prohibited from certain culturally sensitive areas. Guides are not only excellent sources of information but also gracious hosts who can help you avoid making well-intentioned but embarrassing blunders during your visit.

You may also directly contact guides, such as **Bertram Tsavadawa** (928/734-9544 or 928/306-7849, ancientpathways2004@yahoo.com) and **Gary Tso** (928/734-2567, lh-hunter58@hotmail.com), a katsina carver who can introduce you to Hopi artists and take you to their home studios. Professional anthropologist **Micah Loma'omvaya** (928/734-0230 or 928/734-9549, info@hopitours.com or hopianthro@yahoo.com) offers archaeological tours to ruins and other sites on the reservation, starting at $75 per person for a half day. For those arriving from the west, the Legacy Inn in Moenkopi (the westernmost Hopi village near Tuba City) can also arrange a variety of tours.

You'll need a guide if you want to see **Dawa Park** (also known as Taawaki), one of the most fascinating archaeological sites in the Southwest. Pecked or carved into the walls of this horseshoe-shaped canyon are thousands of petroglyphs, including animal- and human-like figures and spirals, which may represent the long migrations made by ancestral clans to the center place.

Sipaulovi (meaning "place of the mosquitoes") hosts hour-long village walking tours (reservations requested, $15 pp) beginning at the visitors center (928/737-5426, www.sipaulovihopiinformationcenter.org, 9 A.M.–4 P.M. Mon.–Fri.). To get there from the Hopi Cultural Center, go east on SR 264 to the second stop sign (just past milepost 379) and turn left onto a paved road, driving three miles to the visitors center, located in the heart of the village. General manager Bonnie Secakuku begins tours with a well-produced video about clan migrations and village history.

Shopping

Numerous galleries are scattered along the roads on Second Mesa, including **Sewukiwma's Arts & Crafts** (928/734-0388), east of the Cultural Center, and Alph Sekakuku's **Hopi Fine Arts** (928/737-2222), located at the base of Second Mesa, where SR 264 is joined by SR 87. East of the Cultural Center at milepost 381 you'll find Janice and Joseph Day's **Tsakurshovi** (928/734-2478), a fascinating store with an intriguing selection of Hopi and Navajo work, including many old-style katsina carvings. The Cultural Center may be the mesas' official center of tourism, but Tsakurshovi is an informal (and impeccable) source of information on everything from local artists to regional travel. The Days supply locals with ceremonial and art supplies, which explains the quantities of cottonwood root, turtle shells, furs, and herbs you'll see inside and outside the store.

Accommodations and Food

The **Cultural Center motel** (928/734-2401) has modest but clean rooms for $95–100 ($75–80 Oct.–Feb.). Camping is free—there are no hookups or amenities, but campers can access the public restrooms at the Cultural Center.

The **restaurant** (928/734-2402) serves all meals daily—inexpensive American food and local specialties such as fry bread made from blue corn or *nöqkwivi,* a traditional hominy-and-mutton stew. You may find it difficult to resist the tempting scents wafting across the road from the **Spider Grill.** Don't let appearances dissuade you from trying this local favorite—though currently served tarp-and-tailgate style, fajitas, burritos, and the like are fresh and tasty. The owners plan to build a permanent structure in the future. (An aside: Banks typically don't offer construction loans on the reservation, so enterprising locals start and finish projects as cash flow allows. Hence, you'll see many works in progress on the mesas.)

You'll find **Hilda Burger,** a popular village hangout, in nearby Shungopavi. At the SR 264/87 intersection is a gas station, **post office,** and **LKD's Diner,** serving breakfast and lunch Monday–Saturday in season; Monday–Friday otherwise.

THIRD MESA

The westernmost mesa is home to four villages—Kykotsmovi, Hotevilla, Bacavi, and Oraibi. Many katsina carvers live in these villages, but Third Mesa is also known for wicker basketry and other crafts. Oraibi is arguably the oldest continuously inhabited village in North America. (First Mesa's Walpi and Acoma in New Mexico also make persuasive claims for this title.) For a time, Old Oraibi was the largest village on the three mesas, but in 1906 internal strife split the community. "Friendlies" wanted to cooperate with the U.S. government's Bureau of Indian Affairs, while "Hostiles," led by a conservative villager named Youkeoma, refused. They settled the dispute with a pushing contest: A line was etched in the ground and the groups lined up on either side. At a signal, each started shoving. When the dust cleared, those friendly to the U.S. government had won, and Youkeoma led his people off to found Hotevilla. Third Mesa's youngest village was formed in 1907 by Hotevilla residents who wished to return to Oraibi. Their request was refused, so instead they founded Bacavi, "place of reeds."

Sights

Those who arrive at Third Mesa from the west will pass **Pumpkin Seed Point,** a picnic area with views of the **Hopi Buttes.** These dark, rocky volcanic necks are horizon markers used in the traditional Hopi ceremonial calendar. When the rising sun aligns with a particular point, it signals the appropriate time for events such as Powamuya, when seeds are sprouted inside kivas and handed out during a katsina procession known as the Bean Dance. This ceremony, like others, is layered with meaning. It heralds the growing season not only of crops but also of children, and some are initiated into katsina societies at this time.

At **Old Oraibi** (oh-RYE-bee), inhabited since the 12th century, past meets present in a windswept collection of stone and cinder-block homes. Near the line in the rock where village factions held a pushing contest to decide Oraibi's fate, an inscription reads, "Well it have to be this way now, that when you pass me over this LINE it will be DONE. Sept. 8, 1906."

Several guides offer walking tours of the village. If you choose to explore on your own, park outside the village or at **Hamana So-o's Arts and Crafts** (928/206-6392) and don't wander beyond the central plaza. Oraibi is not a movie set or a museum; be respectful of people's private property. A few residents sell crafts and food from their homes, and they advertise with signs posted in their windows. Look toward the south end of the mesa, where you'll see the ruins of an old Mennonite church, built in 1901 and destroyed by lightning (a second strike) in 1942, which may have pleased many of the village's traditional residents.

Shopping and Services

Third Mesa's largest community is **Kykotsmovi** (kee-KOTS-moh-vee), founded by residents of Old Oraibi near a spring at the mesa's base. Also known as New Oraibi or K-Town, Kykotsmovi (pop. 800) is the home of the modern Hopi government. The **Hopi Cultural Preservation Office** (1 Main St., 928/734-3612) provides visitor information out of the Tribal Headquarters building. Near the intersection of SR 264 and

IR 2, the **Kykotsmovi Village Store** offers sandwiches, pizzas, and other deli items.

A few miles northwest on SR 264 are the mostly residential villages of Hotevilla (HOAT-vih-lah) and Bacavi (BAH-kah-vee). There's a gas station in Hotevilla, considered the most conservative of the Hopi villages, and you may see signs on homes where artists have items for sale. Hotevilla is also the home of Hopi Radio (KUYI 88.1 FM), an enjoyable travel companion with a blend of national news and local programming that might include farming discussions or a teen show.

West of Kykotsmovi on the way to the turn-off to Oraibi, you'll find **Sockyma's Arts and Crafts** (928/734-6667), **Calnimptewa Gallery** (928/734-2406), and **Monongya Gallery** (928/734-2344), which has one of the largest selections of kachina carvings around. South on the Leupp (pronounced "Loop") Road, IR 2, is **Quotskuyva Fine Art and Gifts.**

IR 2 heads south from Kykotsmovi to Leupp and IR 15. From Leupp, IR 15 leads to Winona (of the Route 66 song), which is only a short distance from Flagstaff. This lovely, quiet drive between Flagstaff and Third Mesa is paved the entire way. A couple miles south of Kykotsmovi, just west of IR 2, the aptly named **Hungry Bear** restaurant (928/734-1239) serves hearty meals.

FIRST MESA

SR 264 winds around the base of First Mesa to **Polacca** (po-LAH-kah, "butterfly"). Many Hopi potters live there or in the three mesa-top villages, and you will likely see signs noting "potteries for sale." Most residents of Polacca, founded in 1890, are aligned with clans and societies from Hano, Sichomovi, or Walpi, the three older villages atop the mesa. Intersecting SR 264, a steep and narrow paved road climbs to the top of First Mesa, just over a mile. The road is suitable for passenger cars, but RVs and other large vehicles must be parked at the bottom.

The village at the edge of the mesa is **Hano,** founded by Tewa Indians from the Rio Grande pueblos. Fleeing the Spanish after the Pueblo Revolt of 1680, the Tewa were allowed to settle there by the Hopi if they agreed to guard access to the mesa. This was the home of the famous Hopi-Tewa potter Nampeyo, born in 1860, who based her designs on ancient pottery shards dug up by archaeologist Jesse Walter Fewkes. Thanks to the efforts of the Fred Harvey Company, which displayed her work at the Grand Canyon, she became famous and traveled around the country demonstrating her craft. Nampeyo eventually became blind, but her daughters learned her techniques and handed them down to the present generation. Just beyond Hano, **Sichomovi** (see-CHO-mo-vee) was founded in 1750 by residents of **Walpi** (WAHL-pee), the centuries-old village perched on the southernmost tip of the mesa.

Sights

Ponsi Hall (928/737-2670, 9 A.M.–3 P.M. Mon.–Sat.), located on the main road that enters the mesa-top villages, has a few parking spaces out front, and inside there are displays about Hopi culture. There you can join a **guided walking tour** ($13) that leads from Sichomovi through Walpi, which is otherwise closed to visitors. Walpi, meaning "the gap," refers to the narrow causeway of stone that isolates the tiny village almost completely from the rest of the mesa—and, it seems, from the modern age as well. The village, which dates back to A.D. 900 by some accounts, lacks running water and electricity. Only a few villagers live there today, but many others consider Walpi home, returning for special occasions such as the Snake Dance ceremony (closed to the public). With nothing but sky and stone in every direction, Walpi offers a striking panorama that has hardly changed over the centuries.

Shopping and Services

A few residents often bring crafts to sell on the steps of Ponsi Hall or along the route to Walpi. Several artists live in First Mesa villages, and you may note signs in windows or doorways indicating art for sale. In some cases, the quality is not equal to that offered by galleries and shops, but prices will be lower. Groups interested in having a traditional Hopi meal can make advance arrangements with First Mesa's administration services (928/737-2670).

At the base of First Mesa in Polacca, the Circle M convenience store has gas pumps. The Hopi Health Care Center (928/737-6000) is located along SR 264. Most days around noon, local cooks arrive at the picnic ramadas next to the parking lot with inexpensive (and tasty) burritos, sandwiches, turnovers, popcorn, and other treats still warm from the oven. You can put together a home-cooked meal for less than $5.

KEAMS CANYON

The natural oasis of **Keams Canyon,** called Pongsikya by the Hopi, was originally known to Anglo settlers as Peach Orchard Springs. This off-reservation town is named for Englishman Thomas Keam, once a trooper under Colonel Kit Carson (whose 1863 signature is inscribed on the canyon wall). Keam opened a trading post there in 1869 and married a Hopi woman. He quarreled with the Bureau of Indian Affairs superintendent, who demanded that the Hopi stop their ceremonies and send their children to the nearby BIA boarding school under threat of force. The superintendent was eventually dismissed.

Shopping and Services

Keams Canyon hosts tribal and federal offices in addition to a hospital, post office, and **Keam's Canyon Shopping Center.** The shopping center incorporates gas pumps, a grocery store, and a small café. **McGee's Indian Art Gallery** (928/738-2295, www.hopiart.com) is centered around Keam's original trading post, displaying an excellent selection of local crafts, particularly kachina carvings. Follow the road up Keams Wash 1.5 miles to a shelter on the west (left), marking the **Kit Carson inscription.**

EVENTS

Annual events include **foot races,** long a part of Hopi culture. Distance running is a skill that goes back to ancient times, when runners pursued game or traveled between fields and villages. Hopi runners were among those who alerted villages on the eve of the Pueblo Revolt of 1680. In the early 20th century, wage workers "commuted" between their mesa villages

and jobs at the Grand Canyon or Flagstaff. Today foot races are held not only as part of certain ceremonies or celebrations but also to promote youth programs and traditional community values. The Oraibi 8K race, held each August, is open to runners of all abilities and ages. The Lewis Tewanima race, held in Shungopavi over Labor Day weekend, honors the 1912 Olympic silver medalist. The challenging Paatuwaqatsi relay climbs to the ancient village of Walpi each September.

Usually held on Columbus Day weekend at the Hopi Veterans Memorial Center (just off SR 264 about five miles east of Kykotsmovi), the Hopi Tuhisma **arts-and-crafts market** is a lively event combining food and entertainment with opportunities to meet carvers, silversmiths, potters, and other artists.

It is a privilege to be able to attend a Hopi **ceremony or dance.** Most social dances (such as the basket dances held each autumn) are open to non-Hopis, though some require a personal invitation from a tribe member. Many kachina dances, on the other hand, are closed to visitors. Each village may have a different open/closed policy regarding a particular ceremony. The Hopi Cultural Center on Second Mesa may be able to help you find out which are open to the public, and a village usually posts a sign at its entrance indicating whether a ceremony is open or closed.

When you attend a ceremony, be aware that you will be considered a part of the collective spiritual effort, so you should act and dress respectfully. This means no shorts, short skirts, or T-shirts, no loud talking, and no striding across the plaza to get a closer look at one of the dancers. (And it bears repeating: No recording of any kind, including photographs or note-taking.) Plaza and rooftop seating is reserved for family and friends. Stand or sit in non-reserved areas and don't block entries to the plaza or get in the way of the ceremonial procession. If you misbehave, you may be asked to leave, or—perhaps worse—you may be publicly schooled in manners by *koshares,* the clowns who serve as social police.

The Painted Desert and Route 66

As much a state of mind as it is a physiographic area, the Painted Desert extends in a narrow arc for about 160 miles from Cameron to the Petrified Forest, between the Little Colorado River and the Hopi tablelands. Encompassing nearly 100,000 acres, much of it on the Navajo reservation, the desert is named for the colorful buttes and badlands eroded from the late-Triassic Chinle Formation. The Navajo call it *halchíítah,* "among the colors."

Shades of gray, green, lavender, red, orange, and pink become vibrant at sunrise and sunset. Most of the soils were laid down as silt and volcanic ash, and are marked by clays that shrink and swell so much when they get wet and then dry out that hardly anything can grow. Reds, oranges, and pinks come from iron and aluminum oxides concentrated in slowly deposited sediments, while blues, grays, and purples are the results of rapid events, such as floods, that removed oxygen from the soils.

Rugged hills and mesas dotted with junipers continue past the Petrified Forest and Painted Desert to the southern end of the Defiance Plateau at the state line. Though this high, arid country looks empty and inhospitable, humans have passed through there for centuries. The southern edge of the Painted Desert is traversed by I-40, the same corridor once traveled by Route 66, before that by army trails, and before that by prehistoric Indian trade routes.

METEOR CRATER

About 50,000 years ago, a meteorite 150 feet across slammed into the Arizona plain at upwards of 30,000 mph, igniting an explosion more powerful than 20 million tons of TNT. The impact threw 175 million tons of stone into the atmosphere, uplifted the bedrock by 150 feet, and turned graphite into diamond at pressures of over 20 million pounds per square inch—and it left a really, *really* big hole in the ground. You can fit 20 football fields into the crater, which is 2.5 miles in circumference and deeper than the height of the Washington

Monument. The crater was originally thought to be volcanic in origin, but the tireless research of Philadelphia mining engineer Daniel Barringer convinced the world otherwise, making this the first-proved meteor crater in the world.

Visiting Meteor Crater

The crater is six miles south of I-40, exit 233. The site is privately owned, and perched on its edge is a well-designed **visitors center** (928/289-5898 or 800/289-5898, www.meteorcrater.com, 7 A.M.–7 P.M. daily, 8 A.M.–5 P.M. mid-Sept.–Memorial Day, $15 adults, $8 children) with a widescreen theater, exhibits on astrogeology and space travel, a gift store, and a sandwich shop. Admission includes guided walks a third of a mile around the rim trail. On the crater floor, a dummy figure in a space suit provides a sense of scale; Apollo astronauts trained there before going to the moon. On the way there from the interstate you'll pass the **Meteor Crater RV Park** (928/289-4002 or 800/478-4002) with 71 sites ($30), a gas station, showers, laundry, Wi-Fi, and the Hole Enchilada restaurant.

WINSLOW

The town of Winslow had its beginnings in 1882 as a railroad stop near Sunset Crossing, one of the few places where wagon trains, soldiers, and other travelers could ford the sandy-bottomed Little Colorado River. Winslow hit its stride in the early 1900s, when cross-country traffic poured in off the new Route 66 and local ranchers shipped their stock out through the rail terminal. In 1930 the Fred Harvey Company opened La Posada, perhaps the prettiest of its regional-style hotels, where train travelers spent days or weeks, often exploring the area on the company's Indian Detours. That same year, Charles Lindberg flew to Winslow Airport, which he had designed as a stop between Chicago and Los Angeles.

Though once considered ideally situated for exploring the Grand Canyon and Indian

© METEOR CRATER, NORTHERN ARIZONA, USA

Meteor Crater is deeper than the height of the Washington Monument.

Country, the town declined when traffic began to pass by on the interstate. Still, you've heard of Winslow if you've ever listened the Eagles sing their hit "Take It Easy." Today Winslow (pop. 9,900) has a border-town ambience, with quiet streets and weathered historic brick buildings. The restoration of La Posada has injected a sense of vitality into the town, and a number of interesting sights are within day-trip distance.

Sights

The corner that Jackson Browne and Glenn Frey sang about is commemorated at the **Standin' on the Corner Park** at 2nd Street (old Route 66) and Kinsley Avenue. You can have your photo taken next to the statue of one of the Eagles holding a guitar, or the "girl, my Lord, in a flatbed Ford" painted in a two-story mural on the facing wall. This part of downtown plays up its Route 66 heritage, with shops offering everything from souvenirs to fine Navajo and Hopi arts and crafts.

The quirky **Old Trails Museum** (212 Kinsley St., 928/289-5861, www.oldtrailsmuseum.org,

11 A.M.–3 P.M. Tues.–Sat., free) is housed in a 1921 bank building nicknamed Winslow's attic. An interesting collection includes dinosaur bones, Route 66 memorabilia, prehistoric artifacts, and the still of a local moonshiner who lived to the age of 97 on a daily breakfast of black coffee, raw eggs, and a shot of his own firewater.

A couple of miles northeast of Winslow on the banks of the Little Colorado River is **Homolovi Ruins State Park** (928/289-4106, http://azstateparks.com, 8 A.M.–5 P.M. daily, $7 per car). The four main pueblo ruins were inhabited in the 13th and 14th centuries by ancestral Hopi clans who eventually migrated north to the three Hopi mesas. The Hopis refer to Ancestral Puebloans (or Anasazi) as Hisatsinom ("the Old Ones"), and Homolovi is part of the Hopis' vast homeland. More than 300 archaeological sites have been uncovered there, and three pueblos are open to the public, with short trails leading to the ruins. There's a visitors center and a 53-site campground that can accommodate RVs up to 83 feet long ($10–35). To get there, take I-40, exit 257 to

Highway 87, go north 1.3 miles to the entrance on the left, and then proceed another two miles to the visitors center.

For a drive-up view of the Painted Desert, continue northeast on SR 87 to milepost 360, where you'll find the **Little Painted Desert County Park** (daily, dawn–dusk). The park is small (660 acres), but it has picnic ramadas and big views from its overlook, particularly at the golden hours of sunrise and sunset.

South of Winslow at **Clear Creek,** you can swim, fish, or bring a canoe or kayak and paddle into deep, rocky Clear Creak Canyon. Free camping is available at McHood Park (928/289-5714), five miles from town. Take Route 87 south to Highway 99 and turn left.

Shopping and Events

Roadworks Gifts & Souvenirs (101 W. 2nd St., 928/289-5423) overlooks the Corner Park. This upstairs shop stocks every kind of Route 66 souvenir you can think of, plus a few hundred more, from books to bumper stickers. Look for the late Bob Waldmire's postcards and Route 66 map. His eccentric and detailed drawings are works of art.

If you're there in late September, don't miss the **"Standin' On the Corner" Festival,** with music, arts and crafts, an auction, and a car show.

In 2011 the Navajo tribe broke ground on nearby Twin Arrows Casino, its first gaming establishment in Arizona. (The tribe operates two casinos in New Mexico.) In addition to gaming and entertainment, the $150 million project will eventually include a hotel and golf course.

Accommodations and Food

Architect Mary Colter designed her masterpiece hotel **◖ La Posada** (303 E. 2nd St., 928/289-4366, www.laposada.org, $120–190) for the Fred Harvey Company in 1930. Built in the style of an old Spanish hacienda, the "Last Great Railroad Hotel" counted among its guests such luminaries as Albert Einstein, Howard Hughes, Dorothy Lamour, Harry Truman, and the Crown Prince of Japan. All trains between Chicago and Los Angeles stopped in Winslow, and so did planes before

better designs let them make the trip without refueling. When Route 66 traffic increased, the hotel's main entry shifted from the train tracks to face the highway. But after I-40 bypassed downtown Winslow, newer hotels sprang up along the freeway, and the railway turned La Posada into office space. The hotel was closed for 40 years and nearly razed before it was put on the historical preservation list and rescued from the wrecking ball in the late 1990s.

Thanks to the tireless efforts of owner Allan Affeldt and his wife, artist Tina Mion, La Posada is well on its way to recapturing its former glory. Suits of armor, religious icons, and Tina's large, intriguing paintings make up an eclectic art collection, and the hotel's gardens invite strolling. The **◖ Turquoise Room Restaurant** (928/289-2888, all meals daily) serves contemporary Southwest cuisine as well as recipes from the Harvey heyday of the 1930s, all presided over by a chef nominated for a James Beard award. Dishes ($18–35 for dinner) use local and sustainably raised ingredients such as Churro lamb. Next to the gracious foyer is a martini lounge, and the hotel boasts two gift shops offering everything from Spanish Colonial–style decorative items to Fred Harvey memorabilia and Indian art. This is a special place, well worth a stop if only for lunch.

Winslow has many inexpensive hotels, including a **Motel 6** (520 W. Desmond St., 928/289-9581, $60–70) and an **Econo Lodge** (1706 N. Park Dr., 928/289-4687, $50–130). The **Quality Inn** (1701 N. Park Dr., 928/289-4638, $70–100) has DJ's Restaurant and Lounge (928/289-3274, lunch and dinner Mon.–Sun., entrées $8–18) and an indoor pool.

Family-owned for a half century, the **Casa Blanca Café** (1201 E. 2nd St., 928/289-4191, lunch and dinner daily) serves authentic Mexican food every day of the week. Entrées are $6–16. You can grab a burger or burrito at **BoJo's Grill & Sports Club** (117 W. 2nd St. 928/289-0616, lunch and dinner daily) and settle down to watch the Arizona Diamondbacks play.

Information

The **Winslow Chamber of Commerce** (101 E.

Second St., 928/289-2434, www.winslowarizona.org, 8 A.M.–5 P.M. Mon.–Fri.) has maps, brochures, and souvenirs.

Getting There

Amtrak trains still stop twice daily in Winslow, but the station (next to La Posada on East 2nd St.) isn't staffed; call 800/872-7245 for information. **Greyhound** buses stop at McDonald's restaurant (1616 N. Park Dr., 928/289-5710).

HOLBROOK

Though it may seem tame today, Holbrook (pop. 5,400) was once the epitome of the wild and woolly West. This ranching center was founded with the arrival of the railroad in 1881. The second-largest outfit in the county, the Hashknife, was based nearby, where cowboys herded up to 60,000 cows and 2,000 horses across two million acres. A spread this size naturally attracted rustlers, and for a time Holbrook was known as the "town too tough for women and churches." Until 1914, this was the only county seat in the country without a house of worship, though there were plenty of saloons and soiled doves. In 1886 the Bucket of Blood Saloon earned its name due to a lead-filled poker disagreement involving a member of the notorious Dalton Gang. A year later, Holbrook was the site of one the deadliest events of the infamous Pleasant Valley War, a decade-long feud between cattlemen and sheepmen. During the gun battle, Sheriff Perry Owens (considered a bit of a dandy when he first arrived in Holbrook) single-handedly killed three members of the Cooper-Blevins gang and wounded a fourth.

Except for a couple of ghosts said to roam the old courthouse, Holbrook's dangerous characters are long gone, and the town is best known for its easy access to the Petrified Forest and the Navajo, Hopi, and Zuni reservations.

Sights

Holbrook's stately 1898 county courthouse has been turned into the **Navajo County Museum** (100 E. Arizona St., 928/524-6558, 9 A.M.–5 P.M. daily, free). Collections focus on Holbrook's colorful Wild West past, and the walls of the claustrophobic jail downstairs are scrawled with prisoners' graffiti. On weekday evenings in summer, the courthouse lawn hosts Native American dances.

Though renamed and updated, the route of the Great Mother Road is marked by vintage signs and historic homes and businesses in Holbrook (Hopi Drive), Winslow (Second St.), and Joseph City (Main Street). More miles of **Old Route 66** have been preserved in Arizona than in any other state. To drive a segment of the original roadway and get a dose of road trip kitsch at the same time, leave I-40 west of Holbrook at exit 269 and head for the **Jackrabbit Trading Post** (a curio store), where you can saddle up on a larger-than-life rabbit. (The Jackrabbit sign may tug at your memory strands—it was used in the animated *Cars* and *Cars 2*.)

Archaeology buffs and historians can step back in time at the **Rock Art Ranch** (928/288-3260), located along Chevelon Canyon roughly 20 miles southwest of Holbrook. The privately owned ranch preserves one of the Southwest's largest concentrations of petroglyphs and a bunkhouse used by the storied Hashknife Cattle Company. The property remains a working ranch, and the owners are selective about visitors. Reservations are required, and directions to the ranch are given when the reservation is made. If you visit with a group, you can arrange for a horseback tour, roping demonstrations, and a chuckwagon dinner.

Entertainment and Events

Holbrook's **Old West Days** in June brings re-enactors, music, crafts, dancing, and bike and foot races. In September the **Navajo County Fair** arrives, and the **Christmas Parade of Lights** illuminates downtown the first Saturday in December. In January the **Hashknife Pony Express Ride** carries mail on horseback along the historic express route from Holbrook to Scottsdale. Riders hand off mailbags every couple of miles en route to the Scottsdale post office, where letters continue to their destinations via regular mail. Even if you can't be there to watch the annual ride, you can send a letter via pony express. Address and stamp the letter as you would normally; then mark the envelope "Via Pony Express" in the lower left-hand corner and enclose it in a second envelope addressed to Postmaster, Holbrook, AZ 86025. (Pony express mail must be received at the Holbrook post office before the January ride.)

Shopping

Nearby Petrified Forest National Park protects a mere 10 percent of the area's petrified wood. Though collection is illegal inside the park, private landowners in the Holbook area can sell their rainbow-colored treasures, and local rock shops offer a bounty of petrified wood, fossils, and other geological curiosities. A few stores are curiosities themselves, including the **Rainbow Rock Shop** (101 Navajo Blvd., 928/524-2384). Look for the herd of dinosaurs guarding its entrance near the train tracks.

Accommodations and Food

Hopi Drive and Navajo Boulevard are Holbrook's main commercial arteries, where you'll find most of the town's hotels and restaurants. The **Wigwam Motel** (811 W. Hopi Dr., 928/524-3048, www.galerie-kokopelli. com/wigwam, $52–58) looks like a classic car collection parked among a forest of big fake tepees. Built in the 1940s and now listed on the National Register of Historic Places, the wigwams still have their original furniture and all their Route 66 charm. **America's Best Inn** (2211 E. Navajo Blvd., 928/524-2654, $45–52) is another inexpensive option.

Along I-40, the **Travelodge** (2418 Navajo Blvd., 928/524-6815) has rooms in the $50–100 category, and rooms at the **Best Western Arizonian Inn** (2508 Navajo Blvd., 928/524-2611) are $75–125. A Good Sam park, the **OK RV Park** (1576 Roadrunner Rd., 928/524-3226, $29) has 136 sites. There's also a **KOA Kampground** (102 Hermosa Dr., 928/524-6689 or 800/562-3389, $23–35) with 208 sites.

Diner fare befitting Holbrook's location on Old Route 66 is what you'll find at **Joe & Aggie's Café** (120 W. Hopi Dr., 866/486-0021, all meals Mon.–Sat.). From the honey bottles for

the sopapillas to the chicken-fried steak platters, Holbrook's oldest restaurant (since 1946) does Mexican and American road food. Sandwiches are $4–8, dinners $5–15, and breakfasts $5–10. **Mesa Italiana** (2318 E. Navajo Blvd., 928/524-6696, dinner daily, $9–20) serves traditional Italian dishes, pizza, and steak.

Information

The offices of the **Holbrook Chamber of Commerce** (100 E. Arizona St., 928/524-6558 or 800/524-2459, 9 A.M.–5 P.M. daily) are located in the old county courthouse.

Getting There

The local **Greyhound** stop (928/524-3832) is at the Circle K at 101 Mission Lane off Navajo Boulevard.

PETRIFIED FOREST NATIONAL PARK

This park, extending both north and south of the interstate, protects one of the world's largest and most colorful concentrations of petrified wood. The petrifaction process was so exact that in some trees the original cell structure is still clearly visible. A wealth of late-Triassic fossils, plus ruins and petroglyphs from 10,000 years of human habitation, complete the picture. This treasure trove of science and history was declared a national monument by President Theodore Roosevelt in 1906, and in 1962 it was designated a national park.

Over 200 million years ago, this sparse grassland was a lushly vegetated tropical river system, crawling with giant reptiles and fish-eating amphibians. Some of the first dinosaurs plodded among cycads, ferns, and early conifers. Huge trees, many up to 200 feet high, were uprooted by wind or old age and swept down into a vast floodplain and buried in silt and mud. Over time, silica-bearing groundwater seeped through the wood and replaced it, cell by cell, with silica. Different minerals tinted the silica a rainbow of brilliant colors. Erosion eventually exposed the fossilized logs in the hills and badlands of the Painted Desert. Native legends regarding the logs' origins are

© KATHLEEN BRYANT

Navajo legend says that petrified wood fragments are the bones of a monster slain by the Hero Twins.

even more colorful: Navajos consider the logs to be the bones of the giant Yeitso, killed by the Hero Twins, while the Pauite told how they were the arrow shafts of the god Shuav.

Visiting the Park

The park's backbone is a 28-mile drive arcing from I-40 (exit 311) to U.S. 180 east of Holbrook, connecting several fascinating sites, scenic overlooks, and short trails. Very few people venture off this road, but backpacking is permitted (with a free permit) in the colorful Petrified Forest National Desert Wilderness Area north of the interstate and near the Rainbow Forest area at the south end of the park.

At the northern end of the drive, the **Painted Desert Visitor Center** (928/524-6228, www.nps.gov/pefo, 8 A.M.–5 P.M. daily, 7 A.M.–7 P.M. in summer, $10 per vehicle) has an introductory video, bookstore, snack bar, restrooms, and general information on the park. Rangers lead tours and hikes year-round, and on summer

Saturdays, cultural demonstrations may feature dancers, weavers, silversmiths, carvers, or other artisans. For two weeks around the summer solstice (June 21), rangers guide visitors to a spiral petroglyph, where a shaft of sunlight marks the longest day of the year.

A short distance beyond the visitors center is the **Painted Desert Inn** (8 A.M.–5 P.M. daily), a National Historic Landmark that once lodged weary Route 66 travelers and is now a museum and bookstore. For a time, this was a Harvey House, and Mary Colter redesigned its interior, collaborating once again with artist Fred Kabotie, who painted murals depicting Hopi legends. Nearby, the old roadbed is visible, lined with telephone poles.

Across the interstate in the central portion of the park, you'll find **Puerco Pueblo** ruins and **Newspaper Rock** petroglyph site. The pueblo is believed to have been occupied twice, A.D. 1100–1200 and 1300–1400. **The Tepees** are cone-shaped rock formations. A short side road leads to **Blue Mesa,** with panoramic viewing points and a mile-long interpretive loop trail. Farther down the main road, **Agate Bridge** is a large petrified log spanning an eroded gully.

In the southern part of the park, you'll see the most striking examples of petrified wood. A trail starting near the Rainbow Forest Museum leads to the popular **Long Logs Trail** and **Agate House,** an eight-room structure built by ancient inhabitants entirely out of petrified wood, which has been partially restored. The **Rainbow Forest Museum** (8 A.M.–5 P.M. daily, extended hours in summer) displays astounding fossils. Behind the museum is the short **Giant Logs Trail,** true to its name—one stone trunk is nearly 10 feet across at the base. Across the road, **Fred Harvey's Curios and Fountain** sells souvenirs and snacks.

Warnings against stealing petrified wood are posted everywhere inside the park, but some people still violate federal law, even though plenty of specimens gathered from private lands (and thus legal) are for sale inside and outside the park. "Conscience wood" displays showcase pieces that guilt-ridden visitors have returned, often after a rash of mysteriously bad luck. Just outside the park's southern entrance are two places where those with acquisitive cravings can find beautiful petrified wood for sale: the **Petrified Forest Museum Gift Shop** (928/524-3470) and the **Crystal Forest Museum and Gifts** (928/524-3500). Both allow self-contained rigs to camp in their parking lots overnight at no charge, though purchases are appreciated.

NEW MEXICO AND COLORADO

Deep canyons rimmed by broad mesas make up the classic scenery of northwestern New Mexico and southwestern Colorado. Most of this region is part of the San Juan Basin, a shallow bowl that encompasses 7,800 square miles of grassland, sagebrush plains, and rolling, dun-colored hills. The basin has some of the richest deposits of oil and natural gas in the country, and wells share space with thousands of acres of open range. (New Mexico's gas and oil industry ranks fourth in the United States, representing 24 percent of the state's gross domestic product.)

The area also holds some of the nation's richest archaeological treasures. Though marginal rainfall and high-desert extremes in temperature make this seem an unlikely location, it gave rise to two extraordinary cultural expressions. The monumental ruins in Chaco Culture National Historical Park in New Mexico were the grand center of a civilization that built hundreds of miles of roads and traded as far away as Central America. The world-famous cliff dwellings of Mesa Verde National Park on the piney tablelands south of Cortez have been protected since the turn of the 20th century. Smaller archaeological sites like Aztec Ruins near Aztec, Salmon Ruins in Bloomfield, Hovenweep National Monument, the Canyons of the Ancients, and the Anasazi Heritage Center near Dolores, Colorado, can each be easily explored in a day.

The capital city of Indian Country today is without a doubt Gallup, New Mexico, located at the edge of the Navajo Nation. Durango, the largest city in southwest Colorado, is a lively

© RUSS BODNAR, NPS

HIGHLIGHTS

◖ Loop Road and Ruins: Explore the remote and enigmatic remains of the Four Corners's ancient cultural hub in Chaco Culture National Historical Park (page 102).

◖ Aztec Ruins National Monument: Influenced by the Chacoan culture, this smaller site is impressive in its own right (page 110).

◖ Durango & Silverton Narrow Gauge Railroad: For splendid mountain and river views, travel back in time on this marvel of 1880s engineering (page 113).

◖ Mesa Verde National Park: One of the world's archaeological jewels lets you peer into the daily lives of prehistoric cliff dwellers (page 123).

◖ Anasazi Heritage Center: Millions of artifacts, interactive computer displays, and Ancestral Puebloan ruins make up this exceptional museum near Dolores (page 134).

◖ Four Corners Monument: At this Navajo Nation park, you can play interstate Twister—"right foot Arizona, right hand Utah..." (page 135).

LOOK FOR ◖ TO FIND RECOMMENDED SIGHTS, ACTIVITIES, DINING, AND LODGING.

college town enviably close to great skiing, hiking, and biking in the San Juan Mountains. Farmington and Cortez also offer access to hiking, mountain biking, and archaeological sites. Thirty to fifty miles away from Bluff, Utah; Durango, Colorado; and Farmington, New Mexico, the Four Corners Monument marks the only place in the country where four states meet at one remote, arbitrary point.

PLANNING YOUR TIME
Plan 4–5 days to explore this region, more if you're a serious archaeology buff or if you plan to add long biking or backpacking excursions. Durango alone merits a day or two with its

upscale dining and lodging options and nearly limitless outdoor recreation options. A trip on the **Durango & Silverton Narrow Gauge Railroad** to Silverton will take the better part of a day. With a few more days you can visit the **Ute Mountain Tribal Park** or go **rafting on the Animas River.** If you prefer a mellower home base, start in Cortez or Aztec, which are close to the **Anasazi Heritage Center** and **Aztec Ruins,** respectively. **Mesa Verde National Park** requires at least a full day to tour, as does seeing the ruins along the **loop road in Chaco Culture National Historical Park.** Each is worth two days if you have the time. **Hovenweep** can be explored in a day or less, and you can tuck in

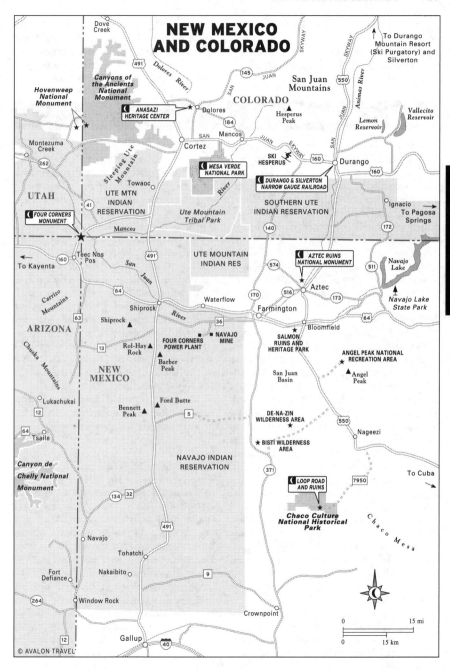

NEW MEXICO AND COLORADO

a visit to the **Four Corners Monument** while you're in the area.

Durango and Cortez are linked by U.S. 160, which joins U.S. 491 in the latter as it heads north to Monticello, Utah, and south to Shiprock and Gallup, New Mexico. U.S. 550 connects Durango to Aztec, Bloomfield, and points southeast, while U.S. 64 runs from west to east near the state line, stringing together Shiprock, Farmington, and Bloomfield.

Gallup and Vicinity

Although it's outside the reservation boundary, Gallup (pop. 20,000) is the Navajo Nation's most important commercial center. This multicultural community along old Route 66 boasts a plethora of arts-and-crafts shops and galleries, along with a good slice of turn-of-the-20th-century history and the country's premiere Native American gathering. Surrounded by the Navajo and Zuni Reservations (and within an hour of the Acoma, Laguna, and Jicarilla Apache Reservations), unpretentious Gallup easily earns its nickname, "Gateway to Indian Country."

History

Coal was discovered in the area near the middle of the 19th century, and the Atlantic & Pacific Railroad chose a route that passed near what was then a tiny stagecoach stop. The town itself was founded in 1881 and named after a railroad paymaster. It quickly became a timber and coal-mining hub. Between 1880 and 1948 more than 50 mines were in operation near Gallup. In 1929 alone, 25,177 railroad cars full of coal left the city's freight station, averaging one 70-car train every day of the year. The coal boom drew people from around the world to Gallup's already diverse ethnic mix, which included members of the Navajo and Hopi tribes and the Acoma and Zuni Pueblos. Descendants of workers from Germany, Italy, Spain, Greece, China, Japan, Austria, Wales, Scotland, Yugoslavia, and other countries continue to call the city home.

Gallup Today

Coal trains still rumble of out Gallup, and the Santa Fe Railroad passes through town every 15 minutes, but the city has shifted its focus to tourism, particularly the rich arts-and-crafts traditions of the nearby Native American tribes. Touted as the "Indian Capital of the World," Gallup boasts more than 100 trading posts, shops, and galleries, along with a few good museums and some 2,000 hotel and motel rooms for the traffic from I-40.

A classic, neon-signed stretch of Old Route 66 parallels the train tracks, serving as Gallup's Main Street. The 12-block downtown area, enclosed by Main Street, Hill Avenue, First Street, and 4th Street, is home to many of Gallup's galleries, trading posts, and public artwork, including the city's ambitious downtown mural project. Motels and restaurants (many serving Mexican-American food) line Route 66/Main Street toward either end of town. Gritty pawnshops sidle up next to high-end craft boutiques, and Navajo cowboys share the sidewalks with tourists hopping off the interstate for a quick browse.

The scourge of drunk driving reaches a pinnacle in Gallup, so keep a sharp eye out behind the wheel, especially on weekend nights.

SIGHTS

The 1918 Santa Fe Train Depot in the center of town was renovated in 1995 and turned into the **Gallup Cultural Center** (201 E. Hwy. 66, 505/863-4131, 8 A.M.–5 P.M. Mon.–Fri., free). The building blends Pueblo and Modernist styles, a nod to El Navajo Hotel, the masterpiece designed by Fred Harvey Company architect Mary Jane Colter and razed in 1957. The Southwest Indian Foundation (800/504-2723, http://southwestindian.com) operates the Cultural Center, hosting events that run the gamut from opera socials to art exhibits. A sculpture of Manuelito, the 19th-century Navajo leader who resisted the tribe's removal to Bosque Redondo, stands in the plaza. The

THE CROWNPOINT RUG AUCTION

On the second Friday of every month, the gymnasium of the Crownpoint Elementary School is lively with Navajo artisans, browsers, and visitors from all over world, gathered for one of the best shopping–and cultural–opportunities on the rez. This event is a social one rather than something staged for tourists (though visitors are welcome), bringing out friends and families for a fun night. Previewing runs 4-6 P.M., and students set up tables with snacks around 5 P.M. Artisans display jewelry, pottery, and other crafts in the halls, but inside the gym the focus is on rugs. You can pick up and examine any one that strikes your fancy and talk directly to its creator. Not only are prices lower here than just about anywhere else, but it is also a major source of income for the weavers, who get the money directly. Rugs sell for under $100 and up into the thousands. The auction starts at 7 P.M. and ends around 10 P.M.

The school is in Crownpoint, 56 miles northeast of Gallup on the way to Chaco Canyon. Head north from Thoreau (I-40, exit 53) for 25 miles on SR 371, turn left (west) at the Crownpoint sign; then take a right at the second four-way stop. The school is on the right–look for the cars. Admission is free, and credit cards aren't accepted for purchases. Cash and traveler's checks are preferred, but personal checks are accepted. For schedule updates and information, contact the **Crownpoint Rug Weavers Association** (505/786-7386, www.crownpointrugauction.com).

Hubbell Trading Post (928/755-3475, www.nps.gov/hutr) in Ganado holds two auctions, in May and September. Auctioned items include contemporary and historic rugs as well as kachina carvings, painting, pottery, and other Indian art from various tribes. Prices begin as low as $20 and reach into the thousands.

second floor houses the Storyteller Museum, with dioramas and displays on trading posts and native crafts, and the Ceremonial Gallery, filled with modern Native American art. Angela's Café (505/722-7526, Mon.–Fri.) serves inexpensive breakfast and lunch items, with later hours and live music on Friday evenings during summer months. The gift shop stocks crafts and souvenirs in a wide range of prices.

The Gallup Historical Society operates the **Rex Museum** (300 W. Hwy. 66, 505/863-1363, 8 A.M.–3:30 P.M. Mon.–Fri., $2 pp) in what was once the Rex Hotel (circa 1900). Vestiges of Gallup's railroad and mining days are on display inside.

The local Chamber of Commerce (106 W. Hwy. 66, 505/722-2228 or 800/380-4989, www.thegallupchamber.com) has brochures detailing self-guided **walking tours** of Gallup's downtown. Some two dozen buildings date to the early 20th century, including the 1925 **Grand Hotel** (306 W. Coal Ave.); the "Pueblo Deco"–style **Chief Theater,** now the City Electric Shoe Shop (228 W. Coal Ave.); **Kitchen's Opera House** (218 W. Hwy. 66),

built around 1890; and the ornate **El Morro Theater** (207 W. Coal Ave.), built in 1928 in the Pueblo Revival style. Throughout downtown, large wall spaces are painted in colorful murals depicting Gallup's history, from its coal-mining days to the Navajo Code Talkers of World War II.

About three miles east of Gallup, inside city-owned Red Rock Park, **Red Rock Museum** (505/863-1337, 8 A.M.–6 P.M. daily in summer, 8 A.M.–4:30 P.M. Mon.–Sat. in winter) has displays on the area's cultural history, from prehistoric artifacts to present-day pueblo, Navajo, and Zuni tribes. Admission is free, though donations are appreciated.

ENTERTAINMENT AND EVENTS

A part of Gallup hospitality for nearly 30 years, free **Indian dances** are held at 7 P.M. daily May–August in the spacious plaza in front of the McKinley County Courthouse (201 W. Hill Ave.). Featured dancers and musicians include the Pollen Trail Dancers (Navajo) and the Cellicion Traditional Dancers from Zuni Pueblo, among many others. The courthouse,

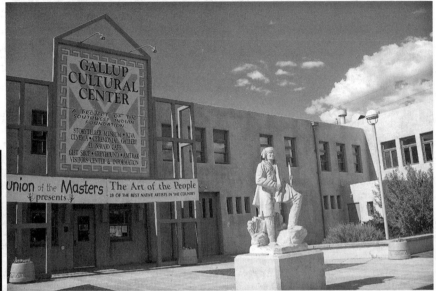

© KATHLEEN BRYANT

A statue of the Navajo leader Manuelito stands in front of the Gallup Cultural Center.

built in 1938, was designed by the firm founded by Henry Charles Trost, a notable Southwestern architect.

The Gallup campus of the University of New Mexico (705 Gurley Ave., 505/863-7500), hosts concerts, lectures, exhibits, and other events. On the second Saturday evening of each month, downtown art galleries hold an **Arts Crawl,** keeping their doors open till 9 P.M. **El Morro Theater** (207 W. Coal Ave., 505/726-0050) screens kiddie matinees and recent releases, but it's also the scene of musical performances and such events as the annual UFO Film Festival held in October. Most weekends you'll find live music at the **Juggernaut** (412 N. Ninth St., 505/726-8104) or three miles east of town at the Navajo-owned **Fire Rock Casino** (505/905-7100 or 866/941-2444). From I-40, take exit 26 and look for the casino next to Red Rock Park. (Or ride the casino's shuttle, which runs daily from various locations in town.) Pick up a copy of the *Gallup Journey,* a free monthly magazine, to find out more about local happenings.

A number of rodeo events ride into town during summer months, including the popular **Lion's Club Rodeo** (www.galluplionsclubrodeo.com), which opens each June with a parade and barbecue downtown. The arena at beautiful Red Rock Park (505/722-3839), three miles east of town, hosts the rodeo and many other events, including the **Red Rock Balloon Rally,** held the first weekend in December, when up to 200 hot air balloons float skyward. It's the second-largest hot air balloon rally in the country and perhaps the most thrilling, with colorful balloons winding among the red and white sandstone cliffs.

But Gallup's grandest event of all takes place in August: The **Inter-Tribal Indian Ceremonial** (505/863-3896 or 800/233-4528) encompasses four days of rodeos, dances, powwows, parades, and art exhibits. Called "The Greatest American Show" by none other than Will Rogers, this celebration of Native American cultures and traditions has been held since 1922. Members of more than 30 tribes come from as far away as Canada to participate.

© MIKE STAUFFER, NEW MEXICO TOURISM DEPARTMENT

Buffalo dancers perform at the Gallup Inter-Tribal Indian Ceremonial.

Tickets to rodeo events and evening performances run $10–25. Exhibits and daily performances are free. Parking at Red Rock Park, where most events are held, is $5 per vehicle. Expect to pay $10 per person to enter, though fees are often waived for certain days or events. Though the recent economic downturn has taken a bite out of attendance, it's still a good idea to get tickets and hotel reservations well in advance.

SHOPPING

Gallup is one of the Four Corners' top shopping destinations, and a stroll down Old Route 66 near the Santa Fe Train Depot is enough to burn a hole in the wallet of any devotee of Southwestern arts and crafts. By some estimates, 80 percent of the world's turquoise trade makes its way through Gallup. If you have time to visit only one trading post, head for the bright red neon sign marking **Richardson's Trading Company** (222 W. Hwy. 66, 505/722-4762). Opened in 1913, this historic post stocks an overwhelming selection of crafts and goods from the creaky wooden floor to the high ceilings. At last count there were 2,000 rugs in the rug room, along with turquoise, silver, pottery, and other treasures. Groups of six or more can make advance arrangements for fascinating behind-the-scenes tours of the post's vaults.

Perry Null Trading Co. (1710 S. 2nd St., 505/863-5249, www.perrynulltrading.com) was started in 1939 as Tobe Turpen's Trading Post. They have tons of jewelry in the pawn vault, along with hundreds of pawned saddles. Among the wide selection at the **Ellis Tanner Trading Co.** (1980 Hwy. 602, 505/863-4434, www.etanner.com), you'll find pawned goods and paintings. The Tanner family traces its trading history back to miner and guide Seth Tanner, who came to the region in the late 1800s at the behest of Brigham Young. Today Tanner's fourth-generation descendants also run the **Shush Yaz Trading Co.** (1304 W. Lincoln, 505/722-0130, www.shushyaz.com), named after Seth's son Joseph, called "Little Bear" by the Navajo. It has a large selection of Pendleton blankets and clothing as well as arts and crafts.

Though Gallup is an undisputed mecca for Indian art, the arts scene includes more than turquoise and silver. Local artists operate a co-op, the **Makeshift Gallery** (213 W. Coal Ave., 505/722-8886, http://makeshiftgallery.com) that, along with the Second Street Gallery (104 S. Second St., 505/728-7924), is often the center of the action during the monthly Arts Crawl.

RECREATION

Recently proclaimed the Adventure Capital of New Mexico, Gallup has a number of hiking and biking trails that lead into gorgeous sandstone cliffs and canyons. The Dawn 'Til Dusk mountain bike endurance race is held each spring, and the Squash Blossom Classic, a combination of bike and foot races, takes place in September. Both events center on the **High Desert Trail System** northeast of town, a 20-plus-mile trail network open to bikers and hikers. The Gamerco (east) trailhead is just north of downtown Gallup. To get there, head north three miles on U.S. 491, and turn left onto Chino Road and then left again at the first turnoff.

The Mentmore (west) trailhead offers access to the High Desert Trail System as well as to the **Mentmore rock climbing area,** which has more than 80 bolted and top-climbs up to 45 feet high and 5.13 in difficulty. To get to the trailhead, take the frontage road (SR 118) six miles west of Gallup; then turn north onto County Road 1/Mentmore and continue for about a mile to the parking area.

The **Northside trail system,** a 22-mile network of technical single-track through the piñon-and-juniper desert, starts behind the Gallup Community Service Center at 410 Bataan Veterans Street. **Sports World Bike Shop** (1500 S. Second St., 505/722-3055) has maps and information about this and other trails.

Two good hiking trails start at **Red Rock Park** (505/722-3829), 640 acres of beautiful scarlet canyons about three miles east of town. (From Route 66, turn north on SR 566, take another left after half mile and follow the signs.) The **Pyramid Rock Trail** is a three-mile

round-trip loop that takes you up to 7,500 feet, and the **Church Rock Trail** (two miles round-trip) offers views over sandstone towers. The park also has a 142-site campground ($12–18), a historical museum, and the 1888 Outlaw Trading Post.

About 20 miles southeast, the Mt. Taylor Ranger District of Cibola National Forest encompasses the Zuni Mountains and McGaffey Lake recreation area, with picnic spots, campgrounds, scenic drives, and miles upon miles of multiuse trails. The **Hilso Trailhead** is the gateway to the trails that make up the Zuni Mountain 100-bike endurance race. To get there, take I-40 approximately seven miles west of town and turn south at exit 33. The trailhead is 11 miles south on NM 400.

ACCOMMODATIONS

Gallup has no shortage of hotel rooms, although some of the cheaper ones along Route 66 are best avoided. If you're looking for historic ambiance, ◖ **El Rancho Hotel** (1000 E. Hwy. 66, 505/863-9311 or 800/543-6351, www.elranchohotel.com) is a sure winner. It was opened in 1937 by director D. W. Griffith's brother and became a second home to movie stars filming nearby during the 1940s, '50s, and '60s. Ronald Reagan, Spencer Tracy, Kirk Douglas, and Katherine Hepburn all stayed there, and their signed photos grace the hallways today. The hotel is a shrine to Hollywood's golden age of Westerns, with a two-story lobby full of Native American art, stone fireplaces, rustic furniture, and a curving twin staircase. On the ground floor, Armand Ortega's Indian Store sells quality crafts, and live music floats from the 49er Lounge, where locals claim you'll find the best margarita in town. Steaks, sandwiches, Mexican-American dishes, and hearty breakfasts are served at the restaurant, open daily for all meals. Rooms inside the historic (and some say haunted) hotel are $90–110.

A number of national hotel chains have staked out Route 66 east and west of town. Rooms at the **Rodeway Inn** (1709 W. Hwy. 66, 505/863-9301) start around $40. In the

$50–100 price range you'll find a **Red Roof Inn** (3304 W. Hwy. 66, 505/772-7765), **Best Western Inn & Suites** (3009 W. Hwy. 66, 505/722-2221), **Days Inn** (3201 W. Hwy. 66, 505/863-6889), and Econolodge (3101 W. Hwy. 66, 505/722-3800), among others. The centrally located **Hampton Inn** (1460 W. Maloney, 505/726-0900) has rooms and suites starting at $130, and rooms at the nearby Quality Inn (1500 W. Maloney, 505/726-1000 or 800/228-5151) are around $100.

RV or tent campers can choose among Red Rock Park, the **USA RV Park** (2925 W. Hwy. 66, 505/863-5021, www.usarvpark.com, $30–35), or the **KOA** (3900 E. Hwy. 66, 505/722-2333, $40). About 15 miles east and south of Gallup, **Cibola National Forest** (505/346-3900, www.fs.usda.gov/cibola) has at-large camping and two no-reservation campgrounds near McGaffey Lake (pull-through sites but no hookups, mid-May–Sept., $5–10).

FOOD

Red or green? When you cross the New Mexico border, be prepared to choose sides, or in this case, sauces. Chile lovers are loyal to their favorite color of heat, and red or green sauce blankets enchiladas, burritos, rellenos—and often burgers, omelets, and other entrées, too. Gallup has a score of restaurants that serve Mexican-American cuisine, and some have been at it for generations. At **Ⓒ Don Diego's Restaurant and Lounge** (801 W. Hwy. 66, 505/722-5517, all meals Mon.–Sat), the Baca family has been cooking up the same great New Mexican food for decades. Dishes are $4–6 for breakfast, $6–8 for lunch, and $8–12 for dinner, including baby back ribs and carne adovada.

Earl's Family Restaurant (1400 E. Hwy. 66, 505/863-4201, all meals daily) is another local landmark, open since 1947. They serve inexpensive Mexican and American family fare. Western BBQ and Navajo tacos have been on the menu of **The Ranch Kitchen** (3001 W. Hwy. 66, 505/722-5696, all meals daily) for four decades.

If you need to take a breather from chile for a meal or two, you'll find plenty of options. The **Coffee House** (203 W. Coal Ave., 505/726-0291), next to the El Morro Theater, is open 7 or 8 A.M.–10 or 11 P.M. (10 A.M.–4 P.M. Sun.). Live music, poetry readings, and local art on the walls make it a cozy neighborhood spot, serving snacks and the usual caffeinated beverages. For fine dining, try **Zen Steak and Sushi** (1212 U.S. 491, 505/722-2628, dinner Mon.–Sat., $10–30) or the **Badlands Grill** (2201 W. Hwy. 66, 505/722-5157, $12–40). Steaks are the specialty there, but they also serve fish, chicken, and decadent desserts.

INFORMATION

For more information on Gallup and the surrounding area, contact the **Gallup-McKinley County Chamber of Commerce** (106 W. Hwy. 66, 505/722-2228, www.thegallupchamber.com). For more information about trails and roads in nearby Cibola National Forest, contact the Mt. Taylor ranger district (505/346-3900, www.fs.usda.gov/cibola). The nearest ranger station is 60 miles east in Grants.

GETTING THERE AND AROUND

Gallup's **Greyhound** station is three miles west of downtown at the Route 66 Mini Market (3060 W. Hwy. 66, 505/863-9078). **Amtrak** is located inside the Cultural Center (201 E. Hwy. 66, 505/863-3244).

Gallup Municipal Airport (2111 W. Hwy. 66, 505/726-6115) is a general aviation airport. **Budget** (505/726-1916) and **Enterprise** (505/722-5280) have offices there, and the airport's flight service (505/863-6578) rents cars to pilots.

ZUNI PUEBLO

The 450,000-acre Zuni Reservation is home to about 10,000 people, most of whom reside in Zuni Pueblo, making it the largest of New Mexico's 19 pueblos. The pueblo is built on the site of Halona, one of the villages visited by Coronado in his 1540 expedition. Though Zuni was the first pueblo to encounter the Spanish, it is the least influenced by Hispanic culture.

The Zuni people, who call themselves A:shiwi (pronounced AH-shee-wee), are very private, but they graciously welcome visitors

ZUNI ARTS AND CRAFTS

Though Zuni ancestors have been making jewelry for more than 1,000 years, the first Zuni silversmith, Lanyade, learned his skill from a Navajo in 1872. Modern Zuni silverwork includes a variety of styles and techniques but is best known for settings with multiple semiprecious stones—dazzling needlepoint and petit point turquoise designs as well as exquisite inlay depicting birds, shalakos, and other motifs.

Fetishes have been carried by Zunis since prehistoric times for use in prayers and ceremonies and also for protection. Fetish necklaces combine small carved animals with *heishe* (shell) beads. Modern fetishes (more accurately known as carvings because they haven't been ritually blessed) may depict snakes, foxes, bears, or other animals.

Pottery also dates back to ancient times.

One traditional design unique to Zuni Pueblo is Deer-in-His-House, which depicts a deer in profile surrounded by arched and linear designs. The deer will likely have a heart line, which represents breath or spirit. Modern Zuni pottery incorporates bold designs on ollas, seed jars, bowls, and effigies. Frogs, dragonflies, and other creatures associated with water are common themes.

Zuni crafts also include beadwork, kachina carvings, paintings, and basketry. When shopping for Zuni or other Indian crafts, be aware that some countries are exporting inexpensive manufactured knockoffs marked as Indian or U.S. made. If you purchase directly from an artist or from an established gallery or trading post, you can ascertain that the work is authentic and handmade.

to art studios, galleries, and local businesses that include a handful of restaurants and convenience stores. An ideal time to visit Zuni is during one of the pueblo's art markets, held during Gallup's Inter-Tribal Indian Ceremonial in August and around various holidays, including Valentine's Day, Mother's Day, and the winter holiday season. Observe all village traditions and restrictions, posted and detailed at the visitor center.

To get there, take SR 602 south from Gallup for 25 miles. Turn right (southwest) on Zuni Route 4 and drive six miles to SR 53. Turn right and continue six miles to Zuni Pueblo. The scenic drive takes in part of the Trail of the Ancients Byway (which continues east to Ramah and El Morro National Monument) and offers classic New Mexico vistas of stacked mesas. As you approach Zuni Pueblo, look for the cliff-sided, pine-topped mesa called Dowa Yalanne, or Corn Mountain. The Zunis took refuge there after the 1680 Pueblo Revolt, consolidating their defenses and preparing to protect their land from reprisals. The mesa rises 1,000 feet above the pueblo and remains an integral part of Zuni life and legend. (A sacred site, it is off limits to non-Zunis.)

Sights

Begin at the **Visitor and Arts Center** (1239 Hwy. 53, 505/782-7238, www.zunitourism.com, 8:30 a.m.–5:30 p.m. Mon.–Fri., 10 a.m.–4 p.m. Sat., noon–4 p.m. Sun.), where you can join a tour (starting at $10 pp) of village sights, including **Old Zuni Mission** (established in 1629 and rebuilt in 1968). With advance arrangements, you can tour the prehistoric Zuni village of Hawikku, see a rock art site and Chaco outlier ($75 for up to four people), or share in a traditional Zuni meal. Photography permits ($10) can be purchased at the visitors center, but be aware that even with a permit, photographs are not allowed in some sites or situations.

If you take a walking tour of the historic Middle Village, you may notice a number of **beehive-shaped ovens** or *hornos*. You'll see the extra-large version of an horno at **Paywa's Zuni Bread** (11A Paywa Dr., 505/782-4849, Wed.–Fri.), a home-based bakery where you can watch traditional breads and pies being made and purchase some to take with you. (If you'd like to assemble a picnic and enjoy some of the reservation's lovely scenery, inquire at the visitors center, where staff members will give you directions to appropriate outdoor locations and trails.)

The **A:shiwi A:wan Museum** (2 E. Ojo Caliente, 505/782-4403, 9 A.M.–6 P.M. Mon.– Fri. or by appointment, admission by donation) has murals and displays illustrating five centuries of Zuni life. The museum does double duty as a community center.

Shopping

Eight out of ten Zuni workers are artisans, creating fetishes, jewelry, basketry, and pottery. A number of trading posts, galleries, and shops carry local arts and crafts, including **Pueblo Trading** (1192 SR 53, 505/782-2296). You can also visit a working studio or the **Zuni Craftsman's Cooperative** (177 W. Hwy. 53, 505/782-4425) and purchase directly from the artist.

The village hosts several **art markets** throughout the year. Market days are especially good times to visit: Vendors sell crafts, home-baked bread and pastries, and garden produce (including chiles), and often there are performances by some of Zuni Pueblo's famed dance groups.

Accommodations

Across the street from the A:shiwi A:wan Museum, rooms at the pretty and historic **Halona Inn** (505/782-2155 or 800/752-3278, http://halona.com) begin at $80.

NORTH OF GALLUP
Highway 491

Once numbered 666 (and earning its unfortunate nickname, the Devil's Highway) U.S. 491 roughly follows the Old Spanish Trail, linking New Mexico, Colorado, and Utah. Heading north from Gallup, the highway parallels the Lukachukai and Chuska Mountains, rising darkly to almost 10,000 feet along the Arizona border. About 40 miles north of Gallup, SR 134 heads west from Sheep Springs. On its way to Window Rock it crosses Narbona Pass, named for the Navajo leader who was killed by the U.S. Army there in 1849 during a peace negotiation, and passes through Crystal, a "rug

town." (For those heading north to Canyon de Chelly, SR 134 and Indian Route 12 combine for a beautiful, peaceful drive.)

The northeastern corner of the Navajo Reservation is a stark lesson in geology. U.S. 491 continues through a bizarre landscape of mesa, monoclines, and volcanic detritus. **Bennett Peak** and **Ford Butte,** on opposite sides of the highway near milepost 64, are both volcanic necks, left behind when softer outer layers eroded away, leaving the harder solid core behind. Dikes of hardened lava radiate from the necks like crazed bicycle spokes across the flat terrain.

As you continue north, look for **Rol-Hay Rock** to the west, sharp little **Barber Peak** and the **Hogback** monocline to the east, and then rising sharply above the relatively flat San Juan Basin—Ship Rock.

Trading Posts

About an hour north of Gallup near Newcomb, more than a half dozen trading posts once operated. Today two posts continue to offer a vintage ambience near the reservation's Two Grey Hills area, where 100 weavers still work in traditional colors and patterns. These aren't tourist spots or galleries but working posts where you may see the first small rug woven by a young girl or a masterpiece made by a skilled weaver. The intricate geometric pattern of the Two Grey Hills regional style incorporates undyed wools in cream, tan, black, and gray, woven so tightly (at least 80 wefts per inch) that they are considered tapestries rather than rugs.

Toadlena Trading Post (505/789-3267 or 888/420-0005, 9 A.M.–6 P.M. Mon.–Sat., 10 A.M.–5 P.M. Sun., shorter winter hours) has operated for longer than a century. The post incorporates a weaving museum in the back room and, like a traditional post, serves the community as a bank, post office, grocery, and social center. Small weavings (less than a foot square) can be purchased for under $100, while larger rugs fetch thousands.

Six miles away, **Two Grey Hills Trading Post** (505/789-3270, 8:30 A.M.–5:30 P.M. Mon.–Sat., or by appointment), established in 1897, was a setting in Tony Hillerman's *The Wailing Wind* (2002). Les Wilson runs this timeless place, which was built in 1897. (If the post looks closed, he suggests driving around back and honking your horn.) Ask to see the rug room, where he stocks a good selection made by local weavers.

To get to either post, drive north on U.S. 491 for 59 miles to Newcomb. At the Shell station, turn left on Indian Route 19 and follow the signs. It's a good idea to call for road conditions before you strike out. These dirt roads are usually suitable for passenger cars, but a high-clearance vehicle would be a better choice.

SHIPROCK

The Navajo Nation's largest town, Shiprock (pop. 9,000), is named for the pinnacle of Ship Rock. The English name comes from early Anglo settlers; the 1,700-foot volcanic dike reminded them of the sails of a 19th-century clipper ship rising above the broad San Juan River valley. The rock is known to the Navajo as Tse Bit A'i (the "rock with wings"). According to one legend, the people sheltered there when being attacked by another tribe, and the rock grew wings and flew them away to safety. It is also known as the place where the twins Monster Slayer and Child Born for Water killed a nest full of monstrous birds preying on their people. (As a sacred site, it is off limits to hiking and climbing.)

Practicalities

The Shiprock area is known for sandpaintings and the rare sandpainting-style or Yei rug, named for the supernatural beings who bring their healing powers to medicine ceremonies, or sings. Another popular regional rug style is the Yei-Bi-Chai design, depicting the dancers who impersonate Yeis. Many Navajo folk artists work in this area, making whimsical and colorful carvings of reservation life, from chickens to rodeo riders.

The Foutz family, one of the oldest trading families on the reservation, runs the **Foutz Trading Co.** (505/368-5790 or 800/383-0615, www.foutztrade.com) with a good selection of Navajo folk art, knives with embroidered sheaths, and Navajo kachinas. The store (west on SR 64) is also full of craft supplies, including a colorful wall of yarn, and has separate rooms for rugs and sandpaintings. They also run the post at Teec Nos Pos, Arizona, 30 miles west on U.S. 160, and Wade Foutz Indian Art (505/598-0380) in Kirtland, just west of Farmington. The **Navajo Arts and Crafts Enterprise** (NACE) operates a store in the Shiprock Shopping Center, at the crossroads of U.S. 64 and U.S. 491, where you'll also find a handful of fast-food restaurants.

The town of Shiprock hosts the **Northern Navajo Fair** in early October. This colorful celebration has been held annually for more than a century, making it the oldest on the reservation. It incorporates six days of events ranging from horse races to arts and crafts displays.

Chaco Culture National Historical Park

Location, location, location. Once the centerpiece of the Ancestral Puebloan world, Chaco Canyon today is a remote outpost. The road to Chaco Canyon is long, rough, and occasionally impassable in bad weather, but the reward for making this journey is that you'll be among the few to explore one of the country's premiere cultural sites. This Ancestral Puebloan hub once teemed with as many as 5,000 inhabitants who lived among stunning public structures that may have functioned something like present-day Washington Mall.

About 4,000 ruins, roads, dams, and petroglyphs have been found in the park, which has been declared a UNESCO World Heritage Site. Chaco's famed "great houses," 16 huge stone masonry complexes, were linked to each other and to many others throughout the region by an intriguing system of roads. Chaco flourished for almost 400 years, peaking in

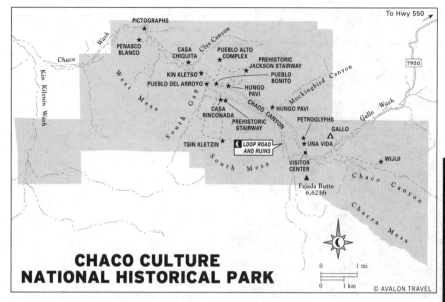

To Hwy 550

7950

PICTOGRAPHS

PENASCO BLANCO

CASA CHIQUITA

Chys Canyon

PUEBLO ALTO COMPLEX

PREHISTORIC JACKSON STAIRWAY

Chaco

KIN KLETSO

PUEBLO DEL ARROYO

PUEBLO BONITO

HUNGO PAVI

Mockingbird Canyon

West Mesa

South Gap

CASA RINCONADA

HUNGO PAVI

CHACO CANYON

PREHISTORIC STAIRWAY

PETROGLYPHS

Gallo Wash

Kin Klizhin Wash

TSIN KLETZIN

LOOP ROAD AND RUINS

GALLO

UNA VIDA

South Mesa

VISITOR CENTER

Chaco Canyon

WIJIJI

Fajada Butte 6,623ft

Chacra Mesa

CHACO CULTURE NATIONAL HISTORICAL PARK

0   1 mi

0   1 km

© AVALON TRAVEL

the 11th century, and its cultural repercussions lasted much longer. An abundance of enigmatic petroglyphs and trade items from far-off lands add to the aura of mystery that surrounds these isolated ruins. From the Pueblo Alto trail overlooking sprawling Pueblo Bonito, it's easy to imagine this dry, windswept canyon bustling with life or haunted by the ghosts of the past.

The Setting

Chaco Wash is a wide, shallow canyon near the center of the San Juan Basin. It drains to the northwest and becomes the Chaco River, an intermittent tributary of the San Juan River. The landscape is dry and uninviting, with escarpments, mesas, and buttes breaking the drab monotony. If you're wondering the obvious—why there?—keep in mind the changing climate and the skill of Chaco's builders in growing crops with hardly any rain. The harsh, unpredictable environment may have made it necessary to organize the agriculture of the entire San Juan Basin, and Chaco may have acted as a buffer, serving as a storage and distribution center where surplus food was held for redistribution during bad harvest years.

History

Humans frequented Chaco Canyon long before the beginning of the Christian era, and people began settling there more or less permanently during the Basketmaker III Period (A.D. 450–750). Underground pit houses evolved into multiroom, multistory surface dwellings and ceremonial rooms (kivas), and by A.D. 900 construction of the characteristic **great houses** began.

Several stories high and containing hundreds of rooms and dozens of ceremonial kivas, the great houses were unlike anything that had been built before in the Southwest. They were planned in detail, oriented to the sun, moon, and stars, and linked by line of sight to each other to ensure direct communications with fires or reflectors. It's not clear what their exact purpose was; in this marginal land; they were too big to be simple farming villages. Their size might have served some greater ceremonial or symbolic purpose—perhaps, as much as anything, to demonstrate the power of their builders and to help unite the Pueblo world. If so, they might have served as public architecture, occupied during times of ceremony or trade.

The great houses of Pueblo Bonito, Peñasco

© KATHLEEN BRYANT

The great house of Pueblo Bonito's remarkable architectural features include this series of doorways.

Blanco, Una Vida, Hungo Pavi, Pueblo Alto, and Chetro Ketl were planned and constructed over decades, and in some cases centuries. New masonry techniques—surrounding thick rubble cores with thin, intricate facing layers, and decreasing wall widths with height—allowed the builders to raise structures as high as four stories. By the 11th century, Chaco was connected to more than 150 other great houses (outliers) throughout the San Juan Basin. Population estimates range from 2,000 to 6,000 people who lived in some 400 settlements in and near Chaco Canyon.

Chaco's importance as a ceremonial and cultural center matched its architecture; social, religious, and commercial activity in the San Juan Basin passed through the valley at some point. A trading network that extended into northern Mexico brought tropical birds, copper, and seashells, exchanged for distinctive turquoise mined nearby and processed into jewelry at Chaco. One archaeologist estimated

that only 20 percent of the exquisite black-on-white pottery associated with Chaco was made there; the remainder may have arrived from the south and west. At least one room appears to have been used to keep live macaws, and nearly every Chacoan great house held evidence of turquoise processing.

The cultural zenith began to fade in the 12th century, when new construction slowed. Though Chaco's influence was still felt into the 13th century to the north, west, and south, in outliers such as Aztec and Salmon, its peak had passed. By 1300 Chaco Canyon was almost completely deserted. Clans migrated to new locations, leaving behind Chacoan ways. As the Mesa Verdean culture grew, Chaco's residents moved south and east, eventually metamorphosing into the Hopi and Rio Grande Pueblo cultures. Modern puebloans still trace a spiritual and biological lineage to Chaco and return from time to time to honor their ancestors. They remember the connection in songs and prayers and also participate in management decisions with the park.

Navajos moved into the canyon in the 1700s and lived there until 1948, and pinpoint the origins of several clans to Chaco, which they call Tse' biyahnii'a'ah ("the home of the great gambler"). The word "Chaco" may be a Spanish corruption of the Navajo word Tsékoh (canyon) or Tzak'aik (white string of rocks), referring to the light-colored sandstone atop Chacra Mesa.

The ruins weren't discovered by Anglos until 1849, when the Washington Expedition under Lieutenant James Simpson surveyed the area. Further photographic expeditions led to excavations near the turn of the 20th century, including some by cowboy archaeologist Richard Wetherill. The Hyde Expedition (1896–1900) from the American Museum of Natural History excavated Pueblo Bonito, and tree-ring dating by a National Geographic party the late 1920s fixed the ages of the sites. The area became a national monument in 1907, a national historical park in 1980, and a UNESCO World Heritage Site in 1987.

NEW MEXICO AND COLORADO

ALL ROADS LEAD TO CHACO

Archaeologists always knew it must have taken a sophisticated transportation system to link the scattered settlements of the Chacoan society, but it took the advent of aerial photography to reveal the amazing extent of the Chaco road system. More than 400 miles of ancient roadway have been identified, linking Chaco Canyon to some 75 surrounding communities. The longest of these reached all the way to Salmon and Aztec Ruins—over 40 miles north—while others seemed to begin and end in the empty desert.

These were not just foot trails, either. Averaging 30 feet across, the roads were built on leveled beds that were raised above sloping terrain, with rock borders or masonry walls to keep the dirt fill in place. They were laid out in amazingly straight lines, and double and quadruple road segments were sometimes built near the great houses. Settlements were spaced about a day's travel apart on the longer north-south routes.

The network must have taken an amazing amount of planning and effort to build and maintain, and it is thought that the roads were more than just ways to move goods and people. Most date to the 11th and 12th centuries, when Chaco's population was expanding, and the roads may have helped bind the burgeoning culture into a cohesive whole. By facilitating communications and bringing spiritual pilgrims to Chaco, the roads may have helped spread the Chacoan religion across the inhospitable landscape and provide yet another way to reflect their worldview in earth and stone.

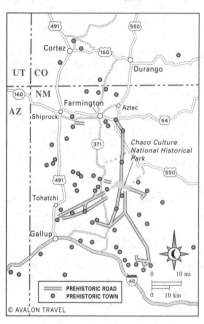

VISITORS CENTER AND VICINITY

The **Gallo Campground,** about 23 miles from Highway 550, is open year-round with 47 sites available on a first-come, first-served basis for $10 per night. Two group sites are available by reservation. The campground has picnic tables and restrooms, and potable water is available at the visitor center. There are no hookups, and no shade. Bring everything you need (gas, food, firewood or charcoal), and be prepared to enjoy the splendid isolation.

A trail from the campground (also a good mountain bike ride) leads 1.5 miles to the pueblo of **Wijiji,** built in the early 1100s. This ruin is unusual in its symmetry and the fact that it seems to have been built in one go, rather than added to over the years. A Navajo legend tells that a Pueblo woman living near there taught the tribe how to weave.

A mile farther is the park **visitors center** (505/786-7014, www.nps.gov/chcu, 8 A.M.–5 P.M. daily, $8 per vehicle, good for one week). The visitors center houses a bookstore, museum, and theater screening two films about Chaco. Check there for information on campfire talks and ranger-guided hikes. You can pick up free permits for hiking longer trails at the visitors center or at trailheads.

Adjacent to the visitors center, the park's observatory lets visitors enjoy Chaco's celebrated

night sky programs, which take advantage of the area's natural darkness. Night sky programs are held at dusk Tuesday, Friday, and Saturday April–October, with special events scheduled throughout the year, including those at solstice and equinox. On certain nights you can look through the park's own 25-inch reflector telescope, and other telescopes set up by dedicated amateurs, to see the stars, planets, and moon as you've never seen them before. Rangers and volunteer stargazers will explain what you're seeing as well as the importance of the night skies in Chacoan culture.

A short trail from the visitors center parking lot leads to the partially excavated **Una Vida** ruin, with about 150 rooms and five kivas. Its backdrop of sandstone cliffs bears petroglyphs of clan symbols still recognized by contemporary Pueblo and Hopi people.

◖ LOOP ROAD AND RUINS

The visitors center is at the beginning of a nine-mile paved loop drive that links five great houses and trailheads leading to others. Heading counterclockwise around the one-way loop, you'll first pass **Hungo Pavi,** an unexcavated ruin, before reaching the parking area for Pueblo Bonito and Chetro Ketl. **Chetro Ketl** was built in the 11th century and enlarged in the early 12th. It has about 500 rooms, 16 kivas, and a huge elevated plaza, fronted by a colonnade reminiscent of Mesoamerican sites.

Pueblo Bonito is the largest and best known of Chaco's great houses. This four-story D-shaped complex was occupied in the 10th–13th century and was built in stages, ending up with about 600 rooms and 40 kivas. Pueblo Bonito is one of the most studied ruins in North America and is a sacred place to native tribes. A leaning sandstone column known as Threatening Rock once loomed over the rear of the pueblo. The Chacoans braced it with earth, timbers, and masonry, and the Park Service monitored its tilt carefully, but in January 1941 it finally made good its promise and fell, crushing about 30 excavated rooms. **Free ranger-guided tours** are led through Pueblo Bonito twice daily beginning at 10 A.M. and 2 P.M., April–October.

For an overlook of Pueblo Bonito and Chetro Ketl, you can hike partway up the Pueblo Alto trail (two miles round-trip). The hawk's-eye view makes it easier to spot interior kivas and differentiate between old and new construction. (The Pueblo Alto Trail begins behind Kin Kletso, about one-third of a mile along the dirt road that leads northwest from Pueblo del Arroyo.) Another short trail leads from Pueblo Bonito along the base of the cliffs to Chetro Ketl, passing many petroglyphs and Richard Wetherill's gravesite.

From the far end of the loop drive, a short spur heads to **Pueblo del Arroyo,** a 280-room complex with more than a dozen kivas, built in a short period around 1100. Near the Pueblo del Arroyo parking lot is a dirt road (closed to private vehicles) leading a quarter mile along Chaco Wash to **Kin Kletso,** which was built in two stages around 1130 and may have been three stories high. Near the ruin are the trailheads for the Peñasco Blanco and Pueblo Alto Trails.

The Peñasco Blanco Trail continues to the **Casa Chiquita** ruins near the mouth of Clys Canyon, past numerous petroglyphs and pictographs, including one that may depict a supernova that occurred in A.D. 1054. **Peñasco Blanco,** 3.6 miles from the trailhead, is one of Chaco's oldest pueblos, begun along with Pueblo Bonito and Una Vida in the 10th century. The Pueblo Alto Trail heads east from Kin Keltso to **Pueblo Alto,** at the intersection of several ancient roads on top of a mesa. The 5.4-mile loop trail offers great views, passing by farming terraces, grinding holes, and prehistoric steps cut into the cliff, now known as the **Jackson Staircase** for photographer William Henry Jackson, who went there in 1877 on a U.S. Geological Survey expedition.

As the road loops to the south side of the canyon on its way back to the visitors center, it passes **Casa Rinconada,** with the largest-known "great kiva" in the park. It would have accommodated hundreds of people. One window was arguably a solstice marker, framing the rising sun on the summer solstice.

From Casa Rinconada, the **South Mesa Trail** leads to **Tsin Kletzin,** dating to the early

12th century. The 4.1-mile loop trail has several good viewing points and reconnects with the loop road at Casa Rinconada.

GETTING THERE AND AROUND

The cities nearest Chaco are Gallup (94 miles), Grants (82 miles), Farmington (69 miles), and Bloomfield (61 miles). Though the southern route appears short and simple on a map, beware: It traverses a 20-mile-long stretch of rocky, rutted dirt road that's challenging under the best of conditions. When wet, this road turns to a nightmarish mire of gumbo.

The more dependable 21-mile-long northern route leaves from U.S. 550 south of Bloomfield. Suitable for passenger cars in dry weather, this route involves 13 miles of dirt road that can become impassable after a storm or snowmelt. Call ahead for road conditions. Following the signs to the park, turn off U.S. 550 onto County Road (CR) 7900 at milepost 112.5 (three miles southeast of Nageezi); then turn south (right) onto CR 7950 and continue to the park boundary.

Timing your visit takes a combination of planning and luck. The best time to travel there is in late September, after the summer monsoon season has passed, or in October, when temperatures are pleasant. May and June are generally dry but hot and shadeless, with daytime highs in the 80s–90s. At any time of year, unexpected storms can change your plans.

Yet another route accesses Chaco from the southeast: paved CR 9 to dirt CR 7900, which is rougher and harder to follow and not recommended for casual visitors (and definitely not for RVs). Serious archaeology buffs equipped with a high-clearance four-wheel-drive vehicle might choose this route if they plan to visit nearby Pueblo Pintado, a Chaco outlier located a couple of miles northwest of Cuba.

There's no public transportation to or within the park. The park's paved nine-mile loop road is a pleasant bike ride, and bikers can also travel the short trails to Wijiji, Casa Chiquita, and Kin Kletso. If you'd rather leave the driving to someone else, a handful of Southwestern tour companies, such as Detours of Arizona

(866/438-6877, www.detoursaz.com), include Chaco Canyon in their itineraries. Bloomfield's Salmon Ruins museum and research center operates a day-long archaeologist-guided tour (505/632-2013, www.chacotours.org) that visits the great houses and Fajada Butte, the site of the solar calendar featured in *Sun Dagger* (1982), a PBS film narrated by Robert Redford. (Erosion, possibly a result of foot traffic, destroyed the calendar in 1989.)

NEAR CHACO
Bisti/De-Na-Zin Wilderness Areas

About 30 miles south of Farmington as the raven flies, a dreamlike terrain of multicolored stone hoodoos spreads between SR 371 and U.S. Highway 550, preserved as the 38,000 acres of the Bisti/De-Na-Zin Wilderness Areas. Bisti means "large area of shale hills" in Navajo, and De-Na-Zin comes from the Navajo word for cranes, since petroglyphs of cranes have been found just to the south. There the landscape looks acid-etched, like a science-fiction movie set, with strange tabletop formations set off against bands of earth the color of burgundy and charcoal. Barely 10,000 people visit per year, so chances are you'll be able to enjoy a sense of solitude in this unearthly landscape. You can camp and hike there (though there are no marked trails), but the wilderness area is off limits to mountain bikes.

To access the Bisti Wilderness via SR 371, drive 36.5 miles south of where it crosses the San Juan River in downtown Farmington; then turn east (right) onto Non-County Maintained (NCM) 7297. Follow the gravel road about two miles to the parking area marked with a BLM wilderness sign. (If you're traveling from the south, the NCM 7297 intersection is about 45 miles north of Crownpoint.) The De-Na-Zin Wilderness is accessible from U.S. Highway 550 and CR 7500, a dirt road that can become slick and muddy in wet weather. For maps and information, contact the Bureau of Land Management's (BLM's) Farmington Field Office (505/599-8900).

Angel Peak Scenic Area

About 20 miles south of Bloomfield on

© BLM/NEW MEXICO

Wind and water have sculpted the Bisti/De-Na-Zin Wilderness Areas.

U.S. 550 is another small but striking area of badlands. The Angel Peak Scenic Area is presided over by a rock spire known to the Navajo as Tsethi Gizhi ("the rock with two prongs on top"). It's easy to zip by the signed turnoff, but fans of striking scenery will be glad they made this side trip. Dirt CR 7175 (okay for passenger cars when dry but impassable in wet weather) follows the rim 6.5 miles, passing several picnic areas en route to a primitive campground with nine tent sites. Overlooks take in an eroded landscape of colorful clay and sandstone. Most of the time you'll have this place all to yourself. Mountain bikes are restricted to main roads, but you can hike along the rim of Kutz Canyon, where the most colorful rock formations are hidden. Contact the BLM's Farmington Field Office (505/599-8900) for maps and information.

Farmington and Vicinity

At the northeastern corner of the Navajo Reservation, the La Plata and Animas Rivers join the San Juan in a landscape of bluffs and mesas called **Totah** ("the place where rivers meet") by the Navajo. Farmington (pop. 43,000), along with smaller Bloomfield and Aztec, forms the urban hub of northwest New Mexico. Across the reservation boundary to the west is Morgan Lake and its two industrial neighbors: the Navajo Mine, one of the largest open-pit coal mines in the world, and the Four Corners Power Plant that feeds on it. (The power plant keeps the waters of the lake at 75°F year-round, to the delight of local windsurfers.)

Millennia ago, Ancestral Puebloan farmers built extensive stone villages along the river corridors, preserved today as Aztec Ruins National Monument and Salmon Ruins and Heritage Park. Navajos lived alongside their Puebloan neighbors in the 18th-century Pueblitos of Dinetah. Anglo settlers arrived in the late 19th century, drawn to the fertile riverside soils. They called their settlement Farmingtown.

The town's early years were lively. In 1883, when a drunken cowboy shot and wounded a Native American within the city limits, local tribes gathered and threatened to take the offenders by force. A war chief arrived just in time to prevent a fight. When the town's first preacher arrived two years later, cowboys shot at the floor around his feet after he refused to drink with them. (He survived and stayed on.) That same year, a prominent Native American named Largo Pete died after riding into a wire fence, and the local militia had to be called out to prevent another clash.

Eventually the *w* was dropped from the town name, and in the 1950s the small farming and ranching town boomed when oil and gas deposits were discovered nearby. Uranium was eventually added to the list. Farmington is now home to San Juan College, with 7,000 students, as well as some of the best mountain biking in the Four Corners area. The historic downtown has several galleries and restaurants, just steps away from a pleasant nature trail that follows the San Juan River.

SIGHTS

Main and Broadway run parallel through Farmington's historic downtown area, where you'll see a few historic buildings, including the 1945 **Totah Theater** (315 W. Main St., 505/327-4145) with its vintage neon sign. Reopened in 2005, the Totah hosts a variety of concerts and plays. Two and a half miles east is the **Gateway Park Museum and Visitors Center** (3041 E. Main St., 505/599-1174, 8 A.M.–5 P.M. Mon.–Sat., $3 pp suggested donation), a big glass-fronted building by the Animas River. The museum has exhibits on local history as well as lectures and art shows. Animated dinosaurs screech and pressure valves hiss within the exhibit titled "From Dinosaurs to Drill Bits," which includes the Geovator, a simulated ride down an oil well that wouldn't be out of place at Disney World. At the end of

an exhibit on the town's history is a replica of a pre–World War II trading post filled with items taken from real posts around the Four Corners.

In Animas Park are the **Riverside Nature Center** (off Browning Pkwy., 8 A.M.–6 P.M. Sat., 1–5 P.M. Sun. in summer, free though admission may be charged for special programs and exhibits), with interpretive exhibits on riverine ecology, and the nearby **Harvest Grove Farm & Orchards Exhibit Barn,** where you can see antique farm equipment on Saturday mornings in summer during the weekly farmers market (or at other times by special arrangement). Kids of all ages can explore the hands-on exhibits at the **E3 Children's Museum & Science Center** (302 North Orchard, 505/599-1425, 10 A.M.–5 P.M. Tues.–Sat., free).

B-Square Ranch (3901 Bloomfield Hwy., 505/325-4275, www.bolackmuseums.com, 9 A.M.–5 P.M. Mon.–Sat., free tours by appointment) encompasses a wildlife preserve, experimental farm, and two museums with antique farm machinery and wildlife displays.

ENTERTAINMENT

Theater performances are staged at the James C. Henderson Fine Arts Center of **San Juan College** (505/326-3311, www.sanjuancollege.edu) on the north side of town. The college also has an art gallery and planetarium (505/566-3430) that gives free shows to the public one Friday evening every month. Ballets, musicals, and theater productions held at the **Farmington Civic Center** (200 W. Arrington Ave., 505/599-1145 or 877/599-3331) include performances by the San Juan Symphony (www.sanjuansymphony.com). Late June–early August the natural sandstone amphitheater at the Lions Wilderness Park stages summer theater productions (5800 College Blvd., 505/599-1140, http://fmtn.org/sandstone, Thurs.–Sun.).

There's no shortage of sports bars and lounges in Farmington, but if you're looking for a place to kick up your heels, the **Top Deck** (515 E. Main St., 505/327-7385) has live music and plenty of dance floor. **St. Clair Winery and Bistro** (5150 E. Main St., 505/325-0711) offers live jazz on summer evenings Thursday–Saturday.

Three **casinos** operate within minutes of Farmington. The **SunRay Park and Casino** (505/566-1200) has 500 slot machines and live horse racing. It's between Farmington and Bloomfield on U.S. 64. West of Farmington, **Flowing Water Casino** (2710 U.S. Hwy. 64, 505/368-2300, 9 A.M.–1 A.M. Sun.–Thurs., till 4 A.M. on weekends), with 125 gaming machines and a restaurant, is the second gaming establishment opened by the Navajo Nation. Upper Fruitland is the site of the Navajo Nation's third casino, Northern Edge. Opened in 2012, it has gaming tables and 750 slot machines.

EVENTS

You'd expect a town named Farmington to have a bounty of local fruits and vegetables, and the weekly **summer growers market** at Gateway Park offers a cornucopia of tasty produce. Throughout summer, Farmington's pleasant city parks are lively with events.

In late May, the annual **Riverfest** brings music, food, art, raft rides, and live entertainment to Animas Park. The **San Juan County Sheriff's Posse Rodeo,** the largest open rodeo in northern New Mexico, rides into the San Juan Rodeo Grounds on SR 516 east of Farmington in June. Every July an annual **Indian Market** showcases local tribes with crafts, performances, and food at Berg Park.

Some of the country's best amateur baseball arrives in August during the **Connie Mack World Series** in Rickett's Park. Later that month is the **San Juan County Fair,** the largest county fair in the state, with livestock, live music, fiddlers, a parade, and more. It happens in McGee Park on U.S. 64 between Farmington and Bloomfield.

The **Totah Festival** celebrates native cultures over Labor Day weekend with a powwow, rug auction, and juried art show. In October the **Road Apple Rally** (www.roadapplerally. com) brings riders from all over the country to try their skill on the loop courses north of the city. This is the oldest continuously held mountain bike race in the United States, and it's open to beginners and veterans alike.

SHOPPING

With the Navajo Reservation on the edge of town and the Ute Mountain Ute, Southern Ute, and Jicarilla Apache reservations nearby, Farmington is a good place to find Native American crafts. Several excellent shops are located in historic downtown. The **Fifth Generation Trading Company** (232 W. Broadway, 505/326-3211) has been operating since 1875 and stocks rugs, kachinas, jewelry, alabaster sculptures, and one of the largest collections of sandpaintings in the Southwest. **Emerson Gallery** (121 W. Main St., 505/599-8597, www.emersongallery.com) displays the vivid paintings of Anthony Chee Emerson as well as folk art by his mother and brother. **Shiprock Trading Company** (301 W. Main St., 505/324-0881), established in 1894, has Navajo rugs, jewelry, baskets, and pottery.

A dozen local artists work on-site at **Artifacts Gallery** (302 W. Main St., 505/327-2907), where you can buy paintings, pottery, furniture, and other items in all price ranges. The Three Rivers Women's Collective operates the **TRWC Arts Center** and gallery (109 N. Allen, 505/716-7660, www.threeriverswomen. com), hosting workshops and displaying members' work.

The unincorporated community of **Waterflow,** 15 miles west of Farmington, is home to the **Hogback Trading Company** (3221 U.S. 64, 505/598-5154). It was established in 1871 by owner Tom Wheeler's great-grandfather Joseph, and the two-story octagonal building has served as a bank, mercantile store, and livestock brokerage over the years. The first floor highlights rugs, and the upstairs gallery has alabaster sculptures, a wagon, and a mock hogan. What's left of the original post stands across the road at the foot of the Hogback. Nearby is **Bob French Navajo Rugs** (3459 U.S. 64, 505/598-5621), where you should head for the back room piled high with rugs of all sizes, styles, and quality. If your budget is tight, ask to see the sale pile of rugs.

Southeast of Waterflow is **Fruitland,** a Mormon community founded in 1877. There you'll find the **Hatch Brothers Trading Post**

(36 Riverside Dr., 505/598-6226), a gem of a place in business since 1949, with an old-style bull-pen layout and just about everything from food to pawned items and rugs for sale. Venerable owner R. S. Hatch says he'll be there for another half century. To get there, take U.S. 64 west of Farmington, turning left onto County Road (CR) 6100/SR 489. Turn left again on CR 6700, which leads to the post along the riverbank.

RECREATION
Mountain Biking

The high-desert landscape of rolling hills, river valleys, and piñon-juniper forests that surrounds Farmington is webbed with great mountain-biking trails. Many of these, including a network of dirt roads built to access petroleum deposits, are on public lands and within easy range of Farmington. Bike trails on the mesa north of San Juan College offer everything from hilly jumps to sandy arroyos. The **Glade Run Trail** is an easy 3.4-mile loop, and there's the longer **Road Apple Rally** loop, a 30-mile New Mexico classic with views of the San Juan Mountains and Ship Rock. Both start from Lions Wilderness Park at the north end of College Avenue. To get there take Piñon Hill Boulevard north from Main Street; then turn onto College Boulevard.

Other popular trails include two loops on **Piñon Mesa,** three miles north of Main Street on SR 170 (look for a large cottonwood on the east side of the road for the trailhead), and **Kinsey's Ridge,** an eight-mile trail (one-way) through scrubby forests that starts at the end of Foothills Drive. A 5.6-mile loop circles **Lake Farmington** northeast of the city. The trail to Hart's Canyon near Aztec, a supposed UFO crash site, is another good local ride.

For more information or trail maps, contact one of the local bike shops, such as **Cottonwood Cycles** (4370 E. Main St., 505/326-0429), **Havens Bikes** (623 E. Main St., 505/327-1727), or **The Hub** (705 S. Allen Ave. 505/327-2620).

Other Recreation

Farmington boasts more than 70 public parks

and facilities, including the highly regarded **Piñon Hills Municipal Golf Course** (2101 Sunrise Pkwy., 505/326-6066), one of a half-dozen public and private courses that make the area a mecca for golfers. A network of **river walks and nature trails** link Animas and Berg Parks, accessed from Fairview Road and Tucker Road south of Main Street. There's a year-round public pool and waterslide at the **Farmington Aquatic Center** (1151 N. Sullivan, 505/599-1167, open daily, $5 adults, $4.50 ages 12–18, $3.25 ages 3–12, children under 3 free).

ACCOMMODATIONS

For about $50 you can get a room at the **Royal Inn** (701 Airport Dr., 505/325-5061). A **Rodeway Inn** (1601 E. Broadway, 505/325-1813 or 800/699-2994) and a **Comfort Inn** (555 Scott Ave., 505/325-2626 or 800/341-1495) both have rooms for under $100.

Much more distinctive is the **Silver River Adobe Inn** (3151 W. Main St., 505/325-8219 or 800/382-9251, www.silveradobe.com), a bed-and-breakfast situated at the confluence of the San Juan and La Plata rivers. The contemporary timber-and-adobe main lodge houses a library and dining area with river views. Organic breakfasts are included with the rooms ($115) and the four-person suite ($175).

The **■ Casa Blanca Bed & Breakfast** (505 E. La Plata St., 505/327-6503 or 800/550-6503, www.casablancanm.com, $135–255) is surrounded by lush gardens on a bluff overlooking downtown. Each room or casita boasts plenty of individual charm, from a kiva fireplace to veranda sitting areas or a private porch. The innkeepers combine regional art and antiques with modern amenities and a Southwestern-style buffet breakfast. Weekly and monthly accommodations are also available.

Even more distinctive is **Kokopelli's Cave Bed & Breakfast** (3204 Crestridge, 505/325-7855, www.bbonline.com/nm/kokopelli, Mar.–Nov.), a 1,650-square-foot cave for rent that's been featured on *The Oprah Winfrey Show* and CNN. It was carved from the sandstone cliff face in the 1980s, originally intended to be the office of a consulting geologist.

Amenities include a waterfall shower and flagstone hot tub, a small kitchen, and outdoor patios where guests can enjoy views from perch 280 feet above the La Plata River. Rates are $260 per night for two people. There's a steep descent to reach the front door, and guests need to sign a liability waiver to stay there.

RVers will find several small campgrounds in Farmington, including **Mom & Pop RV Park** (901 Illinois, 800/748-2807, $20 for hookups, $8 for tent sites) and the tree-shaded Sundowner Mobile & RV Park (201 Airport Dr., 505/327-1671, $29/night). Navajo Lake State Park, 40 miles east, has three camping areas (505/632-2278 or 877/664-7787, $10–18).

FOOD

If Farmington is your first foray into New Mexico and its cuisine, be prepared for some belt-tightening meals. The owners of **Los Hermanitos** (3501 E. Main, 505/326-5664, and 2500 W. Main, 505/327-1919, lunch and dinner daily) are native New Mexicans whose family recipes combine Mexican, Western, and Indian influences. For $5–20 they serve enormous breakfasts as well as such entrées as steak, tamales, *chicharrones,* and *carne adobada,* accompanied by plenty of red or green chiles.

Three Rivers Eatery and Brewhouse (101–113 E. Main, 505/324-2187, lunch and dinner daily) is decorated with artifacts from the 1912 brick building's former tenants: a drugstore and the *Farmington Times-Hustler* newspaper (now the *Daily Times*). It has an outdoor patio and the largest collection of beer labels and coasters in the state. The menu is updated frequently, but burgers, steaks, pasta, and burritos ($6–15) are standbys that go well with the brewery's award-winning beers. The brewery operates a pizzeria next door (505/325-0308, lunch and dinner daily). At **Clancy's** (2701 E. 20th St., 505/325-8176, lunch and dinner daily, $6–20), an Irish cantina, you can leap across cultures to grab a burrito, a pint of stout, or even sushi. Head to **K.B. Dillons** (101 E. Broadway, 505/325-0222, lunch and dinner Mon.–Sat.) for cocktails at the dark bar, or steak, lobster, and other entrées starting at $15.

Farmington isn't all is beef and chiles: Vegetarians are sure to find something at the **Something Special Bakery and Tearoom** (116 N. Auburn, 505/325-8183, breakfast and lunch daily), where there's a vine-shaded patio and a menu that changes monthly. **Mikasa** (400 W. Main, 505/327-2255, lunch and dinner daily) serves sushi ($7–13) in pleasant surroundings, and **Boon's Family Thai BBQ** (321 W. Main., 505/325-5556, Mon.–Sat., $9–16) has curries, pad thai, and other favorites. **Andrea Kristina's Bookstore and Kafe** (218 W. Main St., 505/327-3313, till 7 P.M. Mon.–Sat.) is a friendly and colorful coffeehouse that specializes in all things local—food, books, art, and music. They stay open a couple of hours later on Thursday nights for a weekly open mic night.

INFORMATION

The **Farmington Convention & Visitors Bureau** (505/326-7602 or 800/448-1240, www.farmingtonnm.org, 8 A.M.–5 P.M. Mon.–Sat.) operates a visitors center in the Gateway Park complex at 3041 East Main Street. Stop at the BLM Field Office (1235 La Plata Hwy., Ste. A, 505/599-8900, 8 A.M.–4 P.M. Mon.–Fri.) for information about hiking and camping on public lands.

GETTING THERE AND AROUND

Great Lakes Airlines (800/554-5111, www.flygreatlakes.com) offers flights to Denver, Las Vegas, and Phoenix from the **Four Corners Regional Airport,** west of downtown. Hertz (505/327-6093) and Budget (505/327-9864) have car rental offices at the airport. Farmington's **Greyhound** bus station is at 126 East Main Street (505/325-1009). For getting around town, hop on the Red Apple Transit (505/325-3409) or call KB Cab (505/564-3999).

AZTEC

Hilly streets lined with trees and historic homes make Aztec stand out from its neighbors, as do the signs at the edge of town:

Welcome to Aztec
Pop. 6,378
and Six Old Soreheads

The seat of San Juan County, this charming town began as a trading post on the bank of the Rio de las Anima, and was most likely named Aztec after the distant Mexican civilization that early inhabitants thought had built the ruins nearby. (The river itself may have been dubbed the River of Spirits in Spanish for the same reason.) A farming and ranching center, it shared in the 1950s oil and gas boom and caught the Cold War–era UFO fever. Today Aztec is a quiet and friendly community, misanthropes notwithstanding. The Soreheads are a tongue-in-cheek tradition whose honorees help raise funds for community projects.

Sights and Tours
More brick than adobe, many buildings in Aztec's downtown area date to the 19th century, and 78 structures are listed on the National Register of historic places or the state register of cultural properties. You can pick up a walking tour map at the **Aztec Museum and Pioneer Village** (125 N. Main, 505/334-9829, 9 A.M.–5 P.M. Mon.–Sat., 10 A.M.–4 P.M. in winter, $3 pp). Old buildings, including a sheriff's office and the city's first jail, stand next to a 1920s oil rig, a narrow-gauge railroad caboose, and collections of historic artifacts, fossils, and minerals. A shoot-out that erupted during an early-1900s Christmas party is reenacted at high noon on weekdays in the summer.

Historians can also amble over for a closer look at the 1929 truss-style bridge that crosses the Animal River on SR 516. The Riverside Park Loop travels 1.5 miles along the river and a historic irrigation ditch and pond.

Aztec is surrounded by a dozen **natural arches,** most accessible by passenger car and short hikes. Check the local visitors center (110 N. Ash, 505/334-9551, 8 A.M.–6 P.M. Mon.–Sat. in summer, 8 A.M.–5 P.M. Mon.–Fri. Labor Day–Memorial Day) for maps and hiking directions.

The area's prehistoric sites are the specialty of **Aztec Archaeological Consultants** (210 S. Main St., 505/401-6596, www.aztecarchaeology.com), a tour company that offers half- and full-day journeys to Chaco Canyon, Salmon Ruins, Aztec Ruins, or local rock-art sites starting at $110 for two people.

Events
The visitors center is also a good place to learn about annual events, including the **Aztec UFO Symposium** held in April and the **Aztec Fiesta Days** in June, which include a parade, food, crafts, the election of new Soreheads, and the burning of an effigy of Old Man Gloom. The **Festival of Lights** in December illuminates Aztec's downtown with traditional New Mexican *farolitos* (candles in sand-filled bags).

The **Alien Run mountain bike race** (www.alienrun.com) travels through Hart Canyon, the infamous UFO crash site. *Bike* magazine calls it "one of New Mexico's best unsung trails," and the race is a fundraiser for the Aztec Library.

Accommodations
All of Aztec's hotels are in the $60–100 range. You may have to share your room with a ghost or two at **Miss Gail's Inn** (300 S. Main St., 505/334-3452 or 888/534-3452, www.missgailsinn.com), located in a 1907 building near the center of town. Motel rooms at the **Step Back Inn** (123 W. Aztec Blvd., 505/334-1200 or 800/334-1255, www.stepbackinn.com) begin at $72 and include a continental breakfast. You'll save a few dollars at the no-frills **Enchantment Lodge** (1800 W. Aztec Blvd., 505/325-6143 or 800/847-2194).

RVers will find a few small parks in and around Aztec, but those who plan to tour the ruins can stay virtually next door at the **Ruins Road RV Park** (312 Ruins Rd., 505/334-3160, www.ruinsroadrvpark.com). Other than Wi-Fi, the campground has few amenities, but the setting is pretty and the price is right ($20 for hookups, $10 for tent sites).

Food
Tiny Aztec boasts two Asian restaurants, **Wonderful House** (115 W. Aztec Blvd., 505/334-1832, lunch and dinner Mon.–Sat.)

NEW MEXICO AND COLORADO

and **Basil Thai** (104 S. Main., 505/334-1234, lunch and dinner Mon.–Sat.). **Smokin' J's BBQ** (1415 W. Aztec Blvd. #8-A, 505/334-2552, lunch and dinner Mon.–Sat.) offers slow-smoked ribs, pork, chicken and brisket. For coffee drinks and fresh pastries and quiches, along with frittatas, sandwiches, and soups, head to **Atomic Espresso and Bistro** (122 Main St., 505/334-0109, 7 A.M.–2 P.M. Mon.–Fri., 8 A.M.–noon Sat.). For New Mexican cuisine, try **Rubio's** (116 S. Main, 505/334-0599, all meals daily, $5–25).

Information

The folks at Aztec's **visitors center** (110 N. Ash, 505/334-9551 or 888/838-9551, www.aztecnm.com, 8 A.M.–5 P.M. Mon.–Sat.) will make you feel welcome. (It's also the home of the local Chamber of Commerce.) You can get a feel for what folks there are talking about by browsing through *The Talon,* the local community-input newspaper, available online (www.aztecnews.com).

◖ AZTEC RUINS NATIONAL MONUMENT

Step back in time at this well-preserved Chaco outlier (505/334-6174, www.nps.gov/azru, 8 A.M.–6 P.M. daily, to 5 P.M. in winter, $5 pp), located northwest of Aztec at the intersection of SR 516 and Ruins Road. This outlier is unusual because of its size and the fact that it was inhabited for some two centuries, a relatively long span in the scheme of the prehistoric Southwest. Displays in the visitors center (the former home of archaeologist Earl Morris) present some of the many artifacts recovered at the site.

The first inhabitants were either from Chaco or strongly influenced by that culture. They started modifying the landscape around A.D. 1100 with dozens of small and large structures and earthworks. The largest structure, a great house known today as the West Ruin, is a three-story, 450-room structure that included more than two dozen ceremonial kivas, including the Great Kiva in the central plaza. The site was abandoned by the late 1200s.

Today you can take a short, self-guided walk through the West Ruin, and marvel at the intricate construction of the well-preserved walls—at least those that weren't dismantled by early Anglo settlers to build their own homes. Much of the masonry, ceilings, and timber are original. This abundance of original wood offers many opportunities for tree-ring dating.

The **Great Kiva** was excavated in the 1920s and rebuilt by archaeologist Earl Morris in the 1930s. The only reconstructed great kiva in the Southwest, it offers imaginative visitors a sense of what it must have been like crowded with people, reverberating with drumbeats and dancers' footsteps.

NAVAJO LAKE STATE PARK

Created by the 1963 completion of Navajo Dam, Navajo Lake (505/632-2278, www.emnrd.state.nm.us), about 45 miles east of Farmington, is now a state park. Boasting 150 miles of shoreline, the lake is very popular, particularly on summer weekends. Visitors come to boat, fish, swim, water-ski, and even scuba dive, and they usually start at the visitors center near the dam on SR 511. The San Juan River, flowing west from the lake toward Aztec and Farmington, is famous for its record trout fishing. Get more information on permits and choice spots from **Sandstone Anglers** (888/339-9789, www.sandstoneanglers.com) in Aztec. Fishing licenses are available **Abe's Motel and Fly Shop** (505/632-2194, www.sanjuanriver.com), located at Navajo Dam.

There are 246 developed campsites (http://newmexicostateparks.reserveamerica.com, $10–18) available at the park's three campgrounds: Sims Mesa and Pine among the piñons and junipers along the lake itself, and Cottonwood, downstream along the San Juan River. About half have RV hookups. Primitive camping is permitted along the lakeshore. Fifteen miles of the 35-mile-long lake stretch north across the Colorado border, where it becomes a Colorado's Navajo State Park (www.parks.state.co.us), with rental cabins ($100/night) and an additional three campgrounds (www.coloradostateparks.reserveamerica.com)

© NATIONAL PARK SYSTEM

The Great Kiva at Aztec Ruins is the only reconstructed great kiva in the Southwest.

with 108 RV sites ($20–24) and a few tent sites ($10–16) that overlook the lake.

Most activity centers on the lake, but three miles to the west, off SR 173, Simon Canyon is home to a **pueblito,** a one-room structure dating back to 1754. Pueblitos are usually located in defensible sites (in this case, on top of a large boulder) within Dinetah, the traditional Navajo homeland, and were constructed after the Spanish Reconquest of 1692. The structures blend Navajo and Pueblo cultural traits, and many archaeologists believe they were used by Pueblo refugees who fled their villages, seeking shelter among the Navajos when the Spanish returned.

BLOOMFIELD

Founded in 1877, Bloomfield's story is similar to Farmington's: a farming and agricultural economy supplanted by coal, natural gas, and petroleum discovered in the 1940s and 1950s. To history buffs, Bloomfield is best known as the home of the Stockton Gang, a notorious gang of rustlers who terrorized the town during the late 19th century. Gang leader Port Stockton arrived in Bloomfield fresh off the Lincoln County War down south (where Billy the Kid cut his teeth as an outlaw) with 15 notches already on his gun barrel. Stockton served briefly as Bloomfield's sheriff before hopping the fence and leading a gang in robbing stagecoaches, seizing widows' ranches, and stealing enough cattle to open their own butcher shop in Durango. All the gang members were eventually killed by locals in a brief flurry of violence called the Stockton War.

Though it may not boast the amenities of Farmington or the charm of Aztec, Bloomfield (pop. 7,000) is a convenient place to stay for those planning to make a foray to Chaco Culture National Historic Park.

Salmon Ruins

Don't zip through Bloomfield without stopping at **Salmon Ruins and Heritage Park** (6131 Hwy. 64, 505/632-2103, www.salmonruins. com, 8 A.M.–5 P.M. Mon.–Fri., 9 A.M.–5 P.M. Sat. and Sun. May–Oct., from noon Sun.

© MIKE STAUFFER, NEW MEXICO TOURISM DEPARTMENT

Navajo Lake is very popular, especially on summer weekends.

Nov.–Apr., $3 pp). This choice spot, overlooking the fertile banks of the San Juan River, was originally inhabited by the Chacoans, who stayed for less than a half century. A Chaco outlier built in the shape of a C, the pueblo stood empty for 50 more years, until settlers arrived from Mesa Verde in the late 1100s and added to the construction. By the late 1200s the buildings stood empty again. One reason for the second abandonment may have been a fire around 1263. Based on archaeological evidence, a handful of adults and 35 children were standing on the roof of a kiva, perhaps to escape the flames, when it collapsed, killing them. (The incident is an element in the Anasazi mystery trilogy by Kathleen O'Neal Gear and Michael Gear.) The blaze burned hot enough to fuse the kiva sand into glass, turning the kiva into a virtual time capsule.

Some 250 rooms made up the two-story complex, which measures 430 by 150 feet. The 13-foot-high tower kiva is unusual, with six-foot-thick walls and six log-and-masonry buttresses similar to those found in European cathedrals. You can walk around the ruins themselves and then take a trail down to the **Heritage Park,** where reconstructed dwellings represent the valley's wide variety of inhabitants over the last 10,000 years. Buildings include a Navajo hogan, Jicarilla Apache tepees, a Ute lodge, Basketmaker pit houses, a replica of a trading post, and the original cabin built by homesteader George Salmon near the turn of the 20th century. The museum displays numerous artifacts and holds a research library of 5,000 volumes. You can inquire there about archaeologist-led tours of Chaco Canyon.

Accommodations and Food

A couple of chains (Best Western and Super 8) sit at the U.S. 64/U.S. 550 intersection, where it's a fast 45 miles to the turnoff for Chaco Canyon. The **Desert Rose Resort** (1900 E. Blanco Blvd., 505/632-8339 or 866/459-8339) has RV ($34–37) and tent ($26) sites a couple of miles east of the intersection.

Just west of the intersection on the south side of U.S. 64 you'll find the **Chihuahua Tortilla**

Factory (913 W. Broadway, 505/632-3321), which takes time out from supplying area grocers to cook up home-style Mexican food at reasonable prices. About 15 miles east off U.S. 64, **Wines of the San Juan** (233 NM 511, Blanco, 505/632-0879, 10 A.M.–6 P.M. Mon.

and Wed–Sat., noon–6 P.M. Sun.) is a boutique winery operated by the Arnold family, who welcome visitors to their shady, rustic setting along the river. They host occasional food events and live acoustic music on Sunday afternoons June–August.

Durango and Vicinity

The city of Durango (pop. 16,000) clings to its heritage as it welcomes visitors on their way to Mesa Verde National Park or the skiing, biking, and hiking in the San Juan Mountains to the north. Once listed among the nation's Dozen Distinctive Destinations by the National Trust for Historic Preservation, Durango's colorful past includes ancient ruins, Victorian-era buildings, and a historic railroad.

Venerable it may be, but Durango is far from musty: The 4,400 students attending Fort Lewis College help keep this a young, active place, enviably situated in the Animas River valley between the mountains and the desert and within a hour's drive of ruins, hot springs, and hikes. The city boasts plenty of brewpubs, gear stores, restaurants, and coffee shops, and the scent of pine and patchouli waft through the air.

History

Durango was founded in 1881 by the Denver & Rio Grande Railroad, and in its early years was a rough-knuckled frontier town catering to the cattle and mining industries. Prospectors, gamblers, cowhands, railroad workers, and the occasional desperado crowded the young town's barrooms and dance halls. Brawls and gunfights were common. (An early streetcar line didn't last even a year, according to one historic source, because "the crews were abusive and insulting to patrons, and the cars invariably pulled away from the railroad station before all incoming passengers could get aboard.")

Having faded after the Silver Crash of 1893, Durango found new life in the tourist traffic to Mesa Verde National Park, the restored Silverton railroad, and the lucrative industries spawned by thrill-seeking

recreationists—namely skiing, mountain biking, river-running, and zip-lining, not to mention hiking, camping, and fishing.

SIGHTS
Durango & Silverton Narrow Gauge Railroad

One of Durango's biggest tourist draws, this historic narrow-gauge railroad (479 Main Ave., 970/247-2733 or 888/872-4607, www.durangotrain.com) has been chugging through spectacular mountain scenery for over a century. The experience is authentic down to the 36-inch tracks, restored Victorian coaches, and the steam-spewing engine. At the turn of the last century, the train hauled passengers and freight—including gold and silver ore from Silverton's busy mines. Today scenery is the main draw, from the aspen forest to precipitous bridges over gorges filled with raging water. In summer you'll probably see backpackers hopping off midway at Needleton for the trailhead to Chicago Basin, a six-mile climb to a gorgeous alpine basin surrounded by three 14,000-foot peaks. (The train stops to pick them up on the way back.)

The train runs daily to Silverton early May–mid-October, leaving at 8:30–9:15 A.M. (call or check the website for the current schedule). Hundreds of thousands of people hop on board every year, so advance reservations are a good idea. Standard class is $83 adults ($49 children), but plusher options are available. The trip takes three hours each way, with a two-hour stopover in Silverton, a mining-camp-turned-boomtown now listed on the Historic Register. Winter service to Cascade Canyon, 26 miles up the line, leaves daily late November–early January

NEW MEXICO AND COLORADO

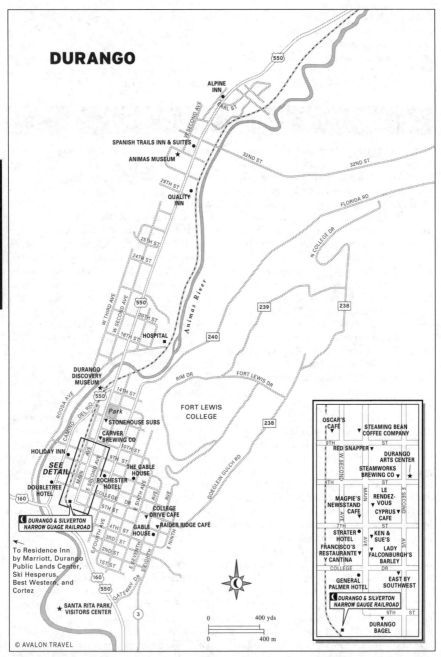

DURANGO

ALPINE INN

EARL ST

W SECOND AVE

550

SPANISH TRAILS INN & SUITES

ANIMAS MUSEUM

32ND ST

32ND ST

FLORIDA RD

29TH ST

QUALITY INN

N COLLEGE DR

25TH ST

24TH ST

Animas River

239

238

W THIRD AVE

W SECOND AVE

20TH ST

550

18TH ST

HOSPITAL

240

ROOSA AVE

CAMINO DEL RIO

DURANGO DISCOVERY MUSEUM

550

14TH ST

RIM DR

FORT LEWIS DR

FORT LEWIS COLLEGE

238

Park

STONEHOUSE SUBS

GOEGLEIN GULCH RD

CARVER BREWING CO

10TH ST

HOLIDAY INN

MAIN AVE

E SECOND AVE

9TH ST

THE GABLE HOUSE

DOUBLETREE HOTEL

ROCHESTER HOTEL

COLLEGE DR

5TH ST

COLLEGE DRIVE CAFE

160

SEE DETAIL

E FIFTH AVE

RAIDER RIDGE CAFÉ

DURANGO & SILVERTON NARROW GUAGE RAILROAD

4TH ST

E SIXTH AVE

GABLE HOUSE

E NINTH AVE

3RD ST

E ELEVENTH

2ND ST

E EIGHTH

E FOURTH AVE

1ST ST

To Residence Inn by Marriott, Durango Public Lands Center, Ski Hesperus, Best Western, and Cortez

160

550

GATEWAY DR

SANTA RITA PARK/ VISITORS CENTER

3

0   400 yds

0   400 m

© AVALON TRAVEL

Detail inset

OSCAR'S CAFÉ

STEAMING BEAN COFFEE COMPANY

9TH   ST

W SECOND

RED SNAPPER

DURANGO ARTS CENTER

STEAMWORKS BREWING CO

8TH   ST

MAGPIE'S NEWSSTAND CAFE

MAIN   AVE

LE RENDEZ-VOUS

CYPRUS CAFE

E SECOND   AVE

7TH   ST

STRATER HOTEL

KEN & SUE'S

FRANCISCO'S RESTAURANTE Y CANTINA

LADY FALCONBURGH'S BARLEY

COLLEGE   DR

GENERAL PALMER HOTEL

EAST BY SOUTHWEST

DURANGO & SILVERTON NARROW GAUGE RAILROAD

5TH   ST

DURANGO BAGEL

The Durango & Silverton narrow-gauge is a marvel of 1880s railroad engineering.

and early March–early May, and Thursday–Saturday early January–early March. Ask about seasonal events, motor coach/train combinations, or the popular photographers' special, when the train stops to allow passengers to take shots of the cars steaming through a backdrop of mountain scenery.

Other Sights

Durango's past, from prehistoric times through the Victorian era and beyond, is preserved in the **Animas Museum** (3065 W. 2nd Ave., 970/259-2402, www.animasmuseum.org, 10 A.M.–6 P.M. Mon.–Sat., 10 A.M.–4 P.M. Tues.–Sat. in winter, $4 adults, $2 ages 7–12, children under 7 free). The county historical society operates the museum in the 1904 Animas City School building, where everything from Pueblo pottery to an intact classroom are displayed.

Located on the banks of the Animas in a repurposed power plant, the **Durango Discovery Museum** (1333 Camino del Rio., 970/259-9234, www.durangodiscovery.org,

10 A.M.–5 P.M. Tues.–Sat., 1–5 P.M. Sun., $9.50 pp) has hands-on exhibits and staged demonstrations about earth science and energy. An interactive play area is geared to kids under four, while older children (and adults) can build a robot or watch a 3-D presentation from NASA.

The **Center for Southwest Studies** at Fort Lewis College has a museum (970/247-7456, http://swcenter.fortlewis.edu, hours vary) with changing exhibits that focus on the region's art, history, and environment. The permanent collection includes a photographic archive and textiles representing 800 years of weaving in the Southwest. Admission is free; campus parking permits are $2 for a full day.

ENTERTAINMENT AND EVENTS

The **Durango Melodrama** (Henry Strater Theater, 970/375-7160, www.durangomelodrama.com) throws together villains, heroes, and vaudeville routines. The action begins at 7:45 P.M. ($24 adults, $19 children), Tuesday–Sunday mid-June–August, and Wednesday–Saturday in September. Advance reservations are a good idea. For a schedule of upcoming events at the **Fort Lewis College Community Concert Hall,** contact the box office (970/247-7657, www.durangoconcerts.com). Recent performances have ranged from ballet to Big Bad Voodoo Daddy.

The **Durango Arts Center** (802 E. Second Ave., 970/259-2606, www.durangoarts.org) hosts workshops and events, including theater performances and changing exhibits of works by DAC members.

The musical stage show at the **Bar D Chuckwagon** (970/247-5753 or 888/800-5753, www.bardchuckwagon.com, $18–32 adults, $9 children) is accompanied by country music and hearty Western cooking. It's nine miles north of Durango at 8080 County Road 250, and the show happens daily at 7:30 P.M. Memorial Day–Labor Day. Reservations are required.

In town, the **Scoot'n Blues Café and Lounge** (900 Main Ave., 970/259-1400, www. scootnblues.com) is a good bet for live music, and claims to have Durango's best happy hour 4–6 P.M. Monday–Friday. The **Abbey Theatre** (128 E. College Dr., 970/385-1711) hosts live shows most weekends, many of them roots-flavored national acts. For the latest on Durango's after-dark scene, pick up a free copy of the *Durango Telegraph* or visit the Durango Late Night website (www.durangolatenight.com).

Snowdown (www.snowdown.org) is a "cabin fever reliever" week of fun in late January or early February. In March the **Durango Independent Film Festival** (970/375-7779, www.durangofilm.org) brings U.S. and world premieres and juried events. That same month, visitors from across the country gather at Fort Lewis College (www.fortlewis.edu) for **Hozhoni Days,** a cultural celebration of the more than 120 tribes represented by the college's student population. Highlights are a powwow and queen pageant.

April brings bluegrass picking and plucking to downtown venues during the **Durango Bluegrass Meltdown** (970/259-7200, www. durangomeltdown.com), and over Memorial Day weekend the **Iron Horse Bicycle Classic** (970/259-4621, www.ironhorsebicycleclassic.

com), one of the 10 largest bicycle events in the country, sees cyclists racing the train to Silverton, a bike swap meet, and other events. In June amateur and professional paddlers participate in a kayak rodeo, races, and a river parade during the weekend-long **Animas River Days** (970/903-5505, www.animasriverdays. org). **Music in the Mountains** (970/385-6820, www.musicinthemountains.com) starts in July and features three weeks of classic music performances at several venues, including the Durango Mountain Resort.

Durango's Wild West roots live on in its many annual **rodeos,** including the Durango Pro Rodeo Series and Lucky Seven Rodeo in June and July. Also in July, the annual **Fiesta Days** (www.durangofiestadays.com) celebrate Western life with a parade and numerous rodeo events. Tractor pulls, auctions, and a livestock show happen in August during the **La Plata County Fair.** August is also the month of the four-day **Railfest,** with visiting locomotives and rail-themed events.

The juried **Autumn Arts Festival** takes over several blocks downtown in mid-September. Early in October, the **Durango Cowboy Poetry Gathering** (970/749-2995, www.durangocowboygathering.org) consists of readings, dances, exhibits, food, and Colorado's largest motorless parade. The **Durango Heritage Festival** (970/382-9298, www.durangoheritagecelebration.org) includes reenactments and other events sure to appeal to fans of La Belle Epoque.

SHOPPING

Many of Durango's art galleries stay open late on Friday evenings in the summer and during gallery walks in May and September. For Western and Native American art, head for **Sorrel Sky** (828 Main Ave., 970/247-3555 or 866/878-3555, www.sorrelsky.com) or **Rain Dance Gallery** (945 Main Ave., 970/375-2708, www.raindancegallery.com), where you can also select a handmade chapeau or custom saddle from **Durango Custom Hats & Saddles** (970/385-8486, www.durangocustomhatsandsaddles.com). The **Toh-Atin Gallery** (145 W. Ninth St., 970/247-8277 or 800/525-0384, www.toh-atin.com) has been in business since 1957 and stocks gorgeous and expensive native and Southwest art and crafts, including piles of Navajo rugs.

Many stores in Durango, such as **Backcountry Experience** (1205 Camino del Rio, 970/247-5830 or 800/648-8519, www.bcexp.com), stock a wide variety of outdoor gear. **Gardenswartz** has two locations: 863 Main Avenue (970/247-2660) and 780 Main Avenue (970/259-6696). **Pine Needle Mountaineering** (835 Main Ave., 970/247-8728 or 800/607-0364, www.pineneedle.com) is another good source of gear and info.

RECREATION
Hiking
Hiking options are many, with the steep, forested slopes of the La Plata Mountains and the San Juan National Forest practically surrounding the city. Backpackers could amble for days in the half-million-acre Wenimuche Wilderness, northeast of town near the Vallecito reservoir. Be warned that most area trails involve at least some steep slopes, and elevations topping 10,000 feet may leave you gasping.

Those unaccustomed to high-altitude hiking can warm up with the mostly level and popular **Animas River Trail,** which runs seven miles along the river and is easily accessed from downtown. Also easy is the one-mile climb to **Raider Ridge** overlooking the Fort Lewis College campus, the city, and the La Plata Mountains. (For the trailhead, take College Drive, turn south on 8th Avenue and then east on 3rd Street, where the trail starts.) The steep, shaley **Hogsback** trail (two miles round-trip) tops out at nearly 7,500 feet, the highest point within the Durango Mountain Park east of town. To get there, go north on Main Avenue past 22nd Street, turn west on Glenisle and south on Leyden. The trailhead is at the end of the street.

As you circumnavigate **Animas Mountain** (6.2 miles round-trip), the scene shifts from great city views to the La Plata range, with peaks among Colorado's famed "14-ers." From downtown, go north on Main Avenue, west on

32nd Street, and north again on 4th Avenue to the trailhead.

In the San Juan National Forest north of town, Haflin Canyon leads to **Missionary Ridge.** This strenuous hike (6.5 miles round-trip) takes you through numerous ecological zones 6,600–9,400 feet. Reach the trailhead by heading east on 32nd Street, turning left on County Road 250 at the end, and driving five more miles to the sign on the right for Haflin Creek.

Just north of Silverton, the spectacular **Ice Lake Trail** (nine miles round-trip) starts at nearly 10,000 feet and climbs steeply above timberline to a basin splashed with wildflowers and surrounded by peaks. If you don't have the time or lung power to make it to the finish, you can call it a day at Lower Ice Lake, just below the tree line. The trail begins at Mineral Springs Campground, two miles north of Silverton off U.S. 550 and FR 585.

Mountain Biking
Durango is one of the most fat tire–happy cities in the country, an infatuation that dates to the 19th-century Durango Wheel Club. In 1990 the city was home to the first-ever Mountain Bike Championships, and in 2001 it hosted one of the World Cup Mountain Biking competitions. Many world-champion riders have lived in town or still do live there. Good rides include the short and long loops at **Log Chutes** (moderately difficult), the tough, steep climb over 11,750-foot **Kennebec Pass** northwest of town (28 miles one-way), and the **Dry Fork Loop** on the edge of town, with six miles of single-track in an 18-mile ride. This is a segment of the 460-mile **Colorado Trail,** which crosses eight mountain ranges, seven national forests, six wilderness areas, and five rivers on its way from Durango to Denver.

Hermosa Creek is another excellent local single-track, running 21 miles from Purgatory to Hermosa, nine miles north of Durango. Two river crossings are involved, which can get deep in the spring and early summer. For more information on biking in the area, stop by **Mountain Bike Specialists** (949 Main Ave., 970/247-4066, www.mountainbikespecialists.com). For

© KATHLEEN BRYANT

The gorgeous and steep Ice Lake Trail begins near Silverton.

bike rentals, starting at $25 per day, head to **Pedal the Peaks** (598B Main Ave., 970/259-6880, www.pedalthepeaks.biz) or **Hassle Free Sports** (2615 Main Ave., 970/259-3874 or 800/835-3800, www.hasslefreesports.com).

Rafting and Kayaking

The Animas River winding through downtown Durango is only the beginning; Durango's river offerings extend to the nearby Dolores and Piedras Rivers as well. You can get inspired watching kayakers tackle the course set up in the Animas River just off Santa Rita Park and then sign up with one of the city's many white-water guide services in kiosks along Main Avenue. These include **Flexible Flyers Rafting** (970/247-4628 or 800/346-7741, www.flexibleflyersrafting.com), **Mountain Waters Rafting** (970/259-4191 or 800/585-8243, www.durangorafting.com), and **Mild to Wild Rafting** (970/247-4789 or 800/567-6745, www.mild2wildrafting.com). Rates for two-hour trips start as low as $23 per person ($23 children).

Skiing

Purgatory at Durango Mountain Resort (970/247-9000 or 800/982-6103, www.duragomountainresort.com) is 25 miles north of Durango on Highway 250. This top-flight resort offers 40 miles of trails spread over 1,360 acres and 2,000 vertical feet, with 11 lifts, including a six-person high-speed quad, to get you to the top. Two terrain parks cater to novice and expert shredders. The resort receives an average annual snowfall of 260 inches, and backcountry Snow Cat skiing trips take advantage of thousands of acres of untracked terrain. Lift tickets start at $65 per day for adults, and a full range of dining, accommodations, equipment rentals, and shopping choices are available at the resort. In summer the slopes are taken over by hikers, mountain bikers, and guests enjoying the alpine slide, mini golf, Frisbee golf, and scenic chairlift rides. Beginning in late November, the resort runs a **skier shuttle** (970/385-8901, ext. 0) from Durango for $10 per person round-trip.

At the other end of the spectrum is the

family-run hill called **Ski Hesperus** (9848 Hwy. 160, 970/259-3711, www.ski hesperus. com), 11 miles west of Durango, with only one lift and a handful of runs. On the bright side, it's cheap (adult passes are $37 per day) and usually much less crowded.

For ski supplies and information in Durango, stop by the **Ski Barn** (3533 Main Ave., 970/247-1923 or 800/796-7472, http:// shopskibarndurango.com) or **Hassle Free Sports** (2615 Main Ave., 970/259-3874 or 800/835-3800, www.hasslefreesports.com). Those are also good places to get the scoop on **cross-country skiing** near Durango, including popular trails at Haviland Lake, Molas Pass, and the Purgatory Ski Touring Center.

Fishing

Surrounded by free-flowing rivers and high mountain lakes, Southwest Colorado has some of the best fishing in the country. Anglers can start with the Animas River in town and fan out to rivers like the San Juan, Dolores, and Piedras. Nearby lakes include Molas, Little Molas, Andrews, Haviland, and Henderson. The Vallecito, McPhee, and Navajo reservoirs are also good spots for trout, salmon, pike, bass, crappie, and bluegill.

Several local outfitters offer guided fly-fishing trips and gear, including **Duranglers** (923 Main Ave., 970/385-4081 or 888/347-4346, www.duranglers.com). Their website is a great source for local fishing info.

Other Activities

Historic **Trimble Hot Springs** (6475 County Rd. 203, 970/247-0111 or 877/811-7111, www. trimblehotsprings.com, $15 adults, $9.50 children) is seven miles north of Durango on Highway 550. They offer spa services in addition to hot and cold soaking pools and are open year-round 9 A.M.–10 or 11 P.M. daily.

For **horseback rides** into the mountains, as well as winter sleigh rides, contact the **Rapp Corral** (970/247-8454, www.rappcorral.com). Rides start at $40 per person for one hour. The **Durango Soaring Club** (970/247-9037, www. soardurango.com) offers glider rides over the Animas Valley mid-May–September, weather permitting, starting at $100 per person for 20 minutes of soaring. **Southwest Adventure Guides** (970/259-0370 or 800/642-5389, www. mtnguide.net) offers rock climbing, backpacking, and mountaineering in summer and ice climbing, mountaineering, and avalanche safety courses in winter.

Soaring Tree Top Adventures (970/769-2357, www.soaringtreetopadventures.com) boasts the largest and highest zip line canopy tour in the country, reachable only via the Durango train. More than two dozen steep zip lines—over a mile and a quarter in all—connect platforms in a pristine Ponderosa forest, crossing and recrossing the Animas River. They added their longest span yet—1,400 feet—in 2008. Guides assist at every platform to make sure you're safely harnessed in. The price ($439 pp) includes round-trip transportation on the train, lunch, and a half day of flying through the trees.

ACCOMMODATIONS

Rates at many of Durango's hotels vary with the season, in some cases dropping almost by half during winter months.

$50-100

Inexpensive motels are easy to find in Durango, particularly on Highway 160 toward the outskirts of town. Places in this price range include the **Alpine Inn** (3515 N. Main Ave., 970/247-4042, www.alpineinn.info) and the **Spanish Trails Inn & Suites** (3141 Main Ave., 970/247-4173, www.spanishtrails.com).

$100-150

This price range is mostly the domain of chain hotels, including **Holiday Inn** (800 Camino del Rio, 970/247-5393), **DoubleTree Hotel** (501 Camino del Rio, 970/259-6580), **Quality Inn** (2930 N. Main Ave., 970/259-5373), and the **Best Western Durango Inn & Suites** (21382 U.S. 160 West, 970/247-3251).

Over $150

Built in 1892, the **Rochester Hotel** (726 E. 2nd Ave., 970/385-1920 or 800/664-1920, www.rochesterhotel.com, $170–260) has 15 renovated rooms and suites in a gentrified area of galleries and cafés. A full breakfast is included with a night's stay. The lobby is decorated with movie posters, recalling Durango's former nickname, "The Hollywood of the Rockies." Built the same year, **The Gable House B&B** (805 E. 5th Ave., 970/247-4982, www.durangobedandbreakfast.com, $155–210), listed on the National Register of Historic Places, is a turreted Queen Anne furnished with antiques. Its shady wraparound veranda looks onto a quiet street in the heart of town.

The **Apple Orchard Inn** (7758 County Rd. 203, 970/247-0751 or 800/426-0751, www.appleorchardinn.com) is located eight miles north of Durango in the lovely Animas Valley near Trimble Hot Springs. The only AAA four-diamond B&B in the Durango area, the inn has four rooms in the main house ($160–185) and separate cottages with covered porches ($210–250). Some rooms have river-rock fireplaces and

The Strater Hotel anchors Durango's historic downtown.

mountain views, along with access to the inn's four-plus acres of gardens and heirloom orchards.

Main Avenue is home to two stately hotels that date back to Durango's 19th-century roots. The AAA four-diamond **❰ General Palmer Hotel** (567 Main Ave., 970/247-4747 or 800/523-3358, www.generalpalmerhotel.com, $120–235) was built in 1898. The hotel retains a period feel with leaded and stained glass, lots of brass and oak, and a gracious lobby. A continental breakfast is included, and you can also head around the corner for a bite at the **Palace Grill** (970/247-2018, lunch and dinner daily, $9–32) or a tipple at the **Quiet Lady Tavern** (970/247-2018, 11 A.M.–closing daily).

On the next block, the **❰ Strater Hotel** (699 Main Ave., 970/247-4431 or 800/247-4431, www.strater.com, $170–250), built in 1887, has been operated since 1926 by three generations of the Barker family, who have amassed an impressive collection of Victorian walnut furniture for the hotel's 93 rooms. The ornate redbrick building also houses two bars, a theater, and a restaurant. At the **Diamond Belle Saloon** (970/247-4431, lunch daily and light fare most evenings), servers dress in Victorian finery and a piano player tinkles ragtime beneath an $11,000 chandelier. (Louis L'Amour wrote a few of his Western page-turners there.) Laid-back but classy, the **Office Spiritorium** (970/247-4431, 4 P.M.–2 A.M. daily) hosts live music most evenings. Award-winning New American cuisine is on the menu at the **Mahogany Grille** (970/247-4433, dinner daily, entrées $18–35). The hotel's Henry Strater Theater is the oldest continually running theatre in the city; contact the hotel for showtimes and offerings.

Campgrounds

No shortage here: There are more than 900 public and private campsites within 40 miles of Durango. The San Juan National Forest's Columbine Ranger District (970/884-2512) administers campsites ranging $14–17 per night; some sites can be reserved (877/444-6777, www.recreation.gov). Many are 20 miles northeast of Durango near the Lemon and Vallecito reservoirs. The popular **Junction Creek campground** (44 sites, 14 with hookups) is a only a few miles northwest of town. To get there from North Main, turn right (west) on 25th Street and continue three miles to a Y intersection; then follow the signs to the campground (another two miles). For information about dispersed camping, contact the San Juan Public Lands Office (970/247-4874).

Private campgrounds include the **Alpen Rose RV Park** (970/247-5540 or 877/259-5791, www.alpenroservpark.com, Apr.–Oct., $40–48), five miles north of town on Highway 550; and the **Durango East KOA** (970/247-0783 or 800/562-0793, $35–50 with hookups), seven miles east of town on Highway 160.

FOOD
Coffee Shops and Cafés
The **Steaming Bean Coffee Company** (915 Main Ave., 970/385-7901, www.thebean.com, 6:30 A.M.–7 P.M. Mon.–Sat., 7 A.M.–5 P.M. Sun.) is a cozy place with Internet computers, local art displays, and a kids corner. Another good place for a caffeinated pick-me-up and a newspaper in the morning is **Magpie's Newsstand Café** (707 Main Ave., 970/259-1159, 7 A.M.–10 P.M. daily), with outdoor seating when the weather is nice. **Durango Bagel** (106 E. 5th St., 970/385-7297) opens daily at 6:30 A.M. near the train station and advertises that "Bikers love bagels because they fit easily on your handlebars." The **College Drive Café** (666 E. College Dr., 970/247-5322) offers breakfast all day, including a half dozen tasty versions of eggs Benedict for under $10 (open for all meals Wed.–Sun.). **Stonehouse Subs** (140 E. 12th St., 970/247-4882, lunch daily), a local favorite, builds sandwiches for $7–20 on freshly baked bread.

A popular breakfast choice, **Oscar's Café** (18 Town Plaza, 970/247-0526, breakfast and lunch daily) serves French toast, burgers, BLTs, chili, and other diner-style delights for under $10. (Bring cash; credit cards aren't accepted.) Fruit smoothies, wraps, salads, and soups ($5–8) are on the menu at the **Raider Ridge Café** (509 E. 8th Ave., #4, 907/375-9727, http://

raiderridgecafe.com, breakfast and lunch daily). Everything is freshly made and under $10.

Brewpubs
Durango calls itself the "Napa Valley of Beer," and four microbreweries are strung along the Animas River: Durango Brewing Company, SKA, Steamworks, and Carver. Hearty breakfasts are a specialty at **Carver Brewing Co.** (1022 Main Ave., 970/259-2545, www.carverbrewing.com, all meals Mon.–Sat., breakfast and lunch Sun.), which has live music and an outdoor beer garden. **Lady Falconburgh's Barley Exchange** (640 N. Main Ave., 970/382-9664, www.ladyfalconburgh.biz, $8–20) stocks more than 100 microbrews and imported beers downstairs in the Century Mall. They open the doors for lunch and keep them open late.

Home-brewed sodas (along with home-brewed beer, of course) are on tap at **Steamworks Brewing Co.** (801 E. 2nd Ave., 970/259-9200, www.steamworksbrewing.com, lunch and dinner daily). They serve a wide-ranging menu, from pizza to Cajun boil (entrées $7–20), on an outdoor patio. **El Rancho** (975 Main Ave., 970/259-8111, 10 A.M.–2 A.M. daily) is a tavern that's been around since 1915, when 20-year-old Jack Dempsey scored his first knockout on the premises before going on to become World Heavyweight Champion. Some historians now say it happened across the street, but in either case a mural on the wall of the old Central Hotel commemorates the event.

Other Restaurants Downtown
With more restaurants per capita than San Francisco, Durango ranks as a foodie town. The ◀ **Cyprus Café** (725 E. 2nd Ave., 970/385-6884) is a charming spot in an old Victorian home that specializes in Mediterranean dishes such as *imam biyaldi* and linguine puttanesca, served daily for lunch and dinner ($10–32). Opened in 1968, **Francisco's Restaurante y Cantina** (619 Main Ave., 970/247-4098) is the oldest restaurant in Durango. Beyond classic Mexican entrées, they serve pasta, chicken, steaks, and seafood for lunch and dinner ($8–26). Steaks are a favorite at the **Ore House** (147

THE SAN JUAN SKYWAY

A spectacularly scenic loop winds for 236 miles through the San Juan and Uncompahgre National Forests north of Durango. This national scenic byway passes historic mining towns, prehistoric ruins, and hot springs as it crosses four mountain passes over 10,000 feet. Depending on the season, take your pick from waterfalls, wildflowers, Victorian mansions, alpine forests, icy peaks, and starry skies. Although you can drive the skyway in a day, the views and outdoor offerings merit at least two or three. It's paved the whole way around, but dozens of dirt roads head off into the hills for bicycling, hiking, backpacking, fishing, rafting, and off-roading.

Starting in Durango, the skyway heads north on U.S. 550, parallel to the Animas River and the rail line past Trimble and Hermosa, before heading on its own toward Purgatory Resort. As you climb over Coal Bank Pass (10,640 feet) and Molas Pass (10,910 feet), you'll appreciate how difficult and expensive the "Million Dollar Highway" was to build. (The name is also thought to come from the value of the ore-bearing fill used to build the road.) The town of **Silverton** is a national historic landmark at the other end of the train line from Durango, with Old West gunfights staged in the street during the summer.

Keep going up U.S. 550 to Red Mountain Pass (11,008 feet), the highest paved pass in the San Juans, which is surrounded by mining ghost towns and alpine scenery. Following the route of an historic toll road, you'll pass through the rust-colored Red Mountain, a collapsed volcanic cone that gave up $750 million worth of gold, silver, and other minerals to early miners. Keep going through the tunnels and wa-terfalls of the precipitous Uncompahgre Gorge to reach **Ouray,** another Victorian-era mining town-turned-tourist magnet. Box Canyon Falls and the Ouray Hot Springs are two of the more popular attractions in the area, and Mt. Sneffels (14,150 feet) rises to the west in the center of its own wilderness area. In winter, Ouray becomes a worldwide hot spot for ice climbing, with the Ouray Ice Festival held every January.

U.S. 550 continues north to **Ridgway,** home to a great public hot spring (this one is outdoors) and authentic enough to be chosen as the film location for classic Westerns like *How the West Was Won* and *True Grit.* Turn left (west) onto SR 62 and cross the Dallas Divide (8,970 feet) to reach **Placerville** on the San Miguel River, where you should take SR 145 southeast. Soon a short side road leads east to the box canyon sheltering the painfully picturesque mining town of **Telluride,** where locals and celebrities rub elbows at music festivals and a world-famous ski resort.

SR 145 continues south over Lizard Head Pass (10,222 feet), with trails leading into the Lizard Head Wilderness near Mt. Wilson (14,246 feet). Picnic pull-outs and historic markers dot the roadway, as does the Ames Power Plant, producer of the world's first commercial supply of alternating current. The road passes more cliffs and waterfalls to tiny **Rico.** Follow the Dolores River, considered one of the top 50 trout streams in the country, southwest to Dolores, home to the Anasazi Heritage Center and only a short hop from **Cortez.** U.S. 160 from Cortez to Mesa Verde National Park and Durango makes up the southern leg of the skyway.

E. College Dr., 970/247-5707, dinner daily, $17–45), which highlights local, sustainable ingredients.

Ken and Sue's (636 Main Ave., 970/385-1801) serves New American fare such as pistachio-crusted grouper and Southwestern Cobb salad ($9–23) for lunch daily and dinner Thursday–Sunday. Dining is available on the patio near the fountain. **Red Snapper** (144 E. 9th St., 970/259-3417) is a sure bet for good seafood, served daily for dinner in an aquarium-filled dining room, along with steak and other hearty dishes ($20–50). Their salad bar is Durango's best and biggest. At **East By Southwest** (160 E. College Ave., 970/247-5533, www.eastbysouthwest.com, lunch Mon.–Sat. and dinner daily), the sushi is surprisingly good for being this far from a coast. The menu extends to include steak, vegetarian dishes, noodles, and 30 kinds of sake.

INFORMATION

Durango's main **visitors center** is run by the **Durango Area Tourism Office** (970/247-3500 or 800/525-8855, www.durango.org) in the Santa Rita Park at the south end of town. During the summer, visit the information kiosk on the 700 block of Main Avenue, near the Durango Coffee Company.

GETTING THERE AND AROUND

For destinations beyond walking distance, hop aboard the free **trolley** that runs up and down Main Avenue every 20 minutes 7 A.M.–10 P.M. in summer, or take one of the **Durango Lift buses** (970/375-4940) that go to Fort Lewis College and elsewhere ($1 pp).

The **Durango-La Plata County Airport** (www.durangoairport.com) is 14 miles southeast of the city on Highway 172, and is served by United Express and Frontier (to Denver), and US Airways (to Phoenix), as well as the Alamo, Avis, Budget, Hertz, and National car rental agencies. Durango's **Greyhound** station (970/247-2755 or 800/231-2222) is located within the city's capacious new transit center at 250 W. 8th Street.

CHIMNEY ROCK ARCHAEOLOGICAL AREA

About 40 miles east of Durango, a rocky ridge marked by pinnacles at either end rises above the Southern Ute Indian Reservation. Spread over the ridge is a 1,000-year-old village, preserved as **Chimney Rock Archaeological Area** (970/883-5359, www.chimneyrockco. org, 9 A.M.–4 P.M. daily, $10 for parking and tours). From May 15 through September, Forest Service rangers and volunteers guide walking tours across the ridge to view the kiva, pueblo, and other rooms, which include a possible guardhouse. Special events include archaeo-astronomy programs and monthly moonrise programs with live flute performances. To get there, take U.S. 160 east about 38 miles, turning south on SR 151. The park entrance is about three miles on the right. Tours begin at the visitors cabin, a half mile from the entrance.

Mesa Verde and Vicinity

◖ MESA VERDE NATIONAL PARK

Between Cortez and the Mancos River looms a series of forested mesas that harbor such a wealth of prehistoric architecture that they have been declared both a national park and a World Heritage Site by UNESCO. Amid the steep canyons that slice across this "green table" (from the Spanish) are more than 4,800 known archaeological sites and many more yet undiscovered. About 600 of these are the famous **cliff dwellings**, built when Mesa Verde reached its height between A.D. 1100 and 1300.

Resembling apartment blocks in a city made of stone, these extraordinary structures are built from the same rock as the huge ledges that soar above them. Natural forces and looters have taken their toll; only a few cliff dwellings have been excavated and reinforced enough to admit visitors, but a stroll down these dusty lanes is enough to make 700 years seem like nothing, and the echo of residents' voices and the smoke of their campfires are more than just a distant memory.

The Setting

The park covers a series of mesas and canyons that form the northern drainage of the Mancos River, which flows through the Ute Reservation to the south. The fingerlike mesas are formed by three sandstone formations, or layers, that together make up the Mesa Verde Group. Most of the large alcoves are found in Ute, Navaho, Soda, and Morefield Canyons, hollowed out of Cliff House Sandstone, the uppermost formation. This sedimentary layer was formed beneath an inland sea between 70 and 100 million years ago. Fine-grained sands deposited in shallow water formed layers of sandstone and

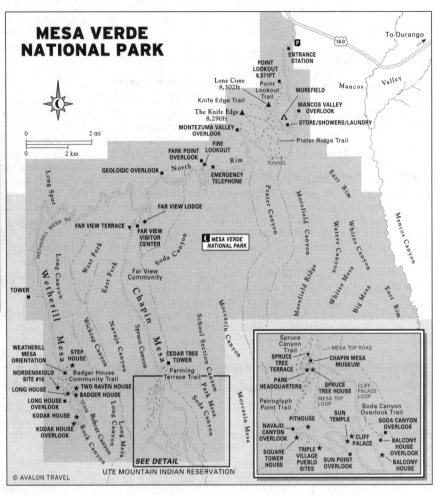

shale. When the softer Mancos Shale beneath it crumbles, the harder sandstone splits away in blocks or, occasionally, huge arches, some of which eventually weather into alcoves reaching back deep into the mesa. This often happens near springs, which help hasten the weathering of the soft sandstone. Percolating rainwater gets redirected horizontally above the less-permeable layer of shale, creating larger alcoves and convenient springs for their inhabitants.

This area is a better place to live than you might think. Sure, the water supply is limited

and no streams run year-round. Most canyons only see flowing water during the summer monsoons or spring runoff. The growing season is long, though—up to 150 days without frost per year, and up this high (7,000 feet) the summer heat isn't so bad, which makes it easier to grow crops. In summer only the front buildings in the alcoves are hit by the sun's vertical rays, leaving the rest back in the cool shadows. In winter, however, the low sun reaches far back into the alcoves, warming the stone walls as well as the alcoves. It's not unusual for it to be 10–20°F warmer up there than in Montezuma Valley to the north, even though parts of the mesa are over 2,000 feet higher. Over the millennia, dust deposited by winds from the southwest covered the mesa tops with a layer of deep red soil. Combine that with the dependable summer rains in July and August, and Mesa Verde becomes a relatively comfortable, fertile place.

The highest portions of Mesa Verde are covered with large Douglas firs, ponderosa pines, and aspen. Utah juniper and piñon pine are the most common trees, and provided wood for building, tools, and fires, as well as tasty, nutritious nuts. Brush species such as mountain mahogany, Gambel oak, and serviceberry are concentrated toward the northern end of the park, and big sagebrush, cacti, and flowers occur in the sandy canyon bottoms. More than 200 species of birds live there, from sociable groups of wild turkeys to hummingbirds. Mule deer and coyotes are common, but bears and mountain lions are rarely seen.

History

Mesa Verde has been occupied for about 1,300 years. Nomadic tribes first arrived there at the fringe of the Rocky Mountains thousands of years ago, but semipermanent dwellings weren't built until around A.D. 500. People dug pit houses in canyon alcoves and on top of the mesas, covering them with flat or raised roofs of logs and soil. They wove outstanding baskets from plant fibers and started to make pottery and use the bow and arrow. By A.D. 1000, these houses were being built primarily aboveground on the mesa tops. Roofed dwellings gradually became grouped together to form small villages, called pueblos (Spanish for "village") by archaeologists. Construction methods changed from mud-covered poles to layered sandstone masonry, and the builders left open courts amid the rooms. Pit houses deepened and changed in function until they became the mostly underground ceremonial chambers called kivas.

Ancestral Puebloan culture reached its climax during the Classic Pueblo Period (A.D. 1100–1300), when the inhabitants moved down into the cliff alcoves and built most of the grand dwellings visible today. (It's strange to think that more people likely lived in the surrounding Montezuma Valley in the 12th century than they do today.) Large alcoves facing south or southwest were advantageous for the sunlight they captured in the winter. If the floor of an alcove was uneven, builders brought in dirt to even out the surface. Kivas were dug for religious rituals and possibly social events and used by both men and women. Rocks too big to move were incorporated into the construction. It obviously took a large population working in harmony to erect buildings like this—Cliff Palace alone had more than 150 rooms and was home to about 100 people. Exquisite pottery was a hallmark of this period, with black geometric designs on a gray or white background. Shell jewelry, turquoise, bone scrapers, and stone tools have all been unearthed in garbage piles or burial sites.

Farming provided most of the food, predominantly the classic trio of corn, beans, and squash, including the violet-striped bean and a variety of corn resistant to drought. The lack of constantly flowing streams meant the Mesa Verdeans had to depend on what little rain fell, but this was usually enough. Archaeologists experimented with growing corn in the park from 1919 to 1972 using dryland farming techniques like those of the Hopi, and the crop failed in only three of those years. Storage rooms were incorporated into the buildings to hold excess harvests over winter.

Drought arrived around A.D. 1273 and lasted until 1296. By this point the masonry had begun to decline in quality. The soil may have become less fertile, overtaxed by the demands of a rising population. Residents began to leave as the local springs dried up, moving south into northern Arizona and New Mexico. Their descendants make up parts of the Hopi and Rio Grande Pueblo tribes. Shortly after A.D. 1300 Mesa Verde was mostly deserted.

The ruins stood empty for centuries. White settlers explored them in the 19th century, after the first official report of the enigmatic sites

FIRE ON THE MOUNTAIN

Wildfires are a natural part of Southwestern ecosystems, so when fighting fires becomes part of the management strategy for places like Mesa Verde, it's no surprise that things can quickly get out of balance. Four-fifths of the park has been burned since a policy of total fire suppression was put into effect in 1908, with an average of eight fires racing across the high mesas every year since 1920. Since 1975 the numbers have climbed to 20-25 burns every year, including four major fires between 1996 and 2002 that burned over half the park.

In July 2000, an unusually hot, dry month, a lightning strike outside the park sparked a blaze that eventually scorched 23,607 acres on the eastern side of Mesa Verde. Three-hundred-foot flames were too hot for flame retardants to work, and the path of destruction eventually covered an area eight miles long and four miles wide. It took 1,106 firefighters nine days to put out the Bircher Fire, and much of the area is still scarred.

Unnaturally large wildfires, caused by a combination of hot, dry weather and the buildup of fuels, are expensive by any calculation. The Bircher Fire cost $5.6 million to fight and closed the park for two weeks, spelling lost revenue to the park and local businesses. Big fires can also alter the local ecology, as plant species vary widely in their response to fire. Plants with light, windblown seeds (like fireweed) easily colonize burn sites. Other species may regrow from surviving below-ground tissues (aspen) or seed stores (raspberry). Some conifers germinate in the heat of a burn, though it may take

centuries for forests to fully regrow. On the bright side, the Bircher Fire burned only a few park buildings, and scorched areas revealed previously hidden archaeological treasures. After a 1996 fire—one-quarter the size of the Bircher Fire—372 new sites were discovered.

© KATHLEEN BRYANT

Fireweed earned its name for being able to grow after a wildfire.

by Professor J. S. Newberry in an 1859 geological report. In 1874 surveyor W. H. Jackson became the first Anglo to enter a cliff dwelling when he crawled inside Two-Story Cliff House (now part of neighboring Ute Mountain Ute Tribal Park). In December 1888 local rancher Richard Wetherill and his brother-in-law Charles Mason rode out onto Sun Point to look for lost cattle. Through the blowing snow they spotted Cliff Palace. They tied together trees to scramble down into the site, and within a

couple days they had discovered Spruce Tree House and Square Tower House as well.

Mesa Verde was declared the first cultural national park in the country in 1906, and it became a World Cultural Heritage Site in 1978.

Entering Mesa Verde

The entrance to the park is off U.S. 160, 10 minutes from Cortez and 45 minutes from Durango. After passing through the entrance station ($15 per vehicle Memorial Day–Labor

© KATHLEEN BRYANT

Mesa Verde's Cliff Palace can be explored on a ranger-guided tour.

Day, $10 otherwise), the park road winds its way up the face of the mesa, reaching the turn-off for **Morefield Ranger Station** and the adjacent **Morefield Campground** after four miles. The ranger station is open late May–August.

From the campground the road continues to wind and climb, passing a viewing point at Park Point before reaching the **Far View Visitor Center** (970/529-5011, 8 A.M.–7 P.M. daily Memorial Day–Labor Day, then 8 A.M.–5 P.M. daily to mid-Oct.), 15 miles from the entrance. The center has exhibits on Native American crafts and conveniences that include an ATM, which is handy for buying tickets to tours of Cliff Palace, Balcony House, and Long House ($3 pp per tour). **Far View Lodge** is across the road from the visitors center.

At the visitors center, the road splits: head left (south) to reach the Far View Sites complex and Chapin Mesa. Go right (west) to reach Wetherill Mesa, which is open Memorial Day–Labor Day.

Chapin Mesa

From the Far View Visitor Center, head south for the road onto Chapin Mesa. At about five miles, after passing turnoffs for **Cedar Tree Tower** and the **Far View Sites Complex,** you'll reach the turnoff to **Park Headquarters** (970/529-4465, www.nps.gov/meve) and the **Chapin Mesa Museum** (970/529-4631, 8 A.M.–5 P.M. daily, to 6:30 P.M. Memorial Day–mid-Oct.). The entire history of Mesa Verde is on display there, with an orientation video shown every half hour. There's also a cafeteria (daily, hours vary seasonally) and a gift shop at Spruce Tree Terrace.

From the museum, a popular half-mile trail descends into Spruce Tree Canyon before leading to **Spruce Tree House.** The third-largest and the best-preserved cliff dwelling in the park, Spruce Tree House had eight kivas and about 130 rooms, and was thought to have 60–90 residents. This is the easiest cliff dwelling to enter. You can tour it yourself for free from spring to fall (rangers are on duty) and take a ranger-guided tour three times a day in the winter.

Two other trails branch off Spruce Tree

© KATHLEEN BRYANT

A ladder protrudes from a subterranean kiva at Spruce Tree House.

Trail, the **Spruce Canyon Trail** (a 2.4-mile loop leading through the canyon ecosystem) and **Petroglyph Point Trail** (an easy 2.4-mile loop), which leads to a petroglyph panel and offers views over Navajo and Spruce Canyons. Both trails are gated—open only during visitor hours—and rangers ask that you register before starting out.

Beyond the museum, the road splits into the two loops that lead to three other large cliff dwellings. The eastern loop leads to the park's most-photographed cliff dwellings, which require tickets to tour. Visitors to **Balcony House** will need to climb ladders and stone steps and crawl through a tunnel, so it's not for the faint of heart or the easily winded. **Cliff Palace,** the largest cliff dwelling in North America and the jewel of Mesa Verde, has 150 rooms and 23 kivas sheltered in an exceptionally large alcove. It's estimated that up to 100 people lived there at its peak. (This tour involves climbing four small ladders.) The **Soda Canyon Overlook Trail** (1.2 miles round-trip, easy) starts along the loop road about a half mile past the Balcony

House parking area, and goes to the canyon edge for views of Balcony House and other sites.

The six-mile **Mesa Top Loop Road** (7:30 A.M.–sunset) passes a dozen sites, including surface dwellings and overlooks with views of cliff dwellings, all reached by short paved trails. From the overlook, it's easy to see how **Square Tower House** got its name. For a few weeks each fall, rangers lead strenuous two-hour hikes down to the ruin ($20 pp, reservations required).

Wetherill Mesa

Though Wetherill Mesa is only 12 miles from the Far View Visitor Center, allow 45 minutes for the winding road (open 9:15 A.M.–4:15 P.M. daily in summer, restricted to vehicles 25 feet and under). You'll find less traffic on this side of the park, and you could easily spend a half day exploring the mesa's trails and sites. The mesa loop is accessible only by tram (leaving every half hour 9:30 A.M.–3:30 P.M. daily), adding to the quiet experience. Amenities include a ranger kiosk, small store, and a snack bar (10 A.M.–4 P.M. daily).

COWBOY ARCHAEOLOGISTS

When the Wetherill brothers spotted the cliff dwellings of Mesa Verde, the experience sparked a passion that changed their lives. For the next several decades, these Mancos Valley ranchers-turned-archaeologists explored and recorded prehistoric sites, including Mesa Verde, Keet Seel, and Chaco Canyon, often neglecting their ranch duties to exhibit artifacts in neighboring towns or to guide visitors to the ruins.

Al Wetherill claimed to be the first of the five brothers to see Cliff Palace, late in the day when he was too weary to explore further. He wrote that the ruined city appeared like a mirage in the fading light: "It would wait. It had waited hundreds of years for the moment of discovery." His brother Richard is usually credited as being the first Anglo to visit the ruin, which he explored in the company of his brother-in-law when they were searching for lost cattle in December 1888.

Over the next day and a half the Wetherill family found two more large villages, Spruce Tree House and Square Tower House. Two years later, they had searched through nearly 200 ruins in the Mesa Verde area and turned their ranch into a small museum. They hosted explorers and travelers who came to visit the ruins. One of their guests was a young Swede named Gustav von Nordenskiold. The son of a scientist, he decided to make a detailed study of Mesa Verde's sites and hired John Wetherill as his foreman. The other four Wetherill brothers helped dig when they could free themselves from ranch chores.

Working with Nordenskiold, the Wetherills learned excavation techniques and rudimen-

tary stratigraphy, the idea that cultural material is deposited with the oldest on the bottom and newest on top. The Wetherills kept notes on each site they explored and were among the first to use a camera to record excavations. Richard often spoke with local Indians, gathering ethnographic information to help answer his questions about artifacts, a practice later used by professional archaeologists.

Applying his knowledge, Richard became the first to identify the Basketmaker culture, the earliest phase of Ancestral Pueblo life. His term was adopted by Alfred Kidder, the archaeologist who in 1927 introduced a cultural timeline still used today. Despite Kidder's report crediting Richard Wetherill for identifying the Basketmakers, more than a few professional archaeologists reviled the brothers as pothunters or dismissed them as "cowboy archaeologists." Undaunted, Richard and John stayed involved in archaeology for the rest of their lives. In 1910 Richard was murdered at Chaco Canyon, where he is buried. John established trading posts in Monument Valley and led expeditions into the Southwest's remote corners until he was an old man. Fred Blackburn, a former BLM ranger-turned-Wetherill historian, credits the brothers for introducing the world to "the archaeological riches of the Four Corners."

The Wetherills' adventures continue to inspire us, perhaps even more now that we know that the cultural resources of the Four Corners are finite in number and therefore precious. The Wetherill family collections are housed at the Anasazi Heritage Center in Dolores, Colorado.

Three trails begin near the ranger kiosk. You can hike to **Step House** for self-guided tours via a steep, 0.8-mile (round-trip) trail. Rangers on duty will explain the evidence of two separate occupations at the site from around A.D. 600 and 1200. The **Nordenskiold #16 Trail** (1 mile round-trip, easy) leads to an overlook of the sites studied by pioneering Swedish scientist Gustaf Nordenskiold, and the **Badger House Community Trail** (2.4 miles round-trip,

easy), which leads around four mesa-top sites. (Rangers at the kiosk can provide maps and describe shorter hike options to Badger House sites from tram stops.) All three trails are accessible from 9:30 A.M.–4:30 P.M. daily.

The tram makes seven stops at overlooks for Nordenskiold #16, the Badger House sites, **Kodak House,** and **Long House,** the second-largest cliff dwelling at Mesa Verde. Tickets ($3 pp, sold at the Far View Visitor Center) are required to tour Long House. The moderately strenuous tour includes a steep 0.75-mile hike to and from the overlook, as well as climbing two 15-foot ladders within the site.

Recreation

Hiking at Mesa Verde is limited to designated trails only, since the ruins and other cultural resources are so fragile. A uniformed park ranger must be present whenever you enter a cliff dwelling, and no backcountry camping is permitted. Several short trails start near the Chapin Mesa museum. Keep in mind that most of the park is over 7,000 feet above sea level. Trails can be steep and the weather hot and dry.

Three trails leave from Morefield Campground, none of which require a permit. **Point Lookout Trail** (2.2 miles round-trip, moderate) begins north of the amphitheater, climbing switchbacks to sweeping views, and the **Knife Edge Trail** (2 miles round-trip, moderate) heads to an overlook of Montezuma Valley, which is especially pretty at sunset. The challenging **Prater Ridge Trail** (7.8 miles round-trip) was scorched by the Bircher Fire but it has been reopened, giving hikers an up-close look at ecosystem recovery.

One way to have the park almost to yourself (aside from touring Wetherill Mesa on a weekday) is to explore in winter on **cross-country skis.** This offers a taste of what the mesas were like when the Wetherills stumbled across Cliff Palace over a century ago, with walls looming in dark alcoves amid the whiteness. Mesa Verde gets 80–100 inches of snow in an average winter, and some roads beyond the Far View Visitor Center are unplowed and open to cross-country skiers. (Stay on roads only, though.) Contact one of the outdoor stores in Durango for ski rentals.

Practicalities

Mesa Verde is open daily, year-round, with limited services in winter. You can book hotel and campground reservations as well as guided bus tours with options that include Cliff Palace ($25–45) through **ARAMARK** (602/441-5210 or 800/449-2288, www.visitmesaverde.com).

Next to the visitors center, ◖ **Far View Lodge** (602/441-5210 or 800/449-2288, www.visitmesaverde.com, Apr.–mid-Oct., $115–160), has rooms with great views and private porches. The lodge encompasses a gift shop and two restaurants, the **Metate Room** (dinner daily) and the **Far View Terrace cafeteria** (all meals daily).

Morefield Campground (800/449-2288, open mid-Apr.–mid-Oct.) is one of the nicest in the national park system. Four hundred sites (starting at $23) are located along loops through a grassy canyon. Reservations are accepted, though the campground rarely fills. There's a grocery store, gas station, showers, and laundry facilities in Morefield Village, as well as the **Knife Edge Café,** which serves breakfast daily May–mid-October.

UTE MOUNTAIN UTE RESERVATION

Colorado's southwest corner cradles this 596,000-acre reservation (www.utemountainute.com) leading up to the Utah and New Mexico borders and a bit beyond each. The reservation is centered around **Sleeping Ute Mountain** (9,977 feet), a laccolithic peak that really does look like a slumbering giant with his head pointing north, complete with headdress, folded arms, and volcanic plugs for toes. **Towaoc** (toe-WAY-ock), which was named for the Ute word meaning "all right," is where most of the reservation's 1,300 residents live, 11 miles south of Cortez.

Sights

One of the tribe's scenic and historic treasures is **Ute Mountain Tribal Park** (970/749-1452 or 800/847-5485, www.utemountainute.com), set aside in 1971 to preserve two beautiful canyons and their prehistoric cliff dwellings and rock art. The tribal park shares a boundary with its more-famous neighbor, Mesa Verde National Park, but in many respects the two are worlds apart. Sites have been left in their natural, unreconstructed state, and the canyons are quiet and lightly visited. The only way to enter the ruins is to hike in with a Ute guide.

THE LEGEND OF SLEEPING UTE MOUNTAIN

© KATHLEEN BRYANT

Sleeping Ute Mountain rises above the eastern horizon at Hovenweep.

In a region where mountain ranges line up like rows of shark teeth, Sleeping Ute is easy to identify by its distinctive silhouette. According to Ute stories, the mountain was once a great warrior god whose violent battle against the Evil Ones threw up the mountains and valleys all around. Wounded, he lay down to rest, and his blood formed the Mancos River and its tributaries. The sleeping god changes his blankets with the season: When his blanket of trees is light green it means spring has arrived; the blanket turns to darker green in summer, red and yellow in fall, and white in winter. When clouds gather atop the peaks and rain falls, it is said that the warrior god is pleased with his people and letting the rain clouds slip from his pockets. The mountain continues to be a spiritual touchstone for the Ute, visible for miles on the skyline of southern Colorado and playing a role in many Ute ceremonies.

The **visitors center** (970/749-1452) is 22 miles south of Cortez at the junction of U.S. 160 and U.S. 491. Tours leave from the visitors center daily at 9 A.M. The half-day tour to **Mancos Canyon** ($28 pp) is easier, while the full-day tour to **Lion Canyon** ($48 pp) involves less time spent driving, proportionally. On this one you'll climb five ladders to visit four cliff dwellings, including the **Eagle's Nest,** as impressive as Mesa Verde's ruins. Bring lunch, water, hiking gear, and your own vehicle; if you don't have your own transportation you can ride with the guide for another $10 per person. Ask about special tours to even more remote sections of the park and make reservations in advance. The park also offers overnight **camping** at primitive sites along the Mancos River ($12).

Practicalities

Towaoc is home to **Ute Mountain Casino and RV Park** (970/565-8800 or 800/258-8007, www.utemountaincasino.com), about 10 miles south of Cortez on U.S. 160, where you'll find food, accommodations, and entertainment. Take your pick from bingo, keno, poker, and blackjack tables and a variety of slot and video-poker machines. Dances are held in the Indian Village outside, including the **Bear Dance** in late May or early June.

The casino's Sleeping Ute RV Park & Campground (970/565-6544 or 800/889-5072) charges $17 and up per night. Accommodations in the 90-room hotel (888/565-8837) are $75–100. Kuchu's Restaurant serves Southwest-style food (open daily for all meals).

At **Ute Mountain Indian Pottery** (800/896-8548), adjacent to the casino complex, tribal artists paint traditional designs on pottery that is poured into ceramic molds before being turned and cleaned. Each artist signs his or her work before it is glazed and fired.

CORTEZ AND VICINITY

The closest city to Mesa Verde National Park and the Four Corners Monument is surrounded by mountains and sage flats, with huge mesas rising to the south. Sleepy Cortez (pop. 8,500) occupies land rich in native history, ranging from the seminomadic Archaic people to the Navajo, who called this spot Tsaya-toh ("rock water") for a nearby spring used to water sheep. Irrigation workers trying to bring water from the Dolores River valley were some of Cortez's first white inhabitants, beginning in 1886. At the turn of the 20th century, when many of the stone buildings that still line Main Street were built, the area was a busy livestock trading center, with herds of sheep and cattle pastured west of town. Today Cortez continues to be a shopping and service center for outlying farms and ranches as well as a primary jumping-off point for visitors to the national park.

Sights

Occupying the ornate 1909 E. R. Lamb & Co. Mercantile Building, the **Cortez Cultural Center** (25 N. Market St., 970/565-1151, www.cortezculturalcenter.org, 10 A.M.–10 P.M. Mon.–Sat., to 5 P.M. Sept.–May) lives up to its name with a museum on the area's rich indigenous heritage, as well as a gallery of local artists and a gift shop. Native dances are held there Monday–Saturday late May–end of August. Other native cultural programs at the center include demonstrations of Navajo sandpainting, flute playing, storytelling, and slide shows or lectures covering the famous World War II Code Talkers and other topics.

About four miles northwest of town is the **Crow Canyon Archaeological Center** (970/565-8975 or 800/422-8975, www.crowcanyon.org, 9 A.M.–4:30 P.M. Mon.–Fri.), a nonprofit organization focusing on the long-term archaeological investigation of the earliest inhabitants of the Four Corners. Most people come to participate in the center's long list of research and educational programs or to use the extensive research library, but if you've ever wanted to play at being Indiana Jones for a week, this is the place. You might even see something you uncover in a museum someday, since every artifact recovered is professionally curated.

The center organizes trips across the Southwest and around the world, though if you have time for only a small taste of archaeology, you can attend a Friday night lecture (free) or make reservations for a day program (Wed. and Thurs. June–Aug., $55 adults, $30 children). To get there, go a half mile north of town on U.S. 491; then take a left on County Road L and two more lefts, following the signs for the center.

Events

Late May brings the **Indian Arts and Culture Festival,** which spreads to Dolores, Mancos, Towaoc, and Mesa Verde National Park with close to a week of music, arts, crafts, and Indian dancing. Highlights include the juried Indian art market and a Navajo rug auction. Cortez's longtime history as a ranching center is celebrated during the **Ute Mountain Roundup** in June, with three days of rodeo events, plus a carnival, parade, and dances.

Saturday mornings June–October there's a local farmers market in the courthouse parking lot. In August and September, festivals featuring regional wines and beers are followed by the three-day Mancos Valley **Balloon and Art Festival,** with mass flights each morning and glows in the evenings.

Shopping

A large selection of high-quality native crafts fills the **Notah Dineh Trading Company and Museum** (345 W. Main St., 970/565-9607 or 800/444-2024, www.notahdineh.com), including pawned items and weaving supplies. Don't miss the museum downstairs, with its display cases full of old guns, beaded leatherwork, and beautiful weavings. The centerpiece is the largest Two Grey Hills rug known (12 by 18 feet), woven by Rachel Curly from 1957 to 1960, a year before the original Notah Dineh opened in the center of town. **Mesa Verde Pottery** (27601 Hwy. 160 E., 970/565-4492 or 800/441-9908, www.mesaverdepottery.com) also has a large selection. More pottery can be found south of Cortez at the **Ute Mountain Indian Pottery** store (156 S. U.S. 160, 800/896-8548, www.utepottery.com).

Accommodations

The **White Eagle Inn** (2110 S. Broadway, 970/565-3333 or 800/659-4608, www.whiteagleinncortez.com) offers very tidy lodgings for around $50. In the $50–100 category, choose from the **Tomahawk Lodge** (728 S. Broadway, 970/565-8521 or 800/643-7705), the **Mesa Verde Inn** (640 S. Broadway, 970/565-3773 or 888/565-3773, www.cortezmesaverdeinn.com), or the **Budget Host Inn** (2040 E. Main St., 970/565-3738).

Ten miles west of town, in McElmo Canyon at the foot of Sleeping Ute Mountain, is a singular bed-and-breakfast called **Kelly Place** (970/565-3125 or 800/745-4885, www.kellyplace.com, $80–190). Guests can opt for guided excursions among more than two dozen archaeological sites on the 100-acre property. The lodge itself is an adobe building graced with roses, orchard, and a courtyard, with seven guest rooms, three private cabins with kitchenettes and private patios, and a two-bedroom apartment. A limited number of RV ($40) and tent ($30) campsites are also available.

On the eastern edge of town is the **Cortez-Mesa Verde KOA Kampground** (27432 E. Hwy. 160, 970/565-9301 or 800/562-3901). Tent sites, teepees, and cabins are $25–55. A heated pool and whirlpool are just a few of the amenities.

Food

Quotations about drinking and fools line the walls at the **Main Street Brewery** (21 E. Main St., 970/564-9112, lunch and dinner daily). They brew their own tasty Mesa Cerveza beers and serve steaks, pizzas, pasta, and burgers for $10–15. **Nero's Italian Restaurant** (303 W. Main St., 970/565-7366, dinner daily) puts a Southwest twist on Italian standbys, with entrées for $7–21. At **Tequila's** (1740 E. Main, 970/565-6868, $8–20), brave souls can ask for a taste of the super-hot chipotle salsa, but have a glass of milk or piece of bread handy to douse the fire. (Experienced chile-heads know that beer or tequila only spread the heat.)

For a step back to the era of beehive hairdos and lawn flamingos, stop by the **Silver Bean** (410 W. Main St., 970/946-4404), a drive-through coffee shop in a gleaming 1969 Airstream International trailer. There are also a few seats inside, where they serve coffee drinks, Italian sodas, smoothies, and a few sandwiches and burritos early morning–mid-afternoon Monday–Saturday. Located between Cortez and Durango, **Absolute Bakery** (110 S. Main, Mancos, 970/533-1200) serves breakfast and lunch, including made-to-order sandwiches on freshly baked bread.

Information

Stop by the **Colorado Welcome Center** (928 E. Main St. at Mildred, 970/565-3414 or 800/253-1616, 8 A.M.–5 P.M. daily, till 6 P.M. in summer), by City Park, for information on local activities and events. You can also try the **Mesa Verde Country Visitor Information Bureau** (970/565-8227 or 800/253-1616, www.mesaverdecountry.com).

NEW MEXICO AND COLORADO

Getting There and Around

Great Lakes Airlines (800/554-5111, www.fly-greatlakes.com) connects the Cortez Municipal Airport (970/565-9510), southwest of town on Highway 160, with Denver. **Hertz** (970/565-2001) and **Budget** (970/564-9012) have rental offices at the airport, and **Enterprise** (970/565-6824) has an office in town.

Dolores

Rio Nuestra Senora de las Dolores, or the River of Our Lady of Sorrows, was named by friars Domínguez and Escalante on their 1776 expedition west from Santa Fe. The town, named for the river, was founded in 1891 when a rail line was established there, linking the mining camps at Telluride, Ridgway, and Durango. Though it is home to fewer than 1,000 residents, this small town packs a big punch in terms of recreation and attractions, from fly-fishing or kayaking the Dolores River to traveling along either of two scenic byways, the San Juan Skyway and the Trail of the Ancients. Nearby McPhee reservoir, the second largest body of water in Colorado, has campgrounds, boat ramps, and picnic areas, while adjacent San Juan National Forest offers miles of trails for hikers, bikers, and equestrians.

◼ Anasazi Heritage Center

In the foothills of the San Juan Mountains near Dolores, this excellent museum (970/882-5600, www.co.blm.gov/ahc, 9 A.M.–5 P.M. daily Mar.–Oct., 10 A.M.–4 P.M. otherwise, $3 pp) covers all the native cultures of the region, particularly the Anasazi. The BLM-operated museum was created during the construction of nearby McPhee dam and reservoir and is used to interpret and archive the more than 1,600 sites researchers studied before the waters rose. More than three million artifacts and records are housed in the museum's research collection. Films, hands-on exhibits, computer programs, and a replica of an ancient pit house are a few of the museum's offerings. The gift shop, operated by Canyonlands Natural History Association (www.cnha.org), has a superb selection of regional books and educational items for children. The museum also serves as the information center for the Canyons of the Ancients National Monument.

From the parking lot, a half mile paved interpretive trail leads uphill to **Escalante Pueblo,** the size of a modest modern house, with 360-degree views of the surrounding countryside and McPhee Reservoir. The smaller **Dominguez Pueblo** is just outside the museum. The ruins and museum were named for the expeditionary friars Francisco Atanasio Domínguez and Silvestre Vélez de Escalante, who set out from Santa Fe in 1776 to find a route to California. (They turned back before reaching the coast, but their route became the Old Spanish Trail.) To get to the museum from Cortez, take U.S. 491 eight miles north and turn east (right) on SR 184 or, from the east side of town, take SR 145 north.

Canyons of the Ancients National Monument

The Anasazi Heritage Center makes an ideal starting point for trips to this 164,000-acre chunk of BLM-managed land (www.co.blm.gov/canm) stretching west of Cortez to the Utah border. Set aside in 2000, the monument protects one of the highest-known densities of archaeological sites in the United States—more than 100 per square mile in some cases—belonging to the Ancestral Puebloan, Ute, and Navajo cultures. Roads are few and many of them are pretty rough. Stop at the Heritage Center for maps and information about current conditions.

The only relatively developed site within the monument is **Lowry Pueblo,** with 40 rooms, eight kivas, and a great kiva. To get there from Cortez, drive 20 miles north on U.S. 491, turning west (left) at Pleasant View onto County Road CC. The ruins are nine miles west. The road changes from pavement to gravel, but it's easily accessible to passenger cars.

Sand Canyon Pueblo, with 420 rooms, 90 kivas, and 14 towers, was estimated to have held more than 700 people at its peak. Not much is visible above the surface today; after excavation and study in the 1980s, the site was

The Anasazi Heritage Center is a treasure trove of information and artifacts.

backfilled to protect walls and other features. However, the road to Sand Canyon makes for a nice mountain bike ride. Take U.S. 491 south of Cortez a few miles to County Road G (McElmo Canyon Road); then go west 12 miles to the trailhead. From there, four miles of slickrock and dirt track lead past several cliff dwellings, though the last mile is too rough to ride.

◖ Four Corners Monument

The only point in the United States where four states meet is a mere speck in a sage-dotted landscape, the nearest settlement being tiny Teec Nos Pos, six miles southwest at the intersection of U.S. 160 and U.S. 64. The Navajo Nation operates the monument at Four Corners (928/871-6647, www.navajonationparks.org, 7 A.M.–8 P.M. daily May 1–Sept., 8 A.M.–5 P.M. daily otherwise, $3 pp), where you'll find a granite-and-brass X marking the spot. This humble intersection of imagined lines draws visitors from all over the world, trickling in by car or arriving by the busload. Vendors sell souvenirs, crafts, and food, and there are picnic tables and restrooms. But the main attraction is watching the various gyrations as people pose for photographs with a hand and foot in each state. Cortez, Farmington, and Bluff are all 30–50 miles away.

Hovenweep National Monument

This remote, little-visited monument straddling the Utah-Colorado border preserves six Ancestral Puebloan villages spread across 20 miles. The word "Hovenweep" is a Paiute/Ute term that means "deserted valley," fittingly adopted by photographer William Henry Jackson in the late 19th century. There, astonishingly well-constructed towers balance on canyon rims and boulder tops, centuries after their original inhabitants moved away. It's a gem for archaeology buffs, a quiet yet visually appealing alternative to Mesa Verde National Park.

Most of the structures there were built between A.D. 1150 and 1300 by groups closely associated with those at Mesa Verde and abandoned soon after. In addition to the square and circular towers, there are many D-shaped homes

© KATHLEEN BRYANT

The flags of four states and the Navajo Nation fly above Four Corners Monument.

and kivas marked by such careful masonry that many structures have survived more or less intact for over 700 years. The classic Hovenweep village is a multistory pueblo situated at the head of a canyon near a perennial spring, often including water-control features such as dams to trap and redirect precious rains into gardens. It remains unclear what purpose the towers served—defensive fortifications, homes, storage structures, signaling stations, celestial observatories, or some combination of all these.

SIGHTS

Start your explorations at the **visitors center** (970/562-4282, www.nps.gov/hove, 8 A.M.–5 P.M. daily, till 6 P.M. in summer, $6 per vehicle), roughly 40 miles west of Cortez. The visitors center has interpretive talks throughout the day and evening programs at the nearby campground.

A short walk from the visitors center is Little Ruin Canyon, where the **Square Tower Group,** the largest collection of ruins in the monument, is located. As many as 200 people may have

lived there. A hiking trail loops two miles along the canyon rim and into the canyon itself, offering up-close views of a number of sites, including the striking two-story Square Tower and sturdy Hovenweep Castle. Allow an hour or two for the moderately challenging trail.

Hovenweep's five outlying groups are accessed by unmaintained dirt roads that may be impassable to low-clearance vehicles (and to any vehicle in bad weather). About five miles from the visitors center, the **Horseshoe Group** includes the Horseshoe Tower and the four-unit Horseshoe House. A short hike east leads to the **Hackberry Group,** where as many as 350 inhabitants may have lived, thanks to a perennial spring in Hackberry Canyon.

Less than a mile farther down the road, the **Holly Group** includes the multistory Tilted Tower and Boulder House, another tower perched on a large boulder at the head of Keeley Canyon. The top floor of the latter fell when the boulder shifted centuries ago. (The Holly Group can also be reached on foot from the visitors center via a one-way, 4-mile trail.)

© RICHARD MAYER

NEW MEXICO AND COLORADO

Hovenweep Castle perches on the edge of Little Ruin Canyon.

It's a 10-mile drive, followed by a 1.6-mile round-trip hike, to the **Cutthroat Castle Group,** which is characterized by an unusually large number of kivas. The **Cajon Group** (ca-HONE), highlighted by a circular tower built on three boulders, lies about nine miles southwest of the visitors center, where you can get driving directions.

PRACTICALITIES

The campground ($10/night) has sites for tents and RVs up to 35 feet long. Hovenweep is open year-round, and passes are good for a week. To get there from Cortez, take U.S. 491 south to County Road G (McElmo Canyon Road) and turn west—a total of 42 miles. From Blanding, take U.S. 191 south and turn east on SR 262, about 45 miles.

SOUTHEAST UTAH

Mention Southeast Utah and most people will conjure images of RVs touring Arches National Park or mountain bikes traversing the Slickrock Trail. But there's so much more: snowcapped mountains tumbling into 1,000-foot river canyons, hot air balloons soaring over desert hoodoos, and backcountry trails leading to ancient ruins and natural bridges. This is the recreation epicenter of southern Utah's canyon country, filled with opportunities to hike, bike, raft, and drive through amazing scenery.

The 12,000-foot peaks of the La Sal and Abajo Mountains tower over two national parks, a national monument, and plenty of other natural wonders that could qualify as either. Scenic drives and overlooks offer panoramas that will take your breath away, even if you don't wander far from your car. But for adventure travelers who live to wander, Southeast Utah is heaven on earth, with acres of open spaces to explore and quiet towns perfectly spaced for the occasional meal and hot shower.

About 35,000 people live in Grand County, San Juan County, and the southern half of Emery County, which together spread over 13,500 square miles. Generally speaking, residents are independent, conservative, and hardy, often descended from the settlers, homesteaders, and ranchers who arrived when this area was almost completely isolated from the rest of the country—there that means well into the 20th century. Even though it's the poster child of Four Corners recreation, Southeast Utah's remoteness and unforgiving landscape still keep much of it off the tourist radar.

© KATHLEEN BRYANT

HIGHLIGHTS

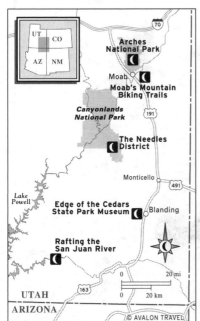

❮ Rafting the San Juan River: See ruins and rock art on a relaxing float from Bluff to Mexican Hat. It's easy enough for first timers (page 143).

❮ Edge of the Cedars State Park Museum: Blanding is home to one of the Four Corners' most extensive archaeological collections, including a reconstructed Anasazi village (page 145).

❮ Moab's Mountain Biking Trails: Moab boasts too many outstanding rides to describe in detail, but the granddaddy of them all is the Slickrock Trail (page 157).

❮ Arches National Park: This world-famous wonderland of arches, fins, domes, and towers is only a short drive from Moab (page 167).

❮ The Needles District: Enjoy some of the best hiking trails in the Four Corners in this gorgeous section of Canyonlands National Park (page 177).

LOOK FOR ❮ TO FIND RECOMMENDED SIGHTS, ACTIVITIES, DINING, AND LODGING.

PLANNING YOUR TIME

Southeast Utah is worth at least a week of travel time, especially given the long distances between towns and parks. Moab is the obvious hub and merits a few days itself with its hiking and **mountain biking trails** and shopping and dining options. You can see the highlights of **Arches National Park** in a day and spend another day at **Canyonlands National Park,** driving to see the views from the Island in the Sky or going on a hike in the Needles district.

If you have more time, take two or three days to explore south of Moab, stopping at the **Edge of the Cedars State Park Museum** in Blanding. Cedar Mesa is cut with canyons that hold ruins and rock art, as well as the impressive spans at Natural Bridges National Monument. For more outdoor fun, consider **rafting the San Juan River** from Bluff to Mexican Hat, an easy-enough expedition for first timers. The Green River from the city of Green River to Moab is another moderate overnight float trip.

U.S. 191 is the region's transportation backbone, with side branches at Monticello (U.S. 491 east to Cortez, Colorado) and Blanding (SR 95 northwest to Hanksville). At Mexican Hat, most travelers continue southwest on U.S. 163 to Monument Valley on the Arizona border, but U.S. 191 continues south from Bluff to cross the vast Navajo Nation.

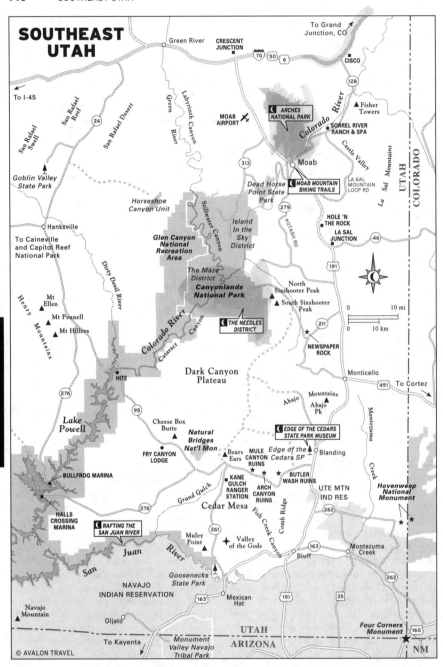

Mexican Hat to Moab

MEXICAN HAT

This tiny town on the San Juan River consists of little more than a few gas stations and hotels, even though it once swelled to as many as 1,000 people during various mining booms in the 20th century. Fewer than 100 live there today, surrounded by geological splendor, from the distinctive rock formation that gives the town its name to the vibrant patterns in the hillsides above and the black cockscomb of Alhambra Rock across the river.

Accommodations and Food

Nestled in the gorge of the San Juan River by the U.S. 163 bridge, the **San Juan Inn** (800/447-2022, www.sanjuaninn.net, $88 d Apr.–Oct., $68 d Nov.–Mar.) has 37 simple but comfortable rooms, including two with kitchens, as well as a small trading post that sells a few groceries along with Native American crafts, books, and outdoorsy clothing. The inn's Olde Bridge Grill has a pool table, a coffee bar, and Internet computers. Sandwiches, Navajo tacos, and burgers are $5–10, and steaks are $10 and up. They're open 7 A.M.–9 P.M. daily, though winter hours may vary.

Across the street from the gas station, the **Mexican Hat Lodge** (435/683-2222, www.mexicanhat.net, $78–104 d) offers a dozen rooms and an outdoor restaurant where you can enjoy a steak cooked on a swinging grill over a cedar-wood fire (platters are $9–27). Once known as the Top O Hat Bar, this place was bought in 1979 by Bobby and Vonnie Mueller, members of a traveling band who fell in love with the area and decided to stay.

Valle's RV Park (435/683-2226), off U.S. 163 behind Valle's Trading Post, has a dozen sites for $16, including all hookups. They also operate a vehicle shuttle service and storage for river trips, and serve pizzas, buffalo wings, and other quick bites starting at $5 in their convenience store.

GOOSENECKS STATE PARK

Just north of Mexican Hat is the turnoff to the west for SR 261, which climbs the vertiginous Moki Dugway up onto Cedar Mesa. A short side road leads to the small park (435/678-2238), which is named for the view: a tortuous series of curves carved 1,000 feet into the desert by the San Juan River. The Goosenecks are a textbook example of an entrenched meander, which begins when a waterway winds across a relatively flat surface. As the landscape is lifted upward, the river cuts deeper and deeper, eventually becoming trapped in the meandering curves. There, the San Juan winds so tightly that it crams five curving river miles into one mile of landscape. Facilities include four free primitive campsites, vault toilets, and ramada-shaded picnic tables.

VALLEY OF THE GODS

Eight miles from Mexican Hat, at the foot of Cedar Mesa, another side road heads east into this flat valley, where dozens of reddish-colored rock formations jut skyward in the mesa's shadow. The 17-mile dirt road is good enough for cars, but impassable when wet, and eventually reconnects to U.S. 163 northeast of Mexican Hat. Along the way you'll pass the ◖ **Valley of the Gods Bed & Breakfast** (970/749-1164, www.zippitydo-dah.com/vog, $135–155), with four rooms in a solar-powered stone 1930s ranch house, more lodging in a two-story converted root cellar next door, and the best porch for hundreds of miles. The owners, experienced hikers, will help you pick out a hiking trail or bike route. Valley of the Gods provides the backdrop for a spectacular hot air balloon rally that takes place each January.

BLUFF

Settled in 1880 on the banks of the San Juan River by members of the Hole-in-the-Rock expedition, this anomalously bohemian enclave has a sense of humor. The

© RICHARD MAYER

Bluff, Utah, was settled by the Hole-in-the-Rock pioneers.

town's welcome sign is a slab of carved sandstone reading "Founded in A.D. 650," the date when the local Ancestral Pueblo population began establishing permanent dwellings. Bluff's tiny size (pop. 400) and dramatic setting give it one of the highest per-capita populations of archaeologists, naturalists, river-runners, backcountry outfitters, and artists in the United States. Restored pioneer homes made from buff-colored sandstone stand along streets lined with majestic cottonwoods, and crazy formations with names like Locomotive Rock loom above. In the center of town, the **Bluff Fort Historic Site** preserves the cabin of Joseph Barton, one of the determined Mormon colonists who settled there after their rugged 1880 journey. Others are remembered at the pioneer cemetery atop an overlooking hill. Just below the cemetery are the partially excavated ruins of what may have been an outlier of Chaco Canyon.

Events

The **Bluff Balloon Festival,** held in mid-January, brings dozens of hot air balloons to Red Rock Country. They lift off from the Valley of the Gods near Mexican Hat, adding splashes of color to an already-vivid palette. The **Utah Navajo Fair & Rodeo** in September includes traditional song and dance, crafts, food, and rodeo events. Writers, artists, filmmakers, and musicians gather for the **Bluff Arts Festival** in late October, when cottonwoods turn gold along the banks of the San Juan.

Shopping

At the foot of a distinctive pair of stone formations on the edge of town, the **Twin Rocks Trading Post** (913 E. Navajo Twins Dr., 435/672-2341 or 800/526-3448, www.twinrocks.com) boasts one of the finest selections of native arts in Southeast Utah. The wide stone building with two cigar-store Indians out front holds plenty of museum-quality merchandise, including knives with inlaid handles, rugs, jewelry, and carvings. Contemporary Navajo baskets, rare elsewhere, are a specialty there.

Across the intersection of U.S. 163 and U.S. 191 is the picturesque **Cow Canyon Trading Post** (435/672-2208, 9 A.M.–5 P.M. daily, though hours may vary). Built in 1954 with stones from an old Mormon house, it has an aura of far greater age, from the vintage cars out front to the low wood-beamed ceilings inside. The owners' eclectic collection of souvenirs, art, and books includes lots of pottery and brightly painted wooden representations of Navajo sandpaintings.

Recreation

The highly recommended **Far Out Expeditions** (7th and Mulberry, 435/672-2294, www.faroutexpeditions.com) offers hikes, backpack trips, and vehicle-supported trips to view rock art and ruins throughout the area, including Monument Valley. Half-day tours with Vaughn and Marcia Hadenfeldt start at $125 per person for two people, and customized day tours are $195 per person. They also offer vehicle shuttles, cookouts, and a guesthouse in a historic home with a kitchen, living room, and two porches ($90 d).

For more than fifty years, **Wild River Expeditions** (101 Main St., 800/422-7654, www.riversandruins.com) has outfitted and guided trips down the San Juan River. Trips run 1–10 days for $165–2,300 per person. **Buckhorn Llama** (970/667-7411, www.llamapack.com) organizes llama pack trips into the backcountry of Southeast Utah and Colorado's San Juan Mountains. Guided trips, such as a 5-day exploration of nearby Grand Gulch, are $350 per person per day for 1–3 people. If you have the skills, experience, and gear to put together your own trip, they will rent the temperamental camelids to carry your packs for $55 per day, after a mandatory getting-to-know-your-llama session ($100). **North Wash Outfitters** (435/672-9942, www.northwashoutfitters.com) will introduce you to the joys of canyoneering for $145 per person and take you on guided day trips starting at $45 per person.

◖ Rafting the San Juan River

The **Sand Island Recreation Area** is a popular put-in point for trips down the San Juan River. The turnoff to this BLM site is three miles west of Bluff on U.S. 191, near mile marker 22. Primitive camping is available there for $10 on a first-come, first-served basis; most of the 27 sites are large enough for RVs and a couple are pull-through. Facilities include a boat ramp, water, and vault toilets. On the cliffs nearby is an impressively large panel of petroglyphs pecked into the stone 800–2,500 years ago— geometric shapes, humanoid figures adorned by three-tiered headdresses, and one half-ram, half-Kokopelli figure brandishing a flute.

The modestly challenging float from Sand Island to Mexican Hat passes through Class III rapids and the famous Goosenecks of the San Juan with lots of rock art and ruins en route. The trip takes 1–3 days. Another five days or so will bring you to Clay Hills Crossing just above Lake Powell, the only viable takeout below Mexican Hat (thanks to a 30-foot waterfall just downstream). You'll need a Bureau of Land Management permit to launch, and mandatory campsites are assigned downstream of Mexican Hat. Contact the Monticello BLM office (435/587-1500) for more details, and pick up a river guidebook from the Canyonlands Natural History Association (435/259-6003 or 800/840-8978, www.cnha.org). Permits are issued by the BLM's river office (435/587-1544, www.blm.gov/ut, mornings only).

Accommodations

The **Recapture Lodge** (250 Main St., 435/672-2281, www.recapturelodge.com, $70) is a comfy place with a pool, hot tub, and occasional slide shows featuring local experts. A light breakfast is available in the lobby on the honor system. For a motel room around $80, try the **Kokopelli Inn** (161 E. Main Street, 435/672-2322 or 877/342-6009, www.kokoinn.com) on U.S. 191 as it passes through town.

Breakfast is included at the ◖ **Decker House Inn** (189 N. 3rd St. E., 435/672-2304 or 888/637-2582, www.deckerhouseinn.com, $85–140). An 1898 home in Bluff's historic district, the Decker House has five rooms with one to three bedrooms each, a guest kitchen,

© KATHLEEN BRYANT

River runners prepare for a trip down the San Juan.

and plenty of space to relax outside. You can't miss the **Desert Rose Inn & Cabins** (701 W. Main St., 435/672-2303 or 888/475-7673, www.desertroseinn.com, $100–140), a three-story porch-fronted building on the western edge of town, with modern rooms and well-equipped cabins.

In addition to the Sand Island Recreation Area along the river, you can camp at the **Cadillac Ranch RV Park** (640 E. Main St., 435/672-2262 or 800/538-6195, www.cadillacranchrv.com, $25) or the **Cottonwood RV Park** (435/672-2287, $16–23, Mar.–Nov. 15), both on U.S. 191.

Food

Bluff restaurants serve some of the finest meals in the Four Corners. Across from the Recapture Lodge, the **San Juan River Kitchen** (281 E. Main, 435/672-9956, dinner Tues.–Sun.) features a revolving menu built around local produce and regional meats. With no microwave on the premises, entrées ($10–15) like roasted red pepper quesadillas or burgers with yam fries

are freshly prepared. Ice cream (made daily), decadent pastries (also made fresh), and Uinta beers round out the menu.

The **Cow Canyon Trading Post and Restaurant** (435/672-2208, dinner Apr.–Nov., call first), located at the intersection of U.S. 191 and SR 162, serves up gourmet Southwest fare with fresh local produce. Their meals are so popular that reservations are often necessary. The dining room is in a glassed-in porch out back of the trading post, looking over green fields on the banks of the San Juan River. You can browse the wares while waiting for your entrée ($10–15).

Flame-grilled steaks, chops, salmon, and home-baked pie ($16–20) are served indoors or out at the **Cottonwood Steakhouse** (Main St. and 4th W., 435/672-2282, from 5:30 P.M. daily Apr.–Nov., $15–25). You can eat out on the porch of the **Twin Rocks Café** (913 E. Navajo Twins Dr., 435/672-2341, all meals daily), next to the trading post of the same name. On the menu are barbecue plates and Navajo tacos ($8–10) as well as a few vegetarian selections and microbrewed beers. **Comb Ridge Coffee** (7th West and Main St., 435/672-9931, 8 A.M.–4 P.M. Wed.–Fri., 7 A.M.–4 P.M. Sat.– Sun.) serves light breakfasts, smoothies, and excellent coffees and displays local artwork.

BLANDING

The largest town in Utah's largest county (geographically speaking) counts about 3,200 residents. Set on White Mesa at the southern edge of rolling sagebrush-covered plains, Blanding has three museums and the scenic byway known as the Trail of the Ancients, leading into the cliffs and canyons of the Ancestral Puebloans. It's also a strongly conservative town where alcohol is forbidden.

Archaeological excavations show that the Ancestral Puebloan culture occupied this area between A.D. 600 and 1200. According to anthropologists, Utes and Navajos arrived sometime after 1400. The Navajos called the location "Sagebrush" because of the prolific Big Sage *(Artemisia tridentata)* that intermingles with piñon-and-juniper woodland at the base of Blue Mountain.

In 1897 a pair of brothers from Bluff established a Mormon community there, naming it Grayson and building an irrigation canal from Johnson Creek. The settlement was renamed under somewhat unusual circumstances. In 1914 a wealthy Easterner named Thomas Bicknell offered a 1,000-book library to any town in Utah that would take his name. In the ensuing scramble, Grayson came in neck and neck with Thurber, near what is now Capitol Reef National Park. Thurber became Bicknell, Grayson adopted Mrs. Bicknell's maiden name of Blanding, and the towns split the books.

Colonization severely impacted the traditional hunting-and-gathering lifestyle of Ute bands. In 1923 an abortive revolt by a desperate group of Utes brought Blanding briefly into the national spotlight as the site of the Posey War, billed (debatably) as the last Native American uprising in the United States.

◖ Edge of the Cedars State Park Museum

Displays on the Ancestral Puebloans, Navajo,

and Utes fill this outstanding museum (660 W. 400 N., 435/678-2238, http://stateparks.utah. gov, 9 A.M.–5 P.M. Mon.–Sat., $5 pp), which serves as the regional archaeological repository for all of Southeast Utah. The extensive collection includes hundreds of everyday objects from sandals to turkey feather blankets. Don't miss the vibrant macaw-feather sash on the second floor. A partly excavated pueblo stands out back. Special events include an Indian market in May.

Dinosaur Museum

Delve even further into the past at the Dinosaur Museum (754 S. 200 W., 435/678-3454, www. dinosaur-museum.org, 9 A.M.–5 P.M. Mon.– Sat. Apr. 15–Oct. 15, $3 adults, $1.50 children), a cavernous building filled with the bones, eggs, tracks, and even fossilized skin of creatures like the allosaurus, Utah's official state fossil. The museum also houses dinosaur sculptures, exhibits on the latest research, and a 360-pound meteorite.

Accommodations

Lodging options include several hotels with rooms for $70–100. Choose from the **Gateway Inn** (88 E. Center St., 435/678-2278 or 866/598-2278, www.gatewayinnblanding. com), the **Blue Mountain Inn** (711 S. Main St., 435/678-3271, www.bluemountaininn-blanding.com), or the **Four Corners Inn** (131 E. Center St., 435/678-3257 or 800/574-3150, www.fourcornersinn.com). Six miles north of town, the solar-powered **Abajo Haven Guest Cabins** (5440 N. Cedar Edge Ln., 435/979-3126, www.abajohaven.com, $70 for cabins, $20 for RV sites) include a free guided hiking tour to a pair of prehistoric sites near the ranch. For an additional fee, the hosts will add a campfire cookout or other guided tours to your stay. The **Blue Mountain RV Park** (1930 S. Main, 435/678-7840 or 435/678-2570, www. bluemountainrvpark.com, Mar. 15–Nov., $35) has full hookups and tent sites.

Food

Disappointed gourmands may think the town's name has something to do with the local cuisine, but you'll find plenty of hearty, home-style cooking and a few fast-food joints in Blanding. The **Old Tymer Restaurant** (733 S. Main St., 435/678-2122, all meals daily) serves mostly Mexican and steaks next to the Blue Mountain Inn. Near the Four Corners Inn is the **Homestead Steak House** (121 E. Center St., 435/678-3456), with a salad bar, Navajo tacos, pizza, ribs, fried ice cream, and homemade pies. Both have entrées for $5–20. Barbecue fans can head for **Fattboyz Grillin** (164 N. Grayson Pkwy., 435/678-3778, lunch and dinner daily, $5–18), serving up popular, plentiful daily specials and saucy ribs.

Information

The Blanding Chamber of Commerce runs a **visitors center** (12 N. Grayson Pkwy., 435/678-3662, www.blandingutah.org, 8 A.M.–8 P.M. Mon.–Sat. in season) on U.S. 191 at the north end of town.

Getting There

About three miles south of town is the **Blanding Municipal Airport** (435/678-2791). There's no train or bus service, but **Moab Luxury Coach** (435/940-4212, www.moabluxurycoach.com) stops morning and evening on its shuttle route to Salt Lake City.

HIGHWAY 95: TRAIL OF THE ANCIENTS

Heading west from U.S. 191 just south of Blanding, SR 95 crosses some of the most scenic backcountry in southern Utah. Built in 1946 but unpaved until 1976, the so-called Bicentennial Highway came with its share of fireworks over opening up beautiful but remote Cedar Mesa to the general, non-four-wheel-drive public. (This road was one target of the environmental saboteurs in Edward Abbey's *The Monkey Wrench Gang*.) The area is particularly rich in archaeology and is one of the easiest routes in the Four Corners to access dozens of canyons filled with ruins and rock art, stone arches, and lovely hanging gardens.

Between mileposts 110 and 111 is a signed parking lot and trailhead for **Butler Wash.** The trail leads a half mile over dirt and slickrock to an overlook, where you'll see a well-preserved pueblo with four kivas. Scan the cliff face to the left of the alcove for a hand-and-foot trail chipped into the rock. West of Butler Wash, the unmistakable barrier of **Comb Ridge,** an 800-foot high jagged sandstone monocline, rises up 80 miles from north to south. The highway crosses the ridge via a gash dynamited through the sheer stone face. There's an overlook between mileposts 108 and 109.

A few miles farther, between mileposts 107 and 108, is a signed turnoff for **Arch Canyon,** where day hikers can spot a ruin just past the canyon mouth. The entire 12-mile-long box canyon is good for two or three days' worth of exploration, with plenty of ruins, arches, and side canyons. Another six miles west on SR 95 brings you to the signed parking area for **Mule Canyon,** where a 12-room dwelling, a kiva, and a two-story circular tower have been excavated and stabilized by the BLM. These structures, occupied more than 800 years ago, are linked by tunnels, a particularly unusual feature. To see the **Mule Canyon Towers** (also known as Cave Towers or Seven Towers), backtrack a short distance east on SR 95 to a gated dirt road (near milepost 102), which leads a half mile to the trailhead. The towers are a short down-canyon walk from the trailhead. If you don't have a high-clearance vehicle, you can park near the gate and walk down the dirt road to the trailhead for a total round-trip hiking distance of about two miles.

Highway 261: Cedar Mesa

Connecting SR 95 with U.S. 163, SR 261 cuts north–south across Cedar Mesa proper, providing access to some of the region's most popular overnight hiking loops before literally dropping off the edge of the mesa via the Moki Dugway. Five miles south of SR 95, the **Kane Gulch Ranger Station** (435/587-1510) marks the starting point for the 23-mile loop hike into **Grand Gulch.** Archaeology buffs know this loop as one of the easiest and prettiest ways to access a veritable feast of ruins and rock art (although all the canyons off SR 261 can boast

© KATHLEEN BRYANT

A kiva is preserved at Mule Canyon Pueblo on Cedar Mesa.

some). This 2–3-day hike connects Kane Gulch with Bullet Canyon and has become so popular that the BLM has instituted a mandatory permit system ($2 pp for day hikers, $5–8 pp for overnighters). The same permit regulations apply to all canyon hikes on Cedar Mesa off SR 261. Contact the BLM's Monticello Field Office (435/587-1510) for details or see their website (www.blm.gov/ut). Maps showing detailed road access are available at the ranger station and other BLM offices.

A scenic 15-mile, 2–3 day loop hike connects **Owl** and **Fish Creek Canyons** to the east of SR 261. This loop, less trafficked and suitable for experienced desert hikers, begins along a dirt road about six miles southeast of the ranger station. The loop is most often hiked clockwise, starting down Owl Creek Canyon. **Slickhorn Canyon,** 11 miles down Highway 261 from the ranger station, is another popular hike, descending 500 feet in 12 miles to the San Juan River to the west. This canyon is rugged, and backpackers can expect to spend four days or more to travel its length. The upper section of

Johns Canyon, beginning seven miles north of the Moki Dugway, makes a good day hike with some moderate scrambling involved.

About 23 miles south of SR 95, SR 261 plunges off the sheer edge of Cedar Mesa in an astounding display of road-building determination known as the **Moki Dugway.** A series of white-knuckled, guardrail-deficient gravel curves descends more than 1,100 feet in three miles to the Valley of the Gods and the town of Mexican Hat. A mining company built the road in 1953 to haul uranium and vanadium from mines on Cedar Mesa. (As you're creeping along, imagine ore-loaded trucks negotiating the 11 percent grade.)

At the top of the dugway, take a detour down a good dirt road five miles to the west to **Muley Point Overlook.** From there you'll have a stunning view off the edge of the plateau as far as the Goosenecks of the San Juan and Monument Valley.

Natural Bridges National Monument

About 35 miles west of Blanding, near the

distinctive double peaks known as the **Bears Ears,** SR 275 leads north from SR 95 to Natural Bridges National Monument (435/692-1234, www.nps.gov/nabr, 8 A.M.–5 P.M. daily, till 6 P.M. May–Sept., $6 per vehicle), where three huge sandstone bridges span White Canyon. The 7,600-acre monument also protects many prehistoric cliff dwellings and storage rooms built by the Ancestral Puebloans. The bridges were formed when the river changed course and cut across tight bends, eventually tunneling through the fins of rock. Sipapu Bridge is the world's second-largest natural bridge. (Glen Canyon's Rainbow Bridge is the largest.) The monument welcomes fewer than 100,000 visitors a year, a fraction of most other Grand Circle parks, but its quiet beauty and winding canyon are enchanting, and with its well-designed visitor center, lingering there a few hours or more is a pleasure.

Originally called President, Senator, and Congressman by prospector Cass Hite in the 1880s, the bridges were briefly renamed Augusta, Caroline, and Edwin before being given their current, native names: Sipapu, Kachina, and Owachomo. The area was set aside by President Theodore Roosevelt in 1908, four years after *National Geographic* magazine sponsored an expedition there, making it the oldest National Park Service unit in the state.

The solar array that powers the Park Service facilities—the largest in the world when it was built in 1980—produces up to 50 kilowatts. Nighttime lighting is kept deliberately low to preserve the incredible starry skies. In 2007 the International Dark-Sky Association designated Natural Bridges as the world's first International Dark-Sky Park when they found it had the least light-polluted night sky they'd ever recorded. Rangers give night-sky talks in the summer, and watching the Milky Way rise above Owachomo Bridge is awe-inspiring.

You can view each bridge from the paved, nine-mile overlook drive, and hike to the base of each bridge via short, steep trails (connected by an 8.6-mile loop trail). The 13-site

Owachomo Bridge is the thinnest of the three spans at Natural Bridges National Monument.

© KATHLEEN BRYANT

campground (for tents and RVs up to 26 feet long, no hookups) is $10 per night. A passport to the Southeast Utah Group of parks costs $25 and gives access to Natural Bridges, Arches National Park, Canyonlands National Park, and Hovenweep National Monument for a year.

Dark Canyon Wilderness/ Primitive Area

This large, rugged canyon system, jointly administered by the National Forest Service and the BLM, is one of the wildest and least-explored in the state. It takes a multiday trip to do it justice, but if you have time, determination, and wilderness skills, you'll be rewarded with 1,000-foot-deep gorges spilling from the western slope of the Abajo Mountains all the way to the high desert along the Colorado River. Water is scarce in the upper canyon, where access points may be snow-covered into early summer. The lower canyon is hikeable year-round, and water is generally available.

The most direct access is via the graded dirt road that heads north from the entrance road to Natural Bridges National Monument through the 8,500-foot pass between the Bears Ears. This road shortly joins forest roads leading to trailheads for Woodenshoe and Peavine Canyons, which cut west from Elk Ridge at 8,200 feet in the Manti-La Sal National Forest. You can descend either canyon, which begin within the 46,000-acre wilderness area administered by the national forest, to reach Dark Canyon. As you descend the main canyon, it becomes progressively narrower and deeper, and you will cross into the 62,000-acre primitive area administered by the BLM.

Dark Canyon is about 30 miles long, and it takes 3–4 days to descend to the uppermost reaches of Lake Powell upstream from Hite. For more information, contact Manti-La Sal National Forest (435/587-2041) or the BLM's Monticello field office (435/587-1500, www. blm.gov/ut). You can find out more about current conditions and water sources by joining the Dark Canyon blog (http://wilderness.net) and perusing recent trip reports.

West of Natural Bridges

From Natural Bridges National Monument, SR 95 follows White Canyon west to Lake Powell. Dark red Organ Rock Shale tops lighter Cedar Mesa Sandstone, making a contrasting backdrop for vibrant green pines. At milepost 75, **Cheesebox Butte** looks like, well, a cheese box. A cairned trail at the end of a short dirt track leads down into White Canyon, which you can cross to ascend **Cheesebox Canyon** and its narrows just a few miles up. Canyoneering obstacles include pools, mud, and boulders that can be bypassed, depending on current conditions. Don't attempt this canyon route if rain is a possibility and allow plenty of time for the return trip if you are day-hiking.

The next major stop along SR 95 is **Hite** on the upper reaches of Lake Powell. There in the northernmost Glen Canyon National Recreation Area, the scenery is an eye-popping spectacle of red, orange, and white mesas, buttes, and spires sandwiched between the waters of the lake and the gray ramparts of the Henry Mountains. A bit farther down the road, two bridges cross what were once the Colorado and Dirty Devil Rivers, the only road crossing for 300 miles between Page and Moab. Before Glen Canyon Dam was built, this was the best natural crossing upriver of Lees Ferry. Prospector Cass Hite dubbed it Dandy Crossing in the 1880s, about the time he discovered gold nearby and opened the only post office in Glen Canyon.

Though there's lake access there, after years of dry conditions, low-water levels have led to the marina's closing. Hite has an intermittently staffed ranger station (435/684-2457), convenience store and gas pumps (435/684-2278), and a primitive campground ($6–12 per night). The recreation area's concessioner, ARAMARK (888/896-3829, www.lakepowell. com), rents furnished condos on a nightly or weekly basis ($250/night). Opposite the former marina, Hite Overlook offers soaring views of the biblical landscape that surrounds the river confluence.

About 15 miles west of Hite, near milepost 33, is the **Hog Springs picnic area.** You can hike up the streambed, surrounded by the canyon's red walls, to a waterfall and plunge pool (about a mile). Keep an eye out for petroglyphs and pictographs.

SR 95 travels a few more miles to the base of the Henry Mountains and the junction of SR 276, which leads south to Bullfrog Marina and Halls Crossing on Lake Powell. SR 95 continues north as the Trail of the Ancients, crossing the Burr Desert to join SR 24 at Hanksville.

Henry Mountains

The last mountain range to be mapped and named in the lower 48 states, the Henrys thrust 2,000 feet above canyon country. Mount Ellen (11,615 feet) is the highest of three peaks over 10,000 feet and the northernmost summit in the relatively small range. John Wesley Powell named the range in 1871 after Joseph Henry, his friend at the helm of the Smithsonian Institution, and assigned geologist Grove Karl Gilbert to study their geology. Out of this came Gilbert's classic "Report on the Geology of the Henry Mountains," published in 1877, which identified the range as laccolithic and made the peaks familiar to geologists worldwide.

Near the turn of the 20th century outlaws hid in the mountains among ranches grazing cows, sheep, and goats. Overgrazing still scars the hillsides, which are now home to a herd of about 200 buffalo. One of the few free-roaming herds in the country, these are descended from 18 released in 1941. The Utah Department of Wildlife Resources manages the herd and organizes a yearly hunt. Rusting equipment and abandoned mine shafts are all that remain of the uranium boom of the 1950s.

The views from the mountains, needless to say, are inspiring, from the tilted layers of the Waterpocket Fold and the Pink Cliffs to the canyons surrounding Lake Powell and the La Sal Mountains. The 68-mile **Bull Creek Pass Backcountry Byway** accesses Burr Point and Angel's Point overlooking the Dirty Devil River. This single-lane dirt road is rough in sections, requiring a four-wheel-drive, high-clearance vehicle. At 10,485-foot Bull Creek Pass (often snow-drifted through July), an alpine hiking trail leads to the summit of Mount Ellen (five miles round-trip). The BLM

maintains three primitive campgrounds in the Henry Mountains: Starr Springs, McMillan Springs, and Lonesome Beaver, which is near the Dandelion Flat picnic area. For more information, contact the BLM's Henry Mountains Field Station in Hanksville (435/542-3461).

MONTICELLO

The seat of San Juan County and its second-largest city, Monticello (pop. 2,000) was founded in 1888 near springs known to travelers for centuries. Mormon settlers, cowboys, and Ute bands were still clashing over control of the springs when the town fathers laid out a town site, planted crops, and began work on an irrigation ditch. Although the community took the name of Thomas Jefferson's Virginia country retreat, locals pronounce it "Mon-ti-SELL-o."

Throughout the 20th century, the town's prosperity rose and fell along with farm prices and mining ventures. Though agriculture continues to be an economic force, Monticello has a growing tourist industry, thanks to its location. It's the closest town to the entrance to the Needles District of Canyonlands National Park and well placed at the foot of the Abajo Mountains, also called the Blue Mountains, for those in search of activities uphill. At 7,069 feet, Monticello is also the loftiest city in Utah.

Events

In March, the **Blue Mountain Triathlon** comes to town, and July brings **Pioneer Day** with games, food, and fireworks. In August the **San Juan County Fair & Rodeo** arrives in a cloud of dust with various livestock-centered events, dances, and agricultural exhibits.

Recreation

Monticello's nonprofit **Four Corners School of Outdoor Education** (800/525-4456, www.fourcornersschool.org) has been running expert-led "ed-ventures" throughout the Southwest since 1984. Rafting, hiking, and backpacking trips to Lake Powell, Chaco Canyon, the Grand Canyon, and Yellowstone all have a strong conservation bent. The list also includes family tours, llama treks, women-only trips, and explorations of native culture, rock art, and geology. Prices and itineraries vary, and trips are guided by professional geologists, archaeologists, anthropologists, and other experts.

Golfers can head for the highly regarded **Hideout** (549 S. Main, 435/587-2200, www.hideoutgolf.com), a lovely 18-hole course that is deceptively challenging, thanks to the elevation.

Monti–La Sal National Forest has miles of dirt roads for scenic drives or mountain bike rides. The 35-mile **Abajo Loop Scenic Backway,** suitable for passenger cars in dry summer conditions, takes a couple hours to travel from Monticello to Blanding. Take SR 191 north to FR 105, traveling west to FR 79 and then south. FR 105 passes campgrounds and picnic areas on its way to the old Blue Mountain Ski Resort. The resort closed a couple of decades back, but backcountry skiers still head there for mountain access in winter months.

Accommodations

Most of Monticello's hotels are located along SR 191 or SR 491. Rooms at the family-owned **Monticello Inn** (164 E. Central, 435/587-2274, $60–105) have refrigerators and microwaves. The **Inn at the Canyons** (533 N. Main, 435/587-2458, www.monticellocanyonlandsinn.com, $85–110) has a heated indoor pool, as does the **Rodeway Inn** (649 N. Main St., 435/587-2489, $85–120).

The **Gristmill Inn** (64 S. 300 E., 435/587-2597, $90–120) is a bed-and-breakfast located in a 1930s flour mill and the millhouse next door. Drive eight miles north of town on SR 191 for the **Runnin Iron Inn and Roughlock RV Park** (435/587-2351, www.canyonlandsbestkeptsecret.com, rooms $60–80, campsites $20, cabins $39), constructed to look like an Old West town. Adjoining the inn, the Line Camp Steakhouse serves steaks, chicken, and fish (starting at $15).

Campsites at the **Bar-TN RV Park** (348 S. Main St., 435/587-1005, www.bar-tn.com) run $15 for full hookups and $10 for tents, and they also have cabins with cable TV for $33. Three

Forest Service campgrounds the Abajo Mountains near Monti Springs and Buckboard are a few m town along FR 105, and Devils Canyo miles south off of Highway 191. Sites ($10 night, no hookups) are open from spring to fall Call the Monticello ranger district (435/587-2041) for more information, or reserve a site by phone or online (877/444-6777, www.recreation.gov).

Food

The **K&A Chuckwagon** (496 N. Main St., 435/587-3468, www.kachuckwagon.com) combines tent and RV camping with cook-out-style meals. Even if you're not staying at their 12-site campground (free with dinner), they welcome drop-ins. Hearty sandwiches and burgers (around $6) are among the offerings at the **MD Ranch Cookhouse** (380 S. Main St., 435/587-3299, hours vary seasonally). Dinner entrées are $9 and up. Expect a hometown atmosphere at family-owned **PJ's Restaurant** (216 E. Center St., 435/587-2335, all meals daily), where you can order a burger or burrito for less than $10 and hang out to play pool, watch TV, or use Wi-Fi. The **Peace Tree Juice Café** (516 N. Main St., 435/587-5063, all meals daily, $5–20) serves vibrant, mostly organic smoothies, wraps, and salads—and a great cup of coffee.

Information

The **Southeastern Utah Welcome Center** (216 S. Main St., 435/587-3401, www.utahscanyoncountry.com, 9 A.M.–6 P.M. Wed.–Mon. Mar.–Oct., 10 A.M.–4 P.M. Thurs.–Sun. Nov.–Feb.) is in the center of town along U.S. 191. The welcome center shares offices with the local chamber of commerce (435/587-2992, www.monticelloutah.info) and a small museum focusing on Monticello's pioneer days.

San Juan County's **multiagency visitors center** (117 S. Main St., 435/587-3235, ext. 4139, or 800/574-4386, www.utahscanyoncountry.com) offers a wealth of information, including trip-planning materials and forest service maps. Contact the **BLM Monticello**

St., 435/587-1500) : hiking at nearby , and other BLM-

can be found in
cello: Dalton
es west of
is 13
per

/940-4212, www. s a regular shuttle
schedule between San Lake City and Moab, with morning (northbound) and evening (southbound) stops in Monticello. Rates start at $90, depending on destination. Tours and charters are also available.

The municipal airport (1639 N. U.S. 191, 435/587-2271) for general aviation is about three miles north of town.

ABAJO MOUNTAINS

The Abajo Mountains were named "below" by the early Spanish explorers who gazed down on them from the higher La Sals to the north. Peaking at 11,362-foot Abajo Peak, this small laccolithic range was formed by an underground magma bulge like the La Sals and Navajo Mountain. Much of the mountainsides lie with in the Monticello Ranger District of Manti–La Sal National Forest, including the Abajo–Harts Draw Recreation Area. Aspens, firs, pine trees, and alpine lakes are the perfect respite from the desert's summer heat, and trees provide splashes of red and yellow in autumn. (Look for the shape of a horse's head formed by the trees toward the north end of the range when seen from Monticello.) **Hart's Draw Road,** a 22-mile paved scenic route, crosses the northeast flank of the range, connecting Monticello with SR 211, the road to the Needles District of Canyonlands.

Moab and Vicinity

The undisputed tourist epicenter of canyon country exerts a force on southern Utah and outdoor lovers everywhere that is far out of proportion to its population of just under 5,000. Moab is a diverse community, with spandex-clad mountain bikers and overall-clad cowboys rubbing elbows with European tourists and frat boys from Boulder. Although still mostly Mormon, the town has a steadily growing liberal bent that keeps alive the spirit of Edward Abbey, who penned the classic *Desert Solitaire* after a few seasons as a ranger in nearby Arches National Park in the 1960s. Set in a narrow, verdant valley where the Colorado River slices between 1,000-foot walls of rock, Moab is surrounded by enough stunning scenery that early settlers' choice of a name ("beautiful land" in Hebrew) makes perfect sense. Moab and its surroundings are definitely photogenic: Dozens of films have been shot in the immediate environs, from the classic (*Wagon Master* and *Cheyenne Autumn*) to the not-so-classic (*Warlock,* anyone?).

History

Spanish Valley was formed when a thick layer of underground salt dissolved, causing the valley floor to sink. Native groups from the Ancestral Puebloans to the Sabuagana Utes lived there for the relatively mild climate, riverside soils, and shallow ford of the Colorado River. Expeditions from New Spain passed through, beginning in 1765 with Juan Maria Antonio Rivera. The easy river crossing was already known to area Indian tribes, but between 1829 and 1848, Santa Fe traders used the route to transport goods (and Paiute slaves) to and from California. In the 1840s explorer John C. Fremont dubbed it the Old Spanish Trail.

Mormon settlers came to stay in 1878 after a previous group of missionaries had been run off by native tribes. The name of Moab was adopted two years later, from the biblical account of the Israelites who rested in the desert kingdom of Moab southeast of Jerusalem after wandering for 40 years. The town's first ferry began operating in 1885, on the south bank of the river near the foot of the La Sal

Mountains. At the turn of the 20th century, the town's economy was based on ranching and farming, including vineyards and orchards. The first bridge spanned the river in 1912, but traffic was sparse.

The town's first economic boom came with the Cold War. The sudden demand for uranium brought hundreds of prospectors to comb the hills with jeeps and Geiger counters. Charlie Steen's 1952 discovery of the multimillion-dollar La Vida mine, in the Lisbon Valley southeast of town, proved there were fortunes to be made. Moab's population more than tripled from 1950 to 1960, and almost overnight the sleepy farming community became known as "The Uranium Capital of the World."

A smaller oil boom lasted into the 1960s, but Moab would have to wait another few decades for its next revolution. It was already obvious that Moab was rich in natural beauty: Arches National Monument had been set aside in 1929 (and made a park in 1971), Canyonlands National Park had been declared in 1964, and river-running was a tourism staple by the early 1970s. In the 1980s word started to get out that the slickrock landscape, so beloved by local motorcyclists and jeep drivers, was perfectly suited to a brand-new sport called mountain biking. Knobby tires stuck to the smooth sandstone like glue, and the endless hills, dips, bowls, and mountain trails were soon recognized as some of the best and most challenging off-road biking terrain in the world.

Thus Moab was reborn yet again as one of the prime tourist destinations in the Southwest, set smack in the middle of an outdoor adventurer's nirvana. Moab sees a million visitors annually. Thousands throng the streets, particularly during festivals celebrating mountain biking or four-wheel-drive vehicles. Drawn by world-class parks and adrenaline sports, enthusiasts arrive from around the world and just next door; they say you can tell spring has arrived when all the license plates in town turn Colorado green. T-shirt and trinket shops are packed from spring through fall, and the town's short Main Street is clotted with mountain bikers and four-wheel-drive vehicles. In the heat

of summer many visitors head up into the La Sals, which tower over town to the east, or to the Colorado River.

SIGHTS

Moab's past is spotlighted at the **Museum of Moab** (118 E. Center St., 435/259-7985, www.moabmuseum.org, 10 A.M.–5 P.M. Mon.–Fri., noon–5 P.M. Sat. and Sun., shorter hours Nov.–Mar., suggested $5 donation). Exhibits on geology, paleontology, and the town's human history include dinosaur bones and a 1907 Moab kitchen. It's across from the Grand County courthouse.

For a break from the desert, visit the **Scott M. Matheson Wetlands Preserve** (934 W. Kane Creek Blvd., 435/259-4629, daily sunrise–sunset, free), a Nature Conservancy site that protects 890 acres of marsh between Moab and the Colorado River. Birding is especially good there from spring to fall; more than 175 species have been noted. A mile-long loop trail leads to a two-story wildlife blind.

ENTERTAINMENT AND EVENTS

As a tourist epicenter, Moab has more nightlife than all the other towns in southern Utah combined—which still isn't saying all that much. For up-to-date listings of music, art, and other events, check out the free monthly *Moab Happenings,* available in print or online (http://moabhappenings.com). At Zax, Eddie McStiff's, or the Moab Brewery, you can start with dinner and a cold one and then follow up with the **Rio** (2 S. 100 W., 435/259-6666) or **Woody's Tavern** (221 S. Main St., 435/259-9323), which has live music on weekends spring through fall. **Frankie D's** (44 W. 200 N., 435/259-2654), set in what looks like an airplane hangar, has pool tables, a dance floor, and a patio with views. For a more upscale (i.e., grown-up) setting, try the **Vista Lounge** 1393 N. U.S. 191, 435/259-5201) inside Buck's Grill House or **The Ghost Bar** (218 N. 100 W., 435/259-3588) above Jeffrey's Steakhouse.

As you'd expect in an area with this much natural beauty, Moab's events center on the outdoors. In late March, runners in the

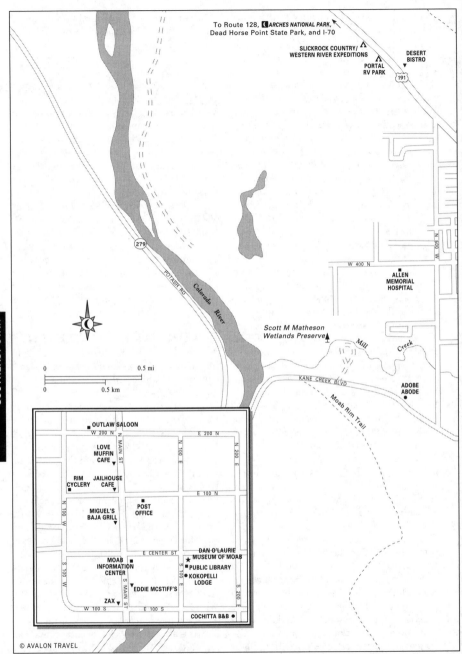

To Route 128, ◖*ARCHES NATIONAL PARK,*
Dead Horse Point State Park, and I-70

SLICKROCK COUNTRY/
WESTERN RIVER EXPEDITIONS

DESERT
BISTRO

PORTAL
RV PARK

191

279

POTASH RD

Colorado River

W 400 N

W 500 N

ALLEN
MEMORIAL
HOSPITAL

*Scott M Matheson
Wetlands Preserve*

Mill   Creek

KANE CREEK BLVD

ADOBE
ABODE

Moab Rim Trail

0   0.5 mi
0   0.5 km

OUTLAW SALOON

W 200 N

LOVE
MUFFIN
CAFE

N MAIN ST

N 100 E

E 200 N

N 200 E

RIM
CYCLERY

JAILHOUSE
CAFE

E 100 N

W 100 W

MIGUEL'S
BAJA GRILL

POST
OFFICE

E CENTER ST

DAN O'LAURIE
MUSEUM OF MOAB

S 100 W

MOAB
INFORMATION
CENTER

S MAIN ST

S 100 E

S 200 E

PUBLIC LIBRARY

KOKOPELLI
LODGE

ZAX

EDDIE MCSTIFF'S

W 100 S

E 100 S

COCHITTA B&B

© AVALON TRAVEL

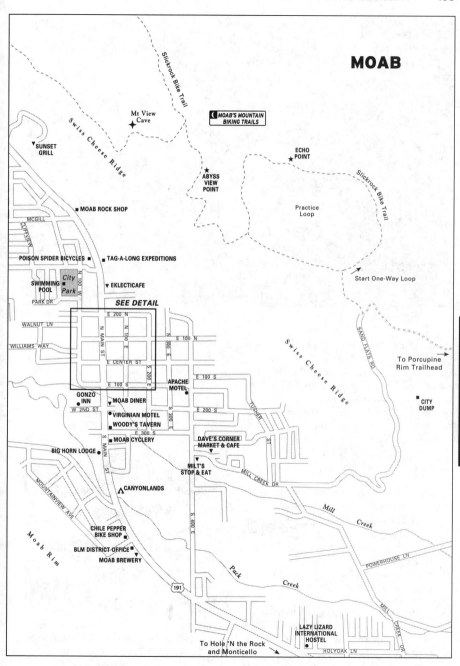

MOAB

- Slickrock Bike Trail
- Mt View Cave
- **MOAB'S MOUNTAIN BIKING TRAILS**
- ★ SUNSET GRILL
- Swiss Cheese Ridge
- ★ ECHO POINT
- ★ ABYSS VIEW POINT
- Slickrock Bike Trail
- ■ MOAB ROCK SHOP
- MCGILL
- CLIFFVIEW
- Practice Loop
- POISON SPIDER BICYCLES ■ ■ TAG-A-LONG EXPEDITIONS
- Start One-Way Loop
- SWIMMING POOL ■ City Park
- N 100 W
- ▼ EKLECTICAFE
- PARK DR
- **SEE DETAIL**
- E 200 N
- N 100 E
- WALNUT LN
- N MAIN ST
- N 300 E
- Swiss Cheese Ridge
- SAND FLATS RD
- WILLIAMS WAY
- E CENTER ST
- S 200 E
- To Porcupine Rim Trailhead
- E 100 S
- APACHE MOTEL ●
- ■ CITY DUMP
- GONZO INN ●
- E 100 S
- ▼ MOAB DINER
- W 2ND ST
- S 300 E
- ● VIRGINIAN MOTEL
- E 200 S
- TUSHER ST
- ■ WOODY'S TAVERN
- E 300 S
- ■ MOAB CYCLERY
- DAVE'S CORNER MARKET & CAFE ■
- S MAIN ST
- ● BIG HORN LODGE
- ▼ MILT'S STOP & EAT
- MILL CREEK DR
- ▲ CANYONLANDS
- Mill Creek
- MOUNTAINVIEW AVE
- Moab Rim
- CHILE PEPPER BIKE SHOP ■
- BLM DISTRICT OFFICE ■
- S 400 E
- ▼ MOAB BREWERY
- POWERHOUSE LN
- MILL CREEK DR
- 191
- Pack Creek
- LAZY LIZARD INTERNATIONAL HOSTEL ●
- To Hole 'N the Rock and Monticello
- HOLYOAK LN

Cliffs surround downtown Moab.

© RICHARD MAYER

Canyonlands Half Marathon thank their guardian angels the desert heat hasn't ramped up to full intensity yet. The **Easter Jeep Safari** in April crams the streets and nearby trails with four-wheelers. April also sees an influx of classic roadsters and rods for the **April Action Car Show**. The **Green River-Moab Friendship Cruise** (http://friendshipcruise. com) on Memorial Day weekend brings a flotilla drifting downstream from the city of Green River. June is the month to catch the **Canyonlands PCRA Rodeo** (www.moabcanyonlandsrodeo.com) at the fairgrounds.

The **Grand County Fair** arrives at the fairgrounds in August, and the **Moab Music Festival** brings the strains of chamber music to the area in early September. In October, artists head outdoors for a **Plein Air painting competition** (www.pleinairmoab.com), and the **Canyonlands Fat Tire Festival,** only one of several annual bike events, welcomes hundreds of bikers from near and far. Later in the month the **Moab Ho-Down** combines bike competitions with film screenings and a Halloween party.

SHOPPING

You'll find outstanding selections of regional books and maps at the multiagency Moab Information Center (25 E. Center St., 435/259-8825 or 800/635-6622, www.discovermoab.com), **Back of Beyond Books** (83 N. Main St., www.backofbeyondbooks.com, 435/259-5154 or 800/700-2859), or its sister store, **Arches Book Company** (89 N. Main St., 435/259-0782). Main Street is lined with souvenir shops specializing in T-shirts, shot glasses, and sunscreen, but if you're looking for something that captures the essence of your travels, the **Tom Till Gallery** (61 N. Main St., 435/259-9808 or 888/479-9808, www.tomtill.com) showcases the work of a local landscape photographer, and the **Hogan Trading Co.** (100 S. Main St., 435/259-8118, www.hogantrading.com) sells Native American and Southwestern arts and crafts. Even if you're not a geology buff, you'll be wowed by the fossils, dinosaur bones, meteorites, mining relics, and minerals at the **Moab Rock Shop** (600 N. Main St., 435/259-7312).

Outdoor Gear

For obvious reasons, Moab has no shortage of shops offering hiking and camping equipment or bikes. You can buy or rent bikes, browse gear, join a guided riding tour, and have your bike repaired at the **Chile Pepper Bike Shop** (702 S. Main St., 435/259-4688 or 888/677-4688, www.chilebikes.com) and **Poison Spider Bicycles** (497 N. Main St., 435/259-7882 or 800/635-1792, http://poisonspiderbicycles.com), which also has showers and a free repair stand out back. The **Rim Cyclery** (94 W. 100 N., 435/259-5333 or 888/304-8219, www.rim-cyclery.com) offers all these services and also sells camping gear.

Gearheads (471 S. Main St., 435/259-4327) is crammed with camping and general outdoor gear, including maps, guidebooks, tents, clothes, and hydration systems. Get your climbing gear at **Pagan Mountaineering** (59 S. Main St., 435/259-1117, www.climbmoab.com), which has more cams than you've probably even seen in one place before. For topo maps and guidebooks, head to one of the local bookstores or prepare with an online shopping spree at Canyonlands Natural History Association (435/259-6003 or 800/840-8978, www.cnha.org).

RECREATION

You're well advised to get a local guidebook, or at least a map, before venturing out into the countryside around Moab. Don't underestimate this landscape—the trails can be highly difficult in spots—and *always* bring enough food and water in case things don't go according to plan in the backcountry. Good map choices available all around town include three published by Latitude 40 (http://latitude-40maps.com)—*Moab East, Moab West,* and *Classic Moab*—and two by Trails Illustrated/National Geographic (www.natgeomaps.com), *Moab North* and *Moab South.*

C Mountain Biking Trails

Moab has enough mountain bike trails to fill a series of guidebooks; these are just a sampling. The granddaddy of all mountain bike routes,

the **Slickrock Trail** actually began as a motorcycle path. Mountain bikers have since taken over, with more than 100,000 riders per year attempting the 12-mile loop up, down, and around the petrified sand dunes northeast of town. This is a difficult trail, with sand traps, sheer drop-offs, few rest spots, and nothing but bare rock if you fall. It's also some of the most fun you can have on two wheels—the pedaling equivalent of interval training on a roller coaster, with great views to boot. If this is your first time, try the two-mile practice loop first. (**Bartlett Wash** northwest of town is another good slickrock area, albeit smaller, that sees much less traffic.)

To reach the Slickrock trailhead from Main Street, head east on 100 South Street; then follow the signs to Tusher Street and Sand Flats Road. You'll have to pay a fee ($10 per car or $2 per bike) to enter the **Sand Flats Recreation Area** (435/259-2444), which is about two miles southeast of downtown Moab. Keep going 6.4 miles past the Slickrock Trail parking lot to reach the trailhead for the **Porcupine Rim Trail,** an exhausting but exhilarating ride that climbs 1,000 feet up into the La Sal Mountains before peaking at a stunning view of Castle Valley from the southern rim. From there it's almost 3,000 feet downhill to SR 128 and back to town. A shuttle to the trailhead is a good idea for the 15-mile ride.

Another relentless climb awaits at the **Moab Rim,** but thankfully this one is shorter: almost 1,000 vertical feet in less than a mile. (One biking guidebook says that this "may well be the toughest mile in the world.") The top of the climb, 1.6 miles from the trailhead along Kane Creek Boulevard, is reward enough, but you can also continue another six technical miles to Hidden Valley and a downhill bike portage to rejoin U.S. 191 south of Moab. Across the canyon is the **Poison Spider Mesa Trail,** overlooking the Colorado above SR 279. A more moderate ride, this one starts near the dinosaur track and climbs 1,000 feet to the top of the mesa. Drink in the view—all the way to Arches National Park—before deciding if you're up for the Portal Trail, where you are highly advised

A mountain biker crosses slickrock near Moab.

© BLM/UTAH

to dismount and walk your bike down a narrow trail (with a sheer drop to one side) to avoid a potentially deadly fall. Via the Portal Trail this is a 12.7-mile one-way ride, rejoining SR 279 closer to Moab. Or you can turn around to make it a 12-mile round-trip ride.

On BLM land near the Island in the Sky are two good easy-to-moderate rides that should take about a half day each. The **Gemini Bridges** are a pair of arches at the edge of a mesa you can walk out onto. The trail leaves Highway 313 on its way out to the Island in the Sky and then coasts steadily downhill for 13.7 miles, passing the bridges and one small uphill en route, to Highway 191, just south of the SR 313 turnoff. You'll need a car shuttle to do the one-way ride. (The bike path along the north side of U.S. 191 will take you just north of the Colorado River bridge past the Arches entrance to the lower trailhead.)

Another easy trail takes you close to **Monitor and Merrimac Buttes** in roughly the same area. Turn off U.S. 191 to the left (west) just north of milepost 141, cross the train tracks

and park after another half mile. The 13.2-mile loop trail (take the right fork initially) leads you past the buttes as well as Determination Towers and the Mill Canyon Dinosaur Trail (also accessed off SR 279). Farther up U.S. 191 from Moab (17.3 miles) is a trailhead on the right (east) to the **Klondike Bluffs,** a steady climb 800 feet up slickrock and dirt to an amazing view over the northern part of Arches National Park. (Look for dinosaur tracks on the way up.) This is a medium-difficulty trail that's 14.4 miles round-trip.

The **Sovereign Trail** is a 20-mile single-track loop north of town that was developed by a group of local motorcyclists who support responsible riding and sharing trails (see www.ridewithrespect.org). Most bikers rate it as moderate in difficulty. It starts from the parking area a few miles out the Willow Springs Road (turn off U.S. 191 to the right just past the SR 313 turnoff). It's possible to make smaller loops by turning around at various intersections. Also north of town is the **Bar-M Loop,** a seven-mile loop that's mostly flat, with some slickrock. This one is good for families and beginners.

When the summer heat sets in, bikers head up into the La Sals, where longer trails such as **Moonlight Meadows** (a nine-mile loop) offer great single-track and lung-busting climbs. The **Burro Pass** trail, an 8–19-mile loop, passes two mountain lakes and viewing points of Arches and Canyonlands National Parks. Another good ride is the **Three Lake Trail,** a 14-mile figure-eight loop of faint single-track past Oowah, Clark, and Warner Lakes.

Mountain Biking Overnight Trips

Several longer trails await riders who are willing to spend a night or more outdoors—and carry everything they need during the day. While more of an undertaking, these trips really let you get far out into the backcountry, far from the day-pedal crowds. You'll need a set of racks and panniers or a bike trailer to carry your gear. The **White Rim Trail** around Canyonlands's Island in the Sky is a 3–4 day ride, and one of the most incredible mountain bike trips in the country. **Kokopelli's Trail** is a 142-mile odyssey from the Colorado mountains to the Moab slickrock. It starts just over the border near Loma, Colorado, 15 miles west of Grand Junction, and roughly follows the Colorado River southwest before climbing into the foothills of the La Sals and descending to Moab. Most people take six days to do the entire ride, which covers everything from fire roads to single-track, but it's possible to resupply, start, or stop at several points along the way. Various maps and guides to this epic journey are available. (You can access parts of this trail from some of the day trails north of town.)

Recommended companies for bike tours in Moab include area bike shops, as well as **Rim Mountain Bike Tours** (1233 S. U.S. 191, 435/259-5223 or 800/626-7335, www.rimtours.com) and **Western Spirit Cycling** (478 Mill Creek Dr., 435/259-8732 or 800/845-2453, www.western-spirit.com). Prices start around $135 per person for half-day trips, including bike rental.

Hiking

Though most people around here hit the backcountry on two wheels (or four), dozens of hiking trails snake through the desert and hills around Moab. From the Jaycee Park Recreation Site four miles down Potash Road (SR 279), it's possible to hike two steep miles up to the **Portal Overlook.** Six miles farther down the road, a steep trail (1.5 miles one-way) leads to **Corona Arch.**

Across the Colorado River on Kane Creek Boulevard, another steep trail leads three miles up to the **Moab Rim** and into the area known as **Behind the Rocks,** a maze of sandstone fins similar to the Fiery Furnace in Arches National Park. Farther down Kane Creek Boulevard, the jeep road up **Pritchett Canyon** leads past (and sometimes through) small pools to a natural bridge, and a moderate two-mile (one-way) trail up **Hunters Canyon** passes Hunter Arch high on the right-hand side above cottonwood trees and pools. (The trailheads for these hikes are 2.6, 3.1, and 7.5 miles from U.S. 191/Main Street, respectively.)

From SR 128 upstream along the Colorado River, look for the turnoff for **Negro Bill Canyon** on the right after three miles. This slickrock gorge leads two miles to **Morning Glory Natural Bridge,** the sixth longest in the country at 243 feet, located in the second side canyon on the right. You can rejoin the main canyon and continue hiking for a few more miles. The canyon was named after William Granstaff, a mixed-race cowboy who ran cattle here in the 1870s. A century later it was the site of a skirmish in the so-called Sagebrush Rebellion, when anti-government locals protested setting the canyon aside as a wilderness area.

Climbing and Canyoneering

Although the Wingate is the only relatively solid sandstone layer in this area, climbers can find plenty of vertical relief within a quick trip of Moab. **Wall Street** is frighteningly close to the traffic on Potash Road but is a good place to experience desert climbing for the first time. Broad, flat **Castle Valley** along SR 128 is punctuated by towers the size of office buildings with names like the Nuns, the Priest, and the Rectory. Castleton Tower is the home of

HIKING TIPS

Wallace Stegner once wrote, "We simply need that wild country available to us, even if we never do more than drive to its edge and look in. For it can be a means of reassuring ourselves of our sanity as creatures, a part of the geography of hope." The Four Corners has that wild country in abundance, and the possibilities for scenery, solitude, and exploration seem limitless. From paved national park paths to terrifying scrambles along canyon ledges, it's all here. You can take a short ramble from your car to a canyon overlook, enjoying the views and natural quiet, or descend into that canyon and its tributaries for weeks without seeing another person.

For those hoping to escape rain or snow, miles of sandstone ledges let you soak up sunshine like a lazy lizard. For those weary of the desert, mountain ranges offer deep summer shade or snow cover from fall to spring. Many trails are developed and accessible even to visitors with disabilities, while countless more are rough, steep, and unmaintained. Remote ruins, petroglyphs, slot canyons, and hidden springs are only a few of the goodies waiting in the backcountry.

The canyon country is a spectacular terrain but not one to be taken lightly. Heed advice regarding heat and water, and be prepared for extreme and changing weather conditions, especially at high altitudes. During the summer monsoon season (roughly July–Sept.), monumental afternoon cloudbursts occur almost daily. Summer temperatures often climb over 100°F, and subzero winter cold is common.

Since you'll be carrying so much weight in water (eight pounds per gallon), it's smart to minimize the weight of the rest of your gear as much as possible. But always carry a map and an emergency survival kit. If you're backpacking, go with companions, especially if it's your first trip or your first trip in high-desert terrain.

Keep yourself safe and also protect the environment by following the guidelines of the **Leave No Trace** program (800/332-4100, www.lnt.org). This includes careful planning (let someone responsible know where you're going and when you plan to return); traveling and camping on durable surfaces (stay off the crypto!); disposing of waste properly (no burning toilet paper); leaving things as you find them (disturbing archaeological sites on federal land is a felony); minimizing the impact of campfires (better yet, use a stove or bring no-cook meals); being considerate of your fellow campers; and leaving wildlife alone.

---

one of the country's classic multipitch tower climbs, leading to a flat top the size of a studio apartment—an incredible spot. Arches and Canyonlands National Park have a few routes, including Washer Woman Arch off the Island in the Sky and Owl Rock in Arches, but be warned that climbing regulations are more restrictive in the parks than outside (no chalk and no new bolts, for starters). **Indian Creek,** en route to the Needles District of Canyonlands, is another world-famous climbing area.

Canyoneering involves boulder-hopping, minor rock climbing, and possible swimming or rappelling to access canyons that would otherwise be too difficult or dangerous to enter. This is not for the uninitiated or faint of heart, but if you know what you're doing—or are with someone who does—a sense of adventure and discovery awaits around every canyon curve.

Buy or rent climbing gear at Pagan Mountaineering (59 S. Main, 435/259-1117, www.climbmoab.com). You can arrange for a guided trip there or schedule instruction and trips from **Moab Cliffs & Canyons** (253 N. Main, 435/259-3317 or 877/641-5271, www.cliffsandcanyons.com) or **Moab Desert Adventures** (471 S. Main St., 435/260-2404 or 877/765-6622, www.moabdesertadventures.com). Prices start at around $100 for a half-day trip for two people. **Desert Highlights** (50 E. Center St., 435/259-4433 or 800/747-1342, www.deserthighlights.com) specializes in canyoneering, from $95 per person for a half-day trip.

CANYONEERING

For a sense of discovery around every turn, nothing beats canyoneering. Though one of the more exciting ways to explore canyon country, it's also one of the most potentially hazardous. Descending or ascending narrow canyons often requires rock-climbing skills and sometimes, technical gear. There's the risk of falling and getting hurting or trapping yourself in some of the most remote wilderness around. Add to this the danger of **flash floods** in monsoon season and the chance of hypothermia, since you may have to wade or even swim to get through some narrow passages.

Flash floods arrive with little or no warning and, even if the sky is blue overhead, can fill a canyon with roiling water, mud, trees, and boulders much quicker than you can escape it. For a reminder of the forces involved, look for tree trunks lodged many yards overhead in narrow canyons by seasonal floods. Flash floods are often preceded by an earthy smell and sound like a train rushing down the canyon. Smaller ones can be fun to watch from a safe vantage point, but large ones are deadly.

Take wading shoes, synthetic clothing (damp cotton is a killer), waterproof bags for your things, and a walking stick or pole for balance and to check for deep holes hidden under muddy water. Only tackle the really wet canyons in hot weather. If necessary, bring ropes and/or nylon webbing and climbing harnesses, and know how to use them or go with someone who does.

Claustrophobes should find something else to do–some slot canyons are so narrow you'll have to remove your backpack and shimmy through sideways. Many excellent guidebooks list canyon hikes in detail. For more information, contact the **American Canyoneering Association** (435/590-8889, www.canyoneering.net), which offers courses, or check out **Canyoneering USA** (435/648-3089, www.canyoneeringusa. com) or the websites www.americansouthwest. net and http://climb-utah.com.

Rafting

Moab's location near the confluence of the two biggest rivers in the Four Corners means that outdoor enthusiasts aren't limited to just dry land. Trips range from easy afternoon floats to serious, multiday white water. Permits are necessary whether you're floating through Canyonlands National Park or BLM land outside park boundaries.

Between Grand Junction, Colorado, and Moab, the Colorado River provides a great introduction to desert rafting. Rapids ranging from Class II to Class IV have names like Sock-It-To-Me, Last Chance, and Room-of-Doom. In all its 131 river miles from the border to Moab, **Westwater Canyon,** from the Westwater Ranger Station (4.5 miles from the border) to the landing at Cisco, requires permits, which are available by phoning the BLM office in Moab (82 E. Dogwood Ave., 435/259-2100, $7 per person). Launches are available two months in advance and are assigned on a first-called, first-served basis. This trip takes

1–2 days. From Dewey Bridge to the boat ramp below the Potash Plant along SR 279 is 46 miles and takes 2–3 days. You don't need a permit for this stretch, but check with the BLM for camping rules. The Potash ramp is the last takeout before Hite Marina on Lake Powell, 118 miles downriver.

After two days of leisurely floating through deep canyons, the Colorado River joins with the Green and explodes into **Cataract Canyon,** where 26 rapids have names like Hell-to-Pay and the Big Drops. This stretch provides some of the best white-water thrills in the country in May and June, its spring surge unfettered by any dam. The still waters of Lake Powell mark the end of the trip. There are no daily launch limits, but reservation fees ($20–30) and permits ($20 pp) are required to cross through Canyonlands National Park. The reservations office (435/259-4351, weekday mornings) will answer questions and help with trip planning. Applications are available online (www.nps.gov/cany).

Moab is full of experienced rafting

companies, which run trips May–September. Prices start around $40 per person for a half day on The Daily (a short and easy white-water run) to around $950 per person on a five-day Cataract Canyon adventure. Westwater Canyon will run you about $400 per person for two or three days.

One of the oldest companies in town is **Tex's Riverways** (691 N. 500 W., 435/259-5101 or 877/662-2839, www.texsriverways.com), which has been operating since 1958 on the Green and Colorado Rivers. They run a jet boat down to the confluence and back on a regular basis that can pick you up if you're doing your own trip. **Tag-a-Long Expeditions** (452 N. Main St., 435/259-8946 or 800/453-3292, www.tagalong.com) has been in business since 1964 and can help you organize self-guided trips. **Sheri Griffith Expeditions** (2231 S. U.S. 191, 435/259-8229 or 800/332-2439, www.griffith-exp.com) organizes women-only raft trips and many other kinds, while **Adrift Adventures** (378 N. Main St., 435/259-8594 or 800/874-4483, www.adrift.net) leads horseback and four-wheel-drive excursions as well as raft trips.

Multisport and Other Tours

Many of the above companies can combine hiking, biking, climbing, and rafting into a customized itinerary. You can also stop by the **Moab Adventure Center** (225 S. Main St., 435/259-7019 or 866/904-1163, www.moabadventurecenter.com), which offers a full buffet of tours from hikes to Hummer safaris to hot air balloon rides.

Hundreds of miles of dirt roads crisscross the rough country of southeastern Utah, and Moab is at the center of it all. Blazed by ranchers and uranium prospectors, many are still popular with four-wheel-drive enthusiasts, who flock to town for the **Easter Jeep Safari. Tag-a-Long Expeditions** (452 N. Main St., 435/259-8946 or 800/453-3292, www.tagalong.com) has driving tours into Canyonlands National Park, including jet-boat/jeep combination day trips.

Adrift Adventures (378 N. Main St., 435/259-8594 or 800/874-4483, www.adrift.net) offers horseback trail rides through the canyons combined with white-water rafting for $950 per adult for five days. Based at the airport, **Skydive Moab** (435/259-5867, www.skydivemoab.com) offers tandem jumps from $215 per person.

ACCOMMODATIONS
In Town

Bear in mind that in this tourist town, hotel prices can fall by as much as half out of season (Nov.–Feb.). For longer stays, rent condos and homes through **Accommodations Unlimited** (www.moabcondorentals.com).

Aside from camping, Moab's cheapest lodging is at the **Lazy Lizard International Hostel** (1213 S. U.S. 191, 435/259-6057, www.lazylizardhostel.com). It's chock-full of character, with a kitchen, laundry, hot tub, and showers ($3 for nonguests). Dorm rooms are $9 per person, and they also have private rooms ($24 d) and log cabins ($29–48 d). Campsites ($6 pp) include full use of the facilities.

While he was in town filming *Rio Bravo*, John Wayne stayed at the **Apache Motel** (166 S. 400 E., 435/259-5727 or 800/228-6882, $45–175), which has suites and kitchenettes in addition to standard rooms. The **Big Horn Lodge** (550 S. Main St., 435/259-6171 or 800/325-6171, www.moabbighorn.com, $50–110) offers package deals that include tours. The **Virginian Motel** (70 E. 2nd S., 435/259-5951 or 800/261-2063, $50–100) is located near Mill Creek, a pretty spot for an evening walk. The **Kokopelli Lodge** (72 S. 100 E., 435/259-7615 or 888/530-3134, www.kokopellilodge.com, $35–80) has eight rooms a block from Main Street.

It's easy to see how the **Adobe Abode** bed-and-breakfast (778 W. Kane Creek Blvd., 435/259-7716, www.adobeabodemoab.com, $140–190) got its name. The distinctive building boasts tile floors and a hot tub, and is located next to the wetland preserve. The attitude of many Moab visitors is summed up in the name of the **Gonzo Inn** (100 W. 200 S., 435/259-2515 or 800/791-4044, www.gonzoinn.com), a more luxurious place with a morning espresso bar and an outdoor pool. Rooms are $150, and the well-appointed suites range $205–340.

A late-1800s Victorian home houses the **Cali**

Cochitta B&B (110 S. 200 E., 435/259-4961 or 888/429-8112, www.moabdreaminn.com, $90–165), offering three rooms, a suite, and two cottages. The AAA four-diamond lodging in town is the ◖ **Sunflower Hill B&B Inn** (185 N. 300 E., 435/259-2974 or 800/662-2786, www.sunflowerhill.com, $165–235). Twelve rooms in two buildings have antique beds (some have private balconies), and wooded pathways lead to an outdoor hot tub.

Outside of Town

Actor Robert Duvall and author Edward Abbey are just two of the notables to grace the **Pack Creek Ranch** (435/259-5091 or 888/879-6622, www.packcreekranch.com) with their presence. Although it dates to the 19th century, this place is still a working ranch, said to have been named after an incident when a pair of prospectors ditched their gear by a nearby stream to escape Native Americans. The 300-acre ranch has a wide variety of lodging options, including rooms in the ranch house, bunk houses, and fully renovated cabins with full kitchens and rock fireplaces—but emphatically *no* phones or TVs. Wireless is available, and there's also a sauna and hot tub. In-season rates range from $95 for a two-person cabin to $175 for a four-person one and $240 for a six-person farmhouse. The ranch is in the foothills of the La Sals southeast of Moab, six miles from the southern end of the La Sal Mountain Loop Road on Highway 191.

Two more luxury properties are 15 miles north of Moab along Highway 128. First is the **Red Cliffs Lodge** (435/259-2002 or 866/812-2002, www.redcliffslodge.com), with 20 one- and two-bedroom cabins ($220–320), at a bend in the river. Cabins have fireplaces and whirlpool tubs, and there's a restaurant, pool, and winery complete with tasting room on-site. (They offer substantial room discounts at certain times throughout the year.)

Next door is the ◖ **Sorrel River Ranch** (435/259-4642 or 877/317-8244, www.sorrelriver.com), where the contrast between rugged setting and deluxe accommodations is so drastic it's almost surreal. The Colorado flows only yards from the porches and balconies of the rooms and suites ($400 and up), while the red towers of Castle Valley and the snowcapped La Sals rise to the east. The 160-acre resort, on the site of a century-old ranch, has a full-service spa, an outdoor pool, an excellent restaurant, and a full slate of activities, including horseback riding, rafting, and mountain biking.

If you want to get away from it all, the **Mt. Peale Inn & Cabins⊛** (435/686-2284, www.mtpeale.com) offers a tranquil alpine retreat on the southeastern slopes of the La Sals, about 30 minutes from the touristy bustle of Moab. Rooms ($90–130) or cabins ($140–210) boast views and easy access to forest trails. The rustic resort has a dining hall (serving dinner and breakfast) and meeting facilities that can accommodate large groups. Massage services and plant medicine workshops are offered.

Camping

These commercial campgrounds are open year-round: **Canyonlands Campground** (555 S. Main St., 435/259-6848 or 800/522-6848, www.canyonlandsrv.com, $25–40), **Portal RV Resort** (1261 N. Hwy. 191, 435/259-6108 or 800/574-2028, www.portalrvresort.com, $21–55), north of town on U.S. 191, and **Slickrock Campground** (1301½ N. Hwy. 191, 435/259-7660 or 800/448-8873, www.slickrockcampground.com), where tent sites are $23, RV sites run $31–38, and cabins with air-conditioning are $49.

In addition to developed campgrounds at **Arches National Park, Canyonlands National Park,** and **Dead Horse Point State Park,** many primitive campsites are available on BLM land near Moab, ranging $8–12 per site per night. There are 11 campgrounds up Highway 128 along the Colorado River, from Goose Island (1.4 miles from the U.S. 191 intersection) to Dewey Bridge (29 miles). Three campgrounds can be found along Kane Creek Road, from Kings Bottom (2.8 miles from the U.S. 191 intersection) to Hunter Canyon (8 miles). Another 33 sites are located in campgrounds along SR 279, from Jaycee Park (four miles from the U.S. 191 intersection) to Gold Bar (10 miles). The Sand Flats Recreation Area

CAMPING

Too often we take for granted the enormous tracts of public land that belong to all of us in the United States. The Colorado Plateau is a prime example. Much of the land out here is owned by the state or federal government, and there's nothing like the freedom of driving for hours, pulling your car off onto a dirt road up in a national forest or across a Bureau of Land Management (BLM)-managed mesa, and finding your own private spot to set up camp just as the sun sets.

Any land managed by the U.S. Forest Service (USFS) and the BLM is open to **dispersed (at-large) camping.** Exceptions are areas specially designated as closed to camping and places that have already been developed with campsites (in these, stay in the campsites only). Dispersed camping ranges from hike-in backcountry sites to clearings alongside roads where you can park a car, camper, or trailer. Fires are often prohibited, particularly in times of drought, and land ownership can be a confusing patchwork of public and private holdings, so check with the local office of the USFS or the BLM for details. Camping is usually free and limited to a maximum stay of two or three weeks.

State and national parks are subject to more regulations; here you often have to stay in developed campsites (often on a first-come, first-served basis) or at least secure a permit for backcountry camping, and you'll probably have to stay in designated zones or campsites once you're out there. **Developed campgrounds** usually include bathrooms, picnic tables, and fire rings, and sometimes can be reserved ahead of time. Fees are $5-15 per campsite.

On private land you are limited to **private campgrounds,** which are still plentiful. These offer tent and RV spaces, including electricity, water, and sewer hookups, and often have showers, laundry services, and other activities and services. Some private campgrounds have small **cabins** with air-conditioning and heat for about the price of a budget motel room. (Usually, you supply the linens and share the campground showers and restrooms.) More elaborate places, typified by **KOA Kampgrounds** (406/248-7444, www.koa.com) come complete with pools, game rooms, hot tubs, saunas, volleyball courts, and even Wi-Fi or cable. Features such as bicycle rental, miniature golf, and summer children's programs cost extra. In the high country, many campgrounds close for winter, and during peak seasons, reservations and/or deposits may be necessary in popular areas like the Grand Canyon. Private campsites cost $20-60, and some can be reserved online.

There are also private cabins or hogans on the Native American reservations (prices vary). Otherwise, you must secure permission from the tribes for backcountry camping ($5 pp per day). On the Navajo Reservation, contact the **Navajo Parks and Recreation Department** office in Window Rock (928/871-6647, www.navajonationparks.org, 8 A.M.–5 P.M.), or the **Cameron Visitor Center** at the junction of U.S. 89 and U.S. 64 in Cameron, Arizona (928/679-2303, 8 A.M.–5 P.M.).

You can reserve campsites in national forests and some national parks online at www.recreation.gov.

near the Slickrock Trail has 120 sites ($10). All are open year-round; contact the BLM's Moab field office (435/259-2100) for more details.

Two seasonal Forest Service campgrounds are located up the La Sal Mountain Loop Road. Small but scenic Oowah campground has 11 first-come, first-served tent sites ($10). For the same price, Warner campground (877/444-6777, www.recreation.gov) has 20 sites large enough for RVs 25 feet or less (no hookups), as well as a cabin ($50). Monti–La Sal National Forest also allows dispersed camping (no fee) for up to 14 days. Call the Moab ranger district (435/259-7155) for more information.

FOOD

Maybe it's all the physical exertion that goes on around here, but Moab has more than its fair share of places to gas up and refuel your internal engines, from vegetarian-friendly ethnic eateries to steakhouses. You can even stop by **Dave's Corner Market** (401 Mill Creek Dr., 435/259-6999, open daily) before heading out for a day on the Slickrock Trail to grab a cup of coffee brewed by mayor Dave Sakrison.

Along Main Street

The ◖ **Jailhouse Cafe** (101 N. Main St., 435/259-3900, breakfast daily, $7–11) occupies a turn-of-the-20th-century courthouse with two-foot adobe walls, serving up ginger pancakes, Southwest eggs Benedict, and other interesting day starters. The outdoor porch at the **Eklecticafe** (352 N. Main St., 435/259-6896, breakfast and lunch daily) has a varied menu that includes Indonesian, Greek, and Southwestern dishes along with burgers and wraps ($7–9). Breakfast is served anytime at the throwback **Moab Diner** (189 S. Main St., 435/259-4006, all meals daily, $6–15), where a long list of burgers, sandwiches, and other traditional favorites round out the menu.

The **Moab Brewery** (686 S. Main St., 435/259-6333, lunch and dinner daily, $8–20) has a separate restaurant area, where they serve steaks, seafood, pasta, and vegetarian dishes. Their brews include Dead Horse Ale and Raven Stout. **Eddie McStiff's** (57 S. Main St., 435/259-2337, lunch and dinner daily, $7–20) has a similar menu, but their organic brick-oven pizzas are especially good.

The **Love Muffin Cafe** (139 N. Main St., 435/259-6833, open daily, seasonal hours) is a hip breakfast-and-coffee spot that also serves sandwiches, soups, and salads for less than $10. They bake their own goodies and roast their own java.

Miguel's Baja Grill (51 N. Main St., 435/259-6546, dinner daily, $12–20) serves great Mexican food, and **Zax** (96 S. Main St., 435/259-6555, all meals daily) offers a varied menu, plus an all-you-can-eat pizza, soup, and salad bar for $13 per person. The outside patio with misters is sweet relief on hot afternoons.

Elsewhere Around Town

If you need a curry fix, head a block east of Main, where Singha Thai (92 E. Center, 435/259-0039, lunch Mon.–Sat., dinner daily,

$12–18) serves mild to spicy standbys like *Tom Yum,* volcano shrimp, and pad thai. **Milt's Stop & Eat** (356 S. 400 E., 435/259-7424, lunch and dinner daily) is an authentic 1954 diner with burgers and sandwiches starting at less than $5.

Uranium millionaire Charlie Steen built his dream home on a hillside overlooking Moab. Today it goes by the name of the **Sunset Grill** (900 N. U.S. 191, 435/259-7146, dinner Mon.–Sat.), serving steaks and seafood (entrées $14–26) with a wonderful view thrown in for free.

Families favor the Wild West show and cowboy supper cookout at the **Bar-M Chuckwagon** (435/259-2276 or 800/214-2085, www.barm-chuckwagon.com, 2–6 nights/week, Apr.–mid-Oct., $28 adults, $14 children), seven miles north of town on U.S. 191. Dinner is served "trail style" on metal plates, and reservations are recommended; the show (faux gunfight and all) starts at 7 P.M.

For those who enjoy the extreme of spending a day sweating on a trail and then sitting down for a tablecloth-and-wine sort of dinner, head to the **Desert Bistro** (36 S. 100 W., 435/259-0756, www.desertbistro.com, dinner most evenings spring–fall, $18–50), which offers a seasonal menu in a cozy setting, or take River Road to the ◖ **River Grill** at Sorrel River Ranch (Milepost 17 on SR 128, 435/259-4642, all meals daily in summer), where dinner entrées are $18–40 and reservations are strongly recommended.

INFORMATION

While each federal land-management agency has an office in town, they've turned over everything tourist-related to the **Moab Information Center** (Main St. and Center St., 435/259-8825 or 800/635-6622, www.discovermoab.com, 8 A.M.–8 or 9 P.M. Mon.–Sat., 9 A.M.–7 P.M. Sun.). "The MIC" is the place to go for just about any question you might have; if they don't have the answer, they know who does. They also sell maps and books.

GETTING THERE AND AROUND
Inter-City Transportation

Moab Luxury Coach (435/940-4212, www.moabluxurycoach.com) has regular shuttle schedules between Moab and Salt Lake City or Grand Junction, Colorado, with stops in Blanding, Bluff, Green River, Monticello, Price, and Provo. Rates start at $70, depending on the destination and offer tours, local transportation on demand 24 hours a day, and charters to far-flung points like Las Vegas or Flagstaff. The closest Amtrak train and Greyhound bus stops are at Green River.

Great Lakes Airlines (800/554-5111, www.flygreatlakes.com) has flights to Denver, Las Vegas, and Page, Arizona, from Canyonlands Field, located 16 miles north of Moab on U.S. 191.

Car Rental

Enterprise (435/259-8505) rents cars at the airport terminal. In town, **Thrifty** rents cars at the Moab Valley Inn (711 S. Main St., 435/259-7317 or 800/847-4389). **Farabee's Jeep Rentals** (35 Grand Ave., 435/259-7494 or 877/970-5337, www.farabeejeeprentals.com) rents four-wheel-drive jeeps starting around $150 per day in season, as does **Cliffhanger Jeep Rental** (40 W. Center St., 435/259-0889, http://cliffhangerjeeprental.com), which also has ATVs.

Shuttle Services

If you're not up for tacking a 10-mile pedal onto each end of your exhausting mountain bike ride, ring up one of Moab's many shuttle services, which can drop you off and/or pick you up at either end. They're also handy for raft trips and getting to and from the airport. Prices start around $10 per person. Ask at any bike shop or contact **Coyote Shuttle** (435/259-8656, www.coyoteshuttle.com) or **Roadrunner Shuttle** (435/259-9402, www.roadrunnershuttle.com), which also drops off boaters.

NEAR MOAB
Highway 279 (Potash-Lower Colorado River Byway)

Late afternoon is an especially good time for this beautiful drive, which snakes southwest along the bank of the Colorado River after leaving U.S. 191 north of the bridge. SR 279 (also known as Potash Road) is paved for 16 miles as it runs within touching distance of the

canyon's north wall. Look for **rock art** panels five miles from the turnoff from U.S. 191, near a popular rock-climbing spot called Wall Street (be careful of parked vehicles and climbers). More petroglyphs and a set of **dinosaur tracks** are signposted at 6.2 miles, and at 9.9 miles is the trailhead to **Corona Arch** and **Bowtie Arch.** Look right at 13.6 miles for **Jug Handle Arch.** The pavement ends at the large evaporation ponds of the Moab Salt Plant, also known as the Intrepid Potash Plant. From here, a dirt road continues to the White Rim Road and the Schaefer Trail inside Canyonlands National Park (high-clearance vehicle recommended).

Highway 128 (Upper Colorado River Byway)

An even more scenic byway, known locally as River Road, heads 49 miles northeast through the Colorado River Gorge from the south side of the U.S. 191 bridge and is paved all the way to I-70. At the turnoff is a picnic area and, just upriver, a natural spring gushing from the canyon wall, where you can refill your water bottles with clear, cold water. Three miles from the intersection is trailhead parking for **Negro Bill Canyon.** At 13 miles, the road passes **Castle Valley,** a filming location used in Westerns and TV commercials. (Red Cliffs Lodge at milepost 14 hosts a free movie museum.) Just before milepost 25, an overlook offers stunning views of the **Fisher Towers,** which rise above **Professor Valley** against the backdrop of the La Sal Mountains.

The road crosses the river at **Dewey Bridge,** where a one-lane suspension bridge of wood and steel built in 1916 was replaced by a concrete span in the 1980s. (The old bridge burned in a 2008 wildfire.) The landscape opens up into barren rolling flatland as SR 128 nears I-70. If you have the time, don't miss the turnoff at milepost 44, leading to the ghost town of **Cisco.**

La Sal Mountains

The second-highest range in Utah rises above the high desert east of Moab, tantalizing sweltering visitors with visions of snowcapped peaks well into summer. (The name, meaning "salt"

in Spanish, is said to have come from Spanish missionaries who couldn't believe there was snow in the midst of such a furnace.)

The paved 62-mile **La Sal Mountain Loop** climbs the mountains' flanks between Castle Valley and U.S. 191, beginning six miles south of Moab and joining SR 128 in the Upper Colorado River Gorge. Mount Peale (at 12,721 feet) is the tallest of six peaks above 12,000 feet, where mountain lakes sparkle amid fir and aspen forests. It's a gorgeous drive with picnic areas, viewing points, and unpaved spur roads its entire length, open late spring–early fall.

En route, more than 60 miles of trails and plenty of back roads tempt hikers, bikers, and horseback riders in summer and skiers and snowshoers in winter. Mountain bikers get a great workout at these elevations; two of the most popular rides each entail about 3,700 feet of elevation change. Many hikers attempt to summit **Mt. Tukuhnikivatz**, a five-mile endeavor up and back that starts at 10,000 feet and climbs another 2,400.

Allow about three hours for the loop—longer if you plan to explore. Hairpin turns make the route unsuitable for large RVs. For current road and trail conditions, contact the Forest Service's Moab Ranger District (435/259-7155).

◀ ARCHES NATIONAL PARK

In the minds of many, Arches National Park is synonymous with the Southwest itself. The image of Delicate Arch—only one of more than 2,000 found within the park—has been emblazoned on everything from license plates to shot glasses. Although natural arches occur around the world, there are more here than anywhere else, along with such geological oddities as spires, fins, pinnacles, and balanced boulders.

To say the least, Arches is a popular park. Besides mountain biking, it's the other reason visitors come to Moab. Its wonders are for the most part easily accessible (i.e., close to a paved road), and the park is just the right size to "do" in a day, making it popular with families and RVers. Expect crowds and a full campground in spring and summer, especially around popular weekends like the Jeep Safari and Fat Tire Festival. The best wa[...] vehicles searching fo[...] rive early or late in [...] at its best.

The Setting

Like most of the Moab region, Ar[...] Park sits on top of an ancient underground sa[...] bed left over from a sea that once covered the Colorado Plateau. Over time, rock layers on top of the salt thrust upward and cracked as the salt shifted and flowed. Water and ice gradually ate away at the exposed cracks to form freestanding fins, many of which are still visible throughout the area (think of them as "proto-arches"). These in turn were carved by erosion until the relatively soft sandstone was worn away.

Sometimes the interplay of weight and balance was just right so that an **arch** was created. The physics are complex, but in a nutshell, chunks of rock dropped away in a curved line, leaving an arch. Horizontal **pothole arches** were cut through by the chemical reaction of rainwater collecting in natural depressions.

Today the park's sandstone spans range in size from 3 feet—the minimum size for something to be considered an arch—to 306 feet, in the case of Landscape Arch. Most are formed from salmon-colored Entrada Sandstone and a few from tan Navajo Sandstone.

Visitor Center

Arches National Park is open 365 days a year, 24 hours a day. The visitors center (435/719-2299, www.nps.gov/arch, 7:30 A.M.–6:30 P.M. mid-Mar.–Oct., 8 A.M.–4:30 P.M. Nov.–mid-Mar.) is five miles north of Moab on U.S. 191. Entrance is $5 per person or $10 per vehicle and good for a week. (The $25 Southeast Utah Passport gives access to Arches, Canyonlands National Park, Hovenweep National Monument, and Natural Bridges National Monument for a year.) The visitors center has exhibits on the park's geology and human history as well as an orientation film shown every half hour. The bookstore also carries maps and gifts. Ask about ranger-guided hikes, such as the popular Fiery Furnace walk, and campfire programs.

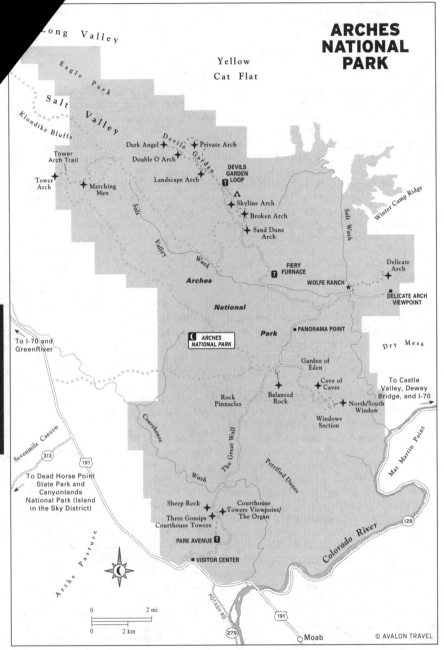

ARCHES NATIONAL PARK

Long Valley

Eagle Park

Salt Valley

Klondike Bluffs

Yellow Cat Flat

Dark Angel

Tower Arch Trail

Tower Arch

Marching Men

Devils Garden

Private Arch

Double O Arch

Landscape Arch

DEVILS GARDEN LOOP

Skyline Arch

Broken Arch

Sand Dune Arch

Salt Valley Wash

Arches

National

Park

FIERY FURNACE

WOLFE RANCH

Winter Camp Ridge

Salt Wash

Delicate Arch

DELICATE ARCH VIEWPOINT

ARCHES NATIONAL PARK

To I-70 and GreenRiver

PANORAMA POINT

Dry Mesa

Garden of Eden

Cove of Caves

To Castle Valley, Dewey Bridge, and I-70

Rock Pinnacles

Balanced Rock

North/South Window

Windows Section

Courthouse Wash

Sevenmile Canyon

313

191

To Dead Horse Point State Park and Canyonlands National Park (Island in the Sky District)

The Great Wall

Petrified Dunes

Mat Martin Point

Sheep Rock

Three Gossips Courthouse Towers

Courthouse Towers Viewpoint/ The Organ

Arths Pasture

PARK AVENUE

VISITOR CENTER

Colorado River

128

POTASH RD

279

191

Moab

0   2 mi

0   2 km

© AVALON TRAVEL

Skyline Arch in Arches National Park is accessible by an easy trail.

Scenic Drive and Hikes

From the visitors center, the park's 18-mile scenic drive zigzags up the steep side of the Moab Fault to climb the mesa where most of the park is located. If this is your first taste of the local scenery, be prepared to be impressed. The high-altitude desert is littered with rock towers and formations of every shape imaginable, backdropped by the La Sal Mountains. It's truly an amazing sight, especially in the early morning or late afternoon, when the sun's low angle sets the stone on fire.

The first turnoff is for **Park Avenue** through the **Courthouse Towers** (a set of giant stone formations reminiscent of a row of skyscrapers). A moderate trail descends into a small canyon and leads for a mile through the towers to rejoin the scenic drive at the **Courthouse Towers Viewpoint.** (You can hike back the way you came or arrange for a ride.) See if you can identify rock formations named the Organ, the Three Gossips, Sheep Rock, and the Tower of Babel.

The scenic drive continues between a set of "petrified" sand dunes to the right (east) and the Great Wall to the west, where you can sometimes spot climbers tackling cracks in the sandstone. About nine miles down the road from the entrance is one of the park's most famous formations: **Balanced Rock,** a 3,600-ton boulder that looks like a gentle breeze could knock it over. An easy 0.3-mile paved trail leads around the rock. The park's original entrance road, now called the Willow Flats road, joins the scenic drive from the west here. This is one of the few opportunities for mountain biking in the park; you can ride this road all the way back to U.S. 191, eight miles north of the visitors center.

Just past Balanced Rock is a side road to the **Windows,** a pair of huge arches that dwarf hikers. En route you'll pass the **Cove of Caves** near a complex of standing rocks called the **Garden of Eden.** At the end of the side road, an easy one-mile gravel trail loops around the North and South Windows and Turret Arch. An alternate primitive loop starts at the South Window overlook and returns the back way to the parking area, where another easy half-mile trail leads to **Double Arch.**

Return to the main road and continue 2.5 miles to reach a second side road. Civil War veteran John Wesley Wolfe built **Wolfe Ranch** near the turn of the 20th century, where he lived with his family for two decades before moving back to Ohio. A nearby petroglyph panel that includes images of men on horseback is attributed to the Ute tribe. From the ranch, a moderate trail (3 miles round-trip) leads up across slickrock to the base of **Delicate Arch,** probably the most famous arch in the world. It takes two to three hours to make the trip out and back, so bring water. Despite its size, Delicate Arch really does look fragile and unbalanced, as if a touch could send it toppling. (Early settlers had more descriptive names for it, including Cowboy's Chaps and Old Lady's Bloomers.) If you'd prefer to view Delicate Arch from afar, drive a mile past the ranch to a parking area where an accessible trail leads 100 yards to an overlook and a moderate trail (one mile round-trip) climbs to the rim of the canyon for a closer view.

Return to the main road and head down into the crazy pastel colors of Salt Valley. At about two miles you'll see an overlook for the **Fiery Furnace,** a labyrinth of stone fins and canyons that are actually cooler in summer than the surrounding desert. There aren't any marked trails here, so you must obtain a permit or sign up for a ranger-led hike, the best and safest way to explore this fascinating corner of the park. Moderately strenuous three-hour excursions leave twice daily mid-March–October They're very popular and often fill up a day or two before; make reservations at the visitors center or online (www.recreation.gov, $10 per adult, $5 children) up to a week in advance.

Three more miles brings you to the turnoff for the unpaved **Salt Valley Road** that heads nine miles northwest to **Klondike Bluffs,** a striking and little-visited corner of Arches that is also accessible via a moderate mountain bike trail from U.S. 191. Out here near the park's boundary, you'll find **Tower Arch** accessed by a strenuous hiking trail (3.4 miles round-trip) that starts from the parking area.

The final mile of the paved scenic drive ends at the campground and a trailhead for **Devils Garden.** The trail is strenuous (7.2 miles round-trip) but takes in a jaw-dropping eight arches. Past **Tunnel Arch** and **Pine Tree Arch,** the trail splits. To the right it quickly becomes primitive (i.e., unmaintained) and loops past **Private Arch** to rejoin the main trail at **Double O Arch.** If you opt to go left, you'll pass what was **Landscape Arch,** the park's largest, an impossibly thin span (only six feet across at one point) that dropped a large piece of rock in 1991. (It's an easy two-mile round-trip hike from the trailhead.) The trail becomes more difficult past this point as it leads to the aptly named **Dark Angel** formation. An easy trail (0.4 mile round-trip) leads to **Skyline Arch** from a parking area near the campground. In 1940 the opening of this arch doubled in size overnight when a huge chunk fell from underneath.

The **Devils Garden campground** is open year-round, with 50 sites ($20/night, no hookups), some suitable for RVs up to 30 feet long. Sites fills quickly in spring and fall, but for an additional $9, you can reserve a site March–October (515/885-3639, 877/444-6777, or 877/833-6777, www.recreation.gov). During the off-season, 24 sites are available on a self-serve basis. There are tables, grills, toilets, and potable water but no showers.

Canyonlands National Park

If one place encapsulates the heart of the Colorado Plateau, it is Canyonlands, the largest of southern Utah's five national parks. From grassy mesa tops to the roiling depths of the Colorado and Green River gorges, Canyonlands encompasses rock art, prehistoric dwellings, sheer-walled ravines, lush riverside thickets, and abundant desert life. And for all there is to see and do, there are almost as many ways to go about it: scenic drives, easy hikes, placid floats, and sweeping vistas give way to four-wheel-drive tracks, steep trails, frothing white water, and claustrophobic slot canyons the farther you push into the backcountry. Covering 527 square miles and ranging 3,700–7,200 feet, Canyonlands is big enough to offer something for just about everyone.

The Y formed by the confluence of the Colorado and Green Rivers neatly divides the park into three sections (four if you count the **River District** itself). The **Island in the Sky District,** north of the rivers and closest to Moab, is a high, wide-open tableland. Connected to the rest of southern Utah by only a narrow causeway, the Island has many scenic overlooks that take in thousands of square miles of canyon country. Most are easily accessible from paved roads and short trails. The 100-mile White Rim Road, suitable for four-wheel-drive, high-clearance vehicles and mountain bikes, loops around the mesa's base. Nearby **Dead Horse Point State Park** gives a taste of the Island in miniature.

The **Needles District,** southeast of the Colorado River, takes its name from distinctive red and white spires of Cedar Mesa Sandstone, jumbled like the skyline of an alien city. This is more of a backcountry district, with plenty of excellent trails and four-wheel-drive roads perfect for overnight trips. West of the rivers, the remote **Maze District** is almost a world in itself.

One $10 fee (per vehicle) gives access to all districts of the park for a week. (A passport to the Southeast Utah Group costs $25 and covers entry to Canyonlands, Arches National

Park, Hovenweep Na[tional] Natural Bridges Nat[ional . . . per] year.) Backpacking pe[rmits for] wheel-drive and mou[ntain-bike per]mits are $30; both are good for 14 days. Some four-wheel-drive roads in the Needles District require permits for day use ($5). For more information, contact the park in Moab (435/719-2313, backcountry reservations 435/259-4351, www.nps.gov/cany). All of the park's visitors centers are open 9 A.M.–4:30 P.M. daily, with extended hours spring–fall.

The Setting

Canyonlands owes its stunning topography to layered deposits, dramatic uplift, and gradual erosion. From the Paradox Formation at the bottom of Cataract Canyon to the Navajo Sandstone on top of the Island in the Sky, the park's geologic history spans hundreds of millions of years. Many of its most outstanding features occur in the Cutler Formation, dating to the Permian Period (245–286 million years ago). The unmistakable White Rim around the Island in the Sky, 200 feet thick and flat as a pancake, and the Cedar Mesa Sandstone formations in the Needles and Maze Districts are both part of the Cutler Formation.

Above the White Rim, in order, are the brownish, silty Moenkopi Formation, the uranium-rich shale of the Chinle Formation, the soaring vertical cliffs of Wingate Sandstone topped by the harder protective layer of the Kayenta Formation, and the creamy curves of Navajo Sandstone, the youngest layer in the park. Another 140 million years of geology above all this is now gone, swept away by wind and water.

History

For such an inhospitable-looking place, Canyonlands has had many inhabitants over the years. The Fremont people left some of the most spectacular pictographs and petroglyphs in the country in Horseshoe Canyon near the Maze and Salt Canyon in the Needles.

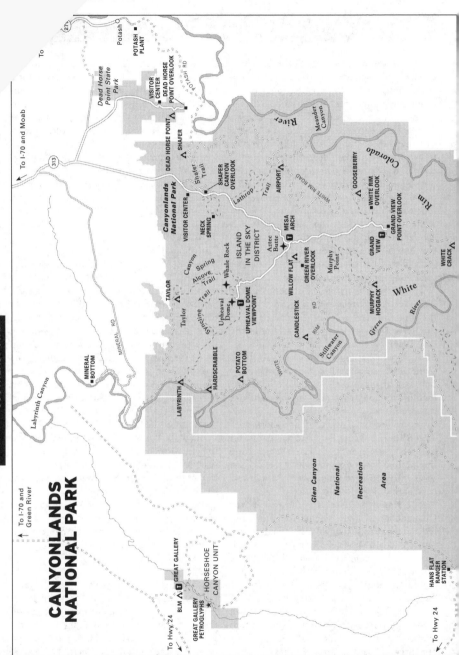

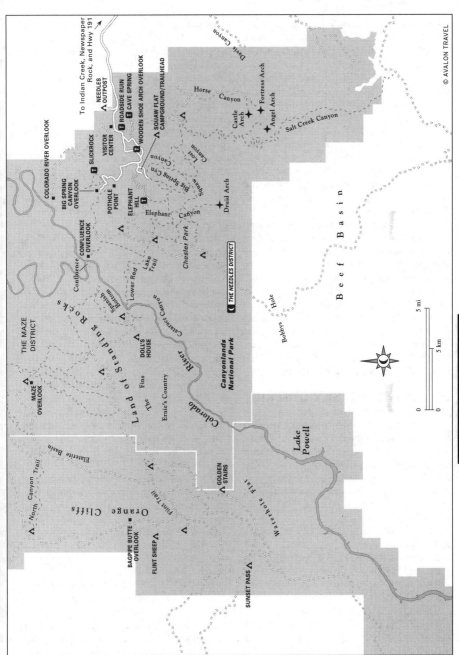

To Indian Creek, Newspaper Rock, and Hwy 191

NEEDLES OUTPOST

ROADSIDE RUIN
CAVE SPRING
WOODEN SHOE ARCH OVERLOOK
SQUAW FLAT CAMPGROUND/TRAILHEAD

SLICKROCK
VISITOR CENTER

COLORADO RIVER OVERLOOK

BIG SPRING CANYON OVERLOOK
POTHOLE POINT
ELEPHANT HILL

CONFLUENCE OVERLOOK

Confluence

Horse Canyon

Fortress Arch
Angel Arch

Castle Arch

Salt Creek Canyon

Lost Canyon

Squaw Canyon

Big Spring Cyn

Elephant Canyon

Druid Arch

Chesler Park

Lake Trail

Lower Red

Spanish Bottom

THE NEEDLES DISTRICT

Cataract Canyon

DOLL'S HOUSE

The Fins

Ernie's Country

THE MAZE DISTRICT

MAZE OVERLOOK

Land of Standing Rocks

Colorado River

Canyonlands National Park

Bobbys Hole

Beef Basin

Davis Canyon

Lake Powell

Elaterite Basin

North Canyon Trail

Orange Cliffs

Flint Trail

BAGPIPE BUTTE OVERLOOK

FLINT SHEEP

GOLDEN STAIRS

Waterhole Flat

SUNSET PASS

5 mi

5 km

0

0

© AVALON TRAVEL

Ancestral Puebloans also left rock art and masonry dwellings, including dozens of small granaries and more-impressive structures like Tower Ruin in the Needles.

Trapper Denis Julien carved his named along the canyons of the Green and Colorado in the 1830s, and on an 1859 expedition to the Confluence, Captain John N. Macomb wrote while overlooking the Needles, "I cannot conceive of a more worthless and impracticable region than the one we now found ourselves in." Undeterred by this, Civil War veteran Major John Wesley Powell led two celebrated and dangerous expeditions down the Green and the Colorado in 1869 and 1871.

Utes and Navajos lived in the canyons until the late 19th century, when cowboys and their cattle crowded them out. At one point, tens of thousands of cattle were grazed in the region, in the lower canyons and up on the Island. Remains of cowboy camps are preserved in the Needles District, and Butch Cassidy and his Wild Bunch hid from the law in Robber's Roost Canyon near the Maze. In 1964, despite considerable opposition from within the state, Canyonlands National Park was signed into existence by President Lyndon Johnson.

ISLAND IN THE SKY DISTRICT

Canyonlands' loftiest district is also the closest to Moab, and thus it sees the largest percentage of the park's annual half-million visitors. The Island is a high mesa that soars 2,000 feet above the river canyons in two giant steps: one from the top of the mesa, at over 6,000 feet, down to the bench known as the White Rim, and another from the White Rim to the rivers themselves.

To reach the Island, take U.S. 191 north from Moab and turn left (west) on SR 313, 6.5 miles north of the Colorado River bridge. This road winds southwest up onto the plateau, a lovely drive through grasslands with views of the La Sals to the east.

About 21 miles later is the Canyonlands park boundary and the Island in the Sky **visitors center** (435/259-4712), where exhibits and an orientation video provide an overview of this district of the park. The visitors center stocks books and maps helpful for those who want to explore. Check the schedule of ranger programs, offered March–October. It's also a good idea to get a weather report, even in summer: At this elevation, lightning is a real danger out in the open, and flash flooding can close roads and trails.

From the visitors center, the road continues another six miles across the top of the mesa and forks near the **Willow Flat Campground,** with 12 sites (no water or hookups, $10), most suitable for RVs up to 28 feet long. The campground is open all year, and in spring and fall all the sites fill early. The views, particularly at sunset, are dazzling.

At the fork, turning right (northwest) will take you another five miles to the road's end at **Whale Rock** and the edge of **Upheaval Dome,** a two-mile-wide crater whose origins geologists have been debating for decades. Most think it is a collapsed salt dome, but some still hold that it is an eroded astrobleme (meteorite crater).

Turn left (south) at the fork, and a six-mile drive will bring you to the edge—**Grandview Point,** one of the great panoramas of the American West. Over 10,000 square miles of canyon country are on magnificent display, including the La Sal and Abajo Mountains, the Needles, Thousand Lake and Boulder Mountains, Ekker and Elaterite Buttes in the Maze, and the Orange Cliffs. It's a vista to lose yourself in, but be careful near the edge: It's a long way down.

The Island has fewer **hiking trails** than the park's other districts. Short trails (under two miles round-trip) lead to the very tip of the mesa at Grandview Point, to an overlook over Upheaval Dome, to the top of the stone domes of Whale Rock and Aztec Butte, and to **Mesa Arch,** perched on the very edge of the precipice. (Watching the sunrise through Mesa Arch is worth getting up early.) Longer trails lead down off the mesa to the White Rim and even to the rivers. If you tackle one of these, remember that you'll have to climb back up whatever you descend, and there is very little water along the way. These include the Syncline Loop around

JOHN WESLEY POWELL

Opening up the last unknown region of the continental United States was just one item on John Wesley Powell's long résumé. The one-armed Civil War veteran also laid the groundwork for some of the fundamental principles of geology and raised a firm (if futile) voice for the wise development of the West and principled treatment of its natural resources and native tribes.

Born in 1834 in western New York, Powell began a series of scientific expeditions into the little-known country of the West in 1867. In 1868 he and a group of students climbed 14,255-foot Long's Peak. Gazing down on the headwaters of the Grand River, as the Colorado was then called, Powell decided that he would descend the river in small boats, despite stories of earlier explorers who had never reemerged from the canyon country.

The country the Colorado River passed through was probably the least known remaining in the lower 48 states. Powell talked with mountain men and Native Americans and studied the few documents that existed on the region. The first expedition set off from Green River Station in the Wyoming Territory on May 24, 1869, with a crew of nine packed into four small boats. They had no idea what lay ahead.

The 1,000-mile journey took only three months, as opposed to the 6-9 they had planned for. Raging rapids tossed the wooden dories like corks, equipment sank as the boats overturned repeatedly, and muddy water worked its way into precious stores of food. One crew member had enough and left after a month. After weeks in the dark depths of the Grand Canyon, three others chose to find an overland route home rather than face another rapid. They were murdered soon after they emerged from the canyon. (Historians debate whether Paiute Indians or Mormon settlers were to blame.) Two days later the remaining five emerged at the mouth of the Virgin River, Arizona, to the astonishment of the nation. The men hadn't been heard from in weeks, and newspapers across the states had reported them dead.

Frustrated by how little scientific data he had been able to collect while trying to keep his party alive, Powell lost no time in readying a second expedition, which set out from Green River Station in three boats on May 22, 1871. In the spring of 1872 the expedition discovered the last unknown river in the country. They named it the Escalante, after the explorer-priest who had traveled the Southwest centuries before, and continued to Lees Ferry, where the river ran high and swift through Marble Canyon. Controlling the boats became so difficult in the surging waters that Powell ended the journey at Kanab Canyon, 144 miles downstream from Lees Ferry. Although abbreviated, the second expedition was a scientific success, with finished topographic maps of the Grand Canyon region and hundreds of photographs recording the group's progress and capturing the canyon's majesty for eager Eastern audiences. The Smithsonian published Powell's *Exploration of the Colorado River of the West and Its Tributaries*, revised as *Canyons of Colorado* in 1895. The book still thrills river runners and history buffs, with page-turning tension and lyrical descriptions of geology and scenery.

As a result of his courageous leadership, Powell had become a national figure. In 1873 he was appointed special commissioner to the tribes in Utah and eastern Nevada, working to improve their education and economic situation. His *Introduction to the Study of Indian Languages* was published in 1877, cementing his reputation as an anthropologist.

Powell's true landmark work, however, was his *Report on the Lands of the Arid Region of the United States* (1878). In this weighty tome, produced for Congress, Powell addressed the problem of settling the arid West. He knew firsthand how unsuited the region was for unplanned settlement, huge populations, and Eastern-style agriculture. With wisdom and great foresight, he advised classifying the land according to its physical characteristics—chiefly rainfall—as well as its economic potential. Most of his advice was ignored in the country's rush to achieve its Manifest Destiny, but Powell's report is recognized today as a watershed document and a milestone of conservation literature.

SOUTHEAST UTAH

© NATIONAL PARK SERVICE

The White Rim Road circumnavigates Island in the Sky.

Upheaval Dome (8 miles round-trip), Lathrop Canyon (22 miles round-trip), Taylor Canyon (21 miles round-trip), and Murphy Loop (11 miles round-trip). You can stop at Murphy Point for the night, but the rest of the overnight routes all involve at least a 1,000-foot descent and steep switchbacks that are often very rough.

It's hard to miss the **White Rim,** a broad geologic layer midway between the Island and the rivers. A dirt track snakes across this mostly level plain, giving the adventurous the opportunity to enter the scenery so many others just look upon. The **White Rim Road** is a 100-mile route gaining fame as one of the best multiday mountain bike rides in the United States. It's also popular with four-wheel-drive enthusiasts and motorcyclists. There are eight campgrounds along the way, and you must reserve sites ahead of time for this popular excursion. (None of the campgrounds has potable water; pack at least a gallon a day per person.) If you go counterclockwise, as most people do, you'll head down the gradually descending Mineral Bottom Road, and at the other end ascend the merciless switchbacks of the Schafer Trail, visible near the visitors center. The entire trail can be driven in a day (though 2–3 days is recommended), but mountain bikers typically take 3–4 days depending on whether they're self-supported or have a support vehicle. (Some superhuman local bikers can ride it in a day.) Many companies in Moab organize trips.

Dead Horse Point State Park

En route to the Island in the Sky, just over 14 miles from the turnoff at U.S. 191, a well-marked left-hand turn leads to this state park, which offers panoramas similar to the Island but on a smaller scale. The name is said to refer to a herd of horses left to graze at the end of the mesa. The herd, unable to find a way down, died of thirst within sight of the river far below. The **visitors center** (435/259-2614, http://stateparks.utah.gov, 8 A.M.–6 P.M., 9 A.M.–5 P.M. in winter, $10 per vehicle), about 45 minutes from Moab, has exhibits, publications, and a seasonal snack bar. Ask rangers to point you toward "Thelma and Louise Point," where the movie heroines (actually, stunt dummies) drove off into what was supposed to be the Grand Canyon. The climbing sequence at the beginning of *Mission: Impossible II* was also filmed there.

The park's Kayenta Campground, open year-round, has 21 sites with electrical hookups and grills (but no water), available by reservation (800/322-3770, $20). The **Intrepid Trail** begins at the visitors center and leads to various overlooks with options for hikes up to nine miles long.

◖ THE NEEDLES DISTRICT

Colorful Church Rock marks the turnoff to the Needles from U.S. 191, 40 miles south of Moab and 14 miles north of Monticello. From there, SR 211 snakes west across the flats before dropping steeply into the valley cut by Indian Creek. This marks the beginning of one of Utah's prettiest drives, Indian Creek Byway, a winding route around the feet of looming mesas. Ten miles in is **Newspaper Rock Recreation Area,** where a rock face bears images pecked and incised into the dark desert varnish. Look for bighorn sheep, a hunter on horseback, and a six-toed foot, representing different cultures and time periods as long as 2,000 years ago.

The soaring red cliffs of Wingate Sandstone along Indian Creek boast the best **crack climbing** in the world, with legendary routes like Supercrack (rated 5.10) slicing upward for hundreds of flawless feet. Keep your eyes out for climbers on the blank-looking walls, and if you're climbing, bring plenty of medium-sized cams and tape up your hands—these are tough, sustained routes.

A few miles farther, historic **Dugout Ranch** sits at the mouth of Cottonwood Creek. Established in 1885, it was bought up by the S&S Cattle Company in 1919 and became part of the largest cattle operation in Utah, with more than 10,000 cows grazing on 1.8 million acres. The Redd family bought the spread in 1967 and in the late 1990s handed it over to the Nature Conservancy to manage on the

condition that it continue as a working, conservation-minded ranch. (Visitors must have an appointment; contact the Conservancy's Moab office at 435/259-4629.)

Continuing northwest, the road passes the unmistakable North and South Six-Shooter Peaks that stand like sentinels just outside the entrance to the Needles. On the other side of the road, heading north, the unpaved road to Lockhart Basin leads a mile to Hamburger Rock, a primitive BLM camping area with eight sites ($6) and great views. Just inside the park boundary is the turnoff to the **Needles Outpost** (435/979-4007, www.canyonlandsneedlesoutpost.com), a privately owned general store, café, gas station, and campground ($20 per night) that's open more or less regularly spring–fall.

Thirty-five miles from U.S. 191 is the Needles **visitors center** (435/259-4711). You can pick up hiking and four-wheel drive permits there, get your bearings at the scale model of the entire park, and check the schedule for ranger programs, offered March–October. The pavement continues another 6.4 miles, passing the turnoff for **Squaw Flat Campground** with 26 sites (water, no hookups, $15) about halfway. Maximum RV length is 28 feet. Sites are on a first-come, first-served basis, and they fill quickly in spring and fall. The pavement ends at the Big Spring Canyon Overlook.

Most visitors come to the Needles for the easily accessible backcountry, and they are seldom disappointed. Four short, self-guided **hiking trails** leave the paved main road for Ancestral Puebloan ruins and an old cowboy camp in a smoke-blackened cave. Over 60 miles of longer trails snake over the slickrock and down into canyon bottoms, easily linked for challenging day hikes or overnight trips. The trail to **Chessler Park** (six miles round-trip) is one of the most popular, leading to an open grassy area surrounded by slickrock. It can be extended to include the **Joint Trail,** so named because it passes through narrow, deep cracks in the rock, for a total of 11 miles round-trip. Other hikes of about 10 miles include the Big Spring to Squaw Canyon Loop, Squaw Canyon to Lost Canyon, Elephant Canyon to Druid Arch, the Peekaboo Trail, and the loop that starts and ends at Squaw Flat campground, heading up Big Spring and back past campsites EC2 and EC1. Lower Red Lake Canyon leads down to the Colorado River just across from Spanish Bottom and the Doll's House in the Maze. You'll have to apply for a permit and reserve a spot at one of more than a dozen backcountry campsites. (Four vehicle campsites are set aside for drivers.)

Mountain bikers are limited to roads, but you can still ride nine miles to the **Confluence Overlook** trailhead, where after a half-mile walk you'll be able to see that the Green River is actually brown and the Colorado flows green. **Elephant Hill,** a short but ridiculously difficult climb in the heart of the district, is also popular with four-wheel-drive enthusiasts, who descend on the park in droves during Easter Jeep Safari. (The back side, even worse than the front, includes a section with such tight corners that vehicles have to shift into reverse and back down part of the way.) Elephant Hill leads to a loop road through the **grabens,** an area of straight-sided, flat-bottomed valleys that look like city streets.

Salt Creek Canyon, one of the most popular drives in the park, was closed to vehicles past the Peekaboo camping area after research showed that its delicate riparian ecosystem—growing around the most extensive perennial water source in the entire park—could be damaged by four-wheel-drive traffic. It's there that the Needle's rich archaeology reaches its apex. Ancient granaries and rock art fill the upper canyon, including the famous red, white, and blue All-American Man pictograph. (The blue is actually charcoal.) The entire canyon takes 2–4 days to hike. Vehicles can still drive up **Horse Canyon** to the east, which leads to Tower Ruin and a pothole (horizontal) arch called Paul Bunyan's Potty, as well as **Davis** and **Lavender Canyons** off of Highway 211. (Salt, Lavender, and Horse Canyons require a permit for day use.)

MAZE DISTRICT

Accessed by river or from SR 24, the Maze is by far the least-visited and least-accessible part of the park. This district, east of SR 24 between Green River and Hanksville, includes the park's separate **Horseshoe Canyon** unit. The Maze offers plenty of opportunity for isolation and adventure—and with its rough roads, faint trails, and rare water sources, it also demands a higher degree of backcountry experience than most parts of the Colorado Plateau. Even if you're driving in, as many visitors do, you *must* be prepared. Always let someone know where you're going and when you will be back—and don't forget to make contact on your safe return.

Three days is considered a minimum to visit the Maze, and you can easily spend a week there. The only services of any kind are at the **Hans Flat Ranger Station** (8 A.M.–4:30 P.M. daily), which is 46 miles from SR 24 along a two-wheel-drive dirt road, about 2.5 hours from Green River. To get there, turn east just south of Goblin Valley State Park (about 24 miles south of I-70.) All you'll find at the ranger station is information—there's no water, food, gas, or entrance fees. A high-clearance four-wheel-drive vehicle is required to travel beyond the North Point Road junction, which is 2.5 miles past the ranger station. It's possible to drive all the way to **The Doll House,** a distinctive rock formation overlooking Spanish Bottom along the Colorado River, but expect the journey to take hours if not days. Plan to be self-sufficient: Bring extra gas, more water than you think you'll need, at least one full-sized spare tire, chains, a shovel, and a high-lift jack; towing bills out there run into the thousands of dollars. The Maze has 20 primitive vehicle campsites; permits are required.

Hiking trails in the Maze are very rugged and not always well marked. Look for rock cairns and be prepared to raise and lower your packs with ropes at some points. Often the main concern is getting from one source of water to the next. Popular destinations include the Land of Standing Rocks and the network of canyons that make up the Maze proper—South Fork, Shot Canyon, and others—where you'll find the famous Harvest Scene pictograph panel. Backpackers camp in at-large

EVERETT RUESS:
LOST WANDERER OF CANYON COUNTRY

Poet, artist, and nomad Everett Ruess saw more of the Southwest in his teens than most do in a lifetime, before vanishing into the very canyons that captured his vivid imagination. Born in Los Angeles in 1914, Everett grew up in a rarified environment of art and philosophy. His mother was a noted art patron and his father a graduate of the Harvard Divinity School. After high school, Everett set out for the Southwest. He bought a burro from a Navajo and explored for months on end the remote reaches of Grand Canyon, Zion, the Painted Desert, the canyons of the Escalante, Monument Valley, and Canyon de Chelly.

Everett captured the wonders he saw in fervent journal entries and lyrical letters to his family and friends. "The wind is in my hair," he wrote, "there's a fire in my heels, and I shall always be a rover." In the days before the parks and monuments, few places were out of bounds. His mother cringed to read of him climbing cliffs to remote ruins and trudging alone across the desert for weeks. "There is a splendid freedom in solitude . . . " he responded. "I can bare my soul to the mountains unabashed . . . and nothing stands between me and the Wild."

Everett quickly won over those he met along the way with his enthusiasm and openness. The Hopi granted him the rare honor of participating in their Antelope Dance, and Everett learned enough Navajo to sing with a medicine man at a sick girl's bedside. He sold paintings and prints of the landscapes he traveled through and spent the winters in California, where the family circle included such luminaries as Edward Weston, Dorothea Lange, and Ansel Adams, all who recognized his potential and encouraged him.

Everett's writings grew more impassioned with every season. His journeys became a spiritual quest, and he began taking greater and greater risks. "I have been flirting pretty heavily with death, the old clown," he wrote, describing premonitions of vanishing into the wild. "I shall go on some last wilderness trip to a place I have known and loved. I shall not return. When I go I leave no trace."

In November 1934 Everett rode into the town of Escalante, where he stocked up on provisions. Intending to spend the winter in Arizona, he then set off down the Hole-in-the-Rock Road as an early blizzard moved in. A week later he camped with a pair of sheepherders. In February his two burros were found in Davis Gulch near what was thought to be his last campsite. Everett had vanished.

Search parties organized by his parents and friends combed the canyons of the Escalante to no avail. An expert tracker agreed that Everett had entered Davis Gulch but found no signs he had ever left. As reports came in of supposed sightings from Moab to Florida, theories flew around canyon country: Everett orchestrated his own disappearance; he was killed in a flood; he died after falling from a cliff. One widely accepted theory is that he was killed for his gear and his body hidden in one of the countless nooks in the country he loved so much. He appeared in the visions of Navajo medicine men and his signature inscription NEMO—meaning "no one" in Latin and probably a reference to the ill-fated captain in Jules Verne's *20,000 Leagues Under the Sea*—kept turning up in caves and canyon walls.

As time passed, Everett Ruess became a canyon country legend. In the early 1960s archaeologists found his canteen and a box of razor blades from the Owl Drug Company of Los Angeles. Scholarly papers, popular books, and lectures have debated his fate. In 2008 a grave site was located near Bluff, Utah. Initially, work by forensic scientists and DNA tests seemed to confirm these were Everett's remains, but a DNA test in October 2009 concluded they were Native American. The story sparked the interest of a new generation of canyon lovers, and the mystery of Everett Ruess endures.

Everett's older brother Waldo oversaw the installation of a plaque high on the wall of Davis Canyon, bearing a quote from Everett's journals:

Oh but the desert is glorious now,
with marching clouds in the blue sky
and cool winds blowing. The smell
of the sage is sweet in my nostrils,
and the luring trail leads onwards.

© NATIONAL PARK SERVICE

Pictographs at the Great Gallery, 1,500–4,000 years old or more, are examples of the Barrier Canyon style of rock art.

zones; permits are required, and reservations fill quickly during spring and fall.

Horseshoe Canyon

This small, separate section of the Maze protects one of the most remarkable collections of rock art in the Four Corners. Turn off SR 24 to the east between Goblin Valley State Park and Hanksville, taking Hans Flat Road (graded dirt) 30 miles to the parking area. You can camp on BLM land at the canyon's western rim. A 6.5-mile (round-trip) trail leads down 750 feet into Horseshoe Canyon along an old four-wheel-drive

route. It's a beautiful, relatively lush canyon filled with cottonwoods. After three miles you'll suddenly catch a glimpse of the **Great Gallery,** an extensive lineup of painted figures up to eight feet tall presided over by the haunting, hollow-eyed "Holy Ghost." This Barrier Canyon style of rock art is believed to have been painted between 2000 B.C. and A.D. 500. Other pictographs and petroglyphs are scattered along the trail. Ranger-guided hikes into Horseshoe Canyon are offered on fall weekends. Contact the Hans Flat Ranger station (435/259-2652) for more information.

Highway 24: Green River to Torrey

Leaving I-70 west of the town of Green River, Utah, SR 24 heads south across the San Rafael Desert. To the west rises the San Rafael Swell, a stone bulge carved by narrow canyons and protected by the serrated barricade of the San Rafael Reef. Goblin Valley State Park and Horseshoe Canyon, a detached portion of the Maze District of Canyonlands National Park, offer two versions of the fantastic on either side of the roadway, but past Hanksville the scenery really starts to get otherworldly. An expanse of badlands make up the western San Rafael Desert, a gorgeous but forbidding wilderness of purples, grays, mustards, and tans. This landscape is so extraterrestrial that the Mars Society, a group dedicated to reaching the Red Planet, has set up a research station near Hanksville. The area is dominated by Factory Butte, a massive wedge of dark Mancos Shale topped with tougher Mesa Verde Sandstone near Caineville. The geology gets older as you continue west along the Fremont River, through the huge monocline of the Waterpocket Fold, the backbone of Capitol Reef National Park.

GREEN RIVER

An easy river crossing is a rarity in canyon country, so this valley south of the Book Cliffs, between Gray and Labyrinth Canyons, has been known since prehistoric times. The Old Spanish Trail forded the river just upstream on its way from Santa Fe to Los Angeles. Because of the easy river access, Major John Wesley Powell launched his expeditions there in 1869 and 1871. Americans began to arrive from the east in the late 1870s, and in 1883 the Denver & Rio Grande Western Railway first dropped off mining supplies and carried away livestock. This ended when the railroad moved to Helper, Utah, and began a pattern of booms and busts that continued through eras of oil exploration, fruit growing, and the establishment of the Utah Launch Complex of the White Sands Missile Base in 1963. Test rockets fired from

along the river landed in White Sands Missile Range in New Mexico until 1979.

Today Green River (pop. 1,000) relies on farming, ranching, and, above all, the traffic off I-70, whose 105-mile run west to Salina is the longest stretch of interstate without services in the country. It has been an obvious supply and staging point for river travel since Powell and his men floated through town. Hot summers, little winter frost, and just the right elevation (4,000 feet) give Green River the ideal climate for growing melons, and the town's famous cantaloupe and watermelons are sold from roadside stands in summer and celebrated during a fall festival.

Sights

The **John Wesley Powell River History Museum** (1765 E. Main St., 435/564-3427, www.jwprhm.com, 8 A.M.–7 P.M. daily Apr.–Oct., winter hours vary, $6 adults, $2 children) celebrates the career of the man whose descents of the Green River put much of this part of the country on the map. Exhibits on the geology and human history of the Green and Colorado Rivers includes the fascinating River Runners Hall of Fame and models of the various boats that have made (or attempted) the difficult descents. A likeness of Powell sits in a chair—his preferred position for scouting the river—on a replica of the *Emma Dean.*

Towering cottonwoods shade green lawns on the east bank of the river at the **Green River State Park** (450 S. Green River Blvd., 435/564-3633, 6 A.M.–10 P.M. daily in summer, 8 A.M.–5 P.M. daily in winter, $5 pp). The park has a picnic area, RV and tent campsites (800/322-3770, www.reserveamerica.com, $16), showers, a nine-hole golf course (435/564-8882), and a boat launch. This is a popular put-in place for trips down Labyrinth and Stillwater Canyons, and marks the start of the Friendship Cruise that floats to Moab every Memorial Day.

Events

Earlier in May, the Outlaw Trails Jamboree (www.outlawtrailsjamboree.com) takes ATV-ers through areas once frequented by the likes of Butch Cassidy and Kid Ricketts. If you're in the area the third weekend in September, keep your eye out for the 25-foot watermelon that's rolled out to help celebrate **Melon Days,** accompanied by music, games, a parade, canoe and foot races, and all the melons you can eat. In late October, Green River hosts runners for the Goblin Valley Ultra Marathon (www.goblinvalleyultra.com), racing over a scenic route that ends in the state park. (Some runners don Halloween costumes for the event.)

Recreation

River-running is the main diversion in Green River, with trips heading in opposite directions: through Desolation and Gray Canyons to the north, and Labyrinth and Stillwater Canyons to the south. **Moki-Mac River Expeditions** (800/284-7280, www.mokimac.com) outfits and guides trips on both the Green and the Colorado Rivers, including the Grand Canyon. Trips last up to 14 days; the shortest are one-day excursions through Westwater Canyon on the Colorado ($150 adults, $135 children) and Gray Canyon ($70 adults, $55 children). If you want to run Labyrinth and Stillwater Canyons on your own, they'll rent you canoes for $25 per day and retrieve up to four people from Mineral Canyon for $350.

Holiday Expeditions (435/564-3273 or 800/624-6323, www.bikeraft.com) is located behind the Comfort Inn off Main St. and offers white-water rafting and mountain bike trips, including guided trips along Canyonlands' White Rim Road that start at $650.

Accommodations

Two of Green River's least-expensive lodgings are known by their classic neon signs: the reclining woman at the **Robber's Roost** (325 W. Main St., 435/564-3452 or 877/342-6099, www.rrmotel.com) and the flower and arrow of the **Sleepy Hollow Motel** (94 E. Main St., 435/564-8189), which welcomes "Hip Cats and Kittens." Both are under $50 per night.

The **River Terrace** (1740 E. Main St., 435/564-3401 or 877/564-3401, www.river-terrace.com, $120–140) has rooms with views of the river as well as the **Tamarisk Restaurant,** serving all meals, downstairs near the pool. Other chain hotels in town include a **Holiday Inn Express** (1845 E. Main St., 435/564-4439, from $100) and a **Motel 6** (1860 E. Main St., 435/564-3436, from $55).

Next to the state park, **Shady Acres RV Park** (350 E. Main St., 435/564-8290 or 800/537-8674, www.shadyacresrv.com) has 101 pull-through sites as well as a Blimpie sandwich shop and a gas station. Tent sites are $20, RV sites run $27–35, and cabins with air-conditioning are $42.

Food

Ray's Tavern (25 S. Broadway, 435/564-3511, lunch and dinner daily) is a classic roadhouse with excellent burgers and other meaty delights under $10, which you can pair with a brew and a few rounds of pool. They have a covered outdoor patio and occasional live music on weekends. Occupying a turn-of-the-century pharmacy across the street, the **Green River Coffee Co.** (25 E. Main, 435/564-3411, breakfast and lunch daily) looks like an old-time soda fountain crossed with a living room. Couches, antiques, and old records give this coffee shop a homey vibe. They serve coffee drinks, snacks, and breakfast and lunches under $10.

At **La Veracruzana** (115 W. Main St., 435/564-3257, lunch and dinner daily), you can get tacos for a couple bucks and saucy dishes like enchiladas or rellenos under $10.

Information

The **Green River Travel Center** (885 E. Main St., 435/564-3427, www.greenriverutah.com) adjoins the John Wesley Powell River History Museum.

Getting There

Moab Luxury Coach (435/940-4212, www.moabluxurycoach.com) has two regular shuttle schedules stops in Green River. Rates start at $70, depending on destination. Tours and charters are also available. Green River's

© NATIONAL PARK SERVICE

Labyrinth Canyon winds below Canyonlands National Park's Island in the Sky.

SOUTHEAST UTAH

Greyhound stop (525 E. Main, 435/564-3421) is the West Winds Rodeway Inn. **Amtrak** (250 S. Broadway, 800/872-7245) passes through Green River morning (eastbound) and evening (westbound) on its California Zephyr route between Chicago and the Bay Area.

LABYRINTH AND STILLWATER CANYONS

If you've cut your teeth on daylong river trips and want to put together a longer trip, this 120-mile stretch of flat-water just might be the perfect step up. It's a calm, winding journey downstream from Green River State Park, with plenty of side canyons to explore and historic artifacts to puzzle over. You probably won't have it all to yourself—powerboats zoom past pretty regularly, and it's popular with the canoe-and-kayak crowd—but for a relaxing, pretty trip that doesn't take all that much planning or expertise, these canyons are hard to beat.

The trip can be done year-round, but try to avoid Memorial Day Weekend, unless you plan to join the Annual Friendship Cruise, which fills the wide canyon with boaters. You'll need a free permit available from the BLM, and you must be completely self-contained, with toilets and a keen eye for collecting all your own garbage. For more information, contact the BLM office in Price, Utah (435/636-3622, www.blm.gov).

Labyrinth Canyon begins south of Green River and winds for 68 miles to Mineral Bottom just north of Canyonlands National Park. Along the way you'll pass an old cabin at Doc Bishop Bottom, the privately owned Ruby Ranch, and the names of early river-runners chiseled into the stone at Register Rock and the post office at the Bow Knot. This section of the river takes 3–4 days to travel, leaving time to explore side canyons. You can arrange a vehicle pickup at Mineral Bottom through rafting or shuttle companies in Green River or Moab. The rafting companies can also arrange guided trips down Labyrinth Canyon.

Stillwater Canyon continues another 53 miles from Mineral Bottom to the confluence of the Green and Colorado Rivers. You'll need a National Park Service permit for this section, since it crosses Canyonlands National Park, and you'll also have to arrange a pickup from one of the jet boats that descend to the confluence daily in season.

CRYSTAL GEYSER

An unsuccessful petroleum test well drilled in the 1930s concentrated bubbling, mineral-rich waters into a cold-water gusher that shoots up to 100 feet in the air 2–4 times per day. It's on the east bank of the river, 4.5 river miles south of the state park, and is surrounded by maroon deposits of travertine. To drive there, turn south onto Frontage Road off Main Street near milepost 4, and head south for three miles until you pass under a railroad overpass. Turn right and go six miles west to the river, on a road that quickly turns to dirt and passes under I-70.

SAN RAFAEL SWELL

This kidney-shaped anticline covers 900 square miles on either side of I-70, stretching for 80 miles from north to south. Its southeastern edge along SR 24 is marked by the **San Rafael Reef,** a jagged line of 1,000-foot cliffs that look like the teeth of some gigantic monster. Two perennial streams cut through this imposing wall, revealing 250-million-year-old Coconino Sandstone—one of the area's oldest exposed rock layers—on their way east toward the Green River.

Pictographs found there, similar to those in Horseshoe Canyon, are estimated to be at least 2,000 years old. In 1853 the head of a railroad survey team charting a route for the transcontinental railroad wrote:

> As we approached the [Green] river yesterday, the ridges on either side of its banks to the west appeared broken into a thousand forms—columns, shafts, temples, buildings, and ruined cities could be seen, or imagined, from the high points along our route.

A member of Powell's second expedition down the Green River wrote in his journal that local Native Americans called the formations of the reef Sau-auger-towip (the "stone house lands"), and conductors on the Denver & Rio Grande Western Railroad pointed out the "silent city" to passengers. Butch Cassidy is only one of dozens of outlaws who sought refuge among the tortuous canyons after various misdeeds. Numerous mineshafts (steer clear) and other remnants of mining for copper and uranium dot the landscape.

Dozens of canyons and hundreds of side canyons lace through the reef as well, making it a canyoneer's playground. But be vigilant about the possibility of flash flooding. Flood debris hangs 50 feet high between the walls of slot canyons. Others are filled with water for most of the year, meaning that if you're truly prepared, you'll find yourself hiking across the desert carrying a wetsuit and an inner tube.

You probably won't be alone in the Swell. With the construction of I-70, the once-remote area became accessible, and off-road vehicle (ORV) use continues to be a contentious issue. The Utah Department of Wildlife Resources helped establish a population of bighorn sheep there (at last count it was some 70 strong), and hundreds of pronghorn antelope live in the desert to the east and occasionally venture into the Swell itself.

Exploring the Southern San Rafael Swell

Always take a topographical map; it's easy to get lost, even in slot canyons, which empty out into a confusing landscape beyond the reef. By far the most detailed guide to exploring the swell is Steve Allen's *Canyoneering: The San Rafael Swell,* the first volume in a series of three covering southern Utah wildlands.

Aside from I-70, the easiest way into the southern reef is the road that leads to Goblin Valley State Park from SR 24. A series of short but spectacular slot canyons cut through the reef in this vicinity. Arguably the finest and easiest to navigate is **Little Wild Horse Canyon.** To get there, take the Goblin Valley Road to the state park boundary. Before you reach the fee station, look for a sign on the right indicating Wild Horse Mesa. Turn right on this good dirt road and travel for five miles to a parking area. Start hiking in the wash, which forks at a half mile. The left fork goes to **Bell Canyon,** the right to Little Wild Horse. You can make an eight-mile loop of both canyons, but if you have time for only a short exploration, fork right for Little Wild Horse Canyon, a gorgeous and easy introduction to narrow slots. The narrows end at about three miles, a good turnaround point for a mild hike. The canyon widens as it continues to the other side of the reef. If you plan to loop back through Bell Canyon, go left 1.5 miles on the faint jeep road that links the two canyons, entering Bell (the next break in the cliffs) to return to the fork in the wash.

Less than a mile farther down the Wild Horse Mesa road is a wash coming from the north. Hike up the wash about 20 minutes to reach the mouths of **Ding** and **Dang Canyons,** a challenging (and less-traveled) pair of slots. Look for pointy Ding Dang Dome at the top of the Ding Canyon, which is your signal to head left (west) and return via Dang Canyon.

Two nearby slot canyons are better accessed from the dirt-surface Behind-the-Reef Road. From SR 24 continue west, past the turnoff for the state park, onto Temple Mountain Road, which cuts through the reef. Look for the unmarked Behind-the-Reef Road on the left. Follow it approximately four miles (or farther, depending on your vehicle) to approach the entrance of **Crack Canyon.** You can make this a turnaround hike or, for a challenging 13-mile loop, combine it with less scenic **Chute Canyon.**

In case you need reminding, do not enter a slot canyon if it's raining anywhere in the vicinity. A storm cell miles away can create flash flood conditions. If you're feeling claustrophobic or cautious, you can hike around **Temple Mountain,** a colorful pointed peak north of the Temple Mountain road about seven miles from the SR 24 intersection. The seven-mile mining road around its base makes a good ramble or mountain bike ride. Keep a wary eye out for open mine shafts.

These hikes are just a taste of what the San Rafael Swell has to offer. Some of the other choices are serious undertakings, and every year some people underestimate them and have to be rescued. West of the reef via the Temple Mountain Road is **Muddy Creek,** with a sinuous, deep section of narrows called simply **The Chute.** One of the best canyon hikes in the Southwest, this involves going down a winding chasm beneath logs jammed high overhead by raging spring floodwaters. The hike from **Hondoo Arch** to the **Hidden Splendor Mine** can be done with a two-car shuttle in a long day. Aside from the spring, the water shouldn't be more than knee deep.

North of I-70, a section of the San Rafael River known as the **Black Box** has 400-foothigh walls that are only 10 feet apart in places. The problem is that this box is full of water and thus requires a wetsuit and inner tubes to avoid hypothermia and drowning. Also north of the interstate (west of mile marker 145) is a dirt road to **Black Dragon Wash,** where an amazing panel of Barrier Canyon–style pictographs is a half mile up.

For more information on visiting the Swell, contact the BLM office in Price (435/636-3600).

GOBLIN VALLEY STATE PARK

About 20 miles north of Hanksville on SR 24, a signed turnoff to the west marks Goblin Valley Road, which leads another 12 miles to one of the odder sights in this landscape of visual extremes. Imagine an amphitheater of house-high chocolate mushrooms left out in the sun, and you'll have a general idea of the crazily eroded sandstone formations that fill this small but detour-worthy park (7 A.M.–10 P.M. daily, $7 per vehicle).

You can admire these geological oddities from a picnic area overlook or hike down among them—best of all, you're even allowed to climb them. Movie buffs might recognize this setting from the sci-fi comedy *Galaxy Quest.* Three hiking trails (all less than three miles round-trip) offer different perspectives of the Jurassic Period formations and some long views of the Henry Mountains.

The park's 21-site campground (800/322-3770, www.reserveamerica.com, no hookups, $16) has showers and back-in RV spaces.

SOUTHEAST UTAH

Check at the visitors center (435/275-4584, 8 A.M.–5 P.M. daily, winter hours may vary) for ranger programs, including twilight walks.

HANKSVILLE

Established in 1882 on the bank of the Fremont River, Hanksville was named for one of its original settlers, Ebenezer Hanks. The only remnant of a string of Mormon communities along the river decimated by floods near the turn of the 20th century, Hanksville has always been a remote town. Mail was once carried by horse from Green River three times a week, with riders making the 110-mile round-trip in two days. Electricity arrived in 1960. Today Hanksville, with a population of about 400, survives on mining, farming, ranching, and, increasingly, the tourist traffic to Lake Powell and parks to the west.

More than a dozen shops, motels, and restaurants go out of their way to make visitors feel welcome. At the intersection of SR 24 and SR 95, the **Hollow Mountain Gas & Grocery** (2 S. SR 95, 435/542-3298) is a gas station and convenience market that has been hollowed out of a sandstone hillside. The **Whispering Sands Motel** (90 S. SR 95, 435/542-3238, www.whisperingsandsmotel.com) has AAA-approved rooms for $70 and up per night.

Ten miles north of town, the Hanksville-Burpee Dinosaur Quarry offers occasional public tours. Recent discoveries include bones from numerous sauropods (the largest land-based animals that ever lived), an *Allosaurus,* and a *Stegosaurus.* For more information, contact the BLM's Hanksville field office (380 S. 100 W., 435/542-3461).

SOUTH-CENTRAL UTAH

Sometimes referred to as America's Outback, Southern Utah is defined by geographical features on a monumental scale. The outlandish cliffs of the Waterpocket Fold in Capitol Reef National Park are evidence of an enormous geological uplift. Passing over the cool evergreen slopes of Boulder Mountain and the Aquarius Plateau, you'll be riding yet another geologic bulge, this one not yet eroded away. From there the tortuous canyons of the Escalante River drain southeast to Lake Powell, and the vast sweep of the Grand Staircase–Escalante National Monument, littered with the leftovers of long-gone cultures, spreads south and west. The vividly named steps of the Grand Staircase march from north to south in the monument's western reaches. Along the way, isolated towns such as Boulder and Escalante are just beginning to see an influx of visitors and new residents drawn by the landscape and seclusion.

For all intents and purposes, the city of Page, Arizona, and the Paria Plateau to the west can be considered part of South-Central Utah. Built to house workers on the Glen Canyon Dam, the tidy little tourist town of Page sits at the southern end of Lake Powell, the region's water-sport mecca, and offers plenty of options for outdoor fun. Canyon explorers flock to the Paria River and its legendary Buckskin Gulch narrows, one of the best canyon hikes in the Four Corners.

Each of these highlights would be worth a trip in itself; fortunately, you can get a tantalizing but substantial taste of them all in a few days' drive along the meandering byways of SR 24 and SR 12, which connect I-70 with U.S. 89

© RICHARD MAYER

HIGHLIGHTS

◖ **Fruita Historic District:** Pick apples and cherries among pioneer cabins in the middle of the red-rock desert in Capitol Reef National Park (page 192).

◖ **Highway 12 from Boulder to Escalante:** Enjoy panoramas of the Escalante canyons on either side of the Hogback, which is barely wide enough for two lanes of pavement (page 200).

◖ **Hiking in Grand Staircase-Escalante National Monument:** The town of Escalante offers easy access to the innumerable canyon hikes—including claustrophobic slots—along the Hole-in-the-Rock Road (page 209).

◖ **Bryce Canyon National Park:** As the sun moves through the sky, watch a changing palette of orange, pink, lavender, and gold at this natural amphitheater crowded with hoodoos (page 211).

LOOK FOR ◖ TO FIND RECOMMENDED SIGHTS, ACTIVITIES, DINING, AND LODGING.

near Bryce Canyon National Park. Page is connected to Kanab, Utah, and Flagstaff, Arizona, by U.S. 89, whose spur, U.S. 89A, crosses south of the Paria Plateau and offers access to the North Rim of the Grand Canyon. These paved roads are only the beginning, however. Most of this area is backcountry—big, beautiful, remote, and nearly empty—and can be explored only by four-wheel drive, horse, mountain bike, or sweat and boot leather.

PLANNING YOUR TIME

"Outback" implies lots of distances to cover, and ideally you'd have a week to explore South-Central Utah—five days minimum. Page, Arizona, is the only city of any size out there,

so it's better to think in terms of road-tripping rather than touring out of a home base. Starting in the east, Capitol Reef National Park merits a few days of exploring. Begin at the **Fruita Historic District,** a haven that contrasts the overwhelming scenery along the Waterpocket Fold with lush orchards. Keep going along SR 12 from Torrey—the stretch from **Boulder to Escalante** is among the most scenic drives in the country. The towns of Boulder and Escalante are jumping-off points for **hiking in Grand Staircase-Escalante.** At the western end of SR 12 you'll find yourself among the stone spires of **Bryce Canyon National Park**—another completely unique sight in this land of visual extremes.

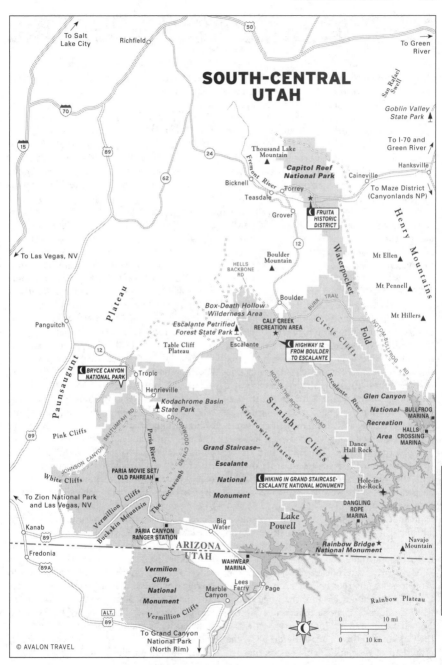

Capitol Reef National Park and Vicinity

Word is starting to get out about Utah's least-known national park, but Capitol Reef still receives far fewer visitors than its more famous neighbors. The long, narrow park—the second largest in the state—follows the Waterpocket Fold, a gigantic north–south wrinkle in the earth's crust that stretches for more than 100 miles. SR 24 bisects the northern end of the park along the Fremont River, but those who venture south past the startling green oasis of the historic Fruita settlement will find a world of dreamlike rock formations, narrow slot canyons, and silent battlements of stone. And the best part is that you stand a very good chance of having it, or at least a sizable chunk of it, all to yourself.

The Setting

Geology is the language of the reef. In all, almost 10,000 feet of sedimentary layers are on display there, ranging from the Permian period (270 million years ago) to the late Cretaceous (80 million years ago). The park's main feature, the **Waterpocket Fold,** is a classic monocline (a single-step fold) and is all that remains of a huge bulge in the planet's surface thrust skyward 65 million years ago. After the fold was formed, it eroded away until only jagged ranks of stone remained along what was once its base.

Since the Waterpocket Fold tilted up to the west, the rock layers are in order of age, with younger layers to the east and older (once deeper) layers to the west. It's easy to recognize the monumental domes of light-colored Navajo Sandstone, like Capitol Dome and the Golden Throne. Cathedral Valley's formations in the north end of the park are formed of darker Entrada Sandstone.

The term "Waterpocket" refers to natural sandstone basins that collect rainwater, and Capitol came about because the huge round white domes of sandstone concentrated in the Navajo Sandstone reminded early settlers of the Capitol building in Washington DC. The other half of the park's name has its roots in

the high-seas experiences of early prospectors: Anything that blocked travel—such as a huge ridge of rock—was called a reef.

VISITORS CENTER AND HIGHWAY 24

SR 24 slices east–west through the park on either side of the **visitors center** (435/425-3791, www.nps.gov/care, 8 A.M.–4:30 P.M. daily with extended summer hours). Various exhibits explain the park's geology, history, and archaeology, and books and maps are for sale. Pick up free backcountry permits there, and check the weather before setting off along any of the park's dirt roads.

West of the visitors center, SR 24 passes **The Castle,** formed of angular Wingate Sandstone, a turnoff to **Panorama Point,** and a very short dirt track leading to the **Goosenecks Overlook** over Sulphur Creek. A 3.5-mile (round-trip) hiking trail circles **Chimney Rock.** The bulbous **Twin Rocks** are the last formation of note before you reach the park's western boundary.

East of the visitors center, SR 24 passes the **Fruita schoolhouse,** built in 1896 and used until 1941, now on the National Register of Historic Places. About a half mile past the schoolhouse, the Fremont people pecked a set of beautiful **petroglyphs** into the canyon wall a stone's throw above the river. (This ancient culture was named after sites found along the river in 1929.) Though you can't approach the rock art panel, the view through binoculars or the telescopes provided is impressive. Deer like to congregate in the grass below and in the orchards across the road. Continue driving east to **Hickman Bridge,** where a steep nature trail (two miles round-trip) leads to the base of the natural bridge. En route, it intersects with the longest trail in the park, climbing the rim to **Navajo Knobs** and back (nine miles round-trip, strenuous). The road passes **Capitol Dome,** an impressive mound of light-colored Navajo sandstone, as it continues to **Behunin Cabin,** built from sandstone in the 1880s. SR 24 eventually leaves the park for the Caineville badlands.

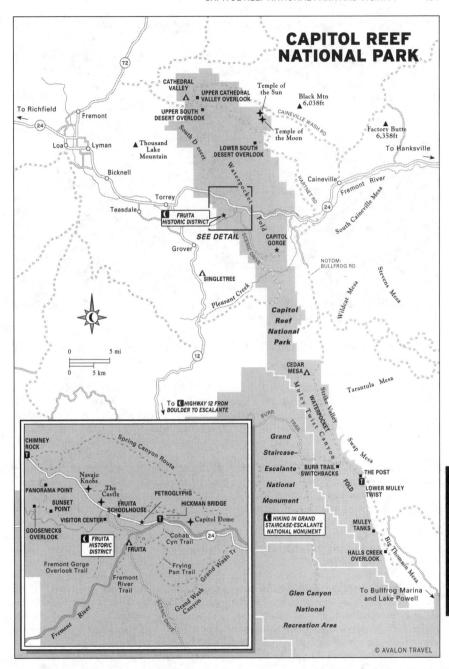

SOUTH-CENTRAL UTAH

© NATIONAL PARK SERVICE

Time your visit right, and you can pick apples in Fruita's orchards.

◖ FRUITA HISTORIC DISTRICT

From the visitors center, continue south to the **historic district,** where Mormon settlers planted orchards on the green banks of the Fremont River in the 1880s. Originally called Junction, as it stood at the intersection of the Fremont River and Sulphur Creek, the settlement quickly became known as the "Eden of Wayne County" around the time when Butch Cassidy and his Wild Bunch are said to have hidden out in the nearby canyons. The settlement changed its name to Fruita in 1902 after the apple, cherry, peach, apricot, mulberry, and pear trees started bearing fruit.

In the early 1900s the population hovered around 10 families, who raised sorghum, alfalfa, and vegetables. Fruit provided most of the income, though only rough tracks connected Fruita with the rest of the world. A barter economy helped the tiny community weather the Great Depression, and the first tractor didn't arrive until World War II. Visitors began to arrive with the declaration of Capitol Reef National Monument in 1937, and the National

Park Service eventually purchased most of the land peacefully by the late 1960s.

Today you can see the historic **school** on SR 24, the **Gifford farmhouse and barn,** the **Holt Farmstead,** and the famous Fruita **orchards.** The Park Service maintains about 2,700 trees with year-round irrigation and care, and each season's bounty is available to visitors on a pick-your-own basis for a small fee. Fruits are ready for harvest anywhere between late June (cherries) and early October (apples); contact the visitors center for a schedule.

At the Gifford farm, about a mile south of the visitors center, there's a pleasantly shady picnic area among the cottonwood and willows by the river. The farmhouse kitchen (added in 1946 to the original 1909 house) is now a gift shop with locally made crafts, reproduction utensils and tools, and preserves, pies, and ice cream. During summer months, interpreters explain and demonstrate various aspects of pioneer life. The Gifford family was the last to leave Fruita in 1969.

A half-dozen hiking trails start from the

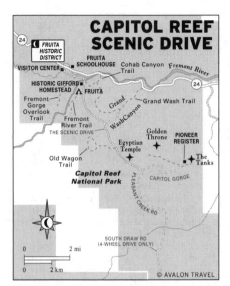

Fruita area, ranging from gentle strolls to steep, cliff-hugging climbs. The nearby **Fremont River Trail** (2.5 miles round-trip) leads through the orchards to an overlook of the valley. The first half mile is easy, but the trail climbs steeply after that, gaining 800 feet.

Another even steeper trail (3.5 miles round-trip) leaves the road to the east just before the campground, climbing up to **Cohab Canyon,** a classic "hanging" canyon that's hard to see from below. The canyon was named after Mormon polygamists who sought refuge from the law there in the 1880s. Short side spurs lead to various overlooks.

Just south of the farm, the year-round **Fruita Campground** has 71 sites (no hookups or showers, $10/night). Sites are on a first-come, first-served basis and often fill by afternoon from spring through fall. The park is free up to this point, but to continue down Scenic Drive you'll have to pay a $5 per car **entrance fee.**

SCENIC DRIVE

The Reef's main thoroughfare starts at the visitors center and heads south for 10 paved miles. Past Fruita, the first major point of interest is the winding mile-long dirt spur into

Grand Wash, accessible to passenger cars in dry weather. Butch Cassidy was said to have a hideout in this narrow, sheer-sided canyon. True or not, there's an arch named after him today, and the trail to **Cassidy Arch** (3.5 miles round-trip) climbs more than 1,000 feet.

Scenic Drive continues south past the **Egyptian Temple** and the **Golden Throne,** two of the park's more unusual landmarks. The Egyptian Temple is a vertical accordion of dark Moenkopi Sandstone topped by the harder Shinarump Layer, and the Golden Throne is an unmistakable dome of gleaming Navajo Sandstone. A demanding trail (four miles round-trip) climbs to the top of the cliffs for panoramic views, including a good look at the base of the Golden Throne.

A short distance farther down the road another dirt spur heads east into **Capitol Gorge,** longer than Grand Wash but just as deep and narrow. This used to be the only way vehicles could cross the Waterpocket Fold before SR 24 was built, and it's probably the closest you will ever come to driving through a slot canyon, weather permitting. The spur ends at two miles, but you can venture farther on the **Capitol Gorge Trail** (2.5 miles round-trip). Look for Fremont petroglyphs and the **Pioneer Register,** where passing settlers carved their names on the canyon wall near the turn of the 20th century.

Scenic Drive ends beyond Capitol Gorge, crossing Pleasant Creek and becoming the unpaved **South Draw Road,** suitable for high-clearance four-wheel-drive vehicles in good weather. The track (closed in winter) makes several creek crossings as it curves around to the southwest, climbing to 8,500 feet to join SR 12 on Boulder Mountain near the Pleasant Creek and Oak Creek Campgrounds in Fishlake National Forest.

CATHEDRAL VALLEY

North of SR 24, the Cathedral District contains some of the national park's most unusual landscapes—and that's saying a lot. To explore this area means traveling via rough roads usually suitable for high-clearance vehicles but

BUTCH CASSIDY AND THE WILD BUNCH

One of the West's most famous outlaws, Butch Cassidy is remembered as much for his wit, charm, and benevolence as for his utter disregard for the law. He was born Robert LeRoy Parker on April 13, 1866, to Mormon parents in Beaver, Utah. Raised on a ranch near Circleville, he fell under the wing of an old rustler named Mike Cassidy before leaving home to seek his fortune by any means necessary. Two years as a cowboy was followed by a stint as a butcher in Rock Springs, Wyoming. By adding his mentor's last name to his profession, Parker came up with the nickname that he would ride to worldwide fame: Butch Cassidy.

In Telluride, Colorado, Cassidy joined forces with another Utahan, Matt Warner, and in 1889 they staged their first major bank robbery in the mountain mining town. Butch served two years in a Wyoming jail for cattle rustling before finding his true calling as the leader of a loosely knit gang known as the Wild Bunch. Several famous outlaws belonged to the Wild Bunch at one time or another, including Ben Kilpatrick (the "Tall Texan"), Harvey Logan ("Kid Curry"), and Butch's best friend, Elzy Lay. When Lay was captured and jailed in 1899, Butch teamed up with Harry Longabaugh, a gunslinger from Pennsylvania better known as the Sundance Kid.

Led by Butch and Sundance, the Wild Bunch embarked on one of the most successful crime sprees in the history of the West. They robbed banks and trains and rustled horses and cattle throughout Colorado, Utah, Wyoming, and the surrounding territories. The gang had a number of hideouts to retreat to when the heat was on, including inaccessible canyons like the grassy Hole in the Wall in northern Wyoming and the remote Robber's Roost in South-Central Utah, south of the San Rafael Swell.

Most of the Wild Bunch eventually found themselves in jail or pine boxes by the turn of the 20th century, but Butch and Sundance kept going. Cassidy's gentlemanly charm no doubt helped, earning him the reputation of a fearless outlaw who never killed anyone and was polite to the ladies. Stories have him helping those in need, including a lost priest whom he helped back home, and ejecting a member from his gang who had stolen a horse from a young boy. He split up his crimes with interludes as a legitimate rancher, but the straight-and-narrow lifestyle never seemed to stick.

As the West filled with settlers and police, the once-easy life of an outlaw became more of an effort. The Pinkerton Agency, hired by the railroads, pursued the pair relentlessly. Butch sought an amnesty first from the governor of Utah and then from the Union Pacific Railroad, but neither worked. Along with Sundance and his girlfriend, Etta Place, Cassidy fled to New York City, where on February 20, 1902, he departed on a steamer for Buenos Aires, Argentina. The trio took aliases and bought a ranch in Patagonia, where they tried to make a go at an honest living. When Etta returned to the United States in 1907, though, Butch and Sundance reverted to their old ways, robbing trains, banks, and rich mine stations in several countries.

The events surrounding the supposed deaths of Butch Cassidy and the Sundance Kid are still debated. On November 4, 1908, the pair found themselves at the Concordia Tin Mines near San Vicente, Bolivia. According to an official document signed by the mayor, a pair of gringos who had robbed a mine payroll holed up in a local house, where they exchanged gunfire with a number of soldiers. When the troops approached the house the next morning, they found both men dead inside, one apparently from a self-inflicted gunshot. The men were quickly buried.

But were they Butch and Sundance? Many say they were actually another pair of outlaws and that it would be just like Butch to spread the word that it had been him and his partner instead. According to this version, the pair returned to the United States and lived out the rest of their lives in peaceful anonymity. Some have sworn they spotted or even met with Butch in the 1920s and 1930s, including his sister Lula and Matt Warner's daughter Joyce. The myth got a boost with the 1969 hit movie starring Paul Newman and Robert Redford, although that telling had them meet their end at the hands of half the Bolivian army. It seems that no one knows for sure what happened but Butch himself, and he probably would have wanted it that way.

sometimes requiring four-wheel drive. And if it's been raining, roads may be impassable to all vehicles. Check with the visitors center for current weather conditions before setting out on this or any other dirt roads in the park.

Most visitors see Cathedral Valley from a 60-mile loop that starts at the **Fremont River Ford,** 12 miles east of the visitors center on SR 24. (One reason to start there: If you can't make the crossing, which can be flooded after thunderstorms or during spring runoff, you won't be able to make the loop.) Be sure to close the gate behind you, and don't park or camp on private property along the road. (Much of the route lies outside park boundaries.)

Continue on **Hartnet Road,** which offers sweeping views over the stark South Desert. About 28 miles from the ford, turn right onto the Caineville Wash Road at **Hartnet Junction,** a half mile from the primitive Cathedral Valley campground (six sites, no fee) at 7,000 feet on the base of **Thousand Lake Mountain.** Notice the changes in the landscape and vegetation as the road gains elevation. Continuing east for 32 miles on the Caineville Wash Road, the loop passes innumerable volcanic dikes and plugs in Cathedral Valley. The sharp spires of the **Temple of the Moon** and the **Temple of the Sun** are the two most striking examples. The loop rejoins SR 24 just west of Caineville.

NOTOM-BULLFROG ROAD

A little more than nine miles east of the visitors center on SR 24, a turnoff leads south for this popular Capitol Reef back road traveling along the east side of the Waterpocket Fold. The 65-mile route to Lake Powell's Bullfrog Marina is paved only on either end; the majority is dirt surface and conditions vary with the weather. About 17 miles south of SR 24 the Notom-Bullfrog Road passes the primitive **Cedar Mesa Campground** (five sites, no fee) and then enters Strike Valley, intersecting the Burr Trail from Boulder after 29 miles. The road offers access to numerous backcountry hikes (permits required), and the best time to explore is in spring or fall.

The trail through Halls Creek Narrows is accessed from the Notom-Bullfrog Road.

Past the Burr Trail switchbacks is the entrance to **Lower Muley Twist,** a popular narrows hike through a canyon so sinuous they say it could tie a mule in knots. If you hike the canyon south of the road, you can exit east to Halls Creek after four miles and climb a cutoff trail back to the road at a parking area on the Notom-Bullfrog Road called **The Post.** With a car shuttle, this six-mile hike can be done in a day. For a very long day hike or overnight trip (15 miles round-trip), start from The Post and head south down the canyon, which becomes more interesting after it joins Halls Creek. Keep an eye out for pour-offs, pools, huge undercuts, and a cowboy camp, and imagine being a Mormon pioneer hauling wagons and cattle through there in the 1880s.

The Notom-Bullfrog Road leaves the park just south of The Post, becoming paved once again as it nears Bullfrog Marina and Glen Canyon National Recreation Area. From the paved southern end, a rough dirt road (4WD recommended) leads four miles across Big

Thompson Mesa to the **Halls Creek Overlook** and the trailhead to another outstanding narrows hike: the **Halls Creek Narrows.** The narrows themselves, three miles long and 328 feet deep, are 11 miles south of the overlook, so getting there and back is best undertaken as a three- or four-day journey, but deep shade and a trickling perennial stream help make it worth the effort. An old wagon trail to Halls Crossing on the Colorado River once ran down this canyon, and ruts are still visible in many stretches.

Two other trails begin at the Halls Creek Overlook. One leads west to **Brimhall Natural Bridge,** a moderately challenging route that's five miles round-trip. The other drops into the canyon and then heads upstream three miles to **Hamburger Rocks,** dark hoodoos of stone that look like burgers on a white stone grill. (Total round-trip distance is nine miles.)

TORREY

Capitol Reef's gateway town stretches for a half mile or so along SR 24 near its intersection with SR 12, about eight miles west of the park. Large cottonwoods and a canal follow the road, along with a growing handful of hotels, restaurants, and other businesses. Torrey (pop. 200) bills itself as Wayne County's biggest little city, and the availability of tourist services is impressive for a town this size. But then there's a lot to see and do: Torrey is situated between Fishlake and Dixie National Forests, with Thousand Lakes Mountain and Boulder Mountain offering numerous recreational opportunities. Though many tourist-related businesses in Torrey close late fall–spring, local outfitters and guides continue to lead outdoor adventures during winter months. Every Fourth of July, Torrey puts on a classic small-town celebration known as Apple Days, encompassing a swap meet, parade, pie-eating contest, and the Big Apple Dance at the town's outdoor dance hall.

Shopping and Services

The Wayne Country Travel Council operates an **information center** (435/425-3365, www.capitolreef.org, 9 A.M.–5 P.M. daily) at the intersection of SR 12 and SR 24. Next door is

Castlerock Coffee & Candy (435/425-2100, www.castlerockcoffee.com, from 7 A.M. daily), serving up coffee drinks, smoothies, and handmade candies and offering a selection of locally made delights from honey and pastries to jewelry, pottery, and photography. **The Torrey Gallery** (80 E. Main St., 435/425-3909, www.torreygallery.com) offers paintings, photography, and sculpture by Utah artists as well as antique and contemporary Navajo rugs.

Backcountry Outfitters (875 E. SR 24, 435/425-2010 or 866/747-3972, www.ridethereef.com) can arrange everything from horseback rides and fishing tips to jeep, ATV, and bike tours and rentals. **Hondoo Rivers and Trails** (90 E. Main St., 435/425-3519 or 800/332-2696, www.hondoo.com) also does multiday trail rides to Capitol Reef, the Escalante canyons, the San Rafael Swell, and other nearby destinations. Alpine Adventures (310 W. Main, 435/425-3660, www.alpineadventuresutah.com) guides hunting and fishing trips to the Henry Mountains and other locations.

For a dose of caffeine and literature, look for the conical roof of **Robber's Roost Books & Beverages** (185 W. Main St., 435/425-3265, www.robbersroostbooks.com). It's a great place to lounge and sip, with couches and a wood-burning stove inside and a glassed-in porch out back. They have a small but well-chosen assortment of titles and many works by local authors. They host **The Entrada Institute** (www.entradainstitute.org), a group that spreads its enthusiasm for the natural and cultural heritage of the Colorado Plateau with a wide range of entertaining and instructive events, including the Saturday Sunset Series and the annual **Cowboy Music and Poetry Gathering,** held in early March.

Accommodations and Food

Starting from the west end of town on SR 24 (aka Main Street), the **Thousand Lakes RV Park** (1050 W. Main St., 435/425-3500 or 800/355-8995, www.thousandlakesrvpark.com, Apr.–Oct.) has tent and RV sites ($18–29) as well as cabins ($35–95). They also boast a heated pool, a grocery store, showers, and Western cookouts

($15–23) five nights a week, and they're a Wi-Fi hot spot to boot. They even rent four-wheel-drive vehicles starting at $95 per day.

The ◖ **Café Diablo** (599 W. Main St., 435/425-3070, www.cafediablo.net, lunch and dinner daily mid-Apr.–Oct.) serves outstanding nouveaux Southwest dishes like pecan chicken and pumpkin-seed trout ($24–30). The outdoor patio is lovely once it starts to cool off at night. Yet another hidden gem of the southern Utah dining scene is the restaurant at the ◖ **Capitol Reef Inn & Café** (360 W. Main, 435/425-3271, www.capitolreefinn.com, all meals daily Apr.–Oct.). Fresh local produce goes into their healthy creations spanning the spectrum from homemade banana bread to 10-vegetable salads and lemon hickory chicken dinners ($6–20). Southwest-style rooms with handmade furniture are $50, complete with satellite movies and a shared hot tub. Elm trees, a waterfall, and a desert garden decorate the grounds, and the owners have built an Anasazi-style kiva next door.

Austin's Chuckwagon Lodge (12 W. Main St., 435/425-3335 or 800/863-3288, www.austinschuckwagonmotel.com) offers rooms for $75 and two-bedroom log cabins, with full kitchens and enough room for six people, for $135. Outdoors is a large heated pool with a whirlpool, and the general store on the premises has a full selection of groceries and a bakery.

About a block north of Main, the sturdy stone masonry **Torrey Schoolhouse** (150 N. Center St., 435/633-4643, www.torreyschoolhouse.com, $110–150), built in 1914, has been recently renovated as a B&B featuring modern conveniences like Wi-Fi and hearty organic breakfasts.

Atop a mesa above the SR 12/SR 24 intersection is the **Sandstone Inn** (955 E. SR 24, 435/425-3775 or 800/458-0216, www.sandstoncapitolreef.com, $70–95), a sprawling complex that boasts 50 rooms, a restaurant, heated pool, hot tub, sauna, and even a small library. Also perched above the intersection on 75 view-filled acres is the ◖ **Sky Ridge B&B** (950 E. SR 24, 435/633-4523 or 877/824-1508, www.skyridgeinn.com, $110–145). Six rooms with names like Juniper and Tumbleweed are eclectically decorated, and a full, tasty breakfast is included.

A few miles east of Torrey toward the national park is the **Best Western Capitol Reef Resort** (2600 E. Hwy. 24, 435/425-3761, $120–160), with 100 rooms available year-round, a restaurant, heated outdoor pool, and tennis courts.

Scenic Byway 12

The most spectacular drive in a land of superlatives, SR 12 is often called the most scenic road in America. The views from this All-American Highway can make you swerve in awe—a definite problem when there's a 500-foot drop from the shoulder. Take turns at the wheel or, if you're alone, stop often to admire the scenery. This is a drive not to be missed.

From Torrey, SR 12 climbs to almost 10,000 feet at the top of the Aquarius Plateau before dropping down to pass through two of the most remote towns in the lower 48, Boulder and Escalante. Meandering across the slickrock expanses of the northern edge of the Grand Staircase–Escalante National Monument, the road passes livestock grazing in green fields near Henrieville, continues west for the neon spires of Bryce Canyon National Park, and climbs the Paunsaugunt Plateau to meet U.S. 89 just south of Panguitch.

You could drive all 124 miles in an afternoon or spend a lifetime exploring the canyons visible from just one of the overlooks. Well worth at least a few days' meandering, SR 12, also known as the "Journey Through Time Scenic Byway," showcases the amazing diversity of what was one of the last blank spots on the map of the United States. For more information, visit the website www.scenicbyway12.com.

WEST ON HIGHWAY 12

On its way up over the flank of **Boulder Mountain,** SR 12 cuts across the eastern edge of the Aquarius Plateau, between Fishlake National Forest and Dixie National Forest, Utah's largest at two million acres. Peaking at 11,322 feet, Boulder Mountain is the highest timbered plateau in North America and is home to hundreds of small lakes above 10,000 feet in elevation. (The mountains around there seem to be deliberately misnamed: Most of the lakes are on Boulder Mountain, and most of the boulders are on Thousand Lake Mountain.) As the road climbs, piñon and juniper gradually give way to aspen, fir, and spruce. Pullouts provide stupendous panoramic overlooks.

About 25 miles east of Boulder, a trio of seasonal campgrounds in the Fremont Ranger District offer special settings for $10/night. **Singletree Campground** has open views of Capitol Reef, followed five miles later by tiny **Oak Creek Campground,** near two trout-stocked reservoirs. After another mile, a spur road leads to **Pleasant Creek Campground** near the **Wildcat Ranger Station,** open in summers. SR 12 tops out at 9,400 feet at Roundtop Flat before dropping down to Boulder, 39 miles south of Torrey.

BOULDER

A cattle ranching community settled in 1889, Boulder (pop. 200) is little more than a wide spot on SR 12. The tiny community, isolated by the canyons of the Escalante River and its tributaries, was the last in Utah to receive its mail by mule train. The river was bridged in 1935 and a year-round road completed in 1939, making Boulder one of the last towns in the United States to gain automobile access. Electric power came to town in 1947.

Today, ranches still spread to the south and west, and Boulder Mountain rises to the north. Huge domes of light-colored Navajo Sandstone, cracked into patterns like the skins of primeval creatures, tower above the town. Boulder itself is a pretty, green oasis that's seen land values rise significantly since President Bill Clinton declared the Grand Staircase–Escalante National Monument in 1996.

Anasazi State Park Museum

One of the largest Anasazi villages west of the Colorado River is on the grounds of the **Anasazi State Park Museum** (460 N. SR 12, 435/335-7308, http://stateparks.utah.gov, 8 A.M.–6 P.M. daily in summer, 9 A.M.–5 P.M. Mon.–Sat. in winter, $5 pp). The museum houses thousands of artifacts, many of which are on display. The excavated and partially reconstructed Coombs Site is believed to have been occupied by up to 200 people A.D. 1160–1235.

Events

Boulder hosts several small-town celebrations during summer months, including the **Heritage Festival** in mid-July, three days of storytelling, music, and a public dig at Anasazi State Park.

Recreation

The **Boulder Mountain Guest Ranch** (3621 Hells Backbone Rd., 435/335-7480, www.bouldermountainguestranch.com) has rooms and cabins ($70–115), an impressive menu at its Sweetwater Café (breakfast, dinner, and box lunches), and an equally impressive menu of outfitter/guide services that include day-hiking, backpacking, and horseback adventures finished off with an optional white-linen "tailgate" package. Day hikes are $90 (including lunch), while overnight trips start at $160/day. Lodging packages and equipment rental are available. The turnoff for the ranch is 3.5 miles up the Hell's Backbone Road.

Red Rock 'n Llamas (877/955-2627, www. redrocknllamas.com) offers 4–5-day guided hikes to Cedar Mesa and the Escalante and Colorado Rivers starting at $850 per person. Llamas carry most of the gear, and are easier on the scenery than horses or mules. Other guide services operating out of Boulder include **Escalante Canyon Outfitters** (888/326-4453, www.ecohike.com), providing canyon trips and "archaeohikes" in conjunction with the Anasazi State Park Museum, and **Earth Tours** (435/691-1241, www.earth-tours.com), with half-day and full-day guided hiking trips in the Escalante and Capitol Reef.

Local fishing guide Steve Stoner runs **Boulder Mountain Fly Fishing** (435/335-7306, www.bouldermountainflyfishing.com) and leads trips in search of the cutthroat and brook trout that fill the many lakes up on Boulder Mountain. He provides all the equipment and charges $350 for two anglers for one day. And if you happen to see a bedraggled group limp into town and head straight for the burgers at Pole's Place, they're probably with the **Boulder Outdoor Survival School** (303/444-9779, www.boss-inc.com). Though based in Boulder, Colorado, their desert survival and Wilderness First Responder (WFR) courses center around two base camps near Boulder.

Accommodations and Food

Campers can choose from 7 sites ($5) at the primitive **Deer Creek Campground** 6.7 miles southeast of Boulder along the Burr Trail or from a number of campgrounds a bit farther out. (For a campground with hookups and spaces large enough for RVs, make reservations in Escalante.)

Just down the road from the Anasazi State Park Museum, **C Boulder Mountain Lodge** (435/335-7460 or 800/556-3446, www.boulder-utah.com, $130–200, discounted Nov.–Mar.) is one of the Four Corner's most enticing getaways. The luxury eco-lodge combines Western coziness with first-class comfort. Tapestries and local artists' works decorate the tasteful interior, and the lodge's stucco and sandstone buildings are arranged around a private waterfowl sanctuary complete with pond and marsh. (Birders can spot ibises from the outdoor hot tub.) The double-height common room has a library, fireplace, and comfy furniture for lounging.

The lodge's **C Hell's Backbone Grill** (435/335-7464, www.hellsbackbonegrill.com, breakfast and dinner Mar.–Nov.) features the finest cooking in this part of Utah. The restaurant has its own no-harm farm and organic garden, supplying a weekly changing menu that may include such delights as chipotle meat loaf and blue corn–crusted trout. Dinner entrées are $17–26.

Across from Anasazi State Park Museum, **Pole's Place** (435/335-7422 or 800/730-7422, www.boulderutah.com, $60–75) combines a gift shop, a motel with 12 guest rooms, and a seasonal café serving burgers and shakes at their walk-up window. The **Burr Trail Grill and Outpost** (10 N. SR 12, 435/335-7503, www.burrtrailgrill.com, lunch and dinner daily, breakfast Fri.–Mon., open seasonally) dishes up New American cuisine for $10–30, with live music Saturday nights. They also serve beer, wine, and homemade desserts. The outpost has a coffee bar, so you can sip while you browse guidebooks or local arts and crafts.

Information

More details about the area's attractions and businesses can be found at the website of the **Boulder Business Alliance** (www.boulderutah.com), the combined Escalante/Boulder Chamber of Commerce (www.escalante-cc.com), and the Garfield County Travel Council (435/676-1102 or 800/444-6689, www.brycecanyoncountry.com).

BURR TRAIL

This old cattle trail winds east from Boulder, crosses the Circle Cliffs and and joins the Notom-Bullfrog Road to reach Bullfrog Marina on Lake Powell after 68 miles. The mostly unpaved backcountry route boasts extraordinary scenery as it crosses Escalante Grand Staircase National Monument, the southern end of Capitol Reef National Park, and enters Glen Canyon National Recreation Area, offering access to dozens of hikes.

The route was blazed by rancher John Atlantic Burr in the late 1800s to move cattle between winter and summer ranges and to market. After the trail was improved by the Atomic Energy Commission to help uranium prospectors access the backcountry, controversy erupted in the 1970s over whether it should be paved its entire length. Garfield County officials held that paving would boost the local economy and improve transportation, while conservationists argued that off-road vehicle (ORV) damage would increase. Things reached

© NATIONAL PARK SERVICE

Passenger cars can travel the Burr Trail switchbacks in dry conditions.

a bitter peak in the 1980s, when directors of the Southern Utah Wilderness Association were hanged in effigy in Escalante, and four county bulldozers were sabotaged near the switchbacks.

The Burr Trail is paved for a few dozen miles on either end, but dirt otherwise, and through the Waterpocket Fold and the park, the going can get rough in inclement weather. In dry weather, the trail is suitable for passenger cars, but steep switchbacks in Capitol Reef make RVs a bad idea. There are no services the entire length, so carry all the water and gasoline you think you'll need, plus some extra. Intermittent posts along the road serve as reference markers for some of the major turnoffs.

Dozens of side roads and trails branch off from the main route. After passing the Deer Creek Campground at mile 6.5, you'll cross **The Gulch** at 10.7 miles, a popular trailhead from which you can reach the Escalante River in about two days. The Burr Trail then follows Long Canyon, a colorful gorge reminiscent of Zion Canyon, for about seven miles. About 30

miles from Boulder, the Burr Trail intersects Wolverine Road, a 28-mile loop through remote, rugged terrain that includes an area of petrified logs on BLM land (collecting any is illegal). Even rougher side roads lead off the Wolverine Loop. The loop rejoins the Burr Trail shortly before crossing into Capitol Reef National Park.

Once inside the park, the Burr Trail turns to dirt. Soon you'll cross **Muley Twist Canyon.** From Muley Twist, the Burr Trail descends a daunting series of switchbacks—800 feet in a half mile—and intersects with the Notom-Bullfrog Road. The view to the east is outstanding. From there the Notom-Bullfrog Road leaves the park and parallels the Waterpocket Fold north and south. Turn south to join SR 276 after 66 miles from Boulder. Lake Powell's Bullfrog Marina is only a short distance ahead.

◖ HIGHWAY 12 FROM BOULDER TO ESCALANTE

The most scenic stretch of SR 12 runs for less than 30 miles between Boulder and Escalante.

Finished by the Civilian Conservation Corps in 1940, the "Million-Dollar Highway to Boulder" allowed the first year-round car access to the towns cut off from the rest of the world by the Escalante canyons. The road wasn't fully paved until 1971.

Drive it and you'll agree the nickname refers to the views as much as the cost: Blond and rosy slickrock undulate toward the horizon, with green lines of cottonwoods following invisible watercourses down canyon bottoms. The Henry Mountains, Navajo Mountain, and the Straight Cliffs stand above it all. Make this drive in early morning or late afternoon to fully appreciate the three-dimensionality of the landscape. Few roads interact with their scenery as spectacularly as this one, and it's worth timing it right.

Shortly after heading west from Boulder, SR 12 is joined by the **Hells Backbone Road,** a 44-mile gravel road (closed in winter) with spectacular views of its own. The highway swings southeast and crosses a winding section called the **Hogback,** a rocky spine just wide enough for the two-lane road, a narrow shoulder, and a few small pull-outs. It then descends from Haymaker Bench to Calf Creek.

Just over 11 miles south of Boulder, the **Calf Creek Canyon Recreation Area,** run by the BLM, has 13 campsites for $8 per night (day use is $2 per car). From there a moderate trail (six miles round-trip) heads up Calf Canyon to **Lower Calf Creek Falls,** plunging 126 feet into a sandy pool. Watch for river otters, reintroduced into the Escalante River in 2005 and occasionally seen in Calf Creek. As you pass beaver-dammed pools lined with reeds, look for ruins and pictographs. The trail offers an accessible peek at the Escalante canyons, so it can get relatively crowded on weekends. Fewer people hike the steep trail (two miles round-trip) to the 90-foot **Upper Calf Creek Falls.** This fairly well-marked trail starts from a short dirt track that leaves SR 12 between mileposts 81 and 82.

Continuing toward Escalante, the highway crosses the river at the start of the popular **Escalante River Trail.** For a pleasant day hike (five miles round-trip), head west (upriver)

from the highway to Escalante Natural Bridge. Expect to get wet; the trail crosses the river several times. Between mile markers 73 and 74, the **Kiva Koffee House** (435/826-4550, www.kivakoffeehouse.com, 8:30 A.M.–4:30 P.M. Wed.–Mon., Apr.–Oct.) is a beautiful round stone and wood building with big windows overlooking the canyon. You can enjoy a coffee drink or some homemade soup while you browse the selection of books and maps, or stay overnight in one of their two guest rooms ($170). Shortly you'll reach **Boynton Overlook,** where you'll have an aerial view of the Escalante River and Calf Creek. (Get out your binoculars and look for a pictograph panel of handprints on the opposite canyon wall, just above the mouth of Calf Creek.) Four miles later, Head of the Rocks overlooks the highway and takes in distant views of Boulder Mountain, the Henrys, and the eastern edge of the Kaiparowits Plateau.

Bare rock gives way to farmland as you pass the turnoff for the **Hole-in-the-Rock Road,** yet another scenic back way. You'll reach the town of Escalante in another five miles.

ESCALANTE

Drawn to the area's mild climate, 6,000 feet high between the Kaiparowits and Aquarius Plateaus, the Mormon pioneers who founded this town in 1875 named it for the nearby river, which in turn was named after the explorer-priest Francisco Silvestre Vélez de Escalante. The settlers nicknamed their new home "Potato Valley" for a local variety of wild tuber and set about exploring the grazing potential of the nearby canyons and benches. Families drew numbers from a hat to decide who got which 1.25-acre lot, logs houses went up, and the new town was off and running. When the Centennial rolled around in July 1876, no one had an American flag yet, so a striped Navajo blanket was hoisted instead. Piped drinking water arrived in 1937. Many of the town's pioneer homes and barns, constructed of stone and logs, are still in use.

Farming and livestock continue to play a strong role in the economy of Escalante (pop.

900), but change began to roll across the horizon like a stampede with the declaration of the huge national monument next door. As the main gateway to the Escalante canyons, the town now boasts many tourist services. Some businesses close in winter, so check ahead if you're visiting November–March.

Sights

If you need a break from the unending swells of slickrock, **Escalante Petrified Forest State Park** (435/826-4466, 7 A.M.–10 P.M. daily, open 8 A.M. winter, $5 pp) has a 130-acre reservoir for fishing and swimming, as well as two short self-guided trails past rainbow-colored chunks of petrified wood and fossilized dinosaur bones. The park is two miles west of Escalante on SR 12 and has campsites, some with hookups, for $16–20 per night (reservations 801/322-3770 or 800/322-3770).

The **Hells Backbone Road** is a 40-mile loop—mostly gravel—that leads up into the 25,000-acre **Box-Death Hollow Wilderness Area** north of Escalante, following sheer ridge tops and crossing gorges lined with orange-gray walls of Navajo Sandstone. The road was completed in 1933 by the Civilian Conservation Corps to provide a route between Boulder and Escalante; today Hell's Backbone affords access to a number of **hikes** in the canyons that flow into the upper reaches of the Escalante River. The southwestern end of the road meets SR 12 at the town of Escalante. The northeastern end meets SR 12 about four miles west of Boulder. About halfway between Escalante and Boulder, the road crosses Hell's Backbone Bridge, which looks down 1,500 feet into Sand Creek canyon. The road (also known as FR 153) is suitable for passenger cars in dry weather and takes a couple hours . . . if you can resist stopping for photos or hikes. You can make the journey from either direction.

Events

The **Escalante Festival and Craft Fair** comes to town at the end of May, followed by the **Pioneer Days Celebration** in late July. In late September, the legacy of Everett Ruess is celebrated with art, lectures, and entertainment during the **Escalante Canyons Arts Festival & Everett Ruess Days** (www.everettruessdays. org). Though Escalante hosts the festival, artists set up their easels in surrounding areas to paint *en plein air* for the exhibition and silent auction that mark the festival's grand finale.

Shopping

An espresso bar isn't the rarity it once was in southern Utah, but the "Esca-Latte" sign at **Escalante Outfitters** (310 W. Main St., 435/826-4266 or 866/455-0041, www.escalanteoutfitters.com) is still a welcome sight to road-tripping caffeine hounds. Along with a pizza parlor, bike rental, and tour packages, this all-inclusive place has Wi-Fi and stocks gear, guidebooks, and microbrews, and has log cabins next door for $45. (Campsites are $16.) They can also arrange lodgings at the charming Vagabond Inn B&B for $130 double.

Right across the street, **Utah Canyons** (325 W. Main St., 435/826-4967, www.utah-canyons.com) offers maps, gear, guidebooks, a small barbecue restaurant, and a wealth of friendly advice about the surrounding countryside. They organize guided day hikes, wilderness skills workshops, and shuttles.

Pick up the *Escalante Arts & Crafts Guide* pamphlet anywhere in town for information on local artists and their galleries. **Brigitte and David Delthony** (1540 W. SR 12, 435/826-4631, www.sculpturedfurnitureartandceramics. com) have a gallery a half mile west of town on SR 12. Brigitte creates pit-fired pottery and ceramics inspired by the area's prehistoric cultures and teaches occasional workshops. David makes beautiful, organically shaped wooden furniture.

Recreation

The town of Escalante offers access to a number of hikes that explore tributary canyons of the Escalante River. One popular day hike along the Hells Backbone Road follows a stretch of narrow, tree-lined streambed called the **Pine Creek Box.** Most people drive up the road about eight miles, descend to the streambed, and follow it back to Escalante in a day. **Death**

Hollow, east of Pine Creek, is a more serious undertaking. Canyoneers need up to five days to do the entire canyon from the trailhead, which is 22.5 miles up the Hells Backbone Road. The route threads through three miles of narrows with pools that may require swimming to cross. This should not be your first canyoneering trip, unless you're on a guided expedition. Both of these hikes are easier with a two-car shuttle.

Another way out of Death Hollow is via the **Boulder Mail Trail,** which until 1935 was the only way the U.S. Postal Service could reach the remote town. Set aside two days for this 16-mile hike, which cuts across the Pine Creek, Death Hollow, and Sand Creek Canyons and the exposed slickrock in between. You'll need some cross-country route-finding ability: Look for sporadic rock cairns and old telegraph wire. The eastern end intersects SR 12 near where the Hells Backbone Road rejoins it at milepost 84.

From the SR 12 bridge over the Escalante River, an easy two-mile trail leads upstream to **Escalante Natural Bridge** on the south side of the canyon. Many people hike down this section of the river from the town of Escalante to the bridge, taking 3–4 days to cover the 16 miles. Be prepared for some scrambling and plenty of wading and bushwhacking. **Phipps Wash,** about 1.5 miles downstream from the bridge, has a natural bridge in a west-side drainage and an arch in an east-side drainage.

Rick Green's **Excursions of Escalante** (125 E. Main, 800/839-7567, www.excursionsescalante.com) specializes in all-day canyoneering courses ($145–165 pp) but also offers guided hikes, photo safaris, and overnight trips. They operate out of the Trailhead Café & Grill.

If you'd like to explore the Escalante canyons but would rather have someone (or something) else carry your pack, sign up with **Escape Goats** (435/826-4652, www.utahpackgoats.com), which offers catered pack trips starting at $550 per person.

Accommodations

Escalante has a number of modest motels with rooms around $50–60, including the **Prospector Inn** (380 W. Main St., 435/826-4653, www.prospectorinn.com). **Escalante's Grand Staircase Bed and Breakfast Inn** (280 W. Main St., 435/826-4890, www.escalantebnb.com, $145) serves hearty breakfasts, with in-room service available on request. The **Rainbow Country Bed & Breakfast Inn** (586 E. 300 S., 435/826-4567 or 800/252-8824, www.bnbescalante.com, $70–100) has great views from the large sundeck. Four guest rooms include a hearty breakfast and access to the pool table and outdoor hot tub.

The owners of **Escalante's Wild West Retreat** (269 S. 200 E., 866/292-3043, www.wildwestretreat.com) took a 1930s barn and turned it into a luxury-rustic getaway with a full kitchen, hot tub, covered porches, and a stargazing upper deck. Rates start at $125, and horses and mules are boarded free. Another private building for rent in the same price range is the **Southwestern Retreat** (435/826-4708, www.southwesternretreat.com, $130). It sleeps seven people in three bedrooms and comes complete with a kitchen, laundry, deck, and entertainment center.

On the southwest edge of town, █ **La Luz Desert Retreat** (435/826-4708, www.laluz.net, $175) is a wedge-shaped vacation home built in the Usonian architectural style of Frank Lloyd Wright. It sleeps up to six people and has wonderful views through many windows.

The **Broken Bow RV Camp** (495 W. Main St., 435/826-4959 or 888/241-8785, www.brokenbowrvpark.com, $25–27) has 38 pull-through sites with hookups, cabins ($45–55), tent sites ($14), showers, and a laundry room. Escalante Outfitters also has cabins and campsites. You can also pitch a tent at the Escalante Petrified Forest State Park, the Calf Creek Canyon Recreation Area, and up in the Dixie National Forest. Fourteen miles from Escalante, the Hell's Backbone Road passes the turnoff for the 8,700-foot **Posey Lake Campground** (www.recreation.gov, 20 sites, $10 per night), and at 17 miles, a turnoff for the 7,800-foot **Blue Spruce Campground** (six sites, $8).

Food

The Prospector Inn's **Ponderosa Restaurant** (45 N. 400 W., 435/826-4775, all meals daily, $6–20) serves American and European dishes. The **Cowboy Blues Restaurant** (530 W. Main St., 435/826-4577, lunch and dinner daily, $10–20) has a Western-style menu and blue margaritas. The **Trail Head Cafe & Grill** (125 E. Main St., 800/839-7567, $5–12) serves up fresh-baked breads, grilled sandwiches and burgers, and coffee drinks on a big stone patio.

Both Utah Canyons and Escalante Outfitters have pleasant patio cafés for eating on-site or grabbing snacks for your pack. If you prefer to outfit yourself, stop by **Griffin Mercantile** (30 W. Main St., 435/826-4226), a mom-and-pop general store, for groceries, ice, and deli selections.

Information

The U.S. National Park Service, National Forest Service, and Bureau of Land Management jointly administer the **Escalante Interagency Visitor Center** (755 W. Main, 435/826-5499, 8 A.M.–4:30 P.M. daily) on the western edge of town (look for the giant lizard out front). Ecology-themed exhibits, interpretive films, a picnic area, and a bookstore make this a pleasant stop for gathering trip information. Direct any other questions to the **Escalante Chamber of Commerce** (435/826-4810, www.escalante-cc.com).

Grand Staircase-Escalante

At 1.9 million acres—almost 3,000 square miles—this 1996 addition to Utah's protected lands dwarfs the surrounding national parks. **Grand Staircase-Escalante National Monument** (GSENM) is almost as big as Delaware and Rhode Island put together, yet few people outside the Four Corners could place it on a map, and few have been lucky enough to venture inside. Word is starting to get out, however, and thousands of visitors are now arriving each year to explore this wonderland of cliffs, canyons, rivers, and desert plateaus. Whatever your interest—archaeology, geology, history, biology, paleontology, desert scenery, or simply escaping into the wild—the monument is more than big enough to accommodate.

GSENM can be roughly divided into three regions from west to east: the Grand Staircase, the Kaiparowits Plateau, and the Canyons of the Escalante.

The Grand Staircase

The southwest corner of the monument is the kind of landscape that makes geologists drool. First described by geologist Clarence Dutton in his classic 1880 *Report of the Geology of the High Plateaus of Utah,* it consists of a series of huge geological steps rising 3,500 feet over 150 miles, from the North Rim of the Grand Canyon to the top of the Paunsaugunt Plateau at Bryce Canyon National Park. More than 250 million years of uplift and erosion are on stark display in five major terraces named for their gaudy colors: the Chocolate Cliffs, the Vermilion Cliffs, the White Cliffs, the Gray Cliffs, and the Pink Cliffs. Five distinct life zones, from Sonoran desert to coniferous forests, shelter a wide variety of plant and animal life, including bald eagles, peregrine falcons, and California condors.

The Kaiparowits Plateau

The monument's vast middle section is its driest and most rugged, one of the largest remaining blank spots on a road map of the Four Corners. Some have likened this region of canyons and mesas to an American Outback, and if it's solitude you're after—and if you can handle yourself in the desert—this is the place to go. Desert bighorn sheep and mountain lions roam among rare plants and remnants of the Fremont and Ancestral Puebloan cultures. In the Paiute language, Kaiparowits means "big mountain's little brother," their name for a point near plateau's north end. The plateau has

THE HOLE-IN-THE-ROCK EXPEDITION

In 1879 Mormon Church president John Taylor called on a group of believers to colonize Montezuma Creek in Southeast Utah to secure a remote corner of the rapidly expanding Mormon empire and "breed goodwill among the Indians." The colonists began to assemble in late November—there were 236 people, many of them recent arrivals to the Western desert, in 82 wagons surrounded by hundreds of horses and cattle. They would undertake one of the most arduous journeys in the history of the American West.

In order to save 250 miles over established routes in the north and south, Silas Smith and other leaders elected to cut straight across the virtually unknown wilderness of the Escalante. Cattle could find little forage in the rough, rocky country, and resourceful Mormon wives, lacking wood, had to burn weeds and sagebrush to cook the food. In December, with snow blocking any hope of retreat through the mountains behind, the main party reached the edge of Glen Canyon. A formidable obstacle faced them: an 1,800-foot drop to the Colorado River, the sheer cliff cut by a narrow crevice. They named it Hole-in-the-Rock.

Scouts who had traveled ahead to assess a possible river crossing believed the crack could offer a way down. Smith and two boys traveled to Salt Lake for blasting powder, mining equipment, and food—it was a six-week journey. Plagued by bitter cold and dwindling food, 60 men set about building a road where, as author Wallace Stegner wrote, "God certainly never intended a road to be." While one team hung from the cliff edge in barrels, chiseling blasting holes to widen and level the existing crack, another team began tacking a road onto the sheer rock face below.

They blasted a small ledge just wide enough for the uphill wagon wheels and then drove two-foot cottonwood stakes into a row of holes gouged every 18 inches into the sandstone. Rocks, dirt, and vegetation were piled on top of the stakes, and gradually a makeshift road began to take shape. At an average angle of 50 degrees, the dizzying route was named Uncle Ben's Dugout for its designer, engineer Benjamin Perkins. Far below, a third work party was busy building a ferry to cross the river.

On January 26, after six weeks of back-breaking labor, the expedition began their descent to the river. Perkins went first, his horses rearing and shying away from the drop-off. (Other accounts say he had to use horses blinded by pinkeye.) About 20 men and boys did what they could to slow the wagons—holding ropes and chains wrapped around the wheels, tying large juniper trees to the frames, and rigging a pulley system from the top. Each wagon smoothed the passage more, making it harder and harder to hold the vehicles back. The remaining men, women, and children climbed down with the expedition's livestock.

By the end of the third day, most of the wagons had been ferried across the river. Amazingly, no lives were lost, but many had been injured and all were exhausted. The passage had worn the road down to almost nothing, so once again there would be no turning back. It took another week to ascend the steep cliffs of Cottonwood Canyon on the other side of the river. There they met a Ute who, on hearing their story, called them liars and rode away insulted.

Though it may have seemed the worst was behind them, more trials awaited. Scouts almost died of thirst and starvation trying to locate the route ahead, which they stumbled on by following a herd of mountain sheep. The final 150 miles took almost four months—an average of two miles a day—as they pulled, pushed, and dragged the wagons over slickrock and through sandy washes. By the time they reached the banks of the San Juan River, the expected six-week trip had taken six months, and nobody had the strength or will to push on another mile. Instead, they settled the town of Bluff, building a cluster of log buildings surrounded by fields and orchards. The historic Bluff Fort town site preserves one of their original cabins and recreates others, offering a glimpse into the day-to-day lives of the Hole-in-the-Rock pioneers. Among the volunteers who staff the fort are several of their descendants.

recently begun to be recognized as a world-class hot spot for late-Cretaceous paleontology, and many prehistoric human sites have also been recorded there.

The Canyons of the Escalante

Dinosaur tracks and historic pioneer routes converge near the maze of canyons of the Escalante River and its tributaries, the last major river to be discovered by Anglo explorers in the contiguous United States. The runoff from the southern edge of the Aquarius Plateau has carved a 1,000-mile labyrinth of converging canyons that eventually drain into the upper reaches of Lake Powell. Many of the monument's 200 or so bird species congregate there along the leafy drainages, including some from the neotropics. This is the easiest part of the monument to access (relatively speaking, of course), and thus it sees the most visitors. It was named after Spanish priest Francisco Silvestre Vélez de Escalante by the Powell survey team in 1872, although the padre didn't see the river during his journeys in 1776.

HISTORY
Early Inhabitants

Humans didn't settle this remote region more or less permanently until about A.D. 500, during the late Basketmaker II period. Both the seminomadic Fremont people and the Kayenta branch of the Ancestral Puebloans took advantage of the wide climatic range and lived in the area around the same time. While the Ancestral Puebloans farmed in the Escalante canyons and up on the Kaiparowits Plateau, the Fremont tended to hunt and gather below the plateau and near the Escalante Valley. Both groups grew corn, beans, and squash, and built brush-roofed pit houses or took advantage of natural rock shelters. The largest Ancestral Puebloan settlements were scattered across the Kaiparowits Plateau near the present town of Boulder, while the Fremont lived in Calf Creek Canyon, Harris Wash, and near the town of Escalante.

Today it's hard to find a corner of the monument without some evidence of early human use, whether it's a prehistoric ruin, a carefully

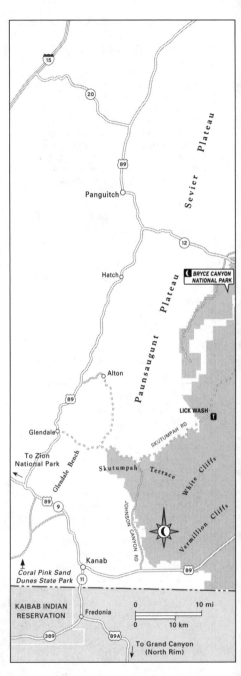

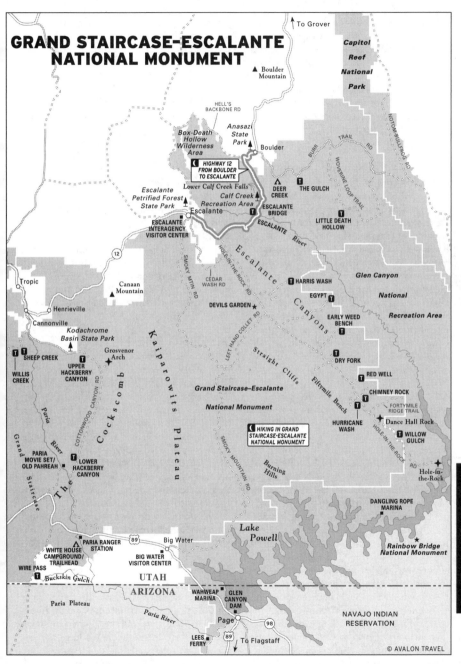

GRAND STAIRCASE-ESCALANTE NATIONAL MONUMENT

To Grover

Capitol Reef National Park

▲ Boulder Mountain

HELL'S BACKBONE RD

Box-Death Hollow Wilderness Area

Anasazi State Park

Boulder

HIGHWAY 12 FROM BOULDER TO ESCALANTE

BURR TRAIL RD

NOTOM-BULLFROG RD

Lower Calf Creek Falls

Calf Creek Recreation Area

DEER CREEK

THE GULCH

WOLVERINE LOOP TRAIL

Escalante Petrified Forest State Park

Escalante

ESCALANTE BRIDGE

LITTLE DEATH HOLLOW

ESCALANTE INTERAGENCY VISITOR CENTER

Escalante River

12

SMOKY MTN. RD

HOLE-IN-THE-ROCK RD

CEDAR WASH RD

Escalante Canyons

HARRIS WASH

Glen Canyon

Tropic

Canaan Mountain

DEVILS GARDEN ★

EGYPT

EARLY WEED BENCH

National

Recreation Area

Henrieville

Cannonville

Kodachrome Basin State Park

LEFT HAND COLLET RD

Straight Cliffs

DRY FORK

SHEEP CREEK

Grosvenor Arch

UPPER HACKBERRY CANYON

Kaiparowits Plateau

Grand Staircase-Escalante

National Monument

Fiftymile Bench

RED WELL

CHIMNEY ROCK

FORTYMILE RIDGE TRAIL

Dance Hall Rock

WILLIS CREEK

COTTONWOOD CANYON RD

HIKING IN GRAND STAIRCASE-ESCALANTE NATIONAL MONUMENT

HURRICANE WASH

HOLE-IN-THE-ROCK RD

WILLOW GULCH

Paria River

PARIA MOVIE SET/ OLD PAHREAH

LOWER HACKBERRY CANYON

The Cockscomb

SMOKY MOUNTAIN RD

Burning Hills

Hole-in-the-Rock

Grand Staircase

DANGLING ROPE MARINA

Lake Powell

Rainbow Bridge National Monument

PARIA RANGER STATION

89

Big Water

WHITE HOUSE CAMPGROUND/ TRAILHEAD

BIG WATER VISITOR CENTER

WIRE PASS

Buckskin Gulch

UTAH
ARIZONA

WAHWEAP MARINA

GLEN CANYON DAM

NAVAJO INDIAN RESERVATION

Paria Plateau

Paria River

Page

89

98

LEES FERRY

To Flagstaff

© AVALON TRAVEL

SOUTH-CENTRAL UTAH

chipped hand- and foothold trail snaking up a rock wall, or a rock art panel with characteristic trapezoidal bodies, animal figures, and abstract designs. Around A.D. 1300, these groups left or were absorbed into other arriving cultures. Groups that would become today's Paiute, Ute, and Navajo tribes entered the area; the Navajo hunted deer and sheep and began herding livestock into the eastern reaches of what would be declared the monument.

European Settlement

The first record of Anglos visiting the region dates to 1866, when Captain James Andrus led a group of cavalry to the headwaters of the Escalante River. Five years later, Jacob Hamblin of Kanab, on his way to the Colorado River to resupply the second Powell Expedition, mistook the Escalante for the Dirty Devil River and thus became the first European to travel the length of the canyon. The unforgiving topography was never demonstrated more clearly than during the 1879–80 Hole-in-the-Rock Expedition. To this day the canyons of the Escalante remain a major barrier to east–west vehicle travel, and the river is bridged only at its upper end.

The 20th Century

Although the Department of the Interior had proposed the creation of a national monument as early as 1936, it took another 60 years for reality to catch up. In September 1996 President Bill Clinton used the authority given to him through the Antiquities Act and created the Grand Staircase–Escalante National Monument. Sparks flew. Utah politicians, no big fans of Washington "meddling" to begin with, were enraged they weren't consulted in the transfer of such a huge chunk of their state to federal jurisdiction. The fact that the declaration was made from the rim of the Grand Canyon, in *Arizona,* just added fuel to the fire.

Tensions have sprouted between local ranchers, miners, and farmers, who feel that their land and way of life is being legislated out of existence, and newly arrived environmentalists and government employees scrambling to

protect the huge area. Many of the latter camp see tourism and tourist dollars as inevitable (and point out that many of the former have quietly stuck their fingers in the tourism pot already). Land values and visitation are already rising.

The monument's proclamation was vague enough on what is and isn't allowed within the boundaries to ensure years of land-use controversies. A few years earlier a Dutch mining company had applied for a state permit to mine the estimated 62 billion tons of coal under the surface of the Kaiparowits Plateau, the largest deposit of its kind in the United States. After the monument's proclamation, the company withdrew its proposal and negotiated federal land exchanges for the leases. In 2000 the monument became part of the National Landscape Conservation System, covering some 40 million acres of BLM-administered lands with special conservation designations. Though the NCLS was signed into law in 2009, legal and political battles are still being fought over land use within the monument.

VISITING THE MONUMENT
Access and Roads

Most access roads branch off SR 12 between Bryce Canyon National Park and Boulder and lead into GSENM's northern edge. A few of these run all the way through the monument to U.S. 89, on the monument's southwest side between Kanab, Utah, and Page, Arizona. Both highways are paved, but the rest of the monument's graded and/or gravel roads can quickly become impassable when wet. Even when dry, they're often rough enough to loosen the bolts on most two-wheel-drive vehicles.

The **Johnson Canyon/Skutumpah Road** connects **Kodachrome Basin State Park** with SR 89 about 10 miles east of Kanab. The 46-mile road (paved for the 18 miles through Johnson Canyon, graded dirt otherwise) offers glimpses of the Grand Staircase and access to trailheads at Sheep Creek, Willis Creek, and Lick Wash. The **Cottonwood Canyon Road** runs for 46 miles along the Cockscomb (aka the East Kaibab Monocline), a huge north–south fold in the earth that divides the Grand

Staircase from the Kaiparowits Plateau. Along this road, which heads southeast from Kodachrome Basin, are trailheads for Upper and Lower Hackberry Canyon and Grosvenor Arch, 17 miles south of SR 12. From Escalante, the **Smoky Mountain Road** winds for 78 rough miles across the Kaiparowits Plateau, providing the best access to the remote area. It eventually joins SR 89 at Big Water.

Perhaps the most popular way to access the eastern half of the monument is via the **Hole-in-the-Rock Road,** blazed in 1879 by a determined band of Mormon pioneers hoping to establish settlements to the southeast. By the time they reached the sheer cliffs of Glen Canyon, they had been journeying for two weeks. It took another 6 weeks to carve a wagon road out of the cliffs at the crevice they called Hole-in-the-Rock, and another 10 weeks to reach the banks of the San Juan, where they established the town of Bluff.

This scenic backway generally follows the pioneer route, running for 57 miles parallel to the Straight Cliffs, which mark the eastern edge of the Kaiparowits Plateau, from SR 12 east of Escalante to the Hole-in-the-Rock itself. In good weather, passenger cars can usually negotiate the graded dirt road except for the last six or so miles, which require a high-clearance four-wheel-drive vehicles. The most dramatic scenery lies east of the road, along side tracks (most requiring high-clearance 4WD) that lead to trailheads for narrow slot canyons heading toward the river.

At 10.4 miles from SR 12, a side road leaves to the east for Harris Wash and a large primitive campsite near a corral. Devil's Garden is just off the main road on the right at 12.1 miles, a small but beautiful area of rock hoodoos and arches. (There's a picnic area, but no overnight camping is allowed.) At 16.5 miles is a turnoff to the Egypt Canyon area, followed by ones for Early Weed Bench (23.6 miles), Dry Fork (25.9 miles), and Fortymile Ridge (36.1 miles).

A half mile past the turnoff to Fortymile Ridge is a natural red-rock amphitheater known as **Dance Hall Rock,** where the original Hole-in-the-Rock pioneers camped and held gatherings. At 50 miles from SR 12 are the access points to Llewelyn, Cottonwood, and David Canyons. Finally, after 56 miles, the road ends at the Hole-in-the-Rock overlook, with great views of Lake Powell. A steep trail leads downward a third of a mile to the rocky lakeshore.

◖ Hiking in Grand Staircase-Escalante National Monument

Entire books have been written about hiking in the monument. Hikers and bikers should acquire a detailed guidebook and maps before heading into this stony expanse and check in with the Escalante Interagency Visitor Center for the most recent route information.

Most of the more popular trails are concentrated along the Escalante River drainage, accessed via the Hole-in-the-Rock Road. Trails descend side canyons to the Escalante canyon itself and either ascend via the same route or else form a loop using the Escalante River or an overland trail as a connector. These include pastoral **Harris Wash,** a relatively easy 2–3-day hike that starts 10.5 miles down the road from SR 12. The **Egypt 3** slot, the next turnoff down the Hole-in-the-Rock Road, is legendarily long and tight, not for beginners, those weighing more than 200 pounds, or anyone freaked out by tight spaces. Return overland to the east of the north–south slot. Also launching from the Egypt trailhead is the triangular route down **Fence Canyon** and then down the Escalante River (some wading required) and back up. **Twentyfive Mile Canyon** is an excellent moderate canyon trip that can be done in two or three days. Don't miss the Golden Cathedral at the end of pretty little Neon Canyon.

Spooky, Peek-a-Boo, and **Brimstone** are three small gulches off the Dry Fork of Coyote Gulch, accessed from the Early Weed Bench Road or the Dry Fork Coyote Trailhead, 26 miles down the Hole-in-the-Rock Road. Along with Egypt, these are three of the best slots in the Four Corners, and all three can be done in a day.

Coyote Gulch is probably the most popular canyon in the Escalante drainage. Tree-lined and wet, it can be hiked down to the Escalante

© BLM/UTAH

In narrow slots, hikers may have to remove packs to continue.

River in a day, but set aside two or three to explore all the side canyons and get back to the trailhead. At 50 miles from SR 12—almost all the way to the Hole-in-the-Rock itself—are the access points to **Llewelyn** and **Cottonwood Canyons,** two difficult slots that lead southeast to Lake Powell. These require 3–5 days and some climbing experience. **Davis Gulch** heads north from the same trailhead and is too narrow for large packs. This is a very long and strenuous day hike or a good two-day venture. Look near the end of the slot for a memorial plaque to Everett Ruess, placed high on the wall to the right.

In the western part of the monument, **Bull Valley Gorge** and **Willis Creek** lie off the Skutumpah Road about 10 miles south of Cannonville. You can explore the narrows in the upper parts of both in a day, or connect them via Sheep Creek for a good overnight hike. (In 1954 three people were killed when their pickup ran off the road at the bridge over Bull Valley Gorge. The truck is still visible, wedged

into the slot.) Farther down the Skutumpah Road toward Kanab is **Lick Wash,** an easy day hike southeast toward No Mans Mesa.

About 13 miles down the Cottonwood Canyon Road from Cannonville is **Round Valley Draw,** a tributary of upper Hackberry Canyon. Explore the upper slots in a day, or else continue down narrow **Hackberry Canyon** on a multiday adventure. It eventually rejoins the Cottonwood Canyon Road after 22 miles. You can explore the side canyons Booker, Stone Donkey, and Pollock (which contains an arch) and look for the old Watson Cabin near the bottom. Keep going down the road from Round Valley Draw to reach the turnoff to the east for **Grosvenor Arch**—actually a cluster of cream-and-gold double arches. (There's a picnic area there.) It's another three miles south to **Cottonwood Creek,** a short slot canyon that runs parallel to the road on the west side for a half mile.

Ten miles west of the Paria Canyon Ranger Station on U.S. 89 is a sandstone obelisk marking the turnoff for Pahreah. The eroded hillsides along this track are a geological kaleidoscope, particularly at sunset. Keep going to the Paria River to find the foundations of the **Pahreah Town Site,** abandoned in the 1930s after nearby gold mines played out and the river kept flooding. The town's graveyard is on the near side of the river, which can often be easily waded, while the town itself is across the water. Hike upriver to **Starlight Arch,** a scenic trip that can be done in a day.

Mountain Biking

With all this backcountry available, mountain bikers may groan to learn that they must stay on roads inside the monument. This still leaves hundreds of miles of remote riding, though. Access roads to trailheads are fair game, although some—particularly the Hole-in-the-Rock Road—see a good bit of dust-raising vehicle traffic. Aim for lesser-used routes like the **Cedar Wash Loop,** a 20-mile back road connecting Escalante to the Hole-in-the-Rock Road, or the **Wolverine Loop Road** off the Burr Trail. Others include the **Egypt** road (10 miles one-way) or the access road up to **Fiftymile**

Bench (27 miles round-trip); it leaves the Hole-in-the-Rock Road at the Willow Tank slide (just past the Hurricane Wash trailhead parking area) and rejoins it just south of Sooner Wash. **Nipple Creek Wash** and **Tibbet Canyon** near Big Water on U.S. 89 are good steep rides, as is the **Smokey Hollow Loop** off the Smoky Mountain Road. **Sand Gulch** leaves U.S. 89 from a corral one mile west of the obelisk marking the turnoff to Pareah. It's 12 mostly level miles round-trip to the old town site and back.

Camping

There are only two developed campgrounds within the monument: Calf Creek and Deer Creek. Other than these and the campgrounds in nearby parks, you're on your own—which is exactly how most visitors to the Escalante like it. Free backcountry permits are required for overnight trips, and minimum-impact camping techniques are crucial to keeping this delicate area as pristine as possible.

Information and Permits

The **Escalante Interagency Visitors Center** (755 W. Main St., 435/826-5600, 7:30 A.M.–5:30 P.M. daily mid-Mar.–mid-Nov., 8 A.M.–4:30 P.M. otherwise) in Escalante is the main source of information for the monument, but additional contact stations are located around the monument's perimeter. The Anasazi State Park Museum in Boulder also has information on the monument and can issue backcountry permits.

Near Bryce Canyon National Park, the **Cannonville Contact Station** (10 Center St., 435/826-5640, 8 A.M.–4:30 P.M. Mar.–Nov.) focuses on Mormon history.

Along U.S. 89 at the southern edge of the monument, the visitors center in **Big Water** (100 Upper Revolution Way, 435/675-3200) focuses on paleontology. The Paria Contact Station (8:30 A.M.–4:15 P.M. daily, mid-Mar.–mid-Nov.) is also located on U.S. 89, about 44 miles east of Kanab.

On the southwestern edge of the monument, the visitors center in **Kanab** (745 E. U.S. 89, 435/644-4680, 8 A.M.–5 P.M. daily in summer) has exhibits concentrating on archaeology and

geology. For more inform[ation] you can also contact mo[nument] in Kanab (190 E. Cente[r] www.blm.gov).

Free **backcountry per**[mits] spend the night in the mo[nument] available at any of these stations and in register boxes at major trailheads. It only takes a few moments to fill one out, and their main purpose is to help to find you if something goes wrong.

KODACHROME BASIN STATE PARK

Surrounded by Grand Staircase–Escalante National Monument, the 2,240 acres of **Kodachrome Basin State Park** (435/679-8562, www.utah.com, 6 A.M.–10 P.M. daily, $6 per vehicle) are a photographer's playground. According to geologists, this area south of SR 12 near Cannonville once had hot springs and geysers like those in Yellowstone National Park. Over time they stopped spurting and filled in with sediment, which outlasted the surrounding terrain and left 67 large vertical pipes of hardened sand, some as tall as 170 feet. Photographers from a 1948 *National Geographic* expedition named the area for a new type of film they used to shoot its colorful arches and chimneys.

The park has a number of trails for hikers, bikers, and equestrians. For a horseback tour through the colorful sand pipes, contact **Red Canyon Trail Rides** (800/892-7923, $30–50). Park accommodations include a 25-unit year-round campground (800/322-3770, www.reserveamerica.com, $16–32) and six cabins (435/679-8536, www.redstonecabins.com, $90) with private baths, refrigerators, and microwaves.

◖ BRYCE CANYON NATIONAL PARK

The Paiute told of the Legend People who lived in a beautiful city but misbehaved and were turned to stone as punishment. They remain standing to this day, filling the gigantic amphitheater of Bryce Canyon National Park with peculiar limestone hoodoos in every imaginable white, yellow, pink, and brown. In ...tion of the geological Grand Staircase, 'ink Cliffs have eroded out of the eastern dge of the Paunsaugunt Plateau, which means they are perfectly placed to catch the gold and red hues of sunset. The park was named for Mormon pioneer Ebenezer Bryce, who tried eking out a living there for a few years in the late 19th century. His droll take on the stunning amphitheater of rock: "It's a hell of a place to lose a cow."

Visiting the Park

The main **visitors center** (435/834-5322, www.nps.gov/brca, 8 A.M.–8 P.M. daily May–Sept., closing earlier fall–spring) has exhibits, a bookstore, and an orientation film. You can pay your entrance fees ($25 per car), get backcountry permits ($5–15), and find out about ranger programs there. An 18-mile (one way) drive follows the rim, offering access to 14 scenic overlooks.

To ease congestion, a free shuttle service runs from the entrance to Bryce Point (every 10–15 minutes, 8 A.M.–7:40 P.M. early May–late Sept.). Another shuttle leaves twice daily for Rainbow Point.

Highlights include astronomy programs that take advantage of the park's natural darkness, offered most Tuesday, Thursday, and Saturday evenings May–mid-October. At the end of June, an astronomy festival features dozens of telescopes and a laser show. Another popular park event is the geology festival in late July.

Recreation

Hikers can choose from 61 miles of trails ranging from 9,100 feet elevation at the rim to 6,500 feet down in the fantasyland of rock. Eight day hiking trails include the easy mile-long section of the **Rim Trail** between Sunrise and Sunset Points and the steep but popular **Navajo Loop** (1.3 miles round-trip), which offers views of **Wall Street** and **Thor's Hammer.** Two trails—the Riggs Spring Loop and Under-the-Rim Trail—are available for overnight

Bryce Canyon's hoodoos create a winter wonderland.

hikes with a permit; backpackers must stay at designated campsites.

In addition to hiking, **cross-country skiing** along the rim is popular in winter, when the park is only lightly visited. Canyon Trail Rides (435/679-8665, www.canyonrides.com) offers guided **horseback rides** for $50 (two hours) to $75 (half day) per person. Rangers lead free **full-moon hikes** June–October.

Accommodations and Food

The rustic but comfortable ◖**Bryce Canyon Lodge** (435/834-8700, www.brycecanyon-forever.com, rooms and cabins $140–245, Apr.–mid-Nov.) is a National Historic Landmark designed in 1925 by Gilbert Stanley Underwood and built near the rim by the Union Pacific Railroad Company. Two campgrounds, one of which is open year-round, combine for a couple hundred tent and RV sites ($15, no hookups). Most sites are on a first-come, first-served basis, but some can be reserved (877/444-6777, www.recreation.gov).

Just north of the park boundary, **Best Western Ruby's Inn** (435/834-5341 or 866/866-6616, www.rubysinn.com, starting at $140) is a sprawling resort incorporating a year-round lodge, RV park, three restaurants, and a general store. Cheaper accommodations and more food choices can be found in the nearby towns of Tropic and Panguitch.

Lake Powell and Glen Canyon

Coming upon Lake Powell unprepared is like stumbling on a mirage. Wavering between red rock and blue sky, the lake's turquoise waters seem outrageously out of place yet are undeniably inviting in the heart of the desert. Regardless of your feelings about damming Glen Canyon, Lake Powell is impressive—the second-largest artificially constructed lake in the country, stretching for 186 miles from Glen Canyon Dam up what used to be the Colorado and San Juan Rivers to Hite Marina. Yet the lake covers only 12 percent of the entire Glen Canyon National Recreation Area. In between is nearly 2,000 miles of convoluted shoreline—longer than the entire West Coast—cut by 96 major canyons.

Around the lake's northern shore, the Glen Canyon National Recreation Area protects the upper reaches of canyons that once took weeks to visit by horseback. Rainbow Bridge, once a week-long journey on horseback, now stands at the very edge of the water. Countless secluded beaches dot the shoreline, giving boaters access to canyons with scenic, natural, and cultural treasures.

Opponents of the dam will point out that the trade-off was drowning one of the most beautiful canyons in the Southwest, along with countless sites of historical and archaeological value. When full, the reservoir can hold enough water to cover 27 million acres a foot deep. An ongoing drought has reduced Lake Powell to drastically lower levels since it first filled completely in 1980—at times less than 50 percent of capacity. In summer 2011 the lake level was 3,660 feet, or about 75 percent. Water-marked cliffs are now exposed around much of the shoreline (dubbed the "bathtub ring"), and boaters are able to reach places not seen since before the lake was filled.

SIGHTS AND RECREATION
Rainbow Bridge National Monument

The largest natural bridge in the world (275 feet across), once one of the most remote spots in the lower 48, now stands at the very edge of Lake Powell—or did, until falling lake levels moved the water's edge 1.5 miles away. If you don't have your own boat, you can book a boat tour at Wahweap Marina or backpack in over Navajo reservation lands (permit required).

Long known to local tribes, the multihued bridge symbolizes rainfall and fertility to the Navajo. It was "discovered" by white men in August 1909, when two Paiute guides led a pair of expeditions that joined forces and surveyed the area.

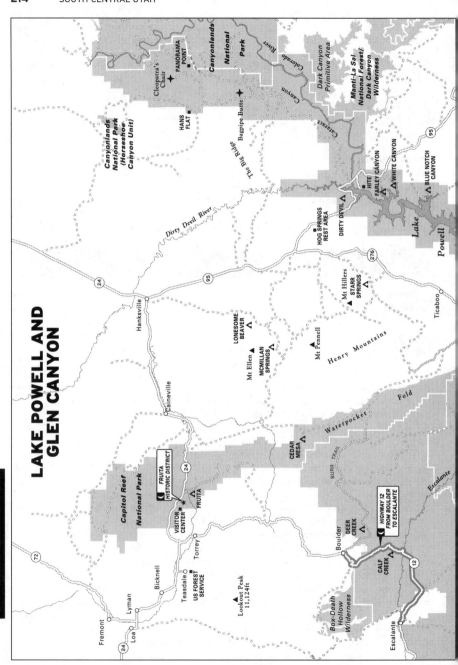

LAKE POWELL AND GLEN CANYON

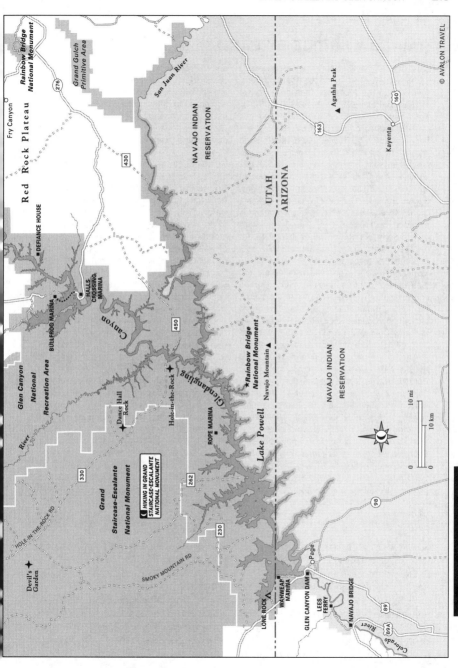

Fry Canyon

Red Rock Plateau

Rainbow Bridge
National Monument

Grand Gulch
Primitive Area

276

430

San Juan River

NAVAJO INDIAN
RESERVATION

Agathla Peak ▲

160

163

UTAH
ARIZONA

Kayenta

DEFIANCE HOUSE ■

Glen Canyon
National
Recreation Area

HALLS
CROSSING
MARINA

BULLFROG MARINA ■

Canyon

450

Rainbow Bridge ★
National Monument

Navajo Mountain ▲

River

Dance Hall
Rock ★

Hole-in-the-Rock ↓

(Gunsight)

NAVAJO INDIAN
RESERVATION

Grand
Staircase-Escalante
National Monument

330

ⓘ HIKING IN GRAND
STAIRCASE-ESCALANTE
NATIONAL MONUMENT

262

ROPE MARINA ■

Lake Powell

HOLE IN THE ROCK RD

Devil's ★
Garden

230

10 mi

10 km

0

0

98

SMOKY MOUNTAIN RD

LONE ROCK ▲

WAHWEAP
MARINA ■

GLEN CANYON DAM ■

○Page

LEES
FERRY

NAVAJO BRIDGE ■

89

Colorado River

89A

© AVALON TRAVEL

RAINBOW BRIDGE BY LAND

Experienced backcountry hikers can reach Rainbow Bridge by looping together two trails, following in the footsteps (and hoof marks) of overland expeditions of the early 1900s. You'll need route-finding skills and a good map (USGS quads recommended); cairns may have been scattered by floods, and rockfalls often obscure trails. The 28-mile loop circles Navajo Mountain, Naatsis'aan. This stately laccolithic dome, visible for miles, has great historical and spiritual significance. For traditional Navajos, the mountain is the head of Changing Woman, the Earth mother. (Climbing to the summit is forbidden.)

The South Rainbow Trail begins off SR 98 between Page and Kayenta. Between mileposts 349 and 350, turn north onto IR 16 (the Navajo Mountain Road) and proceed 32 miles, most of it paved, to a junction. Take the middle fork and continue another five miles to the next fork, turning right and heading for the ruins of the old Rainbow Lodge (which for a time was owned by Barry Goldwater). You'll need a high-clearance 4WD to make the last mile to the trailhead.

The South Rainbow Trail leads west along the side of Navajo Mountain, crossing First and Horse Canyons before heading down into Cliff Canyon at eight miles. In about a mile, you'll reach the first water campsite. Take a side canyon to the right (northeast) another mile down, climbing out and over Redbud Pass, which is marked by a route sign. (The pass was blasted out by an expedition led by John Wetherill party in 1922.) Follow Redbud Creek downstream (left), which shortly joins Bridge Canyon and Bridge Creek, about 13 miles from the trailhead. A spur trail leads right to an alcove with springs and the remains of old Echo Camp. Follow the canyon down to Rainbow Bridge. No camping is allowed within the boundaries of the monument and most definitely not underneath the bridge itself. Rainbow Bridge is considered holy by the Navajos and other tribes; be respectful of this awe-inspiring natural feature.

You can return the same way or take the North Rainbow Trail back to complete the circle. This trail leaves Rainbow Bridge up Bridge Canyon, crossing Oak, N'asja, Bald Rock, and Cha Canyons (all with intermittent water). From Cha Canyon a dirt road takes you to the Navajo Mountain Mission. A vehicle or mountain bike shuttle will save you 10 miles of walking back to the Rainbow Lodge. (Area residents prefer that vehicles not be left at the trailhead.)

Another option is to arrange for one-way boat transportation from Aramark's Wahweap Marina (928/645-2433). Backpacking the entire loop takes 3–5 days, and there is little water away from the lake. Plan to use a water purification system. Spring and fall are the best times to make this journey, avoiding summer heat, winter cold, and most particularly, the late-summer monsoon, when flash flooding is a danger.

Both trails cross the Navajo Reservation. Purchase a backcountry permit ($5 pp per day) in advance from the Navajo Parks and Recreation Department office in Window Rock (928/871-6647, www.navajonationparks.org), the Cameron Visitor Center (928/679-2303), or the Monument Valley Visitor Center (435/727-5870). The local LeChee Chapter office (928/698-2800) can describe current road and trail conditions.

Rainbow Bridge sits 50 miles from Wahweap on a 160-acre national monument (www.nps.gov/rabr) completely surrounded by the Navajo Indian Reservation. Soaring 290 feet above Bridge Creek, the salmon-pink sandstone span is only 32 feet across at its narrowest point. The bridge is an extraordinary sight: It inspired a Zane Grey novel, and Theodore Roosevelt woke several times during a 1913 visit to gaze on it by moonlight.

Boating

The incongruous sight of an SUV towing a boat across the San Rafael Desert starts to make sense at any one of Lake Powell's marinas, where houseboats, fishing boats, kayaks, and personal watercraft vie for space. Houseboats

© RICHARD MAYER

Lake Powell is a water-sport mecca.

are a popular way to explore the lake, with many visitors renting one for a week or more to hole up in their own private side canyon.

Boat rentals are available at Wahweap and Bullfrog Marinas from **Lake Powell Resorts & Marinas** (928/645-2433 or 888/896-3829, www.lakepowell.com). Four classes of houseboats range 44–75 feet and start at about $2,500 for three days. Powerboats, fishing boats, kayaks, and personal watercraft are also available. Boaters must be aware of all state boating regulations as well as those imposed by the National Park Service, which requires a boating permit. Seven miles northeast of Page, **Antelope Point Marina** (928/645-5900, www.antelopepointlakepowell.com) offers houseboat rentals starting at $700 a day. They also rent ski boats, cruisers, and kayaks.

Kayaking

A quieter way to reach the lakeside backcountry is by paddling a kayak. The weather is at its mildest and the powerboaters are fewer September–May. The possibilities are almost limitless; you can take an afternoon to explore the crannies of Wahweap Bay, one of the biggest in the lake, or take a day or two to ascend long, narrow Navajo Canyon east of Page. Crosby Canyon and Antelope Canyon are also popular and within a day of Wahweap, while the lower Escalante and San Juan Rivers are good for multiday trips. Because of the lake's vast expanse, many people start out under power and put in a kayak after anchoring near a side canyon.

Twin Finn (811 Vista Ave., 928/645-3114, www.twinfinn.com) rents kayaks year-round starting at $35/day. **Kayak Powell** (928/660-0778, www.kayakpowell.com, Mar.–Oct.), offers half-day and full-day paddling trips as well as overnighters and rentals. Tours start at $99 per person.

Fishing

The Colorado River's native fish have been largely supplanted by introduced species such as bluegill sunfish, black crappie, walleye, and bass (striped, largemouth, and smallmouth).

Hook and line is the only permitted fishing technique, and if you're over 14 years old a license is required. (Trout require their own additional license.) The lake's now-endangered native fish, including the Colorado squawfish, humpback, and bonytail chub, and the razorback sucker, are off-limits.

FACILITIES AND SERVICES
Wahweap Marina
Just about anything you could do on, under, or near the surface of Lake Powell is available at the main marina just west of Glen Canyon Dam on Lakeshore Drive. Wahweap, which means "bitter water" in the Ute language, is the largest freshwater marina west of the Mississippi. Hundreds of boats bob at anchor in front of the **C Lake Powell Resort** (928/645-2433). Many of the hotel's 350 units ($120–280) have patios or balconies overlooking Wahweap Basin, while the **Rainbow Room** restaurant provides white-tablecloth dining with a panoramic view of the water. They serve all meals daily, with buffets for breakfast and lunch in the Navajo Room and a café for snacks.

Marina services are offered by Aramark's **Lake Powell Resorts & Marinas** (928/645-2433 or 800/528-6154, www.lakepowell.com). Boat rentals and tours are offered at the front desk, ranging from a short cruise to Antelope Canyon ($32 per adult) to all-day tours to Rainbow Bridge ($100 per adult). You can also enjoy a dinner cruise ($75 per adult) aboard the *Canyon King* paddle wheeler. Advance reservations are recommended.

The marina's two campgrounds are open all year, with first-come, first-served tent sites ($23) and sites with full hookups ($40) available by reservation. Primitive camping at **Lone Rock,** six miles northwest on U.S. 89, costs $10 per vehicle, and no-fee dispersed camping is also permitted anywhere along the lake shore beyond the developed areas, with certain restrictions.

Antelope Point Marina
Seven miles uplake from Page, Antelope Point Marina (22 S. Navajo Dr., 928/645-5900,

8 A.M.–5 P.M. daily) has boat rentals, a full-service restaurant, snack bar, fuel dock, and other amenities. The outfitter store sells and rents camping and fishing gear. Tour options there include lake cruises and a boat tour of Antelope Canyon.

Dangling Rope Marina
This outpost, 40 miles east of Wahweap, is accessible only by boat and is the closest to Rainbow Bridge National Monument. There's a ranger station, restrooms, a boat fueling station (the only one between Wahweap and Bullfrog), and limited marina facilities. The marina is closed late November–February.

Halls Crossing Marina
Located on the south side of a popular river crossing, Halls Crossing Marina (435/684-7000) is 95 miles upriver from Wahweap. The crossing was named for Charles Hall, one of the founders of Escalante and the builder of a ferry he operated there 1881–1884. SR 276 connects Halls Crossing with SR 95 at Natural Bridges National Monument, 48 miles to the east. The park service operates a ranger station (435/684-7460) at the marina, which encompasses a campground ($45 with full hookups), condos ($250), snack bar, and general store. The **Charles Hall ferry** (435/684-3088) runs between Halls Crossing and Bullfrog Marina 2–4 times a day spring–fall. Rates start at $10 per person on foot or bicycle, with vehicle fees dependent on length.

Bullfrog Marina
Glen Canyon's second-largest marina is opposite Halls Crossing. The park service operates a ranger station and **visitors center** (435/684-7423, hours vary, Memorial Day–Labor Day) with exhibits on the area's geology and history, and a film about Glen Canyon Dam. The park's concessioner, ARAMARK (435/684-3000), operates the marina and campground ($45 with full hookups) and also offers family-style accommodations in condos ($250) and at the well-equipped **Defiance House Lodge.** Some rooms ($100–165) have views of the lake

and Waterpocket Fold, and the lodge restaurant serves all meals daily in season. You can rent boats there as well. Primitive camping is available nearby for $6 per vehicle.

SR 276 heads north to meet SR 95, 20 miles west of Hite. The **Charles Hall ferry** crosses between Halls Crossing and Bullfrog Marina 2–6 times a day year-round. Rates are $5 per person on foot or bicycle and $20–50 for vehicles, depending on length.

Hite

Though there's still a boat ramp at Hite, Lake Powell's northernmost marina has been closed after falling lake levels left it high and dry. Hite (named for Prospector Cass Hite, who had a gold claim near there in the 1880s) also has a convenience store (435/684-2278), ranger station (435/684-2457), primitive campsites ($6), and RV campground (800/528-6154). Hite sits just off SR 95, 57 miles west of Natural Bridges National Monument, near a pair of highway bridges that cross the flooded mouths of the Dirty Devil and Colorado River Canyons. The historic settlement of Hite City (now underwater) was once a favorite put-in spot for river-runners floating Glen Canyon.

INFORMATION
Fees, Regulations, and Safety

The National Park Service charges $15 per vehicle for entrance to the Glen Canyon National Recreation Area (928/608-6200, www.nps.gov/glca), good for a week. Annual boat and vehicle passes are $30. Life jackets are highly recommended out on the water, and there's no boating after dark. Cliff diving is prohibited.

GETTING THERE AND AROUND

Lake Powell and the Glen Canyon National Recreation Area are accessible by two-wheel-drive vehicles at Lees Ferry off U.S. 89A, at Wahweap Marina near Page, and at Bullfrog and Halls Crossing, both on SR 276 west of Natural Bridges National Monument. Four-wheel-drive vehicles can use the Hole-in-the-Rock Road from SR 12 at Escalante, the Burr Trail from Boulder, or a dirt road that leaves U.S. 89A at Big Water and heads up onto the Kaiparowits Plateau. Passenger cars can reach Hite via SR 95 and the paved access road to the former marina.

Page, Arizona, and the Paria Plateau

PAGE

This tidy little town (pop. 9,000) was built from scratch in 1957 for workers on the Glen Canyon Dam, at the time one of the largest construction projects in the world. Since then, Page has become the tourist center of northernmost Arizona. With an interesting museum and plenty of outdoor activities within easy range, Page makes a good base for visiting the Paria Plateau, Glen Canyon, and Lake Powell, the northern Navajo Nation, and the southern Grand Staircase–Escalante National Monument. Every other vehicle seems to be towing some kind of watercraft, which together with marinas and swimwear shops gives Page a beach town–in-the-desert feel. The town is sandwiched between the dam and the Navajo Generating Station.

The town's economy is largely based on tourism and the generating station, whose three towers jut from the desert plain to the east. Built in 1974, this coal-fired station can produce up to 2,250 megawatts of power for cities such as Tucson, Las Vegas, and Los Angeles. This requires 1,000 tons of coal per hour, brought in by electric train from the controversial mines at Black Mesa, 70 miles south on the Hopi Reservation. In 1991 the Grand Canyon Trust successfully lobbied for scrubbers to be installed on the plant's three generating units. With these in place, sulfur dioxide emissions have been reduced by about 90 percent.

The marinas nearest to Page are Wahweap, seven miles northwest on U.S. 89, and Antelope Point, seven miles northeast.

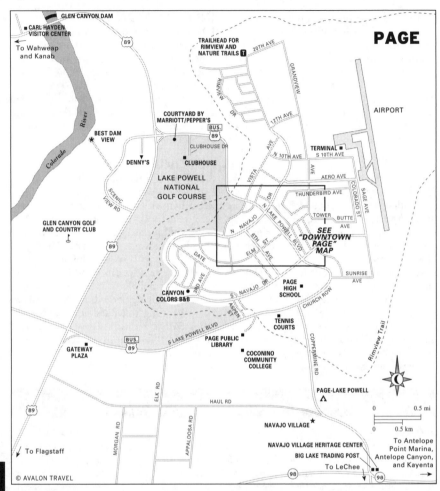

SOUTH-CENTRAL UTAH

Glen Canyon Dam

Page's raison d'être plugs Glen Canyon a few miles west of town with nearly five million cubic yards of concrete, poured around the clock for three years. It was built between 1960 and 1963, stands 710 feet high, and holds back 27,000,000 acre-feet of water when the reservoir is full. Free tours of the dam's cave-cool innards are given at the National Park Service's **Carl Hayden Visitor Center** (928/608-6404, 8 A.M.–6 P.M. daily Memorial Day–Labor Day, to 4 or 5 P.M. otherwise) on the west side

of the U.S. 89 bridge. Depending on the national security alert level, these occur four times daily, with a maximum of 20 people per tour, and take you from the gigantic turbines and transformers to an incongruous patch of green grass at the base. Reservations for the tours, which are guided by the Glen Canyon Natural History Association (928/608-6072, www.glencanyonnha.org), can be made online or by phone up to 24 hours in advance.

The **best dam view** in Page can be found behind the Denny's off U.S. 89. Go down Scenic

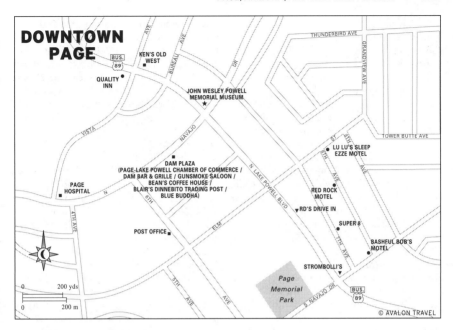

View Drive to the sign for the overlook. To take in the entire sweep of this end of the lake, head west about a mile past the visitors center and then climb the steep but short hill to your right (north). The sight is both startling and impressive: the blue of the lake, the green oasis of Page, the monolithic dam, and Navajo Mountain—all in one grand panorama.

Other Sights

Get a taste of Navajo culture through programs held at **Navajo Village Heritage Center** (928/660-0304, www.navajovillage.com, 9 A.M.–3 P.M. daily Apr.–Oct.), a living museum with a 2.5-hour evening program that includes demonstrations of weaving and silversmithing, and a traditional dinner followed by singing, dancing, and stories around the campfire ($30 adult, $20 students, $5 children). Shorter tours are also offered. The heritage center is located behind Big Lake Trading Post, off SR 98 near its intersection with Coppermine Road.

The **John Wesley Powell Memorial Museum** (6 N. Lake Powell Blvd., 928/645-9496 or 888/597-6873, www.powellmuseum.org, 9 A.M.–5 P.M. Mon.–Fri., $5 adults, $1 children) houses excellent collections on early cultures, explorers and river-runners, and natural history. Exhibits on Powell's life include a "rephotography" display—scenes from his expeditions paired with photos taken a century later to show environmental changes. Kids can grind corn in one hands-on exhibit, and nearby are displays by local artists and a pictorial history of the dam and Lake Powell. The museum is also the local **information center,** and you can make reservations for tours of the lake and Antelope Canyon there as well, with a percentage of the proceeds going to support the museum.

Antelope Canyon, 120 feet deep and only a few yards wide in spots, is probably the most famous slot canyon in the world, thanks to countless photographs of shafts of light penetrating its sensual sandstone curves. The canyon is a Navajo Nation Tribal Park (928/698-2808, 8 A.M.–5 P.M. daily, 9 A.M.–3 P.M. Nov.–Mar., $6 per adult, children under 8 free), and the only way to get inside is in the company of an authorized guide. A ladder is used to reach the bottom of the canyon, but after that it's mostly an easy walk on the flat, sandy canyon floor. The softly lit grottoes and hairpin corners are a photographer's dream—bring a tripod and cable release and try to shoot near noon.

Guides are usually available on site, but you can also arrange for a tour and transportation to the canyon from Page. The canyon is a mile east of the Big Lake Trading Post on SR 98. **Overland Canyon Tours** (695 N. Navajo, 928/608-4072, www.overlandcanyon. com) takes visitors to Antelope Canyon plus the less-visited (and just as impressive) **Canyon X. Waterholes Canyon** is another guided slot option. Navajo-owned **Roger Ekis' Antelope Canyon Tours** (22 S. Lake Powell Blvd., 928/645-9102 or 866/645-9102, www.antelopecanyon.com) visits the upper canyon. Both companies' tours start at $32 for adults ($24 children), including the park fee. Longer custom photography tours are also possible with both outfits.

Like any slot canyon, Antelope is prone to flash flooding from storms upstream, even if the sky is blue overhead. If your guide says get out, listen—something that 11 ill-fated European tourists didn't do in 1997. It took months to recover their bodies from the mud and debris.

Entertainment and Events

Winter months are relatively quiet in Page, but a few local bars host live music on high-season weekends and during spring break, when the lake is frequented by college students. As you might expect, country music is the theme at **Ken's Old West** (718 Vista Ave., 928/645-6150, open till 11 P.M. weekends, 10 P.M. weeknights). **The Dam Bar & Grill** (644 N. Navajo Dr., 928/645-2161, open till 2 A.M.) has a sports bar, pool tables, and a large dance floor with live music Wednesday–Saturday evenings. You can shoot pool or knock down some pins at **The Bowl** (24 N. Lake Powell Blvd., 928/645-2682), which also has a snack bar.

During the off-season (Oct.–Apr.), the **Lake Powell Concert Association** (928/660-3367, www.lakepowellconcertassociation.com) brings live performances to the 800-seat Cultural Arts auditorium of Page High School (500 S. Navajo Dr.). Lake Powell's premiere event, the **Balloon Regatta,** takes place on the first weekend in November, when dozens of hot air balloons float serenely above red sandstone and blue water.

Shopping

A number of local shops stock souvenirs and crafts. Look for art galleries and trading posts, such as **Blair's Dinnebito Trading Post** (626 N. Navajo Dr., 928/645-3008 or 800/644-3008, www.blairstradingpost.com), in the Dam Plaza shopping center. Blair's began as a remote trading post deep in the Navajo Reservation. Along with a large selection of rugs, kachinas, pottery, baskets, and paintings, they also stock raw wool, saddle leather, and pawned jewelry. Ask to see the private collection upstairs, collected over a half century by patriarch Elijah Blair, who helped create the black-background Dinnebito style of Navajo weaving. The old cash registers, guns, historical photos, jewelry, and rugs are not for sale but worth a peek nonetheless.

Hiking

The **Rim Trail** (eight miles round-trip) is a bike- and footpath around the edge of Manson Mesa, with great views of the lake and desert. With several access points, the trail can be hiked in shorter sections. One access is via the nature trail at the north end of town near Lakeview Elementary (at Navajo Drive and 20th Avenue); another is the Rimview Drive trailhead off Lake Page Boulevard.

The **Horseshoe Bend** trail (1.5 miles round-trip) leads to an overlook high above a hairpin turn in the Colorado River. The trail begins at a parking area just south of milepost 545 on U.S. 89. Watch your footing—there aren't any guardrails—and try to visit at sunset, when flocks of birds swarm after insects above the abyss.

The route to **Wiregrass Canyon** (six miles round-trip) follows a steep wash down to Lake Powell. To get there, take U.S. 89 toward Big

Water. Between mileposts 7 and 8, turn right on the dirt road and go about five miles to a parking area. This rocky scramble follows the unmarked wash to the lake. Keep an eye out for arches, balanced rocks, and a natural bridge.

Flat-Water Rafting

Another way to explore the area by water is to navigate the remaining 15-mile stretch of the Colorado River in Glen Canyon below the dam. You can put in a boat at Lees Ferry and travel upstream or sign up for a tour with **Colorado River Discovery** (130 6th Ave., 928/645-9175 or 888/522-6244, www.raftthecanyon.com, $85–155). They lead motorized trips year-round and oar-powered trips during summer months. The peaceful half-day or full-day trips begin at the dam and end at Lees Ferry, floating between the Glen's gorgeous sandstone cliffs and hanging gardens.

Accommodations

Since Page is such a busy tourist hub, it's a good idea to call ahead for reservations, particularly in summer. The summer rates listed here drop dramatically in winter. Plenty of inexpensive accommodations line 8th Avenue, Page's "Street of Little Motels," which originally housed supervisors during the construction of the dam. Clean, comfortable double rooms for under $80 can be found at **Lu Lu's Sleep Ezze Motel** (105 8th Ave., 928/608-0273, www.lulussleepezze.com), **Bashful Bob's Motel** (750 S. Navajo Dr., 928/645-3919, www.bashfulbobsmotel.com), and the **Red Rock Motel** (114 8th Ave., 928/645-0062).

Chain hotels galore are sprinkled throughout the rest of the town; in the $100–150 category are a **Super 8** (75 S. 7th Ave., 928/645-2858) and a **Quality Inn** (287 N. Lake Powell Blvd., 928/645-8851). A pool and patio await at the **Canyon Colors B&B** (225 S. Navajo Dr., 928/645-5979 or 800/536-2530, www.canyoncolors.com, $125), run by a friendly Belgian couple.

On a hillside overlooking the dam and the lake is the **C Courtyard by Marriott** (600 Clubhouse Dr., 928/645-5000, $110–210) with a golf course, heated outdoor pool, and

Pepper's restaurant. The **Page-Lake Powell Campground** (849 S. Coppermine Rd., 928/645-3374, $17–28) is southeast of downtown. More campsites are available west of the dam at Wahweap Marina.

Food

At the Courtyard by Marriott, **Peppers** (928/645-1347, all meals daily) serves Southwest fare (dinner runs $15–25) and a good lunch buffet. On the other end of the price range, **R. D.'s Drive In** (143 Lake Powell Blvd., 928/645-2791, all meals Mon.–Sat.) was the first in town when Glen Canyon Dam was only a dream on paper. This local hangout serves burgers and ice cream, and most items are under $10.

For dependable pizza and pasta head to **Strombolli's** (711 N. Navajo Dr., 928/645-2605, lunch and dinner daily, $7–20). The **Rainbow Room** (928/645-2433, all meals daily, $8–30) at Lake Powell Resort and Marina claims a great sunset out the wide picture windows over the lake. The menu varies from a generous lunch buffet to steak, trout, and pasta for dinner.

You can find beef and carbs at nearly any restaurant in Page, but for something completely different, try **C Blue Buddha** (644 N. Navajo Dr., dinner Mon.–Sat., $8–20), located in the Dam Plaza shopping center. They serve sushi, salads, teriyaki, and, yes, even steak. Also in the Dam Plaza is the **Dam Bar & Grille** (644 N. Navajo Dr., 928/645-2161, lunch and dinner Mon.–Sat., $8–25), serving burgers, ribs, and steaks. Next door, **Bean's Coffee House** (928/645-6858, 6 A.M.–5 P.M. Mon.–Fri., 7 A.M.–5 P.M. Sat., 8 A.M.–noon Sun.) offers breakfast and lunch (less than $10) on weekdays, and coffee and Internet access all hours.

Information

The **Page/Lake Powell Tourism Bureau** operates a visitors center around the corner from the Mesa Theater (647-A Elm St., 928/660-3405 or 888/261-7243, www.pagelakepowelltourism.com, 8 A.M.–6 P.M. Mon.–Sun. in season, to 5 P.M. Mon.–Fri. otherwise). They stock plenty of information and maps about the area and accept reservations for local tours. The **Page Chamber of Commerce** (34 S. Lake Powell Blvd., 928/645-2741, www.pagechamber.com, 9 A.M.–5 P.M. Mon.–Fri.) is another source of information, as is the John Wesley Powell Museum (6 N. Lake Powell Blvd., 928/645-9496, www.powellmuseum.org, 9 A.M.–5 P.M.), where you can book lake- or land-based tours.

For more information on the area's natural and human history, visit the bookstore at the dam operated by the **Glen Canyon Natural History Association** (928/608-6358 or 877/453-6296, www.glencanyonnha.org). GCNHA funds research projects, helps staff visitors centers, and sells books and maps online.

Getting There and Around

The **Page Municipal Airport** (238 10th Ave., 928/645-4337) is served by Great Lakes Airlines (928/645-1355 or 800/554-5111, www.greatlakesav.com), with daily flights to Phoenix and Denver. Classic Aviation (928/645-5357 or 800/444-9220) offers charter flights. Tour companies flying out of Page include Westwind Air Tours (928/645-2494 or 800/245-8668) and Papillon (702/736-7243 or 888/635-7272). Smaller airstrips are located near Lake Powell marinas.

Several local hotels offer shuttles to and from the airport and around town. **Avis** (928/645-2024 or 800/331-1212) rents cars at the Page airport. Locally owned **Buggy Taxi** (928/645-9347) can hook you up with a midsize sedan or, if you're feeling adventurous, a four-wheel-drive. Taxi service is available from **Grand Circle Shuttle** (928/645-6806).

PARIA PLATEAU

As the Grand Staircase marches down to the Colorado River, this plateau between the Kaibab Mountains and the Vermilion Cliffs forms its bottom step. Outlined by U.S. 89 and U.S. 89A, the Paria Plateau marks the eastern end of the Arizona Strip, a slice of the state once isolated by the chasm of the Grand Canyon. The Paria Plateau is centered by the Big Knoll (6,844 feet) and cut neatly in two by the lower reaches of the Paria River, which offers one of

the Four Corners' great canyon hikes. If you're going to do a single overnight narrows hike in the Four Corners, make it this one.

Paria Canyon constricts in its upper reaches into some of the longest and tightest slots in the world, before opening up into a majestic gorge with 1,000-foot walls that empties into the Colorado at Lees Ferry. The BLM manages 112,500 acres as the **Paria Canyon-Vermilion Cliffs Wilderness,** enclosed by the little-known, 293,000-acre **Vermilion Cliffs National Monument.** Permits are required for hiking and backpacking in certain areas, including Coyote Buttes, Paria Canyon, and Buckskin Gulch.

Hiking

The easiest access for hiking the Paria is off U.S. 89, 43 miles east of Kanab and 14 miles west of Big Water. There, near the Paria River Bridge, the **Paria Contact Station** (8:30 A.M.–4:15 P.M. daily mid-Mar.–mid-Nov.) offers advice and sells day-hiking permits ($6 per person per day), maps, and guidebooks, including the BLM's *Hiker's Guide to Paria Canyon.* Reservations for backpacking trips must be made in advance online or by phoning the Arizona Strip District Office (435/688-3200, www.blm.gov/az, $5 per person per day).

Just down the gravel road is the **White House Campground,** where primitive sites are $5. The **Paria River Trailhead** is two miles farther down the road. A trail meanders along the riverbanks, which are wide for four miles before closing in sharply and rising to about 200 feet. The play of light and shadow and the gurgle of water make the seven miles to the Buckskin Gulch confluence an enchanting hike that can be done in one long day.

Two trailheads for Buckskin Gulch are located a few miles west. From the Paria Contact Station, continue west on U.S. 89 for five miles, until the road curves sharply north at the Cockscomb, an unmistakable monocline. A reasonably good dirt road, BLM 700, heads south there parallel to the gigantic ridge; follow it to the **Buckskin Trailhead** (4.5 miles) or the **Wire Pass Trailhead** (8.5 miles). (The road continues all the way to U.S. 89A near Jacob Lake.) There is good at-large camping nearby (but don't sleep in your car at the trailhead; it's prohibited). Wire Pass offers the quickest access to the narrows—less than two miles—which are on most desert rats' lists of the best slot canyons in the Southwest. Deep, dark, and drop-dead gorgeous, Buckskin Gulch gives even slot veterans goose bumps. At points the canyon walls are barely a shoulder's width apart. Day-use permits for Buckskin Gulch and Wire Pass are available at the trailheads for $6 per person (and per dog, if Rover came with you).

From Wire Pass it's 14 miles downstream to the confluence with Paria Canyon, or 16 miles from the Buckskin trailhead. The Buckskin–Wire Pass loop is good for a day hike, but you can make it to White House in a long day. To descend all the way down to Lees Ferry (38 miles) takes 4–5 days.

At the state line, BLM 700 changes to BLM 1065, known as the House Rock Valley Road, an unmaintained dirt road that can be rough in sections and impassable in wet weather. A couple of miles farther south is the access point to **Coyote Buttes,** another popular spot. No doubt you've probably seen eye-popping photos of "The Wave," where red-and-white rock layers swirl like ice cream. Day-use permits are required there as well; 20 are available per day through an online lottery (www.blm.gov). Apply early—four months ahead of time for the peak months of April, May and September. No overnight camping is allowed in the Coyote Buttes permit area.

Campfires are prohibited in the canyons, and "wag bags" (disposal bags for human waste, available with your permit) are required in Paria Canyon. Pay attention to the weather; precipitation is highest July–September, peaking in August, and a cloudburst can fill the narrows much faster than you can get out—notice the logs jammed between the canyon walls high overhead.

Practicalities

Car shuttles can be arranged through Paria Outpost and Outfitters (928/691-1047), Paria Canyon Adventure Ranch (928/660-2674), and others. For more information on authorized guides, shuttles, and permits, contact the BLM's **Arizona Strip Field Office** in St. George, Utah (435/688-3230, www.blm.gov/az, 7:45 A.M.–5 P.M. Mon.–Fri., 10 A.M.–3 P.M. Sat.).

Paria Canyon Adventure Ranch is a friendly, sprawling operation (928/660-2674, www.paria campground.com) located between mileposts 21 and 22 on U.S. 89, near the Paria Contact Station. They offer a wide range of activities; volleyball, horseshoes, horseback riding around the Paria Valley ($55 pp) are a few of the options. Overnight accommodations include a bunkhouse hostel ($15 pp), tent spaces and RV sites ($10 s, $15 d), or a cabin ($40). They also have horse stables and shuttle service for hiking the Paria canyons.

Enjoy the scenery from the big wraparound porch at the **Paria Outpost Restaurant** (928/691-1047, www.paria.com, 5–9 P.M. Fri.–Sat.), which dishes up a Western-style dinner buffet ($13 pp) on weekends and provides other meals on request. The outpost has a guest room ($65), and snacks, drinks, maps, and guidebooks are sold in the general store.

LEES FERRY AND VICINITY

U.S. 89A leaves U.S. 89 105 miles north of Flagstaff and 25 miles south of Page, at the north end of the Echo Cliffs. It heads north across the Marble Platform toward the Vermilion Cliffs. Look for two shining metal arches across the Colorado, flowing deep in a canyon that remains invisible until you reach its edge.

Marble Canyon

Navajo Bridge crosses the river in an area of spectacular scenery and intriguing history. When it was opened in 1929, the original bridge was the highest cantilevered steel arch in the world, soaring 467 feet above the river. During its construction, as the two cantilevered halves were gradually extended across the abyss, drivers had to make an 800-mile trip to travel 800 feet across the river. The bridge's completion was a major event; the opening drew a celebratory crowd of 7,000 to this remote corner

Grand Canyon white-water trips launch at Lees Ferry, which is also the takeout point for flat-water trips down Glen Canyon.

of Arizona. The bridge was christened with a bottle of ginger ale (it was Prohibition), and the road was paved in 1937.

The bridge was replaced in 1995 by a stronger, wider twin—still one of only seven river crossings in 750 miles. The original span is now open only to pedestrians, who can walk across to gaze down at the Colorado River, deep green in color because the river's silt is trapped behind Glen Canyon Dam. You'll often see rafters heading downstream from Lees Ferry. For them, the bridge marks the gateway to the Grand Canyon. (For the condor who likes to hang out in the supports underneath, it's shade.)

Navajo artisans sell jewelry and other crafts on the east end of the bridge. At the opposite end, Glen Canyon Natural History Association operates the **Navajo Bridge Interpretive Center** (928/355-2319, 9 A.M.–5 P.M. daily mid-Apr.–Oct., weekends only in early Apr. and Nov.), stocking an outstanding selection of books and gifts. The Civilian Conservation Corps built the adjoining rustic stone

observation structure in the 1930s. Plaques there commemorate pioneering river-runners and John D. Lee.

Just up the road, **Marble Canyon Lodge** (928/355-2225 or 800/726-1789, www.marble-canyoncompany.com), once a trading post operated by Lorenzo Hubbell, was built in 1929. Rooms ($45–140) are comfortable and basic, though some have kitchenettes, and condo-style lodging is available for guests using the lodge's guide services. On the premises, you'll find a restaurant, gift shop, fly shop, convenience mart, coin-operated laundry, gas station, and post office, with an airstrip across the highway. The **restaurant** (928/355-2225 or 800/726-1789, all meals daily) serves up huge breakfasts off the menu or buffet-style. Dinner entrées ($10–20) include panfried trout. At the convenience market next door, you can grab a snack or order takeout from the restaurant.

A couple of miles farther west, **Lees Ferry Lodge** (928/355-2231, www.vermilioncliffs.com) has 10 rooms (as low as $50 during the

Stormy weather rolls over the Vermilion Cliffs.

off-season) without phones or televisions, though some have a Franklin stove for chilly nights. Larger rooms can accommodate up to five people. Next to the lodge, the **Vermilion Cliffs Bar and Grill** (all meals daily, $8–20) is famous for its lengthy beer menu, featuring brews from Belgium to Brazil. They serve steaks, chops, ribs, chicken, burgers, and even vegetarian fare.

Lees Ferry

The Lees Ferry road descends to the river's edge past house-size rocks balanced on pedestals of compressed earth. Six miles down the paved road, where the Paria River empties into the Colorado, is a small historic district and the major put-in spot for raft trips heading into the Grand Canyon. A ferry operated there—where Glen Canyon transitions to the Grand Canyon—from 1873 to 1928.

The river crossing was named for John Doyle Lee, who is most well known as the engineer—or scapegoat—behind the Mountain Meadows Massacre, one of the darkest chapters in the

history of the Mormon pioneers. In 1857 a party of 137 Arkansas emigrants was crossing southern Utah on the way to California. In early September they were ambushed near Cedar City, Utah, by a group of Paiute and Mormons, angered by U.S. government interference in what they saw as their territory. Led by Lee, the group promised the emigrants safe passage, convinced them to lay down their arms, and then killed everyone except the young children.

Details of the crime were slow in leaking out (and are still debated today), but Lee sought refuge there in 1871. He built Lonely Dell Ranch with the help of Emma, his 17th wife (of 19). The Lees saw a good bit of traffic, partly because their ferry was on the Honeymoon Trail, named for newly married couples traveling by wagon from Arizona settlements to have their marriages officially sanctioned at the temple in St. George, Utah. Lee was eventually tracked down and arrested in 1875, but the trial resulted in a hung jury. He was arrested again the next year, convicted of

THE CONDOR SOARS AGAIN

© KATHLEEN BRYANT

The Vermilion Cliffs rise above House Rock Valley, a condor release site.

If you see a huge silhouette gliding across the skies in canyon country, look at the underside of the wings. If the leading edge is white, you're looking at a California condor *(Gymnogyps californianus)*, whose wingspan can reach more than nine feet across. The genus *Gymnogyps* once ranged over what is now west Texas, Arizona, and New Mexico. Fossilized bones, eggshells, and feathers have been found in the Grand Canyon, dated between 10,000 and 22,000 years ago. By 1982, however, only 22 of the giant birds remained in the mountains of California, making them the most endangered vertebrates in the world.

In a last-ditch effort, naturalists rounded up all the wild California condors and placed them in captivity, hoping the birds could breed themselves back from the brink. In 1996 the Peregrine Fund (www.peregrinefund.org) and other agencies worked jointly to release six birds into the wilds near the Vermilion Cliffs of northern Arizona. The program has seen some success but also some setbacks. Released birds have been killed by predators or power lines; many more have died from ingesting carcasses contaminated with lead shot. (The Arizona Game

and Fish Department encourages hunters in northern Arizona to use non-lead ammunition.) Condors reproduce slowly; they mate for life, and an adult female lays a single egg every other year.

Currently, 68 condors fly over Arizona and southern Utah, and about half the world's population of 360 condors live in the wild. Despite a close brush with extinction, this prehistoric species won't be left in the Stone Age: The Vermilion Cliffs birds have their own Facebook page (www.facebook.com/condorcliffs) and website (www.condorcliffs.org). (And yes, these birds also tweet.)

Condors are scavengers, known to travel up to 100 miles a day in search of food. The Vermilion Cliffs condors range from the Grand Canyon north to Zion National Park. When not flying, condors hang out in roosts. One favors the steel span underneath Navajo Bridge near Lees Ferry. Your next best chance of seeing a condor in the wild is near the release site along the Vermilion Cliffs and House Rock Valley Road, which intersects SR 89A about 15 miles east of Jacob Lake.

first-degree murder, and in 1877 was executed at the site of the massacre.

It's hard to imagine a prettier setting than Lonely Dell, where green cottonwoods and fruit trees contrast with red and gold cliffs and free-flowing water. The Lees' log cabin, built in the 1870s, stands near an orchard of peach, pear, apricot, and plum trees and a stone building built in 1916 for the Bar Z Ranch. The historic ranch site is maintained by the National Park Service and makes a pleasant stroll (about a mile round-trip from the parking area).

From April to October, chances are you will see river-runners loading gear at the boat ramp, the put-in point for commercial and private Grand Canyon raft trips. More than 20,000 people brave the rapids and drink in the scenery (and some of the Colorado) every year. About 100 yards upriver are the remains of a few stone buildings near the sunken carcass of a steamboat brought there in the early 1900s in an unsuccessful attempt to extract gold from the Chinle Shale.

Lees Ferry Campground has 54 designated sites ($12/night) with no hookups, available on a first-come, first-served basis. Sites have grills, and there are toilets and drinking water at the campground, located above the boat launch.

Along the Vermilion Cliffs

On its way to the Kaibab Plateau and Jacob Lake, the gateway to the North Rim of the Grand Canyon, U.S. 89A continues west through a starkly beautiful landscape. North of the highway, huge tumbled Shinarump boulders rest at the foot of the 1,000-foot-high sandstone cliffs. To the south, House Rock Valley drops toward the edge of Marble Canyon, a dark gash running through the relatively level Marble Platform. Overhead, condors soar through the high-desert skies, the site of their release into the wild in 1996.

About 10 miles west of Lees Ferry, **Cliff Dwellers Lodge** (928/355-2261 or 800/962-9755, www.cliffdwellerslodge.com) was built in 1949 by pioneering Glen Canyon boatman Art Greene. Lodge rooms ($80–90) have satellite TVs. A newer guesthouse ($175) has accommodations for groups or families up to six. The nearby "ruins" tucked underneath the huge boulders were part of a trading post dating to the 1920s. You'll find a convenience store/fly shop and gas pumps there, as well as a restaurant (serving all meals daily, $8–20). The patio is a relaxing place to dine on a summer evening.

BACKGROUND

The Land

The Four Corners is part of the larger **Colorado Plateau,** one of the major physiographic provinces of the western United States, covering 130,000 square miles of southern Utah, northern Arizona, northwestern New Mexico, and southwestern Colorado. An uplifted platform with an average elevation of 6,000 feet, the Colorado Plateau is bounded by the Rocky Mountains to the north and east, the Sonoran Desert to the south, and Nevada's Great Basin to the west. Relatively flat, the plateau is sliced by rivers and punctuated by buttes, mesas, isolated mountains, and small ranges. Ninety percent of the vast, semiarid plateau is drained by the Colorado River and its tributaries.

GEOLOGY
Geologic History

The combined forces of weather, gravity, and plate tectonics have filled this region with an amazing variety of topography. If you remember nothing else about the complex surface of the Four Corners, keep these three words in mind: deposition, uplift, and erosion. The Four Corners's stupendous scenery can be summed up in three simple steps. First, deposition: Layers of sediment were laid down like Navajo blankets on a bed. Next, uplift: The various layers were bent, cracked, and generally lifted toward the sky by huge energies below the earth's surface. Finally, erosion: The uplifted

© KATHLEEN BRYANT

GEOLOGIC TERMS

- **anticline:** arch-shaped upfold in rock layers
- **arch:** freestanding stone curve formed by erosion
- **butte:** flat-topped hill with sloping sides
- **concretion:** rounded mineral mass found in sedimentary rock
- **cross-bedding:** linear patterns in sandstone created by shifting wind directions (also called cross stratification)
- **desert varnish:** dark rock coating formed by water and microbes
- **diatreme:** solidified neck of an explosive volcano, later exposed by erosion
- **dike:** vertical ridge of exposed igneous rock formed by fissures filling with magma
- **fault:** fracture or break in a rock mass that has moved
- **graben:** straight-walled canyon formed by downshifted fault blocks (German for "ditch" or "grave")
- **horst:** uplifted block remaining between grabens
- **joint:** fracture or break in a rock mass that has not moved
- **mesa:** flat-topped hill with at least one steeply sloping side
- **monocline:** step-like fold in rock layers
- **natural bridge:** freestanding stone curve formed by flowing water
- **pothole:** shallow water-collecting depression created by erosion (also called a *tinaja* or water pocket)
- **scree:** loose gravel-sized fragments from eroding slopes, similar to talus
- **slickrock:** bare sandstone
- **syncline:** trough-shaped down-fold in rock layers
- **talus:** rock fragments that accumulate at the bottom of eroding slopes or cliffs

layers were stripped by wind, rain, and flowing water, creating the mesas, canyons, and countless other shapes that characterize the region.

In all, some 300 million years of geologic history are visible in the Four Corners, a display with few equals in the world. The region's oldest rocks, at the bottom of the Grand Canyon, date to the middle of the Precambrian Era (4.6 billion–570 million years ago). During the Cambrian, Devonian, Mississippian, and Permian Periods (570–320 million years ago), the region was much closer to the equator, and warm tropical seas left behind layers of early marine fossils. A series of mountain ranges called the Ancestral Rockies rose during the Pennsylvanian Period (320–286 million years ago), including the **Uncompahgre Uplift** in what is now eastern Utah and western Colorado. These were probably as high as today's Rockies and shed sediments into lower-elevation depressions such as the **Paradox Basin,** southwest of the Uncompahgre Uplift, which filled and emptied of water as deep geologic faults shifted well into the Permian Period (286–245 million years ago).

During the Triassic Period (245–208 million years ago), continental drift carried the land north into warmer climates. Increased rainfall fed lakes, streams, marshes, and early forests, some of which were buried and turned to stone. Ferns and early conifers were also covered in silt, mud, and sand along with primitive amphibians and reptiles. Dinosaur fossils were added to the mix during the Jurassic Period (208–144 million years ago), when the local climate cooled somewhat as the continent moved even farther north. By this time the Uncompahgre Uplift had been mostly worn away, and seas flowing in from the west and north created muddy tidal flats whose petrified ripples turn up near sand dunes also frozen by the forces of time.

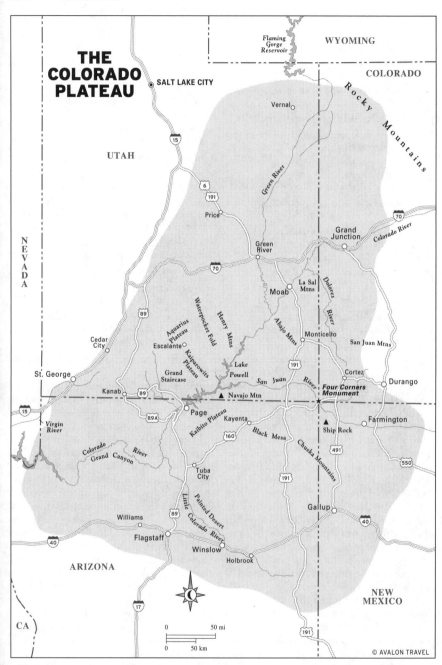

THE COLORADO PLATEAU

Flaming Gorge Reservoir

WYOMING

COLORADO

● SALT LAKE CITY

Vernal

Rocky Mountains

UTAH

NEVADA

Price

Green River

Grand Junction

Colorado River

Green River

La Sal Mtns

Moab

Dolores River

Aquarius Plateau

Waterpocket Fold

Henry Mtns

Abajo Mtns

Monticello

San Juan Mtns

Cedar City

Escalante

Kaiparowits Plateau

Lake Powell

Cortez

Durango

St. George

Grand Staircase

San Juan River

Four Corners Monument

Kanab

▲ Navajo Mtn

Virgin River

Page

Kaibito Plateau

Kayenta

Black Mesa

▲ Ship Rock

Farmington

Colorado River

Grand Canyon

160

Chuska Mountains

Tuba City

Painted Desert

Little Colorado River

Gallup

Williams

Flagstaff

Winslow

Holbrook

ARIZONA

NEW MEXICO

CA

0   50 mi

0   50 km

© AVALON TRAVEL

More marine fossils are found in layers dating to the Cretaceous Period (104–66 million years ago), when waters spread across North America from Alaska to Mexico. The modern Rocky Mountains rose during this period as well, taking 20–30 million years to reach their current heights. More uplift followed during the Tertiary Period (66–2 million years ago), starting with the formation of the **laccolithic mountains** that rise above the plateau today. The La Sals, the Abajos, the Henry Mountains, and Navajo Mountain are all laccolithic peaks, formed over huge blisters of magma that pushed upward without breaking through to the surface.

Beginning about 15 million years ago, the entire plateau, which until now had existed close to sea level, was lifted up about 3,000 feet. Steeper slopes made rivers flow faster, increasing erosion, and rapid downcutting occurred along the course of the Colorado and Green Rivers. About 10,000 feet of sedimentary deposits have eroded in the last 10–15 million years, exposing millions of years of older rock layers. About 5.5 million years ago, the San Andreas Fault opened the Gulf of California, freeing the Colorado River to flow into the ocean to the southwest.

The forces of erosion continued through the Quaternary period (2 million years ago–present), and the youngest geologic features are constantly being created and destroyed. The forces of weather, gravity, and chance shape arches, spires, natural bridges, and hoodoos. Harder limestone or basalt caps protect softer stones underneath, and volcanic necks and dikes are exposed as their softer outer layers wear away. The timescale involved is immense, but change can also happen quickly. Pieces have fallen from arches and towers have collapsed well into the 20th century, and rocks tumble from cliffs on an almost daily basis. The 71-foot-wide Wall Arch, along the Devils Garden Trail in Arches National Park, collapsed overnight in August 2008. The trail leading into Palatki Ruin near Sedona was closed in 2010 when rangers

Rockfalls, like this one at Bryce Canyon, sometimes close trails.

noticed a crack forming in the alcove opening. The alcove's ceiling hasn't fallen . . . yet.

Major Features

Elevations in the Four Corners range from 2,000 feet at the bottom of the Grand Canyon to 14,000 feet in the San Juan Mountains near Durango, but they average 6,000 feet. Dark green forests cover the largest mountain ranges: the **La Sal Mountains** east of Moab, the **Abajo Mountains** west of Monticello, and the **Henry Mountains** east of Capitol Reef National Park. On the Navajo Reservation, **Navajo Mountain** rises south of Lake Powell, and the **Chuska** and **Carrizo Mountains** follow the Arizona–New Mexico border. Boulder and Thousand Lake Mountain form the bulk of the **Aquarius Plateau** in South-Central Utah, near the colorfully named cliffs that make up the **Grand Staircase** to the west. Other dramatic features include stair-step **monoclines** stretching for dozens of miles; the Waterpocket Fold is the largest of these, but the list includes Comb Ridge on Cedar Mesa and the Cockscomb in the southern Escalante. Black Mesa, rich in coal, underlies most of the Hopi Reservation.

Buttes and mesas, looming cliffs and soaring arches, volcanic necks and dikes are among the hundreds of striking geological features that mark the terrain. Long, brown rivers meander for miles before exploding into white water in deep, shaded canyons. Verdant valleys line some sections, while others travel through bare rock. The region's rivers are fed by countless smaller streams and washes, many of which flow only a few days out of the year. The **Colorado River** is the unquestioned champion, even though it has been impounded by dams and reservoirs for much of its length, and its flow has diminished to a trickle in the desert of northern Mexico instead of reaching the Gulf of California. Born in the Colorado Rockies, the Colorado follows a major fault zone running northeast to southwest from Southeast Utah into northern Arizona, and is joined in the heart of Canyonlands National Park by the **Green River,** which flows south from Wyoming. The **San Juan River** runs west across northern New Mexico and Arizona before joining the waters of the Colorado at **Lake Powell,** the huge reservoir sprawling across the Utah-Arizona border behind Glen Canyon Dam. The **Little Colorado River** drains Arizona's White Mountains and the southern Navajo Reservation before it joins the Colorado in the Grand Canyon.

Major Rock Layers

Some of the Four Corners' rock layers, like the sheer walls of Wingate Sandstone near Moab, are easy to recognize. Others aren't, especially when they change character from place to place, like the ubiquitous Navajo Sandstone, deposited as dunes during the Jurassic Period. In Canyonlands and Capitol Reef National Parks, its distinctive rounded contours are the color of chalk and cream. Navajo Sandstone transitions to pink in the lower reaches of Zion Canyon, and the walls of Glen Canyon are salmon-colored even beneath the silty waters of Lake Powell to the south.

A mnemonic device can help you learn geological layers. Heading up the Colorado River from Lees Ferry, apply the phrase "Many canyon walls know no capitalist exploitation" to the layers visible from bottom (oldest) to top: Moenkopi, Chinle, Wingate, Kayenta, Navajo, Carmel, and Entrada. The three most visible layers in Southeast Utah are the red-brown mud/shale of the Kayenta layer, the lighter Navajo Sandstone, and red-brown Entrada Sandstone. If you can recognize these, you're doing pretty well.

CLIMATE

The Colorado Plateau is classified as arid to semiarid, receiving an average of 11.8 inches of rain per year—a little too much to qualify as desert but definitely dry compared to, say, Kansas City, which receives 38 inches annually. This, along with the fact that the plateau sits an average of 6,000 feet above sea level, means that **extreme temperatures** are the norm. Summer heat over 100°F changes to a winter chill below 0°F—and not only that, but the **daily temperature fluctuations** can be tremendous.

Without much cloud cover or vegetation to get in the way, most of the sunlight tends to reach the ground (up to 90 percent, compared to less than 50 percent in other temperate regions). Ground temperatures skyrocket by day, particularly during the sweltering summer months of June–September. At night, however, the dry air lets the heat escape just as quickly and temperatures plummet. A drop of 40°F between noon and night is not unusual.

Precipitation varies across the region, from 5–8 inches yearly in shaley deserts to 20 inches in higher woodlands and forests. The southwest is characterized as much by **seasonal rainfall** as by low rainfall. When it does come, most **precipitation** falls during the **summer monsoon** and winter snows. Monsoon cloudbursts (the "male rain" of the Navajo) are usually heralded by black clouds and anvil-shaped thunderheads visible for miles. Occasionally the air is so dry that rain evaporates before it hits the ground, creating a sheer curtain of moisture known as a virga. Monsoon thunderstorms can dump inches of water in just a few minutes, and the topography channels rain falling over a wide area into narrow gullies. Dry, rocky soil often can't absorb that much moisture that quickly. As a result, rivers suddenly rise, dry washes abruptly flow, and—the most extreme example—**flash floods** can scour a narrow canyon with little or no warning. Winter showers are more gentle (the Navajo's nourishing "female rain") than summer rainstorms. Moisture that falls as snow in the high country is especially precious; annual snowpack is a storehouse of moisture that replenishes rivers and reservoirs and delays the start of fire season, when tinder-dry forests, hot weather, and high winds combine for dangerous conditions across the region.

Flora and Fauna

The Colorado Plateau is blessed with a diverse range of plants and animals, inhabiting everything from bare rock to lush riverbanks and sweltering canyon interiors to snowy alpine tundra. Most of the habitat is dry and high, averaging about 4,000 feet above sea level and only 12 inches of rain per year. The result is an arid landscape whose inhabitants are well adapted to life where water is a precious commodity. Numerous microclimates give rise to special mini ecosystems, including hanging gardens, potholes, and cryptobiotic soil crusts. It helps that this region is one of the largest roadless areas (some say *the* largest) in the lower 48, but human encroachment has taken its toll.

PLANTS

The arid reaches of the Colorado Plateau favor sparse, scrubby vegetation spread widely across the land. There are more than 2,500 species of vascular plants in the region, and more than 200 are endemic. Species from the Great Basin to the west mix with those from the Rocky Mountains to the east. Forests cover the mountains, with different tree communities occurring at different heights, and the banks of streams and rivers are lined with lush vegetation—some native, some not.

Dealing with Drought

A desert (or near desert) calls for a special set of adaptations to collect and store water. Even when it does fall, moisture doesn't stick around for long; heavy rains tend to run off hard, dry soils without soaking in. Between soil evaporation and plant transpiration (water loss during photosynthesis), collectively termed "evapotranspiration," water loss can approach the ridiculous. Regions that receive less than five inches of rain a year may have the potential to lose 120 inches. (In Moab the potential evapotranspiration is over 80 inches per year.) Plants, which can't move on when things get tough, have to make the most of available moisture.

Most plants are able to wait for the right time to throw energy into making flowers or seeds. After a summer thundershower, a seemingly barren plateau can erupt with color as

CRYPTOBIOTIC SOIL

© NATIONAL PARK SERVICE

Cryptobiotic soil can be found at Canyonlands National Park.

The dark, rough covering that grows on undisturbed sandy soil takes its name from the Greek words for "hidden" and "life," and for a long time it was a mystery to biologists. It turns out this crust is a mix of mosses, lichens, algae, and fungi and is crucial to the ecology of the desert. Crypto starts as a dark scattering across the soil and can take centuries to grow three or four inches—it's the ground-level equivalent of old-growth forests. Frost buckling cracks the spongy covering and lifts it into tiny waves that solidify and help trap moisture and windblown seeds and spores. In addition to absorbing and holding water, crypto helps keep the soil from eroding and provides nutrients such as nitrogen that help plants grow. Without it, plant communities would take much longer to develop, or they might not develop at all.

Cryptobiotic crust is very fragile, and a boot print or tire track can trigger a domino-like reaction of wind and water erosion. In some areas, crypto represents more than 70 percent of the living groundcover, making it difficult to bypass. Stay on trails or bare rock or hike in sandy washes to avoid busting the crust: Recent soil studies in southern Utah put minimum recovery times of lichen and moss at 45 to 250 years. It makes us rethink that old saw, "Leave only footprints."

dead-looking plants blossom almost overnight. Grass and flower seeds can lie dormant in the soil for years, waiting until the right amount of precipitation falls. Some plants flower only at night to avoid losing water to the daytime heat.

Many perennials resist drought by eliminating a plant's biggest water wasters: leaves. Thorns on cacti minimize water loss, and small, hairy or scalelike leaves and waxy coverings on other plants cut down on moisture lost to moving air.

Other plants grow only where there is a constant water supply, such as streamside areas or the unique, fragile **hanging gardens** found at springs and seeps, filled with ferns, monkeyflowers, and other species that are rare elsewhere. Willows and cottonwoods send roots deep to reach the water table along rivers and sporadic streams. When rain falls, the best idea is to gather as much as possible, as quickly as possible. The radiating, strap-like leaves of the narrowleaf yucca channel moisture into the plant's center. The extensive, shallow roots of cacti collect water dropped during brief rain showers. The ubiquitous prickly pear can branch along the ground, creating mini dams to slow runoff and help prevent erosion.

Trees and Shrubs

The woody plants of the Colorado Plateau are generally small, widely spaced, and tough. Their roots can split rocks, and they can live up to a century. One of the most common shrubs is **Mormon tea,** an odd-looking broomlike plant that contains pseudoephedrine, a drug used in nasal decongestants. Early settlers boiled this relative of pines and junipers into a bitter but effective medicinal tea. **Blackbrush** is also common, and although it's full of thorns, that doesn't keep desert bighorn sheep from eating it. **Four-winged saltbush** can grow in soils too salty for other plants, which give its leaves a distinctively saline taste. It's an important browse for livestock, pronghorn, elk, deer, and others, and was used by the Hopi to flavor and leaven bread.

Fremont's cottonwood is unmistakable anywhere there is water, with its huge, gnarled trunks and delicate green leaves. It takes its name from the downy, highly flammable cotton produced by female trees and can grow up to 90 feet tall. Other common plants in riparian areas include **netleaf hackberry** and the invasive **Russian olive** and **tamarisk,** which can crowd out native vegetation. One of the most interesting partnerships in the Colorado Plateau involves the **narrowleaf yucca,** which looks like a collection of green swords all pointing outward. Unlike its relative the agave, or

© KATHLEEN BRYANT

Desert willows control erosion by growing in thickets along dry washes.

century plant, which flowers only once before dying, the narrowleaf yucca sends up a towering flower stalk every spring. After mating, female yucca moths gather yucca pollen into a ball and spread it to other yucca plants so that the larvae that hatch from their eggs will have something to eat. In the process, the moths pollinate the plants. Each would be lost without the other: yucca moth larvae feed only on yucca pollen, and the moths are the plant's only pollinators.

Between 4,500 and 5,500 feet, the most common plants are the **juniper** and **piñon.** This woodland, often referred to as "PJ," covers an estimated 75,000 square miles of the dry, rocky West, making it one of the region's most common plant communities. The juniper has needle- or scale-like leaves, and its trunk is covered with shaggy bark that indigenous tribes used as kindling and to line baby cradleboards. It's not a true cedar but a cypress, and it can stop circulation to its twisted outer branches during a drought to keep the rest of the tree alive.

© RICHARD MAYER

Mormon tea, a broomlike plant that contains pseudoephedrine, has been used by people of the Four Corners for centuries.

The scientific name of the piñon, *pinus edulis*, hints at its seasonal treasure: The delicious, protein-rich seeds inside its compact cones are produced in huge crops every 3–7 years—so abundant that animals (including humans) can't possibly eat them all, ensuring that some survive. Roasted or eaten raw, pine nuts have 5,000 calories per pound, making them an important food source. (Some birds breed late or not at all between pine nut crops.) The smallest member of the pine family smells sweet in a campfire, and its pitch was used to seal baskets, mend pottery, and dress wounds.

Other common plants in this zone include the **cliffrose,** with its fragrant cream-colored blossoms; **mountain mahogany,** which has a host of traditional uses, from making farming implements to wool dye; and **big sagebrush,** one of the classic plants of the West. Sage, a fragrant shrub that shelters smaller plants and animals, is indicative of deep soils good for farming and thus has been eliminated from half its historic acreage.

Between 6,500 and 8,000 feet, the most common tree is the **ponderosa pine,** with long needles grouped into threes and thick orange-colored bark that smells like vanilla or butterscotch. Northern Arizona is home to the most extensive ponderosa pine forest in the world, with members averaging about 100 feet tall and 3 feet in diameter. Ponderosas are resistant to the fires that periodically clear the undergrowth, leaving pine forests wide open at eye level. The **Gambel oak, bigtooth maple,** and **Utah serviceberry** are also found in the pine-oak belt.

Higher mountainsides, 8,000–9,500 feet, are the domain of the **Douglas fir** and the **quaking aspen.** Doug fir has distinctive bracts poking out from between its cone scales, and it's not really a fir, but a separate species altogether. In its first two decades, it can grow two feet per year. The white bark and shimmering green leaves of the aspen are unmistakable, and the plants—which grow in clusters that are actually clones of each other, connected underground—are

© KATHLEEN BRYANT

Sacred datura blooms at night to attract pollinator moths.

often one of the first things to grow in land cleared by humans or fire. The aspen-fir zone includes the **white fir** and **berry bushes** such as raspberry, gooseberry, and thimbleberry. The highest plant zone, from 9,500 feet to tree line at 11,500 feet, is home to the **Englemann spruce, blue spruce, subalpine fir, limber pine,** and **lodgepole pine.**

Flowers

Desert flowers are also a hardy bunch and easy to underestimate. Many visitors are amazed to see the plateau's color potential fully realized after a long-awaited downpour. You're likely to see the red blooms of the **Eaton's penstemon** and **Indian paintbrush** or the orange **globe mallow** among various yellow-blooming sunflowers. In addition to several species of **sunflower,** yellow flowers include **rough mule's ear,** and **Newberry's twinpod.** Purples and pinks show up as **milkvetch** and the very similar **locoweed** (which contains an alkaloid that can sicken or even kill grazers), and the easily distinguished **dwarf lupine** and **showy four-o'clock.**

White flowers like the **Apache plume** and the delicate **sego lily** often have a dual purpose: They're pretty and easier for pollinators to see at night. **Evening primrose** and **sacred datura** (also known as moonflower or jimsonweed) also have white blossoms as well as distinctive perfumes to attract pollinators. The bell-like blooms of the datura, the largest flowers in canyon country, are pollinated by moths the size of small birds and contain toxic compounds that have been used to induce shamanic hallucinations. Moths aren't the only pollinators flying around; butterflies, bees, wasps, birds, flies, bats, and beetles are also hard at work, doing good with only their own selfish interests in mind.

Cacti

Cacti are the poster children of desert survivors. Succulent stems and pads expand to store moisture while letting very little evaporate through their waxy coatings. Spines protect the plant, and stomata open only at night to collect carbon dioxide for photosynthesis, conserving even more moisture. The cacti you're most likely to see include the **prickly pear,** with its flattened, palm-sized pads and yellow or red blooms, which appear for only a few days in early summer. The fleshy interior of its red fruit, called *tuna* in Spanish, is eaten by people and animals (be sure you get out all those nearly invisible spines, called glochids). In April or May, the **strawberry hedgehog** bears vivid pink blooms, while the similarly shaped **claret cup cactus,** a favorite of hummingbirds, produces waxy-looking crimson blossoms on densely packed stems.

Invaders

It's hard to believe, but even in this inhospitable land some late-arriving plants have taken root and spread like wildfire. **Tamarisk,** also known as salt cedar, was brought from the Mediterranean in the 19th century and planted as an ornamental and to control streamside erosion. The water-loving shrub took off at 12 miles per year until it was found in nearly every tributary of the Colorado River. Tough and tenacious, it reproduces prolifically, even in poor, salty soils—a mature tree can produce up to 500,000 seeds a year—and if it's cut down or burned it simply sprouts new shoots. It grows in stands so dense that it crowds out other plants and sucks up an astonishing amount of water through taproots that can reach 50 feet. A single tamarisk plant can consume 300 gallons of water a day—more than twice as much water as any native species. Across the Southwest, where the plant is estimated to cover one million acres, tamarisks absorb as much water in a year as 20 million people. To add insult to injury, tamarisks provide little food or habitat for wildlife and burn very easily.

Fighting an invader like this isn't easy (especially when golf resorts and new residents continue to plant them) but some efforts are paying off. Rangers in the Maze District of Canyonlands National Park spray choked waterways with herbicides and have already cleared some canyons of the intruder and increased cottonwood seedling counts. Tamarisk has even inspired Congressional legislation: the Tamarisk Research and Control Act of 2003. The U.S. Department of Agriculture has begun implementing plans to introduce leaf beetles from Asia to 13 Western states to eat tamarisks (and, in theory, leave others alone). One concern is the effect on the endangered Southwest willow flycatcher, which has been forced to nest in salt cedars as native plants have been pushed out.

Shipments of wheat from Europe in the late 1800s brought the first seeds of **cheatgrass,** which now covers some 100 million acres across the West. Since it germinates in fall and spends the winter storing energy and growing roots (as native plants lie dormant), it gets the jump when spring comes. It's also more efficient at using underground water and colonizing areas disturbed by cultivation, overgrazing, or fire. Animals don't like to eat it, and its seed heads have an annoying habit of clinging to hikers' socks. In all, cheatgrass is a formidable competitor and has replaced native grasslands on a scale seldom seen in botanical history. Other invasives include knapweed and Dalmatian toadflax, which crowd out forage plants; pampas grass, which can trigger allergies; and puncture vine, which bears nasty seed heads that can punch through shoes and bicycle tires.

ANIMALS

Though the largest living things you're likely to see in the Four Corners' forests and deserts (aside from other hikers) are mostly birds and the occasional fleeing cottontail, a wide variety of critters call the Colorado Plateau home. Most animals wisely avoid the triple threats of heat, drought, and predators by venturing into the open only at certain times of day or year.

Desert Adaptations

Many animals avoid the stress of daytime temperatures by coming out only at dawn and dusk (crepuscular) or at night (nocturnal). Sagebrush flats and grasslands start hopping near sunset as cottontails and jackrabbits emerge from their burrows, bringing their eager predators, the coyotes. Porcupines, mule deer, and many birds also favor the cooler and dimmer in-between times, while other rodents, bobcats, mountain lions, and foxes wait until full darkness.

Those that do come out by day (diurnal) have other strategies for surviving the heat and dryness. Some animals alter their activity patterns depending on the temperature: Mosquitoes come out at different times of day or not at all, depending on how hot it is. Reptiles such as lizards and snakes are crepuscular in summer, diurnal in spring and fall, and go into a state of semihibernation (torpor) in winter. If the moisture content of their plant food is over 75 percent, pronghorns can survive without drinking any water, as can the nocturnal Ord's kangaroo rat, which can extract all the liquids it needs from the seeds it eats.

Mammals

Desert bighorn sheep, driven close to extinction by livestock diseases and hunting, have been reintroduced into Southeast Utah by the National Park Service. If you venture into the backcountry, you may spot one of the sure-footed ungulates, often in bands of females and young. During the fall and winter rut, males charge each other with a crash of their large curved horns. Herds of **pronghorns** roam the flats, where they can leap up to eight feet high and run up to 65 miles per hour. **Mule deer** thrive throughout the plateau, now that most of their predators have been eliminated. They migrate to high ground in summer, and males sport large racks of antlers. Their odd bounding leap is called "stotting." **Elk** populations, some once driven to extinction from overhunting and habitat loss, are now expanding throughout the mountainous west.

You can tell **desert cottontails** and **black-tailed jackrabbits** apart by size; jackrabbits are larger and more gangly, with long black-tipped ears useful for getting rid of excess heat. Similarly, a **gray fox** is larger than a **kit fox**—the latter's large ears and big bushy tail make it one of the cutest desert creatures. **Coyotes** blend in well with the scenery in their buff and gray pelts. They're as big as medium-sized

© NATIONAL PARK SERVICE

The hooves of bighorn sheep are adapted for traction on rock.

dogs and flourish everywhere from the remote Escalante canyons to urban neighborhoods. A pack of coyotes yipping under the stars is one of the most hauntingly distinctive sounds in the Four Corners.

Ringtails are related to raccoons and have the striped, bushy tails to prove it. They love the cracks and ledges of canyon country, and their incredible agility, balance, and daring, plus hind feet that can rotate 180 degrees for a better grip, let them climb places nothing else can. (Backpackers, take note: A determined ringtail can foil most pack defenses.) A host of chipmunks, squirrels, rats, and mice keeps larger animals well fed. **Deer mice** are infamous for harboring the horrific hantavirus, which killed a handful of people in the region in 1993. You'll probably see the conglomerated nests (middens) of four species of **woodrats** beneath rock overhangs. These are useful to scientists trying to reconstruct the ancient ecology of the Four Corners, since—as their common name, pack rat, suggests—their nests contain everything from broken sticks to shiny objects. The nighttime skies are the domain of close to two dozen types of bats, from the **big brown bat** to the **western pipistrelle,** the smallest bat in the United States.

Beavers and grizzly bears were both once native, but they have been exterminated from the area. On the other hand, the black-footed ferret has been reintroduced, and conservationists hope (and ranchers fear) that it's only a matter of time before reintroduced gray wolves work their way back into the area.

Birds

Those far-off silhouettes soaring on the thermals are hard to distinguish. If it holds its wings in a V and wobbles as it glides, it's a **turkey vulture.** Like condors, their larger cousins, vultures help keep the desert clean of carrion with their excellent eyesight and sense of smell. A large bird with flat wings and an even flight might be a **golden eagle,** with its six-foot wingspan, or a **red-tailed hawk,** the most common large bird of prey in the country. The red-tail's screeching call has added atmosphere to so many classic Westerns that it's become an auditory cliché. Other raptors you might spot include the **sharp-shinned hawk** and **Cooper's hawk,** which look very similar (Cooper's hawks are bigger). Cliff-loving **peregrine falcons,** a once-endangered species making a comeback, dive after prey at 180 mph, making them the world's fastest animal.

The **common raven** disproves the dismissive "birdbrain." Ravens can learn to speak, count to at least 10, and outperform graduate students in tests of memory. You'll often see these clever jet-black birds cavorting in midair, doing barrel rolls or playing tag or catch. The black-and-white **black-billed magpies** are also in the crow (corvid) family and are quite bright. Like ravens, they mate for life and have a wide range of vocalizations. With a smaller vocal repertoire, but one beloved by hikers, the **canyon wren** calls in liquid descending notes that could be the theme song of the Colorado Plateau. The high desert is the domain of brilliant blue **piñon jays** and **western scrub jays,** while **mountain bluebirds** and **western bluebirds** prefer forest edges.

Other common birds on the Colorado Plateau include **hummingbirds** (black-chinned, broad-tailed, and Anna's), **woodpeckers** and **flickers,** and various **chickadees, warblers, flycatchers,** and **towhees.** Usually hunting after dark, the **great horned owl** soars silently after rabbits, reptiles, skunks, and even other birds.

Reptiles and Amphibians

The yellow-and-green **collared lizard** seems enamored with its own beauty, perching prominently on rocks and stumps. (Males are actually defending their territory.) Like other Four Corners lizards, such as the **plateau lizard** and various kinds of **whiptail lizards,** they do push-ups to display their markings and regulate their temperature, and they sprint after insects, spiders, and small arthropods. **Gopher** and **racer snakes** kill their prey through constriction, while **garter** snakes sit in wait near potholes for frogs and tadpoles. There aren't as many poisonous snakes out here as movies and television ads would make you think, and unlike their on-screen counterparts, snakes do not pursue humans. The **midget-faded rattlesnake** packs a potent wallop for its size, however, while the **prairie rattler** migrates miles in search of deer mice to swallow.

Aside from the months of waiting for the rain to fall, the life of a **Great Basin spadefoot toad** doesn't sound so bad: find water, drink to bursting, eat up to half your weight in a single night, and mate like crazy—then burrow back into the mud and do it all again next year. Potholes are often full of their eggs and tadpoles in early summer. **Canyon tree frogs** often sit immobile near water, hoping their excellent camouflage will keep them safe. Like the spadefoot, this frog can survive desiccation and heat that would kill a nondesert amphibian.

Insects and Arachnids

Fierce-looking **tarantulas** grow up to six inches across, and their hairy legs and giant fangs are enough to give arachnophobes screaming fits. But tarantulas bite only when provoked, and the bites are no more dangerous than bee stings. Besides a bad rap, these gentle giants also have to deal with the depredations of the **tarantula hawk.** These wasps paralyze tarantulas and lay their eggs on the living body, which provides food for hatching larvae.

Evolutionarily speaking, **scorpions** are incredibly ancient creatures, and some glow under ultraviolet light; shine one after dark in this area, and you'll be amazed at how many scorpions are out there. The sting of certain species can be fatal to small children or those with weakened immune systems.

Female **black widow spiders** are highly poisonous—steer clear of a black spider with a red hourglass on its abdomen. **Velvet ants** look like colorful, hairy ants but have a bite toxic enough to earn the nickname "cow killer." Shiny black **darkling beetles** (aka stinkbugs) spray a noxious liquid from the end of their abdomen. These very common inch-long beetles raise their rears in a threat posture, but this doesn't deter the grasshopper mouse, which simply sticks the beetle's spraying end in the ground and starts eating the other one.

CONSERVATION ISSUES

Most conservation conflicts in the Four Corners concern public land use, and many have reached heated peaks in southern Utah. Here and elsewhere, longtime residents resent outside influences—be it the federal government, recently arrived residents, or environmental groups based elsewhere—telling them how to manage the vast surrounding federal lands. The other groups point out that generations of land leases and recreational use don't mean the lands are being used sustainably. Lands throughout the Southwest are being grazed, mined, logged, or loved to death. Old ways of life die hard as the economy shifts, and the most beautiful acres on earth have caused some of the most apoplectic arguments you've ever seen.

Monuments and Wilderness Areas

President Clinton ruffled feathers when he created 15 national monuments, including the Canyons of the Ancients (in southwestern Colorado), the Vermilion Cliffs and the Grand Canyon–Parashant (both in northern Arizona), and the gigantic Grand Staircase–Escalante (in southern Utah). A lawsuit by a coalition including the Utah Association of Counties, the Colorado-based Mountain States Legal Foundation, and the Blue Ribbon Coalition, an off-road vehicle (ORV) advocacy group, was defeated in 2002 when a federal court ruled that the president acted within his authority under the 1906 Antiquities Act in authorizing the monuments. Local ranchers refused to remove their livestock from the Grand Staircase–Escalante for years after the monument was set aside, and controversy continues over land use within monuments.

Still up in the air is the fate of millions of acres of desert that environmental groups are hoping to protect under **America's Red Rock Wilderness Act,** first introduced in Congress in 1989 and reintroduced in every session since. This legislation would designate more than nine million acres of southern Utah as off-limits to development and mechanical access. Though the bill has garnered widespread support in the House and the Senate, it has never been debated on the floor of either body. The hitch is a one-sentence statute (R.S. 2477) passed in 1866. Originally intended to give Civil War–era prospectors easy access to claims, the statute states simply, "The right of way for the construction of highways across public lands not otherwise reserved for public purposes is hereby granted," in this case, to the state and country legislatures. The statute was repealed by the 1976 Federal Lands Policy and Management Act, but a grandfather clause continues to honor valid existing rights. R.S. 2477 is invoked by local landowners and counties to prevent the creation of wilderness areas. They argue that an area can be set aside as wilderness only if it has few or no roads.

The result is endless argument over what is and isn't a road. Areas being considered for wilderness protection are marbled with thousands of dirt trails, sandy washes, ORV tracks, seismic exploration lines, and cow paths. In Utah alone, about 15,000 "road" claims are being debated. Passions are high and there is little middle ground. County officials send out bulldozers to improve rights-of-way, and environmental groups sue to stop them.

Off-Road Vehicles

A key issue in the argument over roads is off-road vehicles (ORVs), including motorcycles and "quads," four-wheel all-terrain vehicles (ATVs). (The easily tipped three-wheeled ATVs have been gradually phased out.) Since 2000, the number of ORVs registered in Utah has jumped from 83,000 to more than 200,000, and 94 percent of Bureau of Land Management (BLM) land in the state is open to their use. Popular areas like the San Rafael Swell, however, are still being fought over by ORV groups, who question the worth of wilderness that few people ever see, and their opponents, who cringe at the eroded tracks, noise, and pollution.

Mining and Drilling

The high desert plateaus of the Four Corners hide substantial reserves of uranium, coal, oil,

gas, and other things that take much more than a pick and shovel to unearth. The BLM leases its immense holdings to oil and gas companies to search for new deposits, raising the ire of conservation groups, tribal members, and some local residents. During its final days, the George W. Bush administration directed the BLM to consider opening more public lands in the Rocky Mountains and the Southwest to oil and gas drilling as part of a push to expand national energy reserves. In 2008, as an act of protest, college student Tim DeChristopher faked bids totaling $1.8 million in a BLM lease auction for oil and gas rights on parcels near Arches and Canyonlands National Parks. His arrest by federal agents and subsequent trial gained national attention, raising awareness of the rush toward development and temporarily halting the sale of dozens of parcels. DeChristopher is in prison; his attorneys are appealing his conviction.

Overgrazing

Once, much of the Colorado Plateau was covered by lush grasslands. As they migrated through, native bison and other ungulates not only cropped the shoots but also churned up the earth and fertilized it with their dung. Native herds have been replaced by cows and sheep, which are kept in much smaller areas year-round. Livestock tear up delicate riparian areas and graze anything green and edible down to the ground. Fast-growing invaders such as cheatgrass move in, and delicate ecosystems are drastically changed.

This process was already well underway by the turn of the 20th century, when overgrazing had stopped forest regeneration in the highlands and trampled lowland soils to a bare crust. With improved range management techniques, things have improved over the decades, but only to a limited extent. The effect goes deeper as well—a majority of the Colorado River water still goes to farms to grow feed for livestock, including water-hungry plants like alfalfa. Ranching has always been a marginal enterprise in the West, where alkaline soils and low rainfall add up to a

WATER POCKETS

In *Beyond the Wall* (1984), Edward Abbey wrote, "Nowhere is water so beautiful as in the desert, for nowhere else is it so scarce. By definition. Water, like a human being or a tree or a bird or a song, gains value by rarity, singularity, isolation. In a humid climate, water is common. In the desert each drop is precious."

Whether you call them potholes, or, better yet, water pockets, tinajas, or ephemeral pools, the sandstone basins that pock the Four Corners sit bone-dry and lifeless for much of the year. After a rain, however, these pools become worlds in miniature, with activity that is both astonishing and brief. Eggs, larvae, and small organisms that have survived temperatures from freezing to 140°F burst into life, a span that may be compressed into a few weeks or even days until the water dries up again.

Algae are present even in the smallest pools, providing a bottom rung to the abbreviated food chain. In bigger pools, tadpoles and fairy shrimp larvae wriggle in the muddy depths, backswimmer insects dive for the bottom, and predaceous diving beetles pursue the newly hatched.

These amazing ecosystems are tenacious but delicate, and human use can change the salinity or pH suddenly, disturbing the tiny creatures within. Take a closer look at this almost magical microcosm the next time you encounter a water pocket, but take care not to disturb it. (Unless, of course, it's as key to your survival as it is to the current residents'.)

far preferable to tracts of housing and shopping centers.

Drought

That there's not a lot of surface water in the Southwest is obvious. What's not so clear is how much water there really is, or should be, or the best way to parcel it out. Since the 1990s the Southwest has entered the worst period of drought in over a century. In fact, by some estimates, this may be the worst drought in the past 1,400 years.

According to the U.S. Geological Survey, the period 1999–2009 was the driest in 98 years of recorded history of the Colorado River, the region's main water source. Reservoirs have hit record lows and at times soil moisture levels are barely registering. Bone-dry forests are igniting at the slightest spark, and a plague of bark beetles has decimated drought-weakened trees. Climate models show that global climate change is shifting the weather in the Southwestern United States and parts of northern Mexico in a much drier direction, and the trend could continue into the foreseeable future. Many scientists predict quasi-permanent dry conditions rivaling or exceeding the great drought of the 12th century. Geochemical evidence shows that the Southwest has experienced long dry periods before, but this one appears to be exacerbated by human impact. Some studies suggest that if this climatic trend continues—and if water-use patterns don't change—Colorado River flows will drop in half by 2100.

As a result, Southwestern states are fighting even more fiercely over water, especially water diverted from the Colorado River. This waterway has been over-allotted ever since its average flow was over-calculated and locked into the Colorado River Compact in 1922. (Climatologists now think that the early 20th century was abnormally wet, meaning the calculations that drive the development of the urbanized West were, to put it bluntly, flatout wrong.) "Dust-bowlification," referring to conditions of the 1930s, is a term now being used by the USGS. In summer 2011 six massive

losing equation, and Western beef makes up only a small fraction of the country's supply. But the cowboy's hold on the national identity is a tight one, and the ranching industry, helped by inexpensive grazing permits for federal land, still has political clout far out of proportion to its size. Some environmentalists, however, have come to regard ranchers as partners in preserving the West's open spaces, arguing that well-managed ranchlands are haboobs (dust storms) rolled across Phoenix, grounding and diverting flights, downing power lines, and carrying particulate-laden air into northern Arizona. That same summer, the Wallow Fire burned over a half-million acres in Arizona and New Mexico, and some scientists viewed it as the harbinger of a regional trend toward larger, longer-burning fires.

On the bright side, the West is ideally situated to lead the way in alternative energy research and development. As early as 2004, New Mexico passed a law requiring utilities to get 10 percent of their electricity supply from renewable energy sources, such as solar, by the year 2011. The future of this amazing, austere but still fragile region depends on whether we can find the right balance between leaving it alone, living on its terms, and loving it to death.

History

PREHISTORY
Early Cultures

The history of the Four Corners is largely the history of the Southwest itself, a region that generally includes all of Arizona and New Mexico and parts of Texas, Oklahoma, Colorado, Utah, and Nevada. Some of the oldest records of human occupation in the New World have been found here, dating as far back as 18,000 years ago. As early as 10,000 B.C., small groups of humans lived in the basin of prehistoric Lake Bonneville, an inland sea that covered much of modern-day Utah and left behind the Great Salt Lake. During the **desert archaic** cultural period, starting about 6000 B.C., nomadic hunters and gatherers spread throughout the region in search of game and edible plants, living in caves or temporary brush shelters and leaving little trace of their passing.

Agriculture spread north from Mexico between 2000 and 500 B.C., allowing larger, more permanent settlements to supplement wild forage with a more nutritious diet of squash, corn, and beans. People made crude pottery to cook and store food and water. Farming techniques improved in the 1st millennium A.D., and the construction of partially underground pit houses became widespread.

The Basketmakers

Between about A.D. 100 and 700, the **Basketmaker** culture concentrated on growing crops and domesticating wild animals such as dogs and turkeys, which provided companionship, meat, bones for tools, and feathers for clothing. They wove yucca fibers into cord and sandals and wore ornaments of stones and shells traded from the south. Crops were grown in small garden plots, and large game like deer and elk was taken down with spears thrown using a device called an atlatl. The basketmakers' crafts were true works of art, elaborately decorated and woven tightly enough that, lined with pitch, they could be used for cooking by dropping in red-hot stones. Around A.D. 500 villages grew in size, with many food storage bins and the first **kivas**—round ceremonial chambers built partly underground. These were lined with benches and centered around fire pits and a *sipapu*, a small hole symbolizing the one through which their ancestors had emerged from the underworld.

The Ancestral Puebloans

The Basketmaker culture gradually developed into that of the Ancestral Puebloans, once known as the **Anasazi,** an Athapascan (Navajo) word that translates roughly as "ancient enemies" or "enemies of my ancestors." In the **Developmental period** (A.D. 700–1050), Pueblo culture centered on planned villages that were frequently built on a north–south axis. These often held several hundred people in hundreds of rooms built of stone masonry, as well as pit houses, and were surrounded by tilled fields where cotton may have been grown. Infants were carried on cradleboards, the hard backs flattening their skulls, perhaps on purpose, and pottery grew finer and more elaborately decorated.

© KATHLEEN BRYANT

Pueblo women used stones to grind corn into flour.

Chacoans built many "great kivas" measuring up to 16 feet deep and 70 feet in diameter and developed their pottery skills to new heights.

End of an Era

After a peak around 1300, Chaco and the entire Pueblo culture experienced a startlingly rapid decline that left cliff houses and great houses abandoned. It was as if their inhabitants had simply picked up one day and walked off. (Some researchers think the Chacoans simply moved north to Aztec, where very similar ruins remain, and then south to Casas Grandes in northern Mexico for a third try.) The migration from Chaco was probably due to a combination of factors, including overpopulation, resource depletion, raids by new tribes arriving from the north, widespread droughts in A.D. 1130–1180 and 1276–1299, and changes in religious and political leadership. Though no evidence of organized warfare has been unearthed, this may have been a time of hunger and terror; it's hard to visit some of these inaccessible ruins and not speculate about defensible features such as small doorways, rooftop entries, and interior plazas. Archaeologists have turned up evidence of isolated incidents of violence dating to this period, including some recent controversial finds that indicate cannibalism. This is a touchy subject among many contemporary tribes, who view the dead as something not to be discussed and cannibalism as the worst sort of insult.

During the **Regressive Pueblo** period (1300–1700), a civilization that once numbered in the hundreds of thousands was scattered to the winds. Offshoots rose briefly in this tail-end time, including the **Kayenta people** of northeastern Arizona, who lived in Canyon de Chelly and Navajo National Monument. The **Mesa Verde-style villages** of southwest Colorado and Southeast Utah reached their peak as Chaco faded but suffered the same fate soon after. Though some Ancestral Puebloans may have returned to the foraging lifestyle of their ancestors, most merged with other groups to the south and east, along the Rio Grande and the Hopi mesas. Their descendants continue to live in these areas today.

Settlements expanded into the **Classic Pueblo** period (A.D. 1050–1300), which saw the construction of the great cliff houses that still draw thousands of visitors every year. Built in large natural alcoves in canyon walls, these freestanding structures resembled apartment blocks made of stone, with up to four stories designed so that the roof of one would be the porch for the one above. This period also brought what has been called the **Chaco Phenomenon,** referring to the massive constructions in Chaco Canyon of northwest New Mexico. Perhaps influenced by Central American cultures, the Puebloans built a series of great houses in Chaco unlike anything the Southwest had ever seen. Huge timbers were carried from the Chuska Mountains to serve as floor and roof beams in structures with up to 1,000 rooms. A radiating network of roads made Chaco the Rome of the ancient Southwest, concentrating the religious, cultural, and political energies of some 30,000 people spread over 40,000 square miles. The

Farther north, a group known as the **Fremont** flourished in the western Colorado Plateau and the eastern Great Basin of Nevada in approximately A.D. 750–1250. Originally thought to be a branch of the Ancestral Puebloans, the Fremont have been identified as a distinct culture, albeit a much less cohesive one. They settled in villages, grew similar crops, and made baskets and pottery like their neighbors but left fewer artifacts and constructed nothing approaching the grandeur of the cliff palaces. They were, however, prolific makers of rock art: The Fremont left pictographs (painted) and petroglyphs (carved or pecked) throughout present-day Utah. The Fremont and Ancestral Puebloans did seem to mingle to some extent in South-Central Utah but, probably for many of the same reasons, the Fremont culture faded by A.D. 1500.

More Recent Tribes

As the Ancestral Puebloan and Fremont cultures faded, new cultural groups moved in from the north. These nomadic peoples spoke dialects of the Athapascan languages of western Canada and would eventually evolve into the **Navajo** and **Apache** tribes. The exact timing of the immigration is unclear, but it was definitely under way by the time the Spanish arrived in the 16th century. These groups would become some of the most feared raiders in the history of the Southwest as the cultures of the old and new worlds clashed. Most Apache bands moved south of the Colorado Plateau, but the Navajo stayed in the area around the Four Corners. The Navajos' traditional log hogans have been traced to origins in Asia. For a time they lived among the Puebloans at Dinetah (near present-day Farmington) and adopted many Pueblo customs, including farming, weaving, livestock herding, a matrilineal society, and the clan system. From the Spanish they gained horses, and they learned the art of silversmithing from the Mexicans.

The **Hopis,** along with the pueblo tribes in New Mexico, are considered to be more or less direct descendants of the Ancestral Puebloans. They have an extensive oral history that reaches hundreds of years into the past, and many Hopis recognize clan symbols associated with prehistoric sites or migration trails. **The Zunis** also have an extensive oral history, and they trace clan relationships to the Mogollon culture, whose northern boundary was the Little Colorado River, as well as to the Ancestral Puebloans. The Zuni language is an isolate; that is, while it shares some elements with Hopi and languages spoken in other pueblos (and even Navajo), it is unrelated to any other language.

The origins of the **Ute** tribe are less clear; it is known their ancestors came from the north and west, but when is uncertain. The Ute language is southern Numic, one of the Uto-Aztecan languages shared by many of the Great Basin tribes. Like the Navajo, they gained horses from the Spanish. They remained seminomadic during the colonial period, traveling in bands to hunt and gather seasonal plants, and taking part in the Southwest's extensive slave and horse trade. Later, the Utes established permanent settlements and learned farming techniques from their Mormon neighbors.

THE EUROPEANS ARRIVE

Spanish missionaries and explorers were the first Europeans to traverse the American Southwest. They came in search of souls and gold, respectively, and were spurred in their often miserable and deadly travels by the thousands of "heathens" waiting to be converted and legends of golden cities in the sand. Even more encouraging were the stories of the conquistadores who had already met with success: Hernán Cortés, who in 1521 defeated the entire Aztec empire of central Mexico with only 500 men, and Francisco Pizarro, who helped topple the fabulously wealthy Andean kingdom of the Inca in the 1530s. The legends of El Dorado ("The Golden One") and the Seven Golden Cities of Cibola got a boost from the stories of Alvar Nuñez Cabeza de Vaca who, after being shipwrecked on the Florida coast in 1528, spent eight years wandering across the Southwest with a small group of survivors until eventually reaching the Spanish colonies in Mexico.

Early Explorers

In 1540 **Francisco Vázquez de Coronado**

led a party of 300 into Arizona in search of the cities of gold and to claim the region for Spain. Finding no treasure in the Zuni pueblos, the heavily armed group advanced north, where a side expedition led by García López de Cárdenas became the first Europeans to gaze into the Grand Canyon. Indigenous groups, including the Hopis, may have used the legend of the golden cities to urge the Spaniards onward ("Cibola? Uh, yeah—it's just a few days that way. Keep going, you can't miss it!"). The party advanced through northern New Mexico and Texas and made it as far as Kansas before realizing that the only gold they'd seen was the setting sun reflecting off the walls of the adobe pueblos. Only 100 men made it back to Mexico City, where Coronado died in 1554 after being found guilty of corruption and atrocities against the Indians.

A half century later, in 1598, Juan de Oñate established the colony of New Mexico for Spain. Married to a granddaughter of Cortés, Oñate led 400 settlers across the Rio Grande and sent scouting parties in search of treasure in Quivira (central Kansas). He quickly earned a reputation for brutality among the settlers and made a practice of raiding nearby villages. Residents of Acoma (a pueblo located high atop a mesa in what is now western New Mexico) fought back, killing 11 Spaniards, including one of Oñate's nephews. The furious conquistador laid siege to the sheer-walled mesa and burned the pueblo. Hundreds of Puebloans were killed, children were taken from their parents, and many villagers were sold into slavery. Only a few adult males survived, and Oñate ordered that the right foot of each be cut off. (Feelings are still sore: A modern statue of Oñate erected near Santa Fe had its foot sawed off in 1998 during the quadricentennial festivities marking the anniversary of the colonists' arrival.) In 1601 Oñate returned from an unsuccessful treasure hunt to find his colony mostly deserted. A further quest to the Colorado River and the Gulf of California were also failures. He was recalled to Mexico City in 1606, and tried and convicted for cruelty to both Indians and colonists. Though banished

from New Mexico, he was later cleared of all charges. He died in Spain and is often referred to as "the last conquistador."

SPANISH NEW MEXICO

These early expeditions soured relations between Europeans and native tribes for centuries. The Spanish gradually assumed control over much of the Southwest in the 18th century from their capital city of La Villa Real de la Santa Fe de San Francisco de Asis (today known simply as Santa Fe), founded in 1610. Subsistence agriculture in river valleys, trade with Mexico, and the raising of sheep and horses formed the basis of the economy, despite regular attacks by Apache, Comanche, and Navajo warriors. The effects of missionaries varied: While some served as intermediaries, speaking out for Native Americans' rights in the face of European settlement, others did their best to supplant indigenous cultural traditions with Christianity and suppress all things native.

By the late 17th century, things had reached a head. Continued persecution, punishment, and executions for "witchcraft" and "idolatry" had pushed native tribes to the edge. Abortive revolts in the Zuni, Hopi, and Rio Grande Pueblos served as prelude to a massive uprising in 1680 known as the **Pueblo Revolt.** Led by a Tewa medicine man named Popé, the insurrection was organized by runners carrying knotted strings encoding the fateful date. On August 10 some 17,000 Puebloans, including 6,000 warriors in battle paint, rose against 3,000 Spanish colonists. The furious tribes burned churches and holy icons, threw friars from cliffs, and massacred entire communities as the Spanish survivors retreated to Santa Fe. After a six-day siege, a ragged column was allowed to march south down the Rio Grande valley, leaving some 400 dead amid the ruins. It remains one of the most successful uprisings in the history of the Americas.

Even as they retreated, however, the Spanish were already planning their return, and by 1700 they had reconquered much of the Southwest, extending their New World empire from Panama to California and Santa Fe.

Albuquerque was founded in 1706, and during the 1700s the Spanish population of New Mexico increased to 25,000—many times the size of the Texas and California colonies. Priests once again visited tribes to try and convert them to Christianity, but these efforts met with mixed success. They did discover more about the geography of the region, however, particularly during the **Dominguez-Escalante Expedition** led by Fathers Francisco Atanasio Domínguez and Silvestre Vélez de Escalante. In 1776, as a new nation was declaring its independence on the other side of the continent, 14 men set out to find a northern route between the missions of Santa Fe and Monterey, California.

They made their way through western Colorado, crossing the Green River and going as far north as what is now Cedar City, Utah, before heading west, becoming the first Europeans to venture into Nevada's Great Basin Desert. Bludgeoned by blizzards and starvation, they survived the kindness of groups of Utes and Paiutes before drawing lots to see if they should press on or turn back. The result—turn back—probably saved their lives. The fathers crossed northern Arizona along the Vermilion Cliffs and the Paria River before fording the Colorado River in Glen Canyon, at a spot known as the Crossing of the Fathers (now under the waters of Lake Powell's Padre Bay). In six months and 2,000 miles, they had failed in their goal but added much to European knowledge of the intermountain West.

The colony of New Mexico continued to limp along, far from the resources and attention of Mexico City, the center of Spanish authority in the New World. Spain's colonies relied heavily on slave labor, pitting tribe against tribe and involving Spanish, Mexican, American, and Native American traders. The opening of the **Old Spanish Trail** in the early 19th century allowed the transport of livestock and slaves from Santa Fe to central Utah and, eventually, Los Angeles. Larger tribes that had adopted horses became slave procurers, and small tribes like the Paiutes were frequent targets. Canyon del Muerto in Canyon de Chelly

was named after a slave raid that left hundreds of Navajo women and children dead in 1805. Though slave trading was banned in California and New Mexico in the early 1800s, the lucrative practice continued into the 1850s.

UNITED STATES EXPANSION

Taking advantage of the Spanish colony's relative weakness, explorers, surveyors, and adventurers pushed west from the young United States. Zebulon Pike, John Fremont, and John Gunnison all led parties exploring the intermountain West. A vast territory had been added to the country's borders by the 1803 Louisiana Purchase, and in 1821 the Republic of Mexico's independence from Spain transferred much of the Southwest to new ownership. Anglo settlers continued to trickle in, including Mormons led by Brigham Young, whose wagons entered the Great Salt Lake valley in 1847. Fleeing religious persecution, the Latter-Day Saints busily set about establishing a highly regulated, self-sufficient colony that stretched from the Sierra Nevada to the Rockies and from Oregon to Arizona. Colonists were organized by skill and leadership and sent to settle the farthest corners of the territory to strengthen the church's hold on the land. The unforgiving land made settlement a grueling experience, wrote Wallace Stegner in *Mormon Country:*

> Its destiny was plain on its face, its contempt of man and his history and his theological immortality, his Millennium, his Heaven on Earth, was monumentally obvious. Its distances were terrifying, its cloudbursts catastrophic, its beauty flamboyant and bizarre and allied with death.

In 1846 Brigadier General Stephen Watts Kearny arrived in Santa Fe to proclaim the beginning of American dominion over the Southwest. The **Mexican-American War** (1846–1848) was sparked by unresolved border issues left by the U.S. annexation of the Republic of Texas in 1845. It ended with the **Treaty of Guadalupe Hidalgo,** which transferred the northern half of Mexico—what is today most of California, Nevada, Arizona, New Mexico, and Utah—to American hands. The $10 million **Gadsden Purchase** in 1853 shifted another 30,000 square miles of southern Arizona and New Mexico from Mexico to the United States. The United States now had a Southwest, but by the end of the 19th century, only a relative handful of explorers, trappers, soldiers, miners, and missionaries had ventured onto the Colorado Plateau. The government began to build army posts to protect immigrants, miners, and other settlers from Native Americans. The frontier territories were dominated by cabals that made fortunes off army contracts and the newly laid railroads, while mostly ignoring the needs of native groups.

Thanks to its Mormon settlers, Utah had a head start on the other territories. By 1860 more than 150 communities, with a total of 40,000 inhabitants, had taken root. The desert bloomed with crops grown using ingenious irrigation projects, despite raids by local tribes. The Mormons' autonomy (and their practice of polygamy) rankled the federal government, and in 1857 President James Buchanan declared Utah in rebellion of the U.S. government and sent 2,500 soldiers to the territory to replace Young as governor. Mormon leaders saw this as more religious persecution, declared martial law, and got ready to defend themselves. Young eventually relented and handed over the title of governor to Alfred Cumming, and the **Mormon Rebellion** ended without battle.

RAILROADS AND STATEHOOD

The American Civil War had relatively little impact on the Four Corners, but it was followed by an event of major proportion: the completion of the **transcontinental railroad.** On May 10, 1869, a symbolic golden spike was driven at Promontory, Utah, and the linking of rail lines to both coasts officially closed the American frontier. This had the immediate impact of bringing in immigrants and allowing the transport of products such as timber, minerals, and livestock across huge distances. Where the rail lines went, so did life. Cities, often named after railroad engineers, sprang

up almost overnight along the tracks, bringing jobs and radically altering lives in long-isolated towns and settlements. The Atchison, Topeka, and Santa Fe Railway from St. Louis reached Albuquerque in 1880, northern Arizona in 1883, and Los Angeles in 1885—the same year the Northern Pacific Railway reached Seattle. In 1880 the Southern Pacific Railroad was completed in Tucson, connecting California with New Orleans.

The arrival of the Iron Horse, along with the advent of barbed wire in the 1870s, signaled the end of the traditional lifeways of more nomadic native tribes, who found themselves being crowded from their homelands by Anglo miners, ranchers, and other settlers. Conflict was inevitable, but by sheer force of numbers and technology, Americans rolled over the West and its indigenous cultures in a steady, unstoppable tide.

In 1863 the famous frontiersman and Civil War veteran Kit Carson was ordered to end the problem of Navajo raids once and for all. Once considered a good friend by native groups, Carson began a brutal military campaign that ended with a futile last stand by the Navajo in the Canyon de Chelly. Some 8,000 men, women, and children were then marched 300 miles to Bosque Redondo (later called Fort Sumner), on the Pecos River in eastern New Mexico. Many did not survive the infamous **Long Walk,** and many of those who made it may have wished they hadn't. The poorly planned site was called a reservation but was more of a gulag. Sicknesses and disease compounded a meager wood supply, and worms destroyed the corn crops. Four years of misery ended when Navajo leader Barboncito negotiated the return of his people to their ancestral lands in Arizona and New Mexico in 1868. In return, the Navajo agreed never to raise arms against the United States or her citizens and to send their children to American schools.

The reservation was later expanded to its current boundaries, and in 1882 4,000 square miles out of the center of the Navajo Reservation was set aside for the Hopi tribe. (Land disputes between the two tribes continue to this day.) The Apache were forced onto reservations in the 1880s, despite fierce resistance from bands led by chiefs such as Mangas Coloradas, Cochise, and Victorio. Most famously, the visionary Geronimo and a small band of Chiracahua Apaches eluded 5,000 armed soldiers (a quarter of the U.S. Army) until their surrender in 1886.

The "Wild" West

The last decades of the 1800s encompassed a mythic intersection of time and place, images of which have spread around the world. The real Wild West bore little resemblance to the operatic, fresh-scrubbed version of dime novels and the silver screen. Lawmen like the legendary Pat Garrett and Wyatt Earp were as tough as nails but few and far between, and lawlessness most often took the form of cattle rustling and shady land dealings. Alcohol, prostitution, and gambling dulled the growing pains of a frontier that was no longer really a frontier but in many ways felt like one into the early 1900s. The homestead act of 1862 promised 160 acres to anyone who could live on the land for five years and make improvements. Homesteaders, including many Mormons, eked out a living by farming along streams and rivers. Ranchers grazed thousands of sheep, cows, and horses on the seemingly endless acres of the Colorado Plateau, even though much of it offered substandard forage, moving their herds from the lowlands to the mountains as the seasons shifted. Much of the rural economy centered on trading posts, which served as combination bank, store, and social club.

Powell's Expeditions

The frontier may have closed with the coming of the railroads, but the age of exploration was not yet over. Much of the Four Corners was still terra incognita, the last blank spot on the map of the continental United States. To remedy this, the professor and one-armed Civil War hero **Major John Wesley Powell** led two survey trips down the Colorado River through the Grand Canyon in 1869 and 1871. Braving terrifying rapids in sluggish wooden boats,

Powell's expeditions had little idea what they were getting into. Despite many hardships and dangers, they managed to collect specimens, take photographs, and complete a topographic map of the previously unknown Grand Canyon region. They had the honor of naming the last river (the Escalante) and mountain range (the Henrys) to be added to the map of the United States. Powell wrote his classic knuckle-biter *Exploration of the Colorado River of the West and Its Tributaries* about the experience and went on to direct the U.S. Geological Survey, plead for justice for native tribes as special commissioner to the Native Americans in Utah and Nevada, and argue futilely for the wise use of the West's scant water.

Colorado achieved statehood in 1876, followed by Utah in 1896. Mormon settlers had already applied to join the Union numerous times and were forced to discontinue polygamy and the church's political activities before they were finally admitted.

INTO THE 20TH CENTURY

In 1912 New Mexico and Arizona became the 47th and 48th states, respectively. Both remained very undeveloped—stagecoaches still carried passengers and mules delivered mail to isolated settlements. But the region's stark beauty was starting to gain national attention, thanks to promotion efforts by railroads hoping to increase passenger traffic. This was beginning of the serious Southwest **tourism industry.** Instrumental in opening the region were the restaurants and lodges operated by the **Fred Harvey Company** along the Atchison, Topeka, and Santa Fe Railway. With the help of pioneering architect Mary Colter, the Fred Harvey Company and the railway erected landmark buildings at the South Rim of the Grand Canyon, as well as places like Winslow's La Posada, to cater to the moneyed crowd who came by train for the views, the service, and the Harvey Girls, a famously smart and pretty bunch of waitresses. Not to be outdone, the Union Pacific promoted its Grand Circle Tour, building lodges in Zion, Bryce, and the North Rim of the Grand Canyon, often engaging the services of "the father of parkitecture," Gilbert Stanley Underwood.

With the influx of tourists, retirees, "lungers," and winter residents (dubbed "snowbirds") came the construction of motor courts and "dude ranches" to house them. The Great Depression brought more emigration, along with the relief programs of the New Deal. Artists and writers were employed by the Works Progress Administration to sing the praises of this grubby but gorgeous corner of the country in guidebooks and national park posters, and infrastructure in many parks enjoyed the fruits of cheap, eager labor. Many emigrants moved to California in search of work, traveling the new Route 66, the Mother Road from Chicago to Los Angeles, which ran through Albuquerque and Flagstaff.

Though Native Americans became U.S. citizens with the passage of the Indian Citizenship Act in 1924, relations with native tribes of the reservations remained tense. Things weren't helped by the government's plan of livestock reduction among Navajo ranchers and herders, implemented in the 1930s out of concerns over soil erosion and overgrazing. Thousands of sheep, goats, and horses were slaughtered in front of their horrified owners, who considered them to be almost members of the family. This cemented a long legacy of distrust of the federal government that still lingers.

The Hollywood Version

By the middle of the 20th century, the legend of the Old West was firmly entrenched in the national consciousness, partly as a result of image-crafting by the railroads but also by the **Western movies** Hollywood churned out at an increasing rate. With roots in the radio dramas of the 1930s and 1940s, early oaters often involved singing by the likes of Gene Autry and Roy Rogers. It was the epic films of director John Ford, however, that defined the genre for decades to come. Larger-than-life characters played by actors like John Wayne were shown in clear-cut struggles against evil, set as often as not amidst the sweeping panorama of Monument Valley. Ford and Wayne collaborated on the classics *Stagecoach* (1939), *Rio Grande* (1950), *The Searchers* (1956), and *How the West Was Won* (1962). *Cheyenne Autumn* (1964) was Ford's final tribute to the tribes he had often depicted in a less than positive light. (In some of the films, Navajo actors apparently worked some local humor into their dialogue, which had reservation audiences snickering when they were first shown.)

Fruits of the Land

The pace of change quickened during World War II, when many rural young men—Anglo, Native American, and Hispanic alike—were drafted into the military or found jobs with the government. During the war, several Navajos served as Code Talkers for the Marines in the Pacific, helping ensure a U.S. victory. By the middle of the 20th century, the Colorado Plateau's **resource-based economy** was firmly entrenched, dependent on the extraction and/or processing of natural products such as lumber, minerals, gas, oil, and grass (through grazing). Those activities that required water or power, including agriculture, grazing, and mining, were supported by major public works projects that began with the 1902 Reclamation Act and led to the construction of Roosevelt Dam (1911), Hoover Dam (1936), and Glen Canyon Dam (1966). Much of this region would still be barren desert without the federal government's concerted effort to transform it into a tamed, productive landscape—an important point to remember in light of frequent cries for local autonomy and freedom from federal tyranny. Crops such as cotton, grain, fruit, and alfalfa helped support the rural economies, along with cattle and sheep ranching.

Mining had been important in the Southwest for centuries, particularly in Arizona, where copper reserves were exposed in massive open-pit excavations. The discovery of natural gas and petroleum in Texas and Oklahoma in the early 1900s was only the beginning. Oil was discovered on the Navajo Reservation in 1922, suspicions about coal beneath Black Mesa were proved true, and major oil and natural-gas fields were discovered in the San Juan Basin of northwestern New Mexico and southwestern Colorado in the 1940s. In the 1950s the Cold War brought a sharp demand for **uranium,** a key ingredient in the atomic bomb. Prospectors armed with Geiger counters combed the Colorado Plateau in army-surplus jeeps, opening new roads and occasionally even striking it rich. By 1955 about 800 uranium mines were spread across the plateau, but when the Atomic Energy Commission stopped buying uranium ore in 1970, the market collapsed.

RECENT HISTORY

Rachel Carson's book *Silent Spring,* published in 1962, is often credited with sparking the modern **environmental movement.** Its account of the effects of pesticides on birds struck a nerve with readers around the world and provided the motivation for the passage of a number of environmental laws in the United States, including the Wilderness Act (1964); the National Environmental Policy Act (1969), which created the Environmental Protection Agency; and the Clean Air Act (1970). In 1966, three years after the gates of Glen Canyon Dam were closed, the Sierra Club fought the Bureau of Reclamation's plans to dam the Grand Canyon. In response to the bureau's claim that a dammed river would let tourists get closer to the canyon walls, the Sierra Club ran full-page ads in the *New York Times* and the *Washington Post* asking, "Should we flood the Sistine Chapel so tourists can get closer to the ceiling?" The bold move cost the group its tax-exempt status but boosted membership and helped defeat the plan three years later.

Published in 1968, Edward Abbey's *Desert Solitaire* would do for the Southwest deserts what *Silent Spring* did for birds and forests. The pithy account of two seasons as a ranger

in Arches, liberally laced with calls to protect the Four Corners' natural wonders from the forces of development and "industrial tourism," has become an environmental classic.

Winds of Change

Today the resource economy is struggling, but even as "sustainability" becomes the new buzzword, old ways die hard. The long-term value of the coal deposits beneath Black Mesa on the Navajo and Hopi lands has been estimated as high as $100 billion, but the effects of draining a billion gallons per year from the underground aquifer to carry coal slurry to power plants is being hotly debated. Recent controversies over land use in the San Juan Basin have pitted oil and gas drillers against an unlikely alliance of environmentalists and sixth-generation ranchers. More than 10,000 head of cattle graze in the basin, and ranchers say that oil drilling has contaminated water and led to erosion and the death of livestock. Instead of turning local communities into ghost towns by cutting off access to minerals, the creation of new parks and monuments has brought a new economic boom: **tourism.**

Outdoor recreation is becoming the Four Corners' modern gold mine. Mountain bikers, hikers, river-runners, and families in vans and RVs have discovered the scenic and cultural wonders of the Colorado Plateau and support growing numbers of hotels, restaurants, tour companies, and other businesses. Retirees are drawn to the scenery and climate, particularly in Arizona. As populations rise, the already meager water supply is stretched even thinner.

To make things worse, the region has entered the throes of what may be the worst **drought** in centuries.

Native Cultures

Over a third of all Native Americans live in the Southwest, mostly in Arizona and New Mexico. The tribes you'll encounter in the Four Corners are the Navajo, the Hopi, and the Ute, but other Pueblo tribes, as well as the Apache and Paiute, have reservations nearby. The U.S. government and its citizens have always had a schizophrenic relationship with its native cultures, alternately idealizing and scorning them, while leaving mostly unaddressed the national legacy of guilt over the wholesale destruction during the Euroamerican settlement of the continent. Though the old ways are fading in the face of modern technological civilization, many tribal members strive to preserve traditional culture, arts, and ceremonies.

Some travelers may find a visit to a reservation like a bucket of cold water in the face, replacing hazy romantic notions or harsh stereotypes with the reality of high unemployment and alcohol abuse, low average income, and rough living conditions. Native American reservations may be disheartening places at first glance, but a visit can also be an incredibly enjoyable and enlightening experience, offering a glimpse into a way of life that has endured despite all the odds. Visiting the reservations, which are essentially sovereign nations inside the United States, can also be a humbling reminder of how vast the national experience is and how little we've learned of our own country. Ann Axtell Morris, wife of archaeologist Earl Morris (who worked at Aztec, Canyon de Chelly, and other sites) put it thus: "European historians have a way of taking for granted that America was nothing but a quiescent lump of land until the tracks of the Columbian boots in 1492 stamped CIVILIZATION on its face."

When the Mayflower landed in 1620, thousands of years of cultural traditions had already enriched the Southwest. But it wasn't until the 20th century that the country's rich native prehistory gained respect and protection. In 1906 the Antiquities Act established fines for removing or damaging artifacts and empowered U.S. presidents to set aside lands with features of scientific or historic significance, paving the way for the first national monument at Devils Tower, Wyoming, followed by Arizona's Petrified Forest and Grand Canyon. The 1979 **Archaeological Resources Protection Act** (ARPA) acknowledged that archaeological resources on public lands and Indian lands are "an irreplaceable part of the Nation's heritage," and made it a serious crime to remove or destroy them, with stiff penalties for violators. The **Native American Graves Protection and Repatriation Act** (NAGPRA) of 1990 made it unlawful to disturb or dig up funerary objects and human remains on federal, tribal, or private land. If a tribal affiliation can be determined, the tribe must be given the opportunity to claim the remains. Thanks to this law and a philosophical shift in the practice of archaeology, remains and objects in museums are slowly being returned to the care of their parent tribes, and large-scale excavations are being replaced by smaller projects and less invasive techniques.

In May 2004 a **Resolution of Apology to the Native American Peoples** was introduced in the U.S. Congress, which, among other things, "commends and honors the Native Peoples for the thousands of years that they have stewarded and protected this land" and "apologizes on behalf of the people of the United States to all Native Peoples for the many instances of violence, maltreatment, and neglect inflicted on Native Peoples by citizens of the United States." President Barack Obama signed the resolution into law in December 2009.

NAVAJO
Demography

The Diné, as the Navajo call themselves, are the second-largest tribe in the United States after the Cherokee, with more than 300,000 members. About 165,000 of these live on the country's largest reservation, which covers 25,000 square miles—about a quarter of the state of Arizona and small slivers of New Mexico and Utah. This

NAVAJO CODE TALKERS

During World War II, the obscurity of the Navajo language helped win the battle for the Pacific. The idea came from engineer and World War I veteran Philip Johnston, who had grown up on the Navajo Reservation as the son of a Protestant missionary. Navajo, an extremely complex language with dialect and nuance, was at the time still unwritten. Johnston knew that only a few dozen people outside the reservation spoke the tribe's language and figured it would make an excellent code. He set up a demonstration to convince the Marine Corps, and 30 tribe members were soon recruited as Code Talkers.

Native American languages, including Choctaw, had been used as codes in World War I, but this pilot program took things a step further. Johnston had the idea to use ordinary Navajo words for military terms to add an extra layer of encoding. *Cha* ("beaver") meant "minesweeper," *gini* ("chicken hawk") became "dive-bomber," and *besh-lo* ("iron fish") meant "submarine." More than 400 words were encoded, and multiple Navajo words were assigned to 12 commonly used letters. For example, *be-la-sana* ("apple") and *tse-nil* ("axe") both stood for A. The Code Talkers were drilled repeatedly. There was no room for error; transmissions had to be fast and accurate, and a single mistake could cost lives. Twenty-seven Code Talkers, many of whom had never been off the reservation, were sent to Guadalcanal, and two stayed behind to train others. (One dropped out of training.)

The Code Talkers quickly proved their value. From 1942 to 1945 Navajo soldiers participated in every Marine assault in the Pacific, including Guadalcanal, Peleliu, Tarawa, and Iwo Jima. They transmitted from trenches, foxholes, and jungle redoubts, reporting on battlefield conditions and calling in air support and supplies. The Native Americans were often mistaken for Japanese soldiers and even captured by their fellow Marines in a few cases. Each was given a bodyguard to keep him safe and to prevent the code, which was not written down on the battlefield, from falling into enemy hands. (This arrangement was the basis for the 2002 movie *Windtalkers*.) During the first two days of the battle for Iwo Jima, six Code Talkers worked around the clock to deliver more than 800 messages without error.

The Japanese, experts at breaking codes, were mystified. Even a Navajo soldier captured at Bataan was bewildered by the double code of military jargon, which he termed "crazy Navajo." The code that helped ensure that victory in the Pacific was never broken, and the Code Talkers have only recently been getting the recognition they deserve. One of the first displays on the Code Talkers was at the Burger King in Kayenta, Arizona. (Owner Richard Mike's father, King Mike, was a Code Talker in the Marines' Sixth Division.) In recent years many communities throughout the Four Corners have added memorials or exhibits honoring the Code Talkers, whose story can finally be told.

NAVAJO CODE WORDS

Officers

brigadier general: *so-a-la-ih* ("one star")
colonel: *atsah-besh-le-gai* ("silver eagle")
commanding general: *bih-keh-he* ("war chief")
major general: *so-na-kih* ("two star")

Places

Alaska: *beh-hga* ("with winter")
America: *ne-he-mah* ("our mother")
Australia: *cha-yes-desi* ("rolled hat")
Britain: *toh-ta* ("between waters")
Germany: *besh-be-cha-he* ("iron hat")
India: *ah-le-gai* ("white clothes")
Russia: *sila-gol-chi-ih* ("red army")
Spain: *deba-de-nih* ("sheep pain")

Airplanes

bomber plane: *jay-sho* ("buzzard")
fighter plane: *da-he-tih-hi* ("hummingbird")
torpedo plane: *tas-chizzie* ("swallow")

Ships

aircraft carrier: *tsidi-moffa-ye-hi* ("bird carrier")
battleship: *lo-tso* ("whale")
cruiser: *lo-tso-yazzie* ("small whale")
destroyer: *ca-lo* ("shark")

traditional territory is called Dinetah, meaning "among the People," or Diné Bikeyah, "the land between the sacred mountains," referring to the tribe's traditional territorial boundaries: to the north is Sisnaajinii (Blanca Peak) near Alamosa, Colorado, representing dawn; Tsoodzil (Mt. Taylor) rises near Grants, New Mexico, and symbolizes the daytime sky; Dook'o'oosłííd (the San Francisco Peaks) near Flagstaff signify twilight; and Dibé Nitsaa (Mt. Hesperus) near Durango represents night.

Despite significant natural resources, including massive reserves of coal, natural gas, and oil, the Big Rez is still a very poor place. According to the 2000 census, approximately 40 percent of its residents lived below the poverty line, with one-quarter unemployed and over 30 percent without indoor plumbing. Many tribal members support themselves the way their forebears did, by farming and raising livestock such as goats, sheep, and horses. Tourism and the sale of traditional crafts, including weaving, pottery, and silverwork—mostly to *bilagaana* (Anglos)—are also important moneymakers.

In 1988 Congress approved the Indian Gaming Regulatory Act, and tribes throughout the United States began building casinos to generate much-needed income. But for years afterward, Navajos voted against gambling on the reservation, in part because it is seen as a sickness in traditional teachings. The 2,800-member To'hajiilee band of Navajo (who have their own reservation in New Mexico) decided to go their own way, making plans to build a casino near Albuquerque. Then in 2004 Navajo voters approved a gaming referendum, and in 2009 Fire Rock Casino opened a few miles east of Gallup, New Mexico. A year later Flowing Water Casino opened near Farmington, and Northern Edge, north of Farmington, opened in 2012. Twin Arrows, near Winslow, Arizona, is scheduled to open in August 2013.

Organization

The Navajo Nation is a sovereign entity within the United States, with its own government and courts. Navajo land is held in trust by the federal government, which under the original treaties assumed responsibility for the tribe members' health and welfare. The Navajo Nation is divided into about 110 political divisions called chapters. Elected leaders address local community problems and select delegates for the Tribal Council, based in Window Rock. The Navajo Police have jurisdiction over the reservation, but they share duties with the state and federal law enforcement agencies as well, including the FBI and the Bureau of Indian Affairs (BIA). The BIA still has some administrative and maintenance duties on the reservation, but these are gradually being turned over to the tribe.

Language

Navajos speak an Athapascan language similar to that of the Apaches, their cultural cousins who arrived with them from the north sometime after A.D. 1300. Navajo is a colorful, descriptive language, full of subtle nuance and puns, and it incorporates words from other languages, such as *beeso* for "money," from the Spanish *peso*. Because Navajo is difficult to learn well, it was perfect for a World War II code that remained unbroken throughout the Pacific theater. (It is ironic that mere decades after the war, Navajo children were being punished for speaking their own language in government-run boarding schools, when that very same language helped the United States gain victory.)

Arts

Experts at adapting useful skills from other cultures, Navajos learned weaving from their Pueblo neighbors and silversmithing from Mexican artisans during the Spanish occupation of the Southwest. Handwoven wool rugs have reached an exquisite level of artistry, although fewer and fewer young women are learning the skills and patience to weave like their grandmothers. Navajo silverwork is equally intricate. Other crafts include basketry, pottery, sandpainting, folk art, and kachina carvings based on the Hopi tradition.

Traditional Culture

Traditional Navajo beliefs revolve around the

A LEGENDARY RUNNER

Louis Tewanima (ca. 1880-1969), one of the United States' greatest distance runners, grew up chasing jackrabbits on the Hopi Reservation. It's said that he would run 120 miles to Winslow and back just to see the trains pass. He met the legendary Native American athlete Jim Thorpe at an Indian school in Pennsylvania, where Tewanima once had to run 18 miles to a race after missing the train. (He arrived in time and won the two-mile event.) He went on to represent the United States at the 1908 Olympic Games in London, where he finished ninth in the marathon. At the 1912 Olympics in Stockholm, Tewanima won a silver medal in the first men's 10,000-meter event, setting an American record that stood for 52 years before it was broken by Billy Mills, of Lakota descent.

Tewanima won national races in New Orleans and New York in 1920. At distances between 10 and 20 miles, he was considered the world's fastest man. The "Happy Hopi from Shungopavi" returned to his village, where he died in a fall from a cliff on his way home from a religious ceremony. Every year around Labor Day, the village of Shungopavi and Tewanima's descendants host a footrace (www.tewanima-footrace.org) in his memory.

---

idea that the proper state of the universe is one of order, balance, and happiness called *hózhó,* often translated as beauty or harmony. When hózhó is present, all is well. When it is lost through violence or the breaking of cultural taboos, things swing out of kilter. Particularly stringent rules surround incest and death—a spiritual contagion called *chindi* following the loss of a life can pollute a dwelling if it happens indoors. Disharmony must be put right through rituals called "sings," which have been handed down through generations. Days of chanting, drumming, and ceremonial purification are supervised by a medicine man. Sings include the Blessing Way and the Enemy Way for cleansing after battle, and communal dances with names such as When the Thunder Sleeps are also held.

Often the setting is inside a traditional log hogan, which means "home" in Navajo. These eight-sided, one-room structures have a packed clay floor and a domed roof of mud or sod pierced by a smoke hole. The doorway faces east to greet the rising sun. Hogans are slowly being replaced by modern buildings with tar paper and shingle roofs or plywood walls, but you'll still see traditional hogans out in the countryside, and many public buildings, such as the council chambers in Window Rock, are based on hogan design.

Navajo mythology has a rich cast of characters, including Turquoise Boy, Talking God, Spider Woman, and Water Monster. Origin stories recount a progression through three underworlds into this, the Fourth or Glittering World. Of the Navajo Holy People, one of the most important is Changing Woman *(Asdzaan Nadleehe),* considered the tribe's spiritual mother. Impregnated by the sun, she bore twin sons called Monster Slayer *(Naaee' Neezghani)* and Born for Water *(Tobdjishchini).* The Hero Twins killed a series of monsters to make the earth safe for human beings. Several who pleaded for their lives, including Sleepiness, Hunger, Old Age, and Poverty, were spared as a lesson to humanity.

The Navajos follow a matrilineal clan system, in which kinship is extremely important. There are more than 140 clans today, with names like Bitter Water Clan and the Corn People. Traditional greetings include a recitation of one's mother's ("born-to") and father's ("born-for") clans, and marriages must be to someone outside one's clan. A complex chain of clan relationships can make avoiding this form of "incest" very difficult.

HOPI
Demography
The westernmost group of Pueblo Indians,

once called the Moqui or Moki (a term generally considered derogatory today), occupy a dozen villages on three mesas in the middle of the Navajo Reservation. Most of the approximately 10,000 enrolled tribe members live on the 1.6 million–acre Hopi Reservation. It was created in 1882 with little thought given to the traditional boundaries of the Navajo and Hopi tribes, and subsequent legal rulings have only complicated things. On the Hopi Reservation, the average annual income is $17,500, unemployment is around 25 percent, and more than half of tribe members live below the poverty line. The Hopis live mostly on tourism, mineral leases, tribal enterprises, and farm products such as beans, corn, squash, melons, fruit, and wheat. They also herd cows and sheep. The tribe has repeatedly rejected gambling as an economic opportunity. Instead, the Hopi Economic Development Corporation has focused on adding a variety of tourist-based services in order to fund improvements. While the tribe's traditional culture has had to struggle to survive, core values—and the lofty villages—endure.

Organization

Hopi villages are largely autonomous but are loosely united under the Hopi Tribal Council. The majority rule incorporated by the 1936 Hopi constitution conflicts with the tribe's traditional ways of making decisions, which rely more on building consensus. Like the Navajo Nation, the Hopi tribal government maintains relationships with the federal government, which acts as a trustee for the tribe, as well as with surrounding state and local agencies. Three villages have adopted Western-style governments and others have maintained the traditional Hopi form of government to different degrees. (Hotevilla is considered to be the most traditional.) A chief *(kikmongwi)* oversees each village's social and ceremonial life, while still bowing to community consensus.

Language

The Hopis speak a Uto-Aztecan language, part of a linguistic family that ranges from California to Mexico. Though the Rio Grande pueblos and the Zunis share cultural traits with the Hopi villages, they do not share the same language.

Arts

The most famed Hopi crafts are the carved wooden figurines representing the kachina spirits who reside in the San Francisco Peaks near Flagstaff. Tribe members also make beautiful silver jewelry using an overlay technique, as well as pottery, baskets, and paintings.

Traditional Culture

Hopis live according to the translation of their name, *Hopitu,* which means "peaceful people." Their worldview is based on humility, respect, cooperation, and caring for the earth. This last part is particularly important, since, as farmers without a permanent water supply, they have had to learn dry-farming techniques that take extraordinary care and diligence. In this unforgiving land, it is crucial that the tribe follow the Hopi Way—to ensure not only their own survival but also the well-being of everyone on earth.

The Hopis have an origin story similar in some respects to the Navajos', though details of the story vary from clan to clan. The Bear Clan, it is said, led the Hopi from a *sipapu* (a small opening in the earth) into this, the Fourth World, where they wandered widely before settling in the Tuuwanasave, or "earth center." Here the Hopi people follow the instructions of Maa'sau, the Guardian of the Fourth World, which tell them how to live in harmony and balance with their surroundings. Only a careful balance keeps the world from disaster.

Help is available in the form of the kachinas *(katsinas),* benevolent spirit beings who live in the San Francisco Mountains and appear to the tribe between the winter solstice and mid-July. Hundreds of kachinas serve as messengers between the Hopi people and the spiritual realm by controlling natural forces such as rain and meting out punishment for infringements of Hopi law. The spirits can be personified by men in ceremonies or represented as *tihu* or *tithu* ("dolls" being the closest English translation). Kachina dolls originally were used to teach children, but today most are created for sale. Some kachinas are frightening figures associated with discipline, others are benevolent beings who bring gifts or help crops, while still others serve as comic relief, including the Navajo Clown (Tasavu), who pokes fun at the neighboring tribe.

Hopi society is organized by matrilineal clans, and when a couple marries, the man moves to the woman's home and village. A sophisticated calendar is followed closely, with spiritual leaders calculating ceremonial dates by the position of the sun. As in the New Mexico pueblos, Hopi villages have underground kivas that men's religious societies use for meditation and prayer. Important ceremonies include Soyal (the celebration of the winter solstice) and Niman (the Home Dance), when the katsina spirits return to the San Francisco Peaks. Once all Hopi ceremonies were open to nonmembers, but so many visitors broke the rules against recording that many dances have been

© KATHLEEN BRYANT

Ladders provide access to subterranean kivas in Hopi villages.

closed, including the Snake Dance held every other year in late August. The Snake Dance encompassed nine days of ceremonies in the kivas of the Snake and Antelope clans, concluding when dancers with live snakes in their mouths entered the village plazas.

ZUNI PUEBLO

In 1539 the ancestral Zuni villages were first visited by Europeans, who returned to New Spain with tales about cities of gold. After the Pueblo Revolt of 1680, the Zunis, fearful of reprisals from the Spanish, left their villages and took refuge on Dowa Yalanne (Corn Mountain). After making peace with the returning colonists, the Zunis established a single new pueblo, called Halona Idiwan'a, where many of the reservation's 12,000 members live today. Surrounding Halona (also called the Middle Village) are modern homes and pretty, tree-lined lanes. The tribe is governed by an elected governor, lieutenant governor, and six-member tribal council.

The Zuni reservation occupies 450,000 acres, and many Zunis are farmers or ranchers. The high mesas around the pueblo are pine-covered, and timber is another tribal enterprise. Tourism is a major source of income, and a large percentage of Zunis are artisans.

Though Zunis have adopted contemporary houses and lifestyles, they continue to perform traditional ceremonies. Many ceremonies are closed to outsiders, but others are open by invitation, including some parts of the year's most important shalako ceremonies, held after harvest and before winter solstice. Like the Hopi kachinas, the Zuni shalakos act as intermediaries between the spirit world and humans. The word *shalako* is associated with rain, and shalakos are depicted as towering masked beings.

Zuni pueblo is the southernmost of New Mexico's 19 pueblos. Perhaps because of its greater distance from Santa Fe, the seat of the former Spanish colony, Zuni traditions have been less influenced by Catholicism than those of the Rio Grande Pueblos. (Zuni's mission, destroyed in the 1680 Pueblo Revolt, was eventually reestablished by Spanish priests in 1699.)

Here, as in many pueblos, traditional religion went underground, both in the literal (kiva societies) and in the metaphoric sense. Pottery and jewelry featured designs that may have appeared to Spanish priests to be depictions of the cross, but Zunis recognized the dragonfly, the messenger who carries prayers to the spirit world. Corn, deer, frogs, and other nature symbols all have deeper meanings that tie in to Zuni history and stories.

Traditional design elements are still used today on pottery or jewelry or carved as fetishes, which are perhaps the Zunis' most distinctive craft item. Over the centuries Zuni's adobe mission deteriorated, but in 1970, after the building's restoration, Alex Seowtewa began a gorgeously rendered mural, and today life-size Zuni kachinas dance above the stations of the cross.

UTE

The Ute tribe occupies three reservations, two of them in southwest Colorado and just over the border into New Mexico and Utah. The Utes were once a loose confederation of seven nomadic bands spread across Colorado, Arizona, New Mexico, Wyoming, and Utah, which was named after them. Ute means "land of the sun," and although it is known that they originally came from the north and west, when they arrived is still unclear. The Utes adopted horses from the Spanish and became respected hunters and feared raiders, going after buffalo on the eastern plains and settlers' livestock with equal ferocity. Utes speak a Shoshonean language similar to that of the Shoshones, Paiutes, and Comanches.

The Ute mythos centers on animal deities. In spring, bands would gather for the Bear Dance, which had its origins in a story of a bear who taught the song and dance steps to a young hunter. Spring was a time of reawakening for both man and beast, and after the four-day dance, participants would place plumes they had worn in a cedar tree, symbolically leaving their troubles behind. The Sundance, the most important social and religious ceremony, took place in summer. Participants underwent a four-day fast, called *tagu-wuni* ("standing thirsty"), while dancing inside a special lodge. (Both dances are still held today, but only the Bear Dance is open to the public.)

Two of the bands, the Mouache and the Capote, became the **Southern Ute Tribe** that now inhabits a 700,000-acre "checkerboard" reservation that includes federal land and individually owned homesteads or allotments. The tribe holds the title to over 300,000 acres and counts 1,400 members out of the reservation's total population of 7,900. Tribal headquarters are in Ignacio, Colorado.

The Weeminuche band is now called the **Ute Mountain Ute Tribe.** They occupy a 600,000-acre reservation bordering Mesa Verde National Park, with the anthropomorphic Sleeping Ute Mountain at its center. A population of about 2,000 lives mostly in Towaoc, with a smaller group living in White Mesa.

Both Four Corners Ute tribes are run by elected Tribal Councils and depend on income from agriculture, livestock, construction, forestry, mining, tourism, and casinos on both reservations. (The other four Ute bands became the Northern Ute tribe, which lives on the Uintah-Ouray Reservation near Fort Duchesne, Utah.)

ESSENTIALS

Getting There and Around

In a nutshell, the easiest way to explore the Four Corners is to fly to one of the nearest major airports, such as Salt Lake City or Las Vegas, rent a car, and drive wherever you want to go. It is possible to arrive and get around—somewhat—by bus, train, and local airline, but service is limited to a few cities and the distances involved and the remoteness of many of the region's attractions make a private vehicle the only practical way to travel here. (And in many cases, scenic roads, back roads, and even more remote "back ways" are attractions themselves.) A network of paved highways connects the major cities and points of interest, but this still leaves much of the Four Corners inaccessible to drivers without four-wheel-drive vehicles, or, in many cases, inaccessible to any vehicles, period.

BY AIR

The nearest **international airports** are in Albuquerque (ABQ; 140 miles from Gallup), Phoenix (PHX; 145 miles from Flagstaff), Denver (DEN; 335 miles from Durango), Salt Lake City (SLC; 182 miles from Green River, 235 miles from Moab), and Las Vegas (LAS; 250 miles from Flagstaff, 270 miles from Page). Each of these cities is a major travel gateway served by most major airlines, and all offer a full range of hotels, restaurants,

© KATHLEEN BRYANT

STATE FAST FACTS

ARIZONA

- Total Area (sq. mi.): 113,635 (6th)
- Percent Owned by Federal Government: 41.1% (6th)
- Nickname: Grand Canyon State
- Capital: Phoenix
- Population: 5,580,811
- Population Density (per sq. mi.): 56.3 (33rd)
- Income (per capita): $25,203

COLORADO

- Total Area (sq. mi.): 103,718 (8th)
- Percent Owned by Federal Government: 35.5% (8th)
- Nickname: Centennial State
- Capital: Denver
- Population: 5,029,196
- Population Density (per sq. mi.): 48.5 (37th)
- Income (per capita): $29,679

NEW MEXICO

- Total Area (sq. mi.): 121,356 (5th)
- Percent Owned by Federal Government: 29.4% (9th)
- Nickname: Land of Enchantment
- Capital: Santa Fe
- Population: 2,059,179
- Population Density (per sq. mi.): 17 (45th)
- Income (per capita): $22,461

UTAH

- Total Area (sq. mi.): 82,144 (13th)
- Percent Owned by Federal Government: 63.1% (3rd)
- Nickname: Beehive State
- Capital: Salt Lake City
- Population: 2,763,885
- Population Density (per sq. mi.): 33.6 (41st)
- Income (per capita): $22,684

and tourist-related services. There are smaller **local airports** in Moab (CNY), Cortez (CEZ), Grand Junction (GJT), Flagstaff (FLG), and Page (PGA), with limited service to each other and larger cities.

BY CAR

The Four Corners region is bounded by I-40 to the south, running between Albuquerque and California, and I-70 to the north, which travels from Denver to I-15 in the middle of Utah. I-15 runs from Salt Lake City southwest to St. George, Las Vegas, and beyond. Major travel arteries within the area include highways **U.S. 89** and **U.S. 89A**, which connect Flagstaff to Kanab, located about 75 miles southeast of I-15 at St. George. About 75 miles north of Flagstaff, U.S. 89 intersects **U.S. 160,** which runs northeast to the Four Corners monument, Cortez, and Durango.

From Gallup, **U.S. 491** leads north across the Navajo Reservation, joining briefly with U.S. 160 and eventually meeting U.S. 191 at Monticello. **U.S. 191** joins I-70 near Green River and runs south through Moab and the other towns of Southeast Utah before crossing the state line and the Navajo Reservation. It edges Canyon de Chelly and joins I-40 at Chambers. Other major routes—and out here that includes two-lane paved roads—are **SR 24** and **SR 95** across remote South-Central Utah and the spectacular **SR 12,** which winds across the northern border of the Grand Staircase–Escalante National Monument.

Car rental agencies can be found in the Four Corners' larger cities, including Moab, Durango, Flagstaff, Gallup, and Farmington. When renting a car, consider how far out into the backcountry you want to go. Four-wheel-drive vehicles, available from national

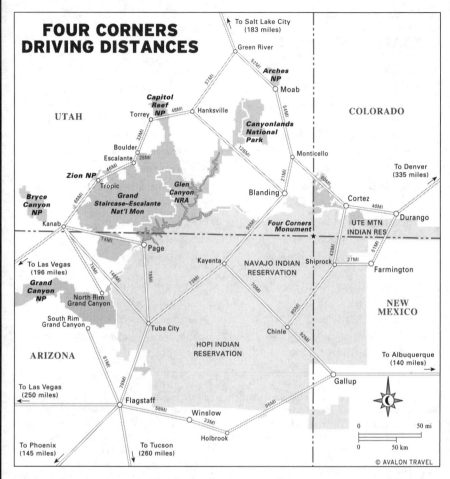

FOUR CORNERS DRIVING DISTANCES

To Salt Lake City (183 miles)

Green River

Arches NP

○ Moab

Capitol Reef NP 48MI ○ Hanksville

Torrey

UTAH

Canyonlands National Park

COLORADO

Boulder

Escalante 28MI

Zion NP

Tropic

Glen Canyon NRA

○ Monticello

To Denver (335 miles)

Bryce Canyon NP

Grand Staircase–Escalante Nat'l Mon

Blanding

Cortez 46MI

○ Durango

Kanab

○ Page

Four Corners Monument ★

UTE MTN INDIAN RES

To Las Vegas (196 miles)

Kayenta ○

NAVAJO INDIAN RESERVATION

Shiprock 27MI ○ Farmington

Grand Canyon NP

North Rim Grand Canyon

NEW MEXICO

South Rim Grand Canyon ○

Tuba City

Chinle ○

ARIZONA

HOPI INDIAN RESERVATION

To Albuquerque (140 miles)

To Las Vegas (250 miles)

○ Gallup

Flagstaff 58MI

Winslow 33MI

Holbrook

To Phoenix (145 miles)

To Tucson (260 miles)

0   50 mi

0   50 km

© AVALON TRAVEL

agencies and local jeep rental outfits, cost more. Increasingly, travelers who plan on sticking to pavement opt to rent a recreational vehicle (RV), which is like piloting your own mobile motel room. You can find developed campsites with water, electric, and sewer hookups for $25–60 per night, or just park on federal land and rough it, relatively speaking. **Cruise America** (800/671-8042, www.cruiseamerica.com) has RV offices in Flagstaff, Phoenix, Albuquerque, Salt Lake City, and Denver, with rentals starting at $50/day.

BY BUS

Bus service is relatively limited in these wide-open spaces. **Greyhound** (800/231-2222, www.greyhound.com) has regular service to cities along the interstates: Green River, Durango, Gallup, Farmington, Holbrook, Winslow, and Flagstaff. Contact them for a schedule and information on special discounts and passes. The Navajo Reservation is served by the **Navajo Transit System** (866/243-6260, www.navajo-transit.com), which sends buses along a dozen routes. Most are under $10 one-way.

A few companies offer bus tours of the Southwest that are very different from the typical Greyhound experience. Both **Adventure Bus** (888/737-5263, www.adventurebus.com) and **Green Tortoise Adventure Travel** (800/867-8647, www.greentortoise.com) have buses that double as rolling hostels. These trips usually include a food fund and communal cooking and concentrate on outdoor activities and national parks.

BY TRAIN

Amtrak (800/872-7245, www.amtrak.com) runs the luxury Southwest Chief line along the path, more or less, of old Route 66. On its way between Chicago to Los Angeles, the Chief stops in Gallup, Winslow, and Flagstaff daily in both directions. Traveling by train is more comfortable but less flexible than traveling than by bus. Fares vary depending on time of year, and a number of discounts are available; contact Amtrak for details.

Tips for Travelers

CULTURAL ISSUES

You'll encounter conservative values in the Four Corners, particularly in southern Utah and on the Native American reservations. In this mostly rural region, tradition is highly valued and flashy displays of wealth and liberal (read: California or East Coast) attitudes may be frowned upon. Gay travelers should avoid overt displays in public. This slower pace of life may be difficult for some visitors to get used to, but do your best—people here are overwhelmingly friendly and accepting. Polygamy still exists in a few pockets near the Utah–Arizona border, where residents may view visitors with distrust.

A visit to a reservation is really a visit to another country, with the expected concerns of cultural sensitivity and personal conduct. The poverty may be startling and the people fascinating, but try to avoid making a camera lens the first thing anyone sees of you. Photography or any other kind of recording is completely prohibited on the Hopi Reservation and allowed only in rare circumstances on the Navajo Nation. Native American culture is by tradition reserved and harmonious—the squeaky wheel gets ostracized, not greased—and older people are viewed with respect. Tribal members may seem aloof at first, and asking too many questions may be off-putting, but give them time to open up, and you won't be disappointed.

TRAVELERS WITH DISABILITIES

The Four Corners is a rough neighborhood, in the sense that many roads are unpaved, trails are steep and crooked, and many buildings are nonaccessible. National hotel chains require their facilities to be accessible, but B&Bs (often in old buildings) and restaurants are another story. Always call ahead and check. The National Park Service does a good job of making its facilities accessible to travelers with disabilities, including most visitors centers and at least a paved trail or two at every location. For more information, check the individual park descriptions on the National Park Service website (www.nps.gov), which list degrees of accessibility, and if you have any more questions, contact the park directly and ask to speak to the accessibility coordinator. The NPS Access Pass offers free lifetime entrance to visitors who are blind or permanently disabled, as well as a 50 percent discount on federal use fees.

For more information on disabled travel, contact **Mobility International USA** (541/343-1284, www.miusa.org) or the **Society for Accessible Travel & Hospitality** (212/447-7284, www.sath.org).

TRAVELING WITH CHILDREN

A trip to the Four Corners is one your kids will remember their entire lives, although it's up to you to make sure it's because of the sunrise over Monument Valley, not the hours spent

DRINKING LAWS

Though relaxed considerably in the past couple years, Utah's liquor laws are still some of the toughest in the states. Don't try to order a double, and if you look like you're under 35, expect your ID to be checked very carefully. Happy hours and drink specials aren't allowed, and restaurants must keep liquor out of sight of patrons. Nor can you order beer at a restaurant without ordering food. But take heart, because Utah makes some truly excellent microbrews that go well with just about anything, and there are two wineries with tasting rooms within minutes of Moab.

Outside of restaurants and bars, beer with a maximum alcohol content of 3.2 percent by weight is sold by grocery and convenience stores. For packaged "heavy" beer, liquor, or wine head for a Utah state liquor store (but not on Sundays, when they are closed).

It is illegal to possess, sell, or consume alcohol on the Navajo, Hopi, and Ute Mountain Ute Reservations. Liquor stores are plentiful in border towns like Gallup and Page, however, and bootlegging (selling alcohol inside reservation boundaries) is a serious problem. In Arizona the U.S. Attorney's office estimates that 99 percent of violent crimes referred to them by tribes are alcohol related. Tribal leaders and community groups are vigilant about eliminating alcohol abuse on the reservation. For that reason, and a host of others, don't even consider bringing alcohol to a reservation event.

driving across the desert looking for a bathroom. To start with, most of this place is like one big rocky jungle gym. Nothing brings out the kids (or the kid in the rest of us) like scrambling over a pile of stones at the edge of a canyon or climbing a trail that overlooks an ancient ruin. Many hikes, bike rides, raft trips, and backpack routes—even some slot canyon journeys—are family friendly. Wild West history is always a surefire hit, from the old-time

melodramas to the trading posts and museums elsewhere. Native cultures are part of that appeal, and include festival dances in the Hopi villages, Navajo-led tours into the Canyon de Chelly, and even a night in an authentic hogan for those so inclined. National parks and monuments foster a child's sense of discovery with the Junior Ranger program, which is free to participants and can help you choose hikes and other activities.

A few things are important to keep in mind—the harsh climate in particular. Always make sure everyone has sunscreen, appropriate clothing, and enough water. (Get kids their own water bottles and make a game out of drinking, drinking, drinking during outdoor activities.) Don't overestimate how far little legs can go on difficult trails, and be aware that the impressively vertical scenery often lacks safety features like guardrails and warning signs. Last but not least, know that it can be an hour or more to the next pit stop when you pile into the car.

Local babysitting agencies can be found in the Yellow Pages or through hotel desks. For more information see blogs such as **Travels With Child** (www.travelswithchild.org) or try **About.com's "Travel With Kids" section** (http://travelwithkids.about.com).

SENIOR TRAVELERS

Many hotels and attractions offer discounts for seniors. Ask at the gate or, better yet, when making reservations. The **American Association of Retired Persons** (888/687-2277, www.aarp.org) is the country's largest seniors' organization, with member discounts for hotels, car rentals, air travel, and tours worldwide. **Road Scholar** (800/454-5768, www.roadscholar.org), the travel/education arm of Elderhostel, Inc., organizes worldwide "extraordinary learning adventures" for people 55 and over. (One half of a couple is sufficient.) Some trips are pure fun, and others are more service oriented, including recording petroglyphs on the Hopi Reservation and cataloging Anasazi artifacts in a Four Corners museum. New additions include adventures geared to multiple generations within a family.

TRAVELING WITH PETS

Smaller pets are allowed at many hotels and motels (usually with a surcharge), but most B&Bs will say no. Remember that pets must stay in vehicles or on paved roads and parking lots in national parks, with very few exceptions. (Be aware that high desert sunshine can heat vehicle interiors to deadly temperatures within minutes.) Pet boarding and doggie day care are often available near parks, in towns such as Moab, Cortez, Durango, and Flagstaff.

TRAVEL INSURANCE

A number of agencies offer specialized travelers' insurance in various combinations of health, accident, trip-cancellation and trip-interruption, and lost-luggage protection. Two dependable choices are **Travel Guard International** (800/826-4919, www.travelguard.com) and **Access America** (800/284-8300, www.accessamerica.com).

VOLUNTEERING

Chronically underfunded as they are, most national parks and national forests gladly accept volunteers for varying positions and time commitments. Either contact the park's volunteer coordinator, or take a look at the park service's **Volunteers-in-Parks** program (www.nps.gov/volunteer). They can sometimes provide housing and (very limited) living expenses. The **Student Conservation Association** (603/543-1700, www.thesca.org) can also place volunteers (not just students) in conservation-related positions.

TOUR COMPANIES

Whether you want to go hiking, biking, horseback riding, off-road driving, river rafting, visit a Native American village, or try your hand at archaeology, you can depend on at least one tour company—and probably a few dozen—willing to help you personalize your trip. Local tour operators are included in the various city listings, and not surprisingly are concentrated in the major tourist hubs of Moab, Durango, Page, and Flagstaff. Several national operations also offer tours of the area, including the Sierra Club, whose **Outings** program (415/977-5522, www.sierraclub.org/outings) offers many nature and cultural trips on the Colorado Plateau, from sightseeing to service programs. **Elderhostel** is a similar organization for travelers over 55, offering educational trips through Road Scholar (www.roadscholar.org). The **Four Corners School of Outdoor Education** (800/525-4456, www.fourcornersschool.org) offers programs, including **Southwest Ed-Ventures,** and in Moab the **Canyonlands Field Institute** (435/259-7750 or 800/860-5262, www.canyonlandsfieldinst.org) has been organizing tours on regional ecology, geology, and native cultures since 1984.

Phoenix-based **Detours** (866/438-6877, www.detoursaz.com) organizes a wide range of cultural and outdoors tours of the Four Corners. Small groups of 6–10 use comfortable, modified vans to get around, and the owners and guides are walking treasure troves of local knowledge. Their roster includes day tours of the Grand Canyon and Sedona and multiday excursions of other national parks, the Navajo Reservation, and Spanish missions. One great option is their Hillerman Country Tour, run with the blessing of the late author himself, which lets fans visit sites from the novels and even meet people who appeared in them. **360 Adventures** (480/722-0360 or 888/722-0360, www.360-adventures.com) is their adventure-travel branch, offering guided rock climbing, hiking, backpacking, mountain biking, and canyoneering trips throughout the Southwest.

For tours of the Navajo reservation, try **Go Navajo Trails** (928/200-5856, www.gonavajotrails.com), featuring 9–11 day tours focusing on scenic sites, archaeology, and Navajo culture, or **Hummingbird Tours** (928/810-8540 or 505/979-1964), with one- or two-day itineraries guided by a mother-daughter team. Will Tsosie runs **Coyote Pass Hospitality** (928/724-3383, http://navajocentral.org), offering bed-and-breakfast accommodations (starting at $85) in traditional Navajo hogans in Tsaile, Lukachukai, and the Chuska Mountains, as well as private tours in your own four-wheel-drive vehicle for $20 per hour.

Health and Safety

HEAT, WATER, AND SUN

In the high desert you have two things working against you whenever you step outside: the strong, nearly constant sunlight and the thin, dry air. It's remarkably easy to get a **sunburn,** so use sunscreen or sun block liberally, and always have a hat with you—the bigger the brim the better. Consider wearing long-sleeved shirts and pants or a skirt, preferably in light colors; they can actually keep you cooler than shorts and T-shirts. A handkerchief is handy to protect your neck if you burn easily. Desert-style hats with built-in neck flaps are available at outdoor gear stores.

Sunburn is the first step on the road to **hyperthermia** (overheating). This progresses through relatively common **heat exhaustion,** with its flulike symptoms such as vomiting and dizziness, to **heat stroke,** a very serious condition in which the body's cooling mechanism breaks down. Heat stroke is marked by a significant change in behavior and brain activity and has an 80 percent mortality rate when untreated. If you suspect that you or someone else has any of these symptoms, get out of the sun, remove any restrictive clothing, and drink plenty of fluids, preferably with salts or electrolytes. If you can, splash cool water on the affected individual or apply cold compresses.

Most visitors to the Four Corners will experience **dehydration** at some point; in this thin, dry, warm air, it's almost inevitable. Pay attention, though, and you'll be able to head off dehydration before it gets serious. One of the earliest and most subtle signs is feeling cranky or out of sorts. One of the clearest signs is, to put it bluntly, the color of your pee. Clear, barely colored urine is good; dark or cloudy urine is bad. Get in the habit of paying attention to this and *hydrate constantly* by taking a few sips of a decaffeinated beverage every so often. Sports drinks such as Gatorade or Cytomax help restore lost electrolytes. Electrolyte mixes are available in powdered or tablet form. Backpack hydration systems make frequent sipping easier. Most people become dehydrated *before* experiencing thirst. Even if you aren't thirsty, drink!

Another thing to keep in mind is that in this dry environment, moisture evaporates rapidly. Even when you're not sweating, you're losing water. During hard exercise in the hot sun—hiking or mountain biking, for instance—it's possible to lose up to two quarts of water per hour, and two gallons of water per day. That's why it's crucial to carry at least **one gallon of water per person per day** when doing these kinds of activities spring–fall. *Always* carry more water than you think you'll need so that you have some extra in case things go wrong. Stashing an extra gallon in the car or a quart in your backpack can make all the difference. Consider staying put or being in the shade, during the hottest part of the day, especially in summer. Night hiking by the light of the moon is cool and magical. Take a water bottle with you whenever you venture off the pavement, even if it's only a short hike to a ruin or overlook. Out there, water is life—don't get caught without it.

OTHER HEALTH AND SAFETY ISSUES
Hypothermia

Temperatures drop amazingly quickly in the dry desert air—a plunge of 40°F from day to night is not unusual. Heat vanishes into the stratosphere as the sun falls, and if your body temperature drops below 95°F, you're in trouble. Shivering is a sign of mild hypothermia. If this happens, remove any wet clothes, find the warmest spot possible, and get the affected person to eat and drink, preferably hot, sugary liquids like Jell-O mix. The "umbles" (stumbles, mumbles, fumbles, grumbles) are signs that cold has affected muscle and nerve function: Cover the victim gently with clothing or a sleeping bag and seek medical attention.

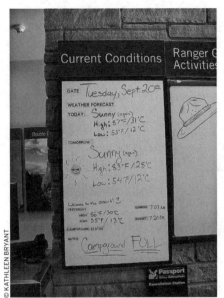

Current Conditions | Ranger Activities

DATE Tuesday, Sept. 20th
WEATHER FORECAST
TODAY: Sunny (again)
High: 87°F/31°C
Low: 53°F/12°C

Sunny (again)
High: 83°F/28°C
Low: 54°F/12°C

Welcome to the desert!!
YESTERDAY:
HIGH: 86°F/30°C   SUNRISE: 7:03 AM
LOW: 55°F/13°C   SUNSET: 7:26 PM
CAMPGROUND STATUS

NOTES: Campground FULL

Passport

© KATHLEEN BRYANT

Check at park visitors centers for current conditions.

Impure Water

Thanks in part to grazing cattle, nearly all natural water sources in the country can be considered contaminated. **Giardia** is the most common bug, causing diarrhea and cramps that can become quite serious. Always filter water or chemically treat it with iodine before drinking it. Rivers like the Colorado, which has been called "too thick to drink, too thin to plow," often carry runoff from fertilized fields and mine tailings rich in heavy metals. If you must drink river water, let the sediment settle before filtering and considering double-treating the water.

In the Backcountry

Getting lost is a very real possibility in the trackless desert and canyon mazes that make up the Colorado Plateau. Always let someone responsible know where you're going and when you plan to return before you head off on a trip, or else you risk having to do something drastic to survive. Consider the case of hiker Aron Ralston, who in 2003 went canyoneering alone

in the Maze District of Canyonlands National Park. When a shifting boulder crushed and pinned his forearm, he was forced to amputate it to escape after five days of exposure.

Keep an eye out for unusual landmarks as you progress, and look back frequently so that you can pick out the way home, if necessary. If you think you've lost the trail, backtrack to your last known point—a tree, a junction, or a trail marker. If this doesn't work, *stay put* and try to **signal** for help. Use your signal mirror, wave brightly colored clothing, and blow your whistle. (Recently, a lost hiker was located when he flashed his camera as search helicopters neared.) As hard as it is to just sit and wait, wandering off makes it more difficult for rescuers to find you.

Always check the weather forecast before venturing into narrow canyons to avoid **flash floods.** Storms cells miles away can create surging runoff in dry, rocky areas.

Plants and Animals

At times it seems like every living thing in the desert either stings, bites, scratches, or impales. Life here is a struggle, and the plants and animals have evolved many ways to secure and protect scant resources—and themselves. A fearsome appearance might be deceiving. For example, tarantulas aren't dangerous to humans. **Rattlesnakes,** however, are often found sunning themselves on ledges or trails to maintain an ideal body temperature of 80–85°F. They're as afraid of you as you are of them, so if you don't startle them—or torment them—you should have nothing to worry about. Simply back off and go another way. The warning rattle is unmistakable, though it can be difficult to pinpoint when the snake is hidden.

Scorpions, centipedes, and poisonous **spiders** like the black widow are also present. The easiest way to avoid these biting creatures is not to put your hands and feet where you can't see where they might be, including on ledges and overhangs and behind logs. Don't leave shoes or clothing lying on the ground, but if you do, shake them out before putting them on or, in the case of sleeping bags, crawling inside.

DESERT SURVIVAL KIT

If you plan on doing any hikes or bike rides in lightly traveled areas, throw these items into a small plastic bag and keep it in the bottom of your pack. Customize the kit to your specific needs (such as an EpiPen, knee brace, spare glasses, etc.).

- compact lighter
- multi-tool or pocketknife
- light source (small flashlight or LED headlamp)
- compass (to go with your map)
- extra food (energy bars, hard candy, or honey packets)
- space blanket (a garbage bag is better than nothing)
- first-aid kit (basic essentials)
- signal mirror (a CD will do in a pinch—practice first!)
- signal whistle
- water purification tablets
- electrolyte tablets
- cash

These are just the basics. Other handy items include safety pins, cord or dental floss, extra zip-top plastic bags, pen and paper. You'll find some fiendishly compact and clever survival kits at gear stores if you'd prefer not to make your own; just remember to replace water purification tablets according to the manufacturer's shelf-life recommendations.

The most you'll probably ever see of a **mountain lion** is a flash of movement, but these large cats are present in the higher mountain ranges and have been spotted in populated national parks like the Grand Canyon. **Coyotes** are ubiquitous but have never been recorded to attack adults (nor have wolves, for that matter). **Black bears** also live in the mountains; store your food in a bear-proof container, and don't leave any food sitting around a campsite. Bears are also drawn to scented items like toothpaste and soap, so be sure to put those away.

Poison ivy grows near rivers, springs, seeps, and ditches; be on the lookout for waxy leaves arranged in groups of three. **Nettles** can also cause severe itching; they grow in drier, rocky locations. The sharp, stiff leaves of **agaves** and **yuccas** can be dangerous if you stumble into them (one species of yucca is called the Spanish Bayonet). **Cacti** are covered with spines, often including tiny ones you can't even see. Needless to say, avoid these plants, particularly the cholla, whose needles leave behind a nearly invisible sheath that itches madly.

Hantavirus

This nasty virus made news in the Four Corners in 1993, when a number of people suddenly developed acute breathing problems. About half died with alarming speed. When health authorities investigated, they realized that heavy snowmelt had caused a bumper crop of piñon nuts, which in turn supported an unusually high deer mouse population. They figured out that the mice droppings carried the airborne virus that causes Hantavirus Pulmonary Syndrome. The symptoms, which appear 1–5 weeks after exposure, include fever, fatigue, aching muscles, nausea, and other flulike symptoms. Left untreated, the virus can be fatal. It is very rare, but to avoid it, minimize your contact with rodents and their droppings, particularly in enclosed spaces like old cabins. Clean up infested areas by wetting the droppings with a bleach solution (wear latex gloves) and mopping them up—don't sweep dry particles into the air. In the backcountry, avoid pack rat middens, and don't encourage critters into your campsite by leaving food within easy reach.

Interestingly, the Navajo were not surprised by the 1993 hantavirus outbreak. In their medical tradition, mice are considered the carriers of an ancient sickness that targets the healthiest and strongest, so they've always been vigilant at keeping rodents out of residences and the food supply. The sickness had struck in 1918 and 1933–1934—years with high numbers of

© KATHLEEN BRYANT

Even the cutest rodent can carry germs or ruin a backpack in search of food.

piñon nuts and mice. Some native elders had even predicted the 1993 outbreak.

CRIME

The most common form of crime in the Four Corners is theft—don't leave anything valuable in view in your car or hotel room—but assaults and robberies do occur. Crime has increased on public lands in recent years, due to a rise in visitors and a decrease in money for law enforcement, particularly in remote areas such as those patrolled by the BLM.

As a rule of thumb, don't sleep at highway rest areas, and keep one eye peeled and one ear open when alone in the backcountry, particularly if you're a woman traveling alone. Lock your hotel door and your car as a matter of habit. Don't let fear ruin your trip; just be aware of your surroundings. Dial **911** from any pay phone, toll-free, in case of emergency.

Information and Services

ELECTRICITY

Homes and businesses in the United States operate on 110–220 volt electricity. Modern outlets are designed to accept either two- or three-prong plug-ins, which include two flat prongs and one round (grounding) prong. Outlets in older buildings, however, may accept only two-prong plug-ins. If you're using an expensive piece of electronics such as a laptop computer, you should get a three-to-two-prong adapter that also protects against power surges.

MONEY

Cash is always the easiest way to pay, but the fraud protection, insurance benefits, and other advantages of **credit cards** make them popular among travelers. Unfortunately, in smaller towns in the Four Corners and on large parts of the Native American reservations, some

TOURISM INFORMATION

ARIZONA OFFICE OF TOURISM
866/275-5816
www.arizonaguide.com

NEW MEXICO DEPARTMENT OF TOURISM
505/827-7400
www.newmexico.org

SOUTHWEST COLORADO TRAVEL REGION
800/933-4340
www.swcolotravel.org

UTAH TRAVEL COUNCIL
800/200-1160
www.utah.com

NAVAJO NATION TOURISM DEPARTMENT
928/871-6436
www.discovernavajo.com

GRAND CIRCLE ASSOCIATION
888/254-7263
www.grandcircle.org

BUREAU OF LAND MANAGEMENT
National office: 202/208-3801
Arizona: 602/417-9200
Colorado: 303/239-3600

New Mexico: 505/954-2098
Utah: 801/539-4001
www.blm.gov

U.S. FOREST SERVICE
National office: 800/832-1355
www.fs.fed.us

NATIONAL PARK SERVICE
Intermountain Region: 303/969-2500
www.nps.gov

ARIZONA STATE PARKS
602/542-4174
www.pr.state.az.us

COLORADO STATE PARKS
303/866-3437
www.parks.state.co.us

NEW MEXICO STATE PARKS
888/667-2757
www.emnrd.state.nm.us

UTAH STATE PARKS & RECREATION
801/538-7220
www.stateparks.utah.gov

NAVAJO PARKS & RECREATION DEPARTMENT
928/871-6647
www.navajonationparks.org

vendors can't accept credit cards. **Travelers checks** are another option, but these can also be somewhat of a problem outside larger towns. They offer the advantage of replacement if they're lost or stolen; American Express and Thomas Cook checks are widely accepted at banks, hotels, and restaurants. Forget about using **personal checks** outside your home state. Foreign visitors should change to U.S. dollars at the earliest opportunity.

On the plus side, almost every town has a bank, service station, or grocery store with an automated teller machine **(ATM)** where you can withdraw cash using your bank card or credit card, as long as you don't mind paying a small fee

every time. The most popular ATM networks are Star, Cirrus, Plus, Visa, American Express, and MasterCard. **Western Union** (800/325-6000, www.westernunion.com) lets you wire money for a fee to any of thousands of locations, as well as by phone and over the Internet. Each state charges a different amount of **sales tax:** Arizona (5.6 percent), Utah (4.65 percent), Colorado (2.9 percent), and New Mexico (5 percent). Not to be outdone, the Navajo Nation charges its own 4 percent sales tax.

Tipping is customary in restaurants, taxis, and whenever someone totes your bags (airports and hotels). A 15 percent tip on restaurant and bar bills is standard, since waiters make considerably less than minimum wage before tips. Leave 20 percent or more for outstanding service, or if you're just feeling nice. Taxi drivers typically receive 15 percent, and airport porters and bellhops at least $1 per bag. Tip tour guides 10–15 percent of the tour cost. Tip on the higher end of that range for adventure trips like river rafting.

PARK PASSES AND FEES

With admission fees climbing ever higher, it's often a good idea to buy an **Interagency Annual Pass** if you plan on visiting more than two or three national parks. At $80, they quickly pay for themselves in entry fees, and they are good for one year for the occupants of any private vehicle at federally operated recreation areas, including BLM and forest service sites as well as national parks. Get one at any park or online (http://store.usgs.gov/pass). You can also buy local **park passports** for parks in certain areas, including the Southeast Utah Group (Arches, Canyonlands, Hovenweep, and Natural Bridges), and the national monuments near Flagstaff (Walnut Canyon, Wupatki, and Sunset Crater), both $25. **State park passes** are also available for each state.

The number of annual **fee free days** increased to 17 in 2011, with the goal of making it easier for families to visit national parks. More than 100 parks waive entrance fees on these days, sometimes around a holiday like Veterans Day or National Public Lands Day but also for the duration of National Park Week each April.

MAPS

The best overall map of the region is the **Guide to Indian Country** map published by the Automobile Club of Southern California. It covers everything in the Four Corners, plus areas to the east (Albuquerque and Santa Fe) and west (to Kingman, Arizona, and St. George, Utah). It's the map Lieutenant Joe Leaphorn fills with pins in Tony Hillerman's Navajo mysteries, and it's indispensable for any long-term exploration of the Four Corners area. You can get it from AAA offices and at bookstores and gas stations throughout the region.

Many travelers swear by the detailed state atlases published by DeLorme (www.delorme.com) and Benchmark (www.benchmarkmaps.com). Local chambers of commerce often publish street maps, usually free, that are helpful for finding hotels, restaurants, and other businesses.

National Geographic's waterproof and tear-resistant **Trails Illustrated Maps** (www.natgeomaps.com) cover most of the major Four Corners hot spots, including Moab, Grand Canyon National Park, and the canyons of the Escalante for about $12 each.

Latitude 40 Maps (303/258-7909, www.latitude40maps.com) has created several recreational topo maps ($8–12), including the invaluable *Slickrock Bike Trail* map. All are available locally and come with trail information on the reverse. Latitude 40 also publishes recreational topo maps for southwest Colorado, Durango, and other areas.

Forest service maps (www.fs.fed.us) are helpful for traveling back roads and locating trailheads (though not especially helpful for trails themselves). Ranger stations and sometimes local gear shops and bookstores sell forest maps; many also carry United States Geological Survey (USGS) maps. For backpacking trips, a USGS quad (http://topomaps.usgs.gov) provides the highest level of topography detail.

TIME ZONES

All four states are in the Mountain Time zone, which is two hours behind Eastern Time (New York), one hour ahead of Pacific Time (California), and seven hours behind Greenwich Mean Time (London). Sound simple? Not so fast. From March to November, Utah, Colorado, and Mexico advance one hour according to daylight saving time ("spring forward, fall back"). Arizonans, however, apparently have enough sunshine, because that state stays on the same time year-round—except for the Navajo Reservation, which *does* participate in daylight saving time. To make things even more confusing, the Hopi Reservation *inside* the Navajo Reservation follows Arizona's lead and ignores daylight saving time. From March

Prepare well before exploring complex canyon systems.

to November, then, set your watch forward one hour if you enter Utah, New Mexico, or the Navajo Reservation from Arizona or the Hopi Reservation. Set it back an hour on entering Arizona. Don't rely on your cell phone to tell you the correct local time. An hour may seem inconsequential when you're on vacation, but if you're headed for a small town and hoping to arrive before restaurants close for the night, or if you have reservations for a tour, that missing hour can make the difference between going hungry and not going at all.

BUSINESS HOURS

Most businesses, aside from restaurants, are open 9 A.M.–6 P.M. Monday–Saturday, with varying hours (if any) on Sunday. In Utah, many businesses, including restaurants, are closed Sunday. Banks and post offices are typically open for the first half of the day Saturday. The seasonal tourism industry means that many businesses close for the winter, or at least significantly reduce their hours. This can also apply in the height of the summer in some

locations, when visitation drops from the heat. It's always a good idea to call ahead October–April to make sure your favorite hotel, restaurant, or trading post hasn't closed up shop for the season.

COMMUNICATIONS

Every incorporated town, no matter how small, has a **U.S. post office** usually open 8:30 A.M.–5 P.M. Monday–Friday and 9 A.M.–noon Saturday (for now). The main telephone **area codes** in the Four Corners are 435 (southern Utah), 970 (southwestern Colorado), 505 (most of New Mexico), and 928 (northern Arizona). **Toll-free numbers** start with 800, 888, 877, and 866, and you can get **directory assistance** by calling 411 (local), or 1 + area code + 555-1212 (long-distance). Toll-free information is 800/555-1212. For **emergencies** dial 911. Cell phone coverage in the Four Corners can be spotty at best outside cities. Your vehicle's GPS unit may be off inside national park boundaries.

Most medium-to-large cities have their own

newspapers, which are a good source of information on local events and attitudes. This includes the *Gallup Independent* (www.gallupindependent.com), Moab's *Times-Independent* (www.moabtimes.com), the Farmington *Daily Times* (www.daily-times.com), and Flagstaff's *Arizona Daily Sun* (www.azdailysun.com). On the reservations look for the *Navajo Times* (www.thenavajotimes.com) and the *Navajo Hopi Observer* (www.navajohopiobserver.com). For alternative views, try the *Canyon Country Zephyr* (www.canyoncountryzephyr.com), the *Four Corners Free Press* (http://fourcornersfreepress.com), or *High Country News* (www.hcn.org).

Internet cafés and Wi-Fi hotspots have spread across the Four Corners. Many coffee shops, hotels, and hostels offer Internet computers for a fee and wireless Internet access for free, but the most dependable place to hop online is still the public library. Ask nicely and they'll put you on the waiting list even if you don't have a library card.

Radio stations always offer an interesting taste of local life, and radio is still an important medium of communication in this wide-open countryside. On KTTN (660 AM), "The Voice of the Navajo Nation," you'll hear mostly country-and-western music interspersed with chants and announcements in Navajo on pertinent topics like the news, weather, and livestock reports. You'll find Hopi Radio KUYI ("water" in Hopi) at 88.1 FM. Like KUYI, Tuba City's KGHR (91.5 FM) broadcasts an interesting mix of country, classical, rock, and Native American music, plus National Public Radio (NPR) programs.

RESOURCES

Suggested Reading

RECREATION
Hiking

Adkinson, Ron. *Best Easy Day Hikes: Grand Staircase–Escalante & the Glen Canyon Region*. Guilford, CT: Globe Pequot (Falcon Guides), 2010. A pocket-size guide listing 19 hikes on Cedar Mesa, the Escalante, and the Paria Plateau.

Adkinson, Ron. *Hiking Grand Staircase–Escalante & the Glen Canyon Region*. Guilford, CT: Globe Pequot (Falcon Guides), 2011. Fifty-nine meticulous trail descriptions across the monument and its surrounding area, with elevation maps and mileage charts.

Grubbs, Bruce. *Best Easy Day Hikes: Flagstaff*. Guilford, CT: Globe Pequot (Falcon Guides), 2009. From half-hour rambles to all-day ventures.

Grubbs, Bruce. *Desert Sense: Skills for Camping, Hiking and Biking in Hot, Dry Climates*. Seattle: Mountaineers, 2005. Techniques for staying safe and happy in the desert.

Grubbs, Bruce. *Hiking Northern Arizona*. Guilford, CT: Globe Pequot (Falcon Guides), 2008. Includes descriptions of dozens of trails in the mountains and national monuments near Flagstaff and the Red Rock Country surrounding Sedona.

Hinchman, Sandra. *Hiking the Southwest's Canyon Country*. Seattle: Mountaineers, 2004. Seven 2–3-week itineraries through the Four Corners region, covering more than 100 hikes. A fun book for planning your next adventure.

Mitchell, Joe, and Mike Coronella. *The Hayduke Trail: A Guide to the Backcountry Hiking Trail on the Colorado Plateau*. Salt Lake City: University of Utah Press, 2005. This 800-mile backcountry trail traverses six national parks and some of the most remote scenery of the Southwest.

Molvar, Erik, and Tamara Martin. *Hiking Zion and Bryce Canyon National Parks*. Guilford, CT: Globe Pequot (Falcon Guides), 2005. Covers 56 hikes in the two parks, as well as in Cedar Breaks National Monument and other nearby areas.

Ray, Cosmic. *Favorite Hikes: Flagstaff & Sedona*. Fifty of this Flagstaff author's preferred trails, including Sedona "vortex hikes." Cosmic Ray Publications, 2008. Available locally.

Schneider, Bill. *Best Easy Day Hikes: Canyonlands and Arches*. Guilford, CT: Globe Pequot (Falcon Guides), 2005. Details of trails to ruins, rock art, and natural wonders.

Various authors. *Grand Canyon Trail Guides*. Grand Canyon, AZ: Grand Canyon Association, 1996–2006. These pocket-size booklets cover individual trails, including Grandview, Hermit, North Kaibab, and South Kaibab. Cultural and natural history is included, along with trail descriptions and maps. A few are available as electronic downloads (www.grandcanyonassociation.org).

Wilson, Dave. *Hiking Ruins Seldom Seen.* Guilford, CT: Globe Pequot (Falcon Guides), 2011. Cultural background and detailed directions to 36 ruins and rock art sites throughout the Four Corners states.

Mountain Biking

Alley, Sarah Bennett. *Mountain Biking New Mexico.* Guilford, CT: Globe Pequot (Falcon Guides), 2001. Covers the whole state, including six rides near Farmington and Chaco Canyon.

Crowell, David. *Mountain Biking Moab Pocket Guide.* Guilford, CT: Globe Pequot (Falcon Guides), 2003. A quick guide to 42 rides, small enough to slip into your CamelBak.

Hurst, Robert. *Mountain Biking Colorado's San Juan Mountains: Durango and Telluride.* Guilford, CT: Globe Pequot (Falcon Guides), 2002. More than 70 mountain bike trails around Durango and in the mountains to the north.

McCoy, Michael. *Mountain Bike! Southern Utah.* Birmingham, AL: Menasha Ridge Press, 2000. About half of the 75 rides in this slim but detailed volume are in Southeast and South-Central Utah.

Peel, John. *Mountain Biking Durango.* Guilford, CT: Globe Pequot (Falcon Guides), 1998. Thirty-nine of the city's best rides, from downtown to lung-busting climbs in the hills.

Ray, Cosmic. *Fat Tire Trails & Tales: Arizona Mountain Bike Trail Guide.* Cosmic Ray Publications, 2010. More than good riding, this is also good reading. Includes several Flagstaff and Sedona trails.

Rider Mel. *Rider Mel's Mountain Bike Guide to Moab.* Self-published, 2011. Includes 40 trails, from family rides to thrillers. Available online (http://ridermel.com) or in Moab stores.

Rock Climbing

Bjørnstad, Eric. *Desert Rock: Rock Climbs in the National Parks.* Guilford, CT: Globe Pequot (Falcon Guides), 1996. Routes in Arches, Canyonlands, Capitol Reef, Zion, and the Glen Canyon National Recreation Area.

Bjørnstad, Eric. *Desert Rock II: Wall Street to the San Rafael Swell.* Guilford, CT: Globe Pequot (Falcon Guides), 1997. Covers short crack routes in the San Rafael area as well as some spots near Moab.

Bjørnstad, Eric. *Desert Rock III: Moab to Colorado National Monument.* Guilford, CT: Globe Pequot (Falcon Guides), 1999. Authoritative and detailed, this guide covers more than 500 routes in all the climbing spots near Moab, from the Fisher Towers to the Island in the Sky.

Bjørnstad, Eric. *Desert Rock IV: Remote Areas of the Colorado Plateau.* Guilford, CT: Globe Pequot (Falcon Guides), 2003. Includes the Valley of the Gods and other even more isolated spots.

Burns, Cameron. *Selected Climbs in the Desert Southwest: Colorado and Utah.* Seattle: Mountaineers, 1999. Access and route info on more than 130 routes in western Colorado and southern Utah.

Macdonald, Dougald, and Chris McNamara. *Desert Towers Select.* SuperTopo, 2002. This detailed guide to 15 tower routes in Arches, Castle Valley, Colorado National Monument, Canyonlands, and Indian Creek is available for download in PDF format for $9.95 at www.supertopo.com and includes free updates for three years.

Canyoneering

Allen, Steve. *Canyoneering: The San Rafael Swell.* Salt Lake City: University of Utah Press, 2000. The definitive guide to exploring the canyons of South-Central Utah. Incredibly detailed and comprehensive.

Allen, Steve. *Canyoneering 2: Technical Loop Hikes in Southern Utah.* Salt Lake City: University of Utah Press, 2002. Seven weeklong routes in South-Central Utah, all covered with Allen's typical thoroughness.

Allen, Steve. *Canyoneering 3: Loop Hikes in Utah's Escalante.* Salt Lake City: University of Utah Press, 1997. Thirty-seven hikes and 14 road descriptions, mostly in the Grand Staircase–Escalante National Monument.

Kelsey, Michael. *Hiking and Exploring the Paria River* (2010); *Non-Technical Canyon Hiking Guide to the Colorado Plateau* (2006); and *Technical Slot Canyon Guide to the Colorado Plateau* (2008). This author's self-published guidebooks are full of information on front- and backcountry destinations throughout the Four Corners. But take time estimates with a grain of salt—Kelsey is clearly fitter and faster than the average bear.

NATURAL HISTORY
General Guides
Williams, David. *A Naturalist's Guide to Canyon Country.* Guilford, CT: Globe Pequot (Falcon Guides), 2002. Covers the geology, flora, and fauna of the canyonlands in one handy volume.

National Audobon Society. *Field Guide to the Southwestern States.* New York: Knopf, 1999. Descriptions and photos of flora, fauna, geology, astronomy, and more for Arizona, New Mexico, and Utah. Travel information for the region's parks, preserves, and other sites is included.

Flora and Fauna
Cunningham, Richard. *50 Common Birds of the Southwest.* Tucson, AZ: Western National Parks and Monuments Association, 1990. If

you're looking for a concise, easy-to-carry guide, this one is excellent.

Fagan, Damian. *Canyon Country Wildflowers.* Guilford, CT: Globe Pequot (Falcon Guides), 1998. Look up that pretty blossom by color in this photo-rich guide that covers the central Colorado Plateau.

Halfpenny, James. *Scats and Tracks of the Desert Southwest.* Guilford, CT: Globe Pequot (Falcon Guides), 2005. Did a bear or bobcat leave that? Find out with this small but intriguing guide.

Hanson, Jonathan and Roseann. *50 Common Amphibians and Reptiles of the Southwest.* Tucson, AZ: Western National Parks Association, 1997. The "most-likely-to" list of reptilian encounters. WNPA publishes similar concise, well-photographed and well-written guides of most anything Western, from critter holes to cacti and birds to butterflies.

Kavanagh, James. *Field Guide to the Grand Canyon.* Blaine, WA: Waterford Press, 2001. A folding, plastic-coated sheet with pictures and descriptions of common plants and animals.

Kavanagh, James. *Southwestern Desert Birds.* Blaine, WA: Waterford Press, 2001. A plastic pocket guide with dozens of illustrations of common species.

Kavanagh, James. *Southwestern Desert Life: An Introduction to Familiar Plants and Animals.* Blaine, WA: Waterford Press, 2001. A folding, plastic-coated sheet with pictures and descriptions of 150 common species.

Geology
Baars, Donald. *A Traveler's Guide to the Geology of the Colorado Plateau.* Salt Lake City: University of Utah Press, 2002. Organized by route, this guide takes you from the Paradox Basin to the High Plateaus and explains everything you see along the way.

Hopkins, Ralph. *Hiking the Southwest's Geology: Four Corners Region.* Seattle: Mountaineers, 2003. A hiking guide with a geological focus, organized by geologic provinces.

Blakely, Ron, and Wayne Ranney. *Ancient Landscapes of the Colorado Plateau.* Grand Canyon, AZ: Grand Canyon Association, 2008. If you wish you could travel back in time to see what the region looked like millions of years ago, this book will take you there through paleogeographic maps and illustrations.

HUMAN HISTORY
Archaeology

Cole, Sally. *Legacy on Stone: Rock Art of the Colorado Plateau and Four Corners Region.* Boulder, CO: Johnson Books, 2008. Links between rock art and imagery in pottery, basketry, and other crafts provide cultural context.

Frazier, Kendrick. *People of Chaco.* New York: W. W. Norton, 1999. One of the best single-volume treatments of the ancient culture, its history, and descendants.

Gardner, A. Dudley, and Val Brinkerhoff. *Architecture of the Ancient Ones.* Salt Lake City: Gibbs Smith, 2000. A beautifully photographed book on design of the Ancestral Puebloan ruins.

Grant, Campbell. *Canyon de Chelly: Its People and Its Rock Art.* Tucson: University of Arizona Press, 1978. Covers prehistoric and Navajo cultures as well as natural history.

Kelen, Leslie. *Sacred Images: A Vision of Native American Rock Art.* Salt Lake City: Gibbs Smith, 2008. More great photos, this time concentrating on Ancestral Puebloan rock art as well as that of the Fremont and the Ute.

Lekson, Stephen. *The Chaco Meridian.* Walnut Creek, CA: Altamira Press, 1999. Explores the implications of the fact that the ruins at Aztec, Chaco, and Paquime, Mexico, are on almost the exact same longitude.

Noble, David Grant. *Ancient Ruins of the Southwest: An Archeological Guide.* Flagstaff, AZ: Northland Publishing, 2000. Rich with background information, this guide covers the ruins of the Ancestral Puebloans, Mogollon, and other cultures.

Roberts, David. *In Search of the Old Ones.* New York: Simon & Schuster, 1997. The author's descriptions of his explorations read like a good novel.

Anthropology

Fergusson, Erna. *Dancing Gods: Indian Ceremonials of New Mexico and Arizona.* Albuquerque: University of New Mexico Press, 2001. Visiting details and background information on native ceremonies open to the public on the Navajo, Hopi, and Apache Reservations and the Zuni and Rio Grande Pueblos.

Locke, Raymond. *The Book of the Navajo.* Los Angeles: Mankind Publishing, 2002. Addresses Navajo history, spirituality, and other aspects of traditional Navajo culture.

Pettit, Jan. *Utes: The Mountain People.* Boulder, CO: Johnson Books, 1990. Tribal history with rare archival photographs and extensive cultural detail.

Water, Frank. *Book of the Hopi.* New York: Penguin, 1977. The tribe's historical, spiritual, and cultural history, touching on creation stories, clan migrations, and the ceremonial cycle.

Native American Art

Berholz, Richard C. *Old Trading Posts of the Four Corners.* Lake City, CO: Western Reflections, 2007. Includes a history of trading on the Navajo, Hopi, and Ute reservations with maps and information on visiting trading posts today.

Day, Jonathan. *Traditional Hopi Kachinas.* Flagstaff, AZ: Northland Publishing, 2000. Includes a history of carving with a focus on the revived "old-style" kachina dolls and their carvers.

Hayes, Allan, and John Blom. *Southwestern Pottery: Anasazi to Zuni.* Flagstaff, AZ: Northland Publishing, 1996. A definitive guide to all major indigenous styles of pottery in the Southwest, with photos and interesting historical anecdotes.

Kosik, Fran. *Native Roads: The Complete Motoring Guide to the Navajo and Hopi Nations.* Tucson, AZ: Rio Nuevo, 2005. Bursting with fascinating details, this guide takes you down all the major roads on the reservations and many of the not-so-major ones.

Lamb, Susan. *Guide to Navajo Rugs.* Tucson, AZ: Western National Parks Association, 1992. Pocket-sized book with a good overview of weaving history and regional styles.

McManis, Kent. *Zuni Fetishes & Carvings.* Tucson, AZ: Rio Nuevo, 2010. Excellent information from a longtime trader, combined with beautiful photographs.

Page, Jake and Susanne. *Indian Arts of the Southwest.* Tucson, AZ: Rio Nuevo, 2009. A broad overview of native crafts, with cultural history and beautiful photographs.

Simpson, Georgiana Kennedy. *Guide to Indian Jewelry of the Southwest.* Tucson, AZ: Western National Parks Association, 1999. Pocket-sized but inclusive—like a field guide for jewelry shoppers.

Wright, Barton. *Hopi Kachinas: The Complete Guide to Collecting Kachina Dolls.* Flagstaff, AZ: Northland Publishing, 1977. A classic guide with photographs and descriptions of major kachina figures.

Memoirs and Narratives

Bergera, Gary, ed. *On Desert Trails with Everett Ruess.* Salt Lake City: Gibbs Smith, 2000. A selection of Ruess's poems and letters, with commentary, photos, and woodcuts.

Clark, H. Jackson. *The Owl in Monument Canyon.* Salt Lake City: University of Utah Press, 1993. Fascinating stories and memories from the author's four decades as a trader on the Navajo reservation during the mid-20th century.

Ellis, Reuben, ed. *Stories and Stone: Writing the Anasazi Homeland.* Boulder, CO: Pruett Publishing Company, 1996. An anthology of writing about the prehistoric Southwest, with contributions from Barry Lopez, Willa Cather, Robert Frost, Leslie Marmon Silko, and others.

Miller, David. *Hole in the Rock: An Epic in the Colonization of the Great American West.* Salt Lake: University of Utah Press, 1959. The author's careful research brings to life the hardships faced by Mormon settlers.

Roberts, David. *The Pueblo Revolt: The Secret Rebellion That Drove the Spaniards Out of the Southwest.* New York: Simon & Schuster, 2005. This account of Pope's rebellion against colonial Spain incorporates Puebloan prehistory and culture.

Rusho, W. L., ed. *Everett Ruess: A Vagabond for Beauty & Wilderness Journals.* Salt Lake City: Gibbs Smith, 2002. The combined edition of both books about the teenage wanderer includes letters and journal entries from his all-too-brief life.

Warner, Ted, ed. *The Dominguez-Escalante Journal.* Salt Lake City: University of Utah Press, 1995. The story of the incredible 1776 journey in the padres' own words, with annotations and maps.

Land Use, Development, and Water Issues

Fradkin, Philip. *A River No More: The Colorado River and the West.* Berkeley: University of California Press, 1996. The story of the Colorado River and its tributaries, and their impact on the ranches, towns, and cities of the region.

Martin, Russell. *A Story That Stands Like a Dam: Glen Canyon and the Struggle for the Soul of the West.* Salt Lake City: University of Utah Press, 1999. The colorful story of the construction of Glen Canyon Dam and the controversy that has arisen in its wake.

Reisner, Marc. *Cadillac Desert: The American West and Its Disappearing Water.* New York: Penguin Books, 1993. The highly entertaining tale of water use, and misuse, in the West.

Wilkinson, Charles. *Fire on the Plateau: Conflict and Endurance in the American Southwest.* Washington, DC: Island Press, 2004. Written by a former attorney, this book recounts some of the Southwest's most heated and heart-wrenching struggles over land use and natural resources on Indian lands.

GOOD READS
Southwest Classics

Abbey, Edward. *Beyond the Wall: Essays from the Outside.* New York: Henry Holt, 1984. A collection of essays on life in the West, in Abbey's trademark cantankerous, reverent style.

Abbey, Edward. *Desert Solitaire.* New York: Ballantine, 1991. The classic story of the author's sojourn at Arches before the crowds arrived. Should be required reading for all visitors.

Abbey, Edward. *The Journey Home: Some Words in Defense of the American West.* New York: E. P. Dutton, 1991. More essays, with a focus on the desert Southwest.

Dunaway, David King, and Sarah Spurgeon. *Writing the Southwest.* New York: Penguin, 1995. An excellent introduction to regional literature, with pieces by Edward Abbey, John Nichols, Barbara Kingsolver, Tony Hillerman, and others, as well as a selected bibliography.

Powell, John Wesley. *The Exploration of the Colorado River and Its Canyons.* Washington, DC: National Geographic, 2002. The exhilarating firsthand account of one of the most incredible voyages of discovery in American history.

Stegner, Wallace. *Beyond the Hundredth Meridian: John Wesley Powell and the Second Opening of the West.* New York: Penguin, 1992. Probably the best account of Powell's life, adventures, and struggles.

Stegner, Wallace. *Mormon Country.* Lincoln: University of Nebraska Press, 1992. Essays on Southern Utah, both historical and modern, in the author's gorgeous prose.

Telford, John, and Terry Tempest Williams. *Coyote's Canyon.* Salt Lake City: Gibbs Smith, 1981. Telford's photographs and Williams's prose do a wonderful job of evoking the grandeur of the Four Corners' landscapes.

Fiction

Edward Abbey's *The Monkey Wrench Gang* (1975) and its sequel *Hayduke Lives!* (1989) detail the exploits of a band of eco-saboteurs fighting against the industrialization of the Colorado Plateau. Both novels have been reprinted and are widely available.

Tony Hillerman's best-selling series of police mysteries, set on the Navajo Reservation, gives a fascinating glimpse into modern Navajo culture—and they're darn good reading as well. Titles include *A Thief of Time, The First Eagle, Sacred Clowns, The Dark Wind, The Fallen Man, Listening Woman, Skinwalkers, Hunting Badger, Dance Hall of the Dead, Coyote Waits, The Blessing Way, Talking God, People of Darkness, The Ghostway, Skeleton Man, The Sinister Pig,* and *Wailing Wind.* Hillerman died in 2008, but for voracious readers of Southwestern fiction, many other writers do a fine job of combining mystery and Native American culture. Among them:

Nevada Barr set *Ill Wind* (2004), starring roving ranger Anna Pigeon, in Mesa Verde National Park.

James D. Doss writes mysteries featuring Charlie Moon, a Ute rancher and police investigator. The series, now at 16 books, begins with *The Shaman Sings* (1994).

Kathleen O'Neal Gear and **Michael Gear,** both former archaeologists, are known for dozens of historical novels about America's first people. Among them is an Anasazi mystery trilogy—*The Visitant* (1999), *The Summoning God* (2000), *Bone Walker* (2001)—that speculates about the cultural changes sweeping through the Four Corners at the close of the 12th century.

Another husband-wife writing team, **Aimee and David Thurlo,** pen mysteries featuring Navajo policewoman Ella Clah. Now numbering 17, the series began with *Blackening Song* (1995).

MAPS
Topographical Maps
For an extended backcountry trip, the most detailed map is the 7.5-minute 1:24,000 **U.S. Geological Survey quadrangle** matching your route. You can buy USGS quads in numerous outdoors stores and visitors centers or order them directly from USGS (888/275-8747, http://store.usgs.gov).

Alternately, you can print topo maps yourself using National Geographic's TOPO! software (www.natgeomaps.com). Other good sources include **TopoZone** (www.topozone.com) and MyTopo (www.mytopo.com), which let you create and download custom topographic maps based on the USGS line.

National Geographic's **Trails Illustrated Maps** are waterproof and tear-resistant, with good topographical detail, trails, and highways. Among Four Corners sites are maps for Moab and the canyons of the Escalante.

Latitude 40 Maps (303/258-7909, www.latitude40maps.com) has created several recreational topo maps for southwest Colorado and other areas, including a map detailing the *Slickrock Bike Trail* near Moab.

Driving Maps
State travel bureaus and local chambers of commerce often hand out free maps that are helpful for finding highways, hotels, restaurants, and other businesses. But the handiest map for a road trip of the Four Corners is the **Guide to Indian Country** map published by the Automobile Club of Southern California. It covers everything between Albuquerque and Santa Fe west to Kingman, Arizona, and St. George, Utah.

If you plan to spend a lot of time camping, hiking, and biking in a single national forest, **USDA forest service maps** (www.fs.fed.us) are best for showing the networks of dirt roads and two-tracks used for logging, fire management, etc.

Atlases
Atlases are tough to stuff in a backpack, but for a near-encyclopedic combination of topography, travel information, highways, backcountry roads, and land management boundaries, they're hard to beat. **Delorme** and **Benchmark** publish atlases for Arizona, Colorado, New Mexico, and Utah.

Internet Resources

NATIONAL PARKS AND MONUMENTS

Recreation.gov
www.recreation.gov
This government website provides information on federal recreation areas, including many in the Four Corners. It's searchable by state and activity and has been expanded to include data on state, tribal, and local recreation areas. You can also make reservations for several park and forest campgrounds here.

National Park Service
www.nps.gov
Check official National Park Service websites (always preceded by www.nps.gov) for the latest fee information, road conditions, closures, and events. Many park sites include links for downloading maps, brochures, or trail guides, and some even offer audio files or streaming videos on subjects from history to river running.

Arches National Park
www.nps.gov/arch

Aztec Ruins National Monument
www.nps.gov/azru

Bryce Canyon National Park
www.nps.gov/brca

Canyon de Chelly National Monument
www.nps.gov/cach

Canyonlands National Park
www.nps.gov/cany

Capitol Reef National Park
www.nps.gov/care

Chaco Culture National Historic Park
www.nps.gov/chcu

Glen Canyon National Recreation Area
www.nps.gov/glca

Grand Canyon National Park
www.nps.gov/grca

Hovenweep National Monument
www.nps.gov/hove

Hubbell Trading Post National Historic Site
www.nps.gov/hutr

Mesa Verde National Park
www.nps.gov/meve

Natural Bridges National Monument
www.nps.gov/nabr

Navajo National Monument
www.nps.gov/nava

Petrified Forest National Park
www.nps.gov/pefo

Rainbow Bridge National Monument
www.nps.gov/rabr

Sunset Crater Volcano National Monument
www.nps.gov/sucr

Walnut Canyon National Monument
www.nps.gov/waca

Wupatki National Monument
www.nps.gov/wupa

Bureau of Land Management (BLM)
www.blm.gov
For more information about Canyons of the Ancients National Monument, Vermilion Cliffs National Monument, Paria Canyon–Vermilion Cliffs Wilderness Area, or Grand Staircase–Escalante National Monument, start with the BLM's Arizona and Utah pages. The BLM also manages Cedar Mesa, the San Rafael Swell, Newspaper Rock, and many other scenic and historic areas in the Four Corners.

PARKS PARTNERS

Cooperating nonprofit associations work with national parks to staff visitor centers, fund programs and interpretive publications, and produce a host of materials ranging from trail guides and histories to canvas shopping bags.

Bryce Canyon Natural History Association
www.brycecanyon.org

Canyonlands Natural History Association
www.cnha.org

Capitol Reef Natural History Association
www.capitolreefnha.org

Glen Canyon Natural History Association
www.glencanyonnha.org

Grand Canyon Association
www.grandcanyon.org

Mesa Verde Museum Association
www.mesaverde.org

Western National Parks Association
www.wnpa.org

NATIONAL FORESTS

See forest service websites for information about hiking trails, scenic drives, picnic areas, and campgrounds. Many of these sites post current notices about road closures, fire restrictions, and other issues.

Cibola National Forest
www.fs.usda.gov/cibola

Coconino National Forest
www.fs.usda.gov/coconino

Dixie National Forest
www.fs.fed.us/dxnf

Fishlake National Forest
www.fs.usda.gov/fishlake

Kaibab National Forest
www.fs.usda.gov/kaibab

Manti-La Sal National Forest
www.fs.usda.gov/mantilasal

San Juan National Forest
www.fs.usda.gov/sanjuan

NATIVE AMERICAN CULTURES
Hopi Mesas
www.experiencehopi.com
The tribe's recently completed hotel in Moenkopi is the main focus on this website, but those planning to visit the Hopi Mesas will find helpful information about villages, heritage sites, and guide services. The cultural center (www.hopiculturalcenter.com) also has helpful information about visiting the reservation. The tribe's official website (www.hopi-nsn.gov) has recent news releases and information about tribal government.

Navajo Nation
www.navajonationparks.org
Learn more about visiting the Navajo Nation's tribal parks, including Antelope Canyon and Monument Valley. The site has information about hunting and fishing permits and fee schedules for camping and hiking on tribal lands. Traditional stories and cultural history are included on the tribe's tourism department website (www.discovernavajo.com), which also has information about lodging, attractions, events, and tours. For information about tribal government, visit the Navajo Nation's official website (www.navajo-nsn.gov).

Navajo Central
http://navajocentral.org
Computer systems analyst Larry DiLucchio has compiled an extensive collection of information on the Navajo tribe and reservation. Having lived in Chinle for over 15 years, he has assembled an excellent list of questions and answers on daily life on the reservation from an outsider's perspective.

Southern and Ute Mountain Utes
www.southern-ute.nsn.gov
www.utemountainute.com
The West's three Ute reservations include two along the southern Colorado border near the Four Corners. The Ute Mountain Ute Tribal Park adjoins Mesa Verde, and tribal members guide tours of the cliff dwellings in Mancos Canyon.

Zuni Pueblo
www.zunitourism.com
The department of tourism's site includes cultural history and helpful information about visiting Zuni Pueblo. The tribe's official site (www.ashiwi.org) has information about tribal enterprises and government.

FOUR CORNERS TRAVEL
State Travel Councils
Find out about upcoming events and festivals, request printed brochures, or explore links to towns, museums, sights, and businesses.

Arizona Office of Tourism
www.arizonaguide.com

Colorado Tourism Office
www.colorado.com

New Mexico Tourism Department
www.newmexico.org

Utah Travel Industry
www.utah.com

Regional Background
DesertUSA
www.desertusa.com
An excellent online resource for information on the deserts of the American Southwest, with everything from cultural history to shopping. It's updated with new articles regularly and includes maps, wildflower reports, current festivals, and a message board.

Bill Leverton's TravelSW.com
www.travelsw.com
Journalist Bill Leverton's site is packed with articles and information for independent travelers in the Southwest.

The American Southwest
www.americansouthwest.net
This well-organized site covers the parks and scenic spots of Arizona, California, Colorado, Nevada, New Mexico, Texas, and Utah. Articles feature excellent photography and detailed visiting instructions, and there's a particularly good section on slot canyons.

Out West
www.outwestnewspaper.com
Editor/reporter Chuck Woodbury spent much of the period 1987–2000 roving around the American West in his 24-foot motor home. After driving over 200,000 miles, he had logged a million words on the people, places, and things he encountered off (sometimes far off) the beaten path. He offers many links of interest to RVers.

Canyons, Cultures, and Environmental Change
www.cpluhna.nau.edu
Subtitled "An Introduction to the Land Use History of the Colorado Plateau," this website is full of information of the natural and human history of the Four Corners. It's produced by NASA, the USGS, and Northern Arizona University, and it covers everything from uranium mining to endangered species.

OUTDOOR RECREATION
GORP
http://gorp.away.com
The Great Outdoor Resource Page is the place to go for details on anything and everything in outdoor recreation. You can browse by destination or by activities, and you can book trips online—just be ready for plenty of advertisements.

Canyoneering
www.canyoneeringusa.com
Everything you could ever want to know about canyoneering in the American West. The site also has an online store that sells canyoneering gear and a bulletin board to trade tips.

Wilderness Areas
www.wilderness.net
Information and inspiration about wilderness areas in the United States, including Dark Canyon, Bisti/De-Na-Zin, and Paria Canyon–Vermilion Cliffs. Some of the wilderness areas listed have associated blogs with recent travel reports.

Leave No Trace
www.lnt.org
This national organization explains and promotes low-impact ethics for responsible use and active stewardship of the outdoors.

Index

List of Maps

www.moon.com

DESTINATIONS | ACTIVITIES | BLOGS | MAPS | BOOKS

MOON.COM is ready to help plan your next trip! Filled with fresh trip ideas and strategies, author interviews, informative travel blogs, a detailed map library, and descriptions of all the Moon guidebooks, Moon.com is all you need to get out and explore the world—or even places in your own backyard. While at Moon.com, sign up for our monthly e-newsletter for updates on new releases, travel tips, and expert advice from our on-the-go Moon authors. As always, when you travel with Moon, expect an experience that is uncommon and truly unique.

f ➤ KEEP UP WITH MOON ON FACEBOOK AND TWITTER
JOIN THE MOON PHOTO GROUP ON FLICKR

MOON FOUR CORNERS
Avalon Travel
a member of the Perseus Books Group
1700 Fourth Street
Berkeley, CA 94710, USA
www.moon.com

Editor and Series Manager: Kathryn Ettinger
Copy Editor: Jade Chan
Graphics Coordinator: Darren Alessi
Production Coordinator: Darren Alessi
Cover Designer: Darren Alessi
Map Editor: Albert Angulo
Cartographers: Chris Henrick, June Thammasnong, Kaitlin Jaffe, Claire Sarraillé
Indexer: Rachel Kuhn

ISBN: 978-1-59880-598-7
ISSN: 1543-7000

Printing History
1st Edition – 2003
4th Edition – August 2012
5 4 3 2 1

Text © 2012 by Kathleen Bryant and Avalon Travel.
Maps © 2012 by Avalon Travel.
All rights reserved.

Some photos and illustrations are used by permission and are the property of the original copyright owners.

Front cover photo: Rock formations in Monument Valley © Don White / SuperStock
Title page photo: © Dan Monaghan, New Mexico Tourism Department
Interior color photos: pages 4 © Kathleen Bryant; page 5 (top) © Kathleen Bryant, (bottom) © Natalia Bratslavsky/123rf.com; page 6 (inset) © Richard Mayer, (bottom) © Mike Stauffer, New Mexico Tourism Department; page 7 (top and bottom right) © Kathleen Bryant, (bottom left) © Dan Monaghan, New Mexico Tourism Department; page 8 © Kathleen Bryant; page 10-11 © Kathleen Bryant; page 12 © Richard Mayer; page 13-14 © Kathleen Bryant; page 15 © Richard Mayer; page 16 © Kathleen Bryant; page 17 © James Orr, New Mexico Tourism Department; page 18 (bottom left) © Sven Brunso, (bottom right) © Kathleen Bryant; page 19 Mike Stauffer, New Mexico Tourism Department; page 20-21 © Kathleen Bryant; page 22 © Richard Mayer; page 23 © National Park Service; page 24 (top three) © Kathleen Bryant, (bottom) © Richard Mayer

Printed in Canada by Friesens

KEEPING CURRENT

If you have a favorite gem you'd like to see included in the next edition, or see anything that needs updating, clarification, or correction, please drop us a line. Send your comments via email to feedback@moon.com, or use the address above.

MAP SYMBOLS

▭ Expressway	🅒 Highlight	✕ Airfield	⚲ Golf Course
▭ Primary Road	○ City/Town	✈ Airport	🅟 Parking Area
▭ Secondary Road	◉ State Capital	▲ Mountain	▲ Archaeological Site
▭ Unpaved Road	⊛ National Capital	✛ Unique Natural Feature	⛪ Church
▭ Trail	★ Point of Interest		🅖 Gas Station
▭ Ferry	• Accommodation	🗻 Waterfall	Glacier
▭ Railroad	▼ Restaurant/Bar	▲ Park	Mangrove
▭ Pedestrian Walkway	▪ Other Location	🅣 Trailhead	Reef
▭ Stairs	▲ Campground	⛷ Skiing Area	Swamp

CONVERSION TABLES

°C = (°F - 32) / 1.8
°F = (°C x 1.8) + 32
1 inch = 2.54 centimeters (cm)
1 foot = 0.304 meters (m)
1 yard = 0.914 meters
1 mile = 1.6093 kilometers (km)
1 km = 0.6214 miles
1 fathom = 1.8288 m
1 chain = 20.1168 m
1 furlong = 201.168 m
1 acre = 0.4047 hectares
1 sq km = 100 hectares
1 sq mile = 2.59 square km
1 ounce = 28.35 grams
1 pound = 0.4536 kilograms
1 short ton = 0.90718 metric ton
1 short ton = 2,000 pounds
1 long ton = 1.016 metric tons
1 long ton = 2,240 pounds
1 metric ton = 1,000 kilograms
1 quart = 0.94635 liters
1 US gallon = 3.7854 liters
1 Imperial gallon = 4.5459 liters
1 nautical mile = 1.852 km